Land and Freedom

LAND AND FREEDOM

*Rural Society, Popular Protest, and
Party Politics in Antebellum New York*

Reeve Huston

UNIVERSITY PRESS

2000

OXFORD
UNIVERSITY PRESS

Oxford   New York

Athens   Auckland   Bangkok   Bogota   Bombay   Buenos Aires
Calcutta   Cape Town   Dar es Salaam   Delhi   Florence   Hong Kong
Istanbul   Karachi   Kuala Lumpur   Madras   Madrid   Melbourne
Mexico City   Nairobi   Paris   Singapore   Taipei   Tokyo   Toronto

and associated companies in
Berlin   Ibadan

Copyright © 2000 by Reeve Huston

Published by Oxford University Press, Inc.,
198 Madison Avenue, New York, New York 10016

Oxford is a registered trademark of Oxford University Press

Library of Congress Cataloging-in-Publication Data
Huston, Reeve, 1960–
Land and freedom : rural society, popular protest, and party politics in
antebellum New York / Reeve Huston.
p. cm.
Includes bibliographical references and index.
ISBN 0-19-513600-4
1. Land tenure—New York (State)   2. Antirent War, N.Y., 1839–1846.
3. Agriculture—Economic aspects—New York (State)   4. New York/
(State)   —Politics and government—19th century.   I. Title.
HD211.N2 H87 2000
333.3'09747—dc21   99-088532

9 8 7 6 5 4 3 2 1

Printed in the United States of America
on acid-free paper

To my mother,
Patricia Reeve Huston
and to the memory
of my father,
John Schee Huston

ACKNOWLEDGMENTS

L ike all intellectual projects, this one has been shaped by many hands. As a graduate student, I was blessed with advisors who shared a commitment to high standards of scholarship, a willingness to devote prodigious time and energy to their students, and a disposition to let each student find his or her own voice. David Montgomery encouraged my interest in rural society and my desire to write a different sort of political history; he voiced his faith in the importance of this project, even when my own conviction was flagging. He read several drafts with care, encouraging me to tease out the broader significance of the anti-renters' story. His own work, especially *Beyond Equality*, has deeply influenced this work; so have his guidance and friendship. Bill Cronon offered humane counsel during the early stages of this project, allowed me to tap his deep knowledge of U.S. agricultural history, pushed me to think through my assumptions and concepts, and encouraged me to strive for elegance of expression. Emilia da Costa encouraged me to bring out the broad significance of the Anti-Rent Wars and rightly challenged some early interpretations. Her comments on my drafts, as well as numerous discussions over her superb dinners, had a decisive influence on this work. Although not officially an advisor, Jack Wilson was in on the conversations with Emilia. In addition to offering an exquisite barbecued lamb and that high, lonesome sound, he read numerous drafts and provided critical guidance. Several of his comments planted the seeds for important themes in this work. Finally, David Brion Davis had faith in the importance of the Anti-Rent Wars from the start, and extended encouragement and advice.

Since completing this work as a dissertation, numerous scholars have offered generous advice. John Brooke, Christopher Clark, Elisabeth Clemens, Edward Countryman, Harry Watson, and two anonymous readers each read a complete draft of this work and offered comments that ranged from the helpful to the pivotal. Eric Arnessen, Pete Daniel, Philip Deloria, Sarah Deutsch, William Forbath, Ronald Formisano, Michael Goldberg, Julie

Greene, Steven Hahn, Yvette Huginnie, Susan Johnson, Bruce Laurie, Gunther Peck, Karen Sawislak, William Shade, and Carol Sheriff read parts of this work in the form of chapters, conference papers, or articles and offered important advice. When contacted by a young scholar working on the Anti-Rent Wars, Charles McCurdy could have acted in a territorial manner. Instead, he allowed me to read his superb book manuscript on the Anti-Rent Wars and New York's lawyer-statesmen and read my pentultimate draft of the book, saving me from several errors of fact. Two exceptionally talented graduate students helped as well. Cathleen Dooley assembled data from the 1860 manuscript census; both she and John Shaw did some eleventh-hour proofreading. Many thanks, too, to Thomas LeBien, formerly of Oxford University Press, who read my work carefully and helped make the manuscript shorter, tighter, and more accessible.

I also owe a debt of gratitude to several archivists and librarians who responded with efficiency and good humor to my floods of requests and frequent appearances at their desks. Many thanks to Bill Evans, Jim Folts, Jim Corsaro, Paul Mercer, and their colleagues at the New York State Archives and the Manuscripts Division of the New York State Library; Joanne Chaison, Nancy Burkett, Dennis Laurie, and Marie Lamoureaux at the American Antiquarian Society; and the staff at the Delaware County Historical Association, the New-York Historical Society, the Albany Institute of History and Art, the New York Historical Association, Cornell University Library's Department of Manuscripts and Archives, the Rensselaer Polytechnic Institute Archives and Special Collections, the New York Public Library, the Delaware County Clerk's Office, the Albany County Hall of Records, the offices of the Roxbury and Westerlo town clerks, and Beinecke Library at Yale University.

I have also received important help from a number of institutions, for which I am grateful. A Mellon Fellowship in the Humanities, administered by the Woodrow Wilson Foundation, funded a year of work on the dissertation from which this book emerged. A small grant from the Social and Behavioral Sciences Research Institute at the University of Arizona funded a summer of mop-up research, while a junior sabbatical, funded by the University of Arizona's College of Social and Behavioral Sciences, provided time for a final revision and a start on the next project. A grant from the Author's Support Fund, funded by the Office of the Provost, University of Arizona, paid for most of the illustrations and indexing. Parts of chapters 5, 6, 7, 8, and 9 first appeared in different forms in Eric Arnessen, Julia Greene, and Bruce Laurie, *Labor Histories: Class, Politics, and the Working-Class Experience* and in the *Journal of the Early Republic*. Those materials have appeared here by permission of University of Illinois Press and the *Journal of the Early Republic*.

Finally, a number of friends and family members have seen me through this project and a lot else. Gunther Peck, Jenny Price, Peg and Phil Deloria, Mary Renda, Susan Johnson, and Michael Goldberg made graduate school a humane and humorous place and have continued to offer support and friendship since then. My sisters, Jenny and Katina, offered emotional support; my mother, Patricia Huston, provided some financial support as well. I'm indebted to all three. Since graduate school, Gunther Peck and David Waldstreicher have been at once friends, colleagues, and political compatriots; I'm grateful to both for their support for all my selves and hope that I've reciprocated. Sally Deutsch has seen me through the last stages of the dissertation and everything since with generosity, humor, and a remarkable capacity for joy. She has listened, sympathized, advised, proofread, and taken on more than her share of the child care. More recently, Isaac Deutsch Huston has been more fun than I could have imagined. Both he and his mother have kept me focused on the pleasures of the day.

CONTENTS

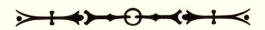

Land and Freedom

INTRODUCTION

Whent he arrived in Sand Lake, a village in the foothills of the Tagkhanic mountains just east of Albany, Governor William Bouck was dismayed to find a crowd waiting for him. Brightly colored banners and transparencies filled the village square with strange icons, pictures of Indians, and mottoes like "Down with the Rent!" and "The Land is Mine, Sayeth the Lord." As the governor arrived, some of the celebrants began firing a six-pound cannon; between one and two thousand people greeted him, "in various ways demonstrat[ing] their high respect for their chief magistrate." Most distressing of all, at the edge of the crowd stood a hundred men dressed in pantaloons, calico gowns, and painted muslin masks. "Parti-colored patches, furs, etc." decorated their robes, and brass rings and strings of beads hung from their false ears and noses. The men carried "swords, knives, bits of scythes, . . . threatening looking cheese knives, . . . clubs . . . muskets, . . . [and] pistols."[1]

The governor had expected his visit to be secret; the crowd's presence meant that news of his trip would get back to Albany, exposing him to political attacks for abetting lawless agrarians. The people who greeted him were anti-renters, tenants dedicated to destroying New York's leasehold estates and distributing the land to those who farmed it. More than a score of estates existed in New York, covering two million acres in the Hudson Valley and the surrounding hills, the Catskill piedmont, and the Mohawk and Susquehanna Valleys. Some 260,000 tenants—about a twelfth of New York's population— farmed on long-term leases in exchange for cash rents or payments in produce and labor. In 1839, tenants on the 750,000-acre manor of Rensselaerwyck began organizing to resist their landlords' demands. Sand Lake was on Rensselaerwyck; when the governor arrived there in August 1844, the movement was rapidly spreading to other estates. Within a year, it would claim between 25,000 and 60,000 supporters in 11 counties. Everywhere they organized, anti-renters initiated a rent boycott, began lobbying the legislature, and sought ways to challenge their landlords' titles in court. They also created bands of disguised men like those at the edge of the crowd in Sand Lake. These were the "Indians," who forcibly prevented lawmen from evicting tenants or seizing their personal property to cover their overdue rent.[2]

Bouck had come to meet with the anti-rent leaders. For three hours, he tried to negotiate a formula for settling the tenants' dispute with their landlord. In this he failed. But he did inform them that he had directed the sheriff of Rensselaer County not to serve any process against tenants without consulting the attorney general and the chief justice of the state supreme court. This order, all knew, would end prosecution of tenants in the county. When their meeting ended, the anti-renters held a rally. Joseph Gregory, a local anti-rent leader, exhorted the assembled tenants to "continue to resist any attempt to enforce the payment of their rents by all possible means." The "Indians" made a spectacular entrance to the meeting, "galloping furiously into the village under another discharge of the six-pounder." When the assembly ended, the anti-renters once again crowded around the governor, shaking his hand and thanking him for his support.[3]

That a sitting governor would meet with the leaders of a movement dedicated to resisting the laws of his state is remarkable. That he would order a sheriff to suspend civil process is astounding. Bouck was impressed by the anti-renters' growing organization and sympathetic to their desire to replace great estates with small, family-owned farms. His visit to Sand Lake was part of an effort to forge an informal alliance between the insurgents and his conservative faction of the New York Democrats. But he hoped to do so without explicitly endorsing the movement, for many members of his own party bitterly opposed the anti-renters as a threat to property rights and the sanctity of the law. Bouck's support and his opponents' hostility attested to the power of the anti-renters and the importance of the issues they raised. They also bore witness to the capacity of the movement to affect electoral and legislative politics—not least by fostering divisions in the established political parties.

Whether they supported or denounced the anti-renters, New Yorkers of all stripes agreed that the movement was important. James Fenimore Cooper devoted a fictional trilogy, *The Littlepage Manuscripts,* to exposing the dangers that the movement posed to social order and American national destiny. To Horace Greeley in 1845, the insurgents were "the unknown Gracchi of a rural neighborhood" who had transformed "the pregnant language of the Declaration of Independence" into an agrarian attack on the laws of property. He worried that this "*rebellion*" could be "pushed into a Revolution" and called for sending lecturers to the leasehold district to "expose the fallacies and misrepresentations of the anti-rent orators." Within a year, however, he had embraced an altered version of the land reform advocated by the most radical anti-renters and had begun working to cement a political alliance between the insurgents and his reform wing of the Whig party. The movement's capacity to inspire hope and fear reached beyond New York's borders. To the

South Carolina planter William Elliot, nonslaveholders' defense of their "common right" to hunt, fish, and forage on unenclosed land owned by others was a sign of "the principle of the anti-rent excitement . . . at work with us." For many observers, the Anti-Rent Wars represented an opportunity to free the United States from ancient forms of bondage. For others, the movement embodied the greatest dangers confronting American society: demagoguery, the excesses of democracy, and popular attacks on private property, contracts, and the rule of law.[4]

Given the importance of the Anti-Rent Wars to antebellum Americans, contemporary historians' lack of attention to them is striking.[5] One of the aims of this book is to renew appreciation for their importance. Part of their significance lay in their sheer scale. Tenants on leasehold estates numbered 260,000 in the late 1840s—at least a twelfth of the population of New York, the nation's most populous state.[6] And the anti-rent movement won the support of tens of thousands of those tenants. Twenty-five thousand people signed anti-rent petitions in 1845; a movement newspaper claimed that 50,000–60,000 tenants actively supported the cause. This made the Anti-Rent Wars one of the most powerful social movements of the antebellum era and the largest and most sustained farmers' movement in American history before the 1870s.[7]

The insurgency's import also lay in its political impact. During the 1840s, anti-renters elected scores of local and state officials, provided the swing votes to sweep a governor into office, and helped rewrite the state's constitution. In the process, they left an indelible mark on party alignments, policies, and ideologies in New York. And no state's leaders enjoyed more influence in national affairs than those of the Empire State. The anti-renters shaped the careers, ideas, and policies of Martin Van Buren, Silas Wright, Horace Greeley, William Seward, and several others. Through them, they influenced national politics.[8]

As one of the more powerful popular insurgencies of the antebellum era, the Anti-Rent Wars provide a window onto broader social and political developments. First and foremost, they allow us to examine one of the most important but understudied conflicts of the antebellum era: the contest for land. In the half century before the Civil War, farmers from New York to California fought great proprietors, land companies, speculators, and railroads for access to the soil; tens of thousands of urban workers and middle-class reformers supported movements for land reform. These were conflicts over an issue at the foundation of the social order: the distribution of the means of production. Taken together, they rivaled in level of support the other great social movements of the era. But we know very little about the ideas and strategies of agrarian insurgents and reformers; nor can we say much about their impact on the broader social and political order. The anti-rent movement was the most extensive of these struggles; its story can begin to tell us about the broader conflict of which it was a part.[9]

The Anti-Rent Wars also provide a close look at the ideas and aspirations of one large group of farmers at a moment of decisive economic change. After 1815, capitalist social relations (in which the majority of those who labor do not own the land, factories, or workshops in which they toil but are employed for wages by those who do own them) became the norm in the cities and factory towns of the northeast. At the same time, the expansion of markets for produce brought the anti-renters and other northeastern farmers more fully into a national market, tying them in numerous ways to a broader, increasingly capitalist economy. As this happened, increasing numbers of rural producers hired wage laborers and rented their land to propertyless neighbors, thus engrafting some elements of capitalist social relations onto a preexisting family system of labor.[10]

Christopher Clark and others have shown how northeastern farmers' changing economic practices helped bring about this new order and how their values and practices changed (and often failed to change) in adjusting to it. Their focus has been on practices and values rather than on social and political thought—on *mentalité* rather than ideology. The Anti-Rent Wars, on the other hand, provided a rare moment when ordinary farmers and their leaders debated what kind of society they wished to inhabit. By listening to them, we can learn a great deal about how the consolidation of a capitalist economy affected the social and economic ideas of one large group of farmers. Just as important, while historians of farmers and the "Market Revolution" have focused on rural producers' attitudes toward credit and exchange, the Anti-Rent Wars brought property rights and the distribution of land to the center of debate. In examining the insurgents' ideas about these issues, we can learn about what place, if any, they envisioned for themselves in the broader capitalist order.[11]

The Anti-Renters did not just respond to a changing economic system, however; they sought to shape it. They sought to do so primarily through electoral politics and, as Governor Bouck's visit to Sand Lake makes clear, they won significant concessions from political leaders. But they did not pursue their goals through electoral politics alone: they also created an alternative politics through the "Indians." Their movement thus provides both a window onto antebellum popular politics and an avenue for exploring the place of "the People" in the politics of Jacksonian America. Progressive and neoprogressive historians depict the ideologies and platforms of antebellum parties as more or less unmediated reflections of the aspirations of particular constituencies; in their narratives, the hopes and demands of urban wage earners and frontier farmers found expression in the program of the Democratic party. Practitioners of the "new social history," on the other hand, either ignore formal politics (thus implicitly depicting it as irrelevant to the experience of people who worked with their hands) or portray it as an arena in which popular demands were routinely coopted and silenced. Most recently, Glenn C. Altschuler and Stuart M. Blumin have depicted Jacksonian party politics as dominated by a tiny activist cadre and argued that large numbers *democratic but not jacksonian*

of rank-and-file voters approached electoral politics in a spirit of "engaged disbelief," viewing it as little more than entertaining humbug.[12]

Each of these interpretations has much to recommend it. One can find ample evidence of popular demands making their way into party platforms and rhetoric, and equally plentiful examples of party leaders silencing and coopting initiatives from below.[13] For their part, Altschuler and Blumin have injected a critical element into the debate about antebellum democracy: the existence of widespread criticism of the partisan political order.[14] But the anti- renters' simultaneous enthusiasm for Governor Bouck and for resisting the law, as well as the transformation of Horace Greeley's thinking in the face of their insurgency, suggest that the relationship between Jacksonian party leaders and their plebeian constituents was more complex than any of these interpretations suggest. Rather than being simply represented, coopted, or cynically amused by partisan activists, the anti-renters' relationship to those activists was a dialectical one, in which each appropriated and reshaped the ideas, demands, and platforms of the other. Examining their relationship promises a more nuanced understanding of how Jacksonian democracy worked, sketching in sharp lines the extent and limits of political power enjoyed by white men of the antebellum "producing classes." Doing so will also uncover a hitherto unexamined source of dynamism in the Jacksonian political order, showing how the give and take between popular movements and partisan activists could shape, divide, and even help destroy the major parties.[15]

Finally, the Anti-Rent Wars provide important insight into the social and political origins of free-labor ideology in the northern United States. During the late eighteenth and early nineteenth century, northerners began to draw sharp distinctions between "free" and "unfree" forms of labor; in doing so, they simultaneously transformed northern labor systems, distinguished themselves in new ways from the slave South, and provided a powerful ideological buttress for the emerging capitalist order.[16] By midcentury, most northerners were convinced that their society was uniquely friendly to "free labor." This belief informed the ideologies of both the northern Democratic and Republican parties and largely set the terms by which northerners understood the sectional crisis and the Civil War.[17]

Historians have argued that these ideas originated in the efforts of courts and industrial employers to legitimize the emerging system of wage labor.[18] While they offer a compelling account of how contention over new employment relations helped create new ideals of freedom, they err in attributing the origins of these ideals *entirely* to conflicts over wage labor. Both Republicans and northern Democrats saw petty proprietorship among farmers as the cornerstone of free labor, and Republicans backed up their commitment to independent farming by placing the land question, in the form of a homestead act, at the center of their program.[19] It is worth asking whether these aspects of free-laborism, like the Republicans' legitimization of wage labor, emerged out of social conflict, and what part farmers played in creating these ideas. A good place to start is in conflicts over land.

In telling the story of the Anti-Rent Wars, this book thus offers new interpretations of three key issues in the history of the early American republic: northeastern farmers' place in the emerging capitalist order, the workings of Jacksonian politics, and the origins of free-labor thought and practice. At the center of this story, and key to each of these broader themes, is the anti-renters' ideas about land and freedom. To insurgent tenants, these two concepts were sacred and inseparable; the former was essential to the realization of the latter. In thinking this way, the anti-renters were participants in a broad, international trend, as rural people throughout the modern world translated ancient desires for land into the languages of republican, liberal, or socialist revolution. But the specific meanings farmers assigned to "freedom," their proposed rules regarding access to land, and the impact of their ideas were determined by national and regional cultures and conditions. This book explores the working out of internationally shared desires for land and freedom in a specific context: New York's leasehold estates as they were integrated into a broader capitalist economy and a new system of partisan democracy. It examines how these ideals emerged; how they changed; how insurgents debated them and sought to enforce them in public life; how political leaders received, deflected, and sought to transform them; and how they changed (and failed to change) society and politics in New York.

In the hope of conveying the broad contours of the Anti-Rent Wars while grounding that picture in a detailed analysis of social and political change, I have combined a regionwide study of the movement with a focused examination of two counties: Albany and Delaware. Anti-renters in these counties were among the most militant in the leasehold district; here, all three wings of the movement—the anti-rent associations, the "Indians," and the anti-rent electoral organizations—were most powerful. These counties were at the core of the two areas where the movement was strongest: the hill towns above the Hudson Valley and the foothills of the Catskills. Excluded from close scrutiny are the leasehold towns along the Mohawk and Susquehanna rivers, where the movement was weaker. Where intensive statistical analysis was required, I focused on one town in each county: Westerlo in Albany County and Roxbury in Delaware County. Each of these towns was among the anti-rent "banner towns" of its county.

Roxbury and Westerlo were representative of anti-rent strongholds in another way: they were both hill towns that had been settled after the Revolution. Although Hudson Valley leasehold communities offered significant support to the movement, they never matched the militance or unanimity of the hill towns. Hill and valley communities had significantly different ethnic and linguistic profiles. Both were home to a mix of Yankees, Yorkers (New Yorkers of Dutch, German, and Huguenot extraction), and German-speaking immigrants. But Yorkers were the earliest settlers in the valley towns and remained an important presence well into the nineteenth century. The hill towns, on the other hand, were dominated by Yankees from the start.[20]

Just as important, hill and valley communities gave rise to starkly different economies. Blessed by fertile soil and easy transportation to market, the Hudson Valley gave rise to a prosperous commercial agriculture 40 years before independence. After 1825, valley residents switched to a more varied but equally prosperous agriculture. Hill towns, on the other hand, were on the frontier of settlement during the late eighteenth century; their residents suffered from all the problems of frontier farmers: lack of capital and infrastructure, poor access to markets, and poverty. Declining soil fertility, deforestation, and population growth made their transition to a more market-centered economy more painful than it was in the valley.[21] It is in the poorer, Yankee-dominated hill towns that the main story of the Anti-Rent Wars is to be found.

Chapter 1

LANDLORDS AND TENANTS,
1785 – 1820

In early November 1785, Stephen Van Rensselaer turned 21 and inherited the Manor House, a Georgian granite and marble structure overlooking the Troy Road in Watervliet. His father, who died when Stephen was five, had built the house in 1765 for his bride, the former Catherine Livingston. The issue of one of the colony's great families, Catherine had been no ordinary woman; and this was no ordinary house. The facade displayed a central, columned portico, bordered top and bottom with marble balustrades and fronted by a flight of steps that widened gracefully at the bottom. Two stories above lay a windowed gable, which was echoed gently by peaked cornices above the second-story windows; smaller gabled, columned, and balustraded porticoes at the front of each wing restated both gable and entryway more forcefully. Just inside the front door lay an entrance hall, 24 by 46 feet, its wallpaper covered with scenes copied by hand from Vernet, Lancret, and Pannini. Beyond lay a library, a massive reception room, several drawing rooms, and a dining hall capable of seating nearly a hundred guests. Everyone agreed that this was one of the grandest houses in the new republic.[1]

What made such grandeur affordable was a small and more unassuming building just north of the house. The Manor House, of course, had a manor—750,000 acres in Albany and Rensselaer counties known as Rensselaerwyck. Every New Year's Day, the manor's thousand-odd tenants were required to visit the manor office and pay their rent. Stephen's father had commissioned both buildings during a period of rapid growth in the manor population and had funded their construction with his expanding rent income. The Revolution had halted the expansion of the estate, and most tenants had stopped paying rent. But in the peace following the treaty of Paris, Stephen forged plans to renew the manor's growth and to compel his tenants to resume their payments. Looking east or west from the upper stories of his home, Van Rensselaer could glimpse the hills that he planned to fill with loyal, paying tenants.[2]

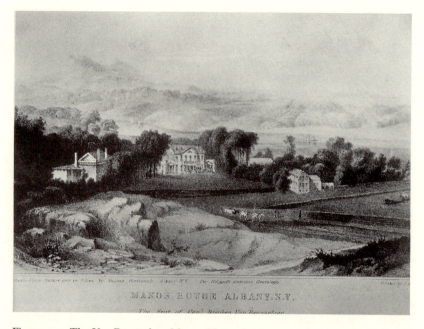

Figure 1.1. The Van Rensselaer Manor House in the early nineteenth century. To the left of the Manor House is the manor office. Behind the house is the Hudson River and, beyond that, the hills of the East Manor, in Rensselaer County. *Manor House, Albany, New York, Seat of Gen'l Van Rensselaer,* by Eugene Sintzenich. © Collection of the New–York Historical Society.

One of the people who moved to those hills was Daniel Shays. A Revolutionary veteran and the owner of a small farm in Pelham, Massachusetts, Shays had led his neighbors in a movement for debt and tax relief during the depression of the early 1780s. Shays and his followers had been convinced that merchant-creditors and their allies in government had deliberately pursued a policy of deflation after the Revolution in order to profit from the labor of indebted small producers. They believed that the only sure basis for individual liberty was independent proprietorship—a proprietorship that the government's policy of hard money, high taxes, and strict enforcement of contracts was threatening. They had fought to retain their hold on property. And they had lost. Spared the hangman's noose by a governor's pardon, Shays left Pelham and joined the flood of migrants moving west out of New England. Along with his fellow emigrants, Shays sought the secure proprietorship that had eluded him in Massachusetts.[3]

Since its origins, New York had been a meeting ground of Indian and European, Dutch and English, slave and free. Beginning in the late 1780s, it became a meeting ground between two groups, with two sets of beliefs regarding the distribution of land, the structure of class relations, and the contours of freedom. Rensselaerwyck was one of several tenanted estates inherited from the colonial period, each of them stark social and political hierarchies based on a single family's control of the land. The configuration of the Manor House and manor office hinted at the landlords' ideal of class relations: a relationship of great men and subordinates, marked by tribute, deference, and social distance. The expansion of these estates after the Revolution brought new settlers, many of whom had come to question such subordination during the Revolution. Like Daniel Shays, they cherished a landed, patriarchal egalitarianism and had come to see small-scale, independent proprietorship as the only sure basis for individual freedom. Their arrival began a process of accommodation and conflict between these two groups, one that yielded a delicate truce.

The Resurgence of the Estates

Estates like Rensselaerwyck originated in the seventeenth- and eighteenth-century land grants of the Dutch and English colonial governments. Van Rensselaer's estate was founded under the government of New Netherlands, but most originated in the years between 1670 and 1760, when English governors granted tens of millions of acres to their favorites. While some grantees sold their lands, others created leasehold estates—tracts on which tenant families held their land through long-term leases. Spurred by a growing population and a booming trade in wheat and timber, these estates developed rapidly after 1710. By 1776, they encompassed two million acres and some seven thousand tenant families. Settlement was limited to the Hudson Valley, where fertile soil and easy access to the Hudson River allowed tenants and landlords to prosper by supplying the timber and grain markets of Albany and New York.[4]

The American Revolution halted this growth and threatened the very existence of the estates. Farmers in Dutchess and Albany counties rebelled during the 1750s and 1760s, claiming the land as their own. Most proprietors in the southern Hudson Valley sided with the crown and found themselves hounded and humiliated by revolutionary committees. Northern landlords took a leading role in the patriot cause but quickly lost control of the movement to popular Whigs. The popular wing of the movement attacked "aristocracy" and gave a new, political voice to ideals of economic independence. The new state legislature legitimized these ideals, outlawing primogeniture, entail, and "feudal tenures" while confiscating the estates of loyalist landlords and selling them to small farmers. Most patriot landlords in the southern counties sensed the hostility to their estates and wisely sold their lands as well.[5]

Attacks like these destroyed all but a handful of leasehold estates elsewhere in the new United States, but not in New York. There, the landlords' dominion was saved by two developments: western migration and the politics of Federalism. During the mid-1780s, patriot landlords and other members of the gentry united behind the conservative nationalist movement headed by Alexander Hamilton. In 1788, they passed a federal constitution that put strict limits on legislators' ability to abridge the rights of property. Soon thereafter, they regained control over their tenants' votes. With these accomplishments, Federalist proprietors were well positioned to contain further challenges to their estates.[6]

Where a politically united gentry strengthened the leasehold against political challenge, western migration gave it new economic life. With war's end, migrants began pouring out of New England. Plagued by a soil declining in fertility, crop pests, timber shortages, a dense population, and high land prices, Yankees left their homes for cheaper, more fertile farms to the west. They were joined by German-speaking and Yorker farmers from New York, as well as by Scottish, Swiss, and German immigrants. Their movement was spurred by booming grain and timber prices beginning in the mid-1780s, the result of bad harvests and warfare in Europe. High prices meant that migrants could more easily attain prosperity in their new homes. They also meant that the sparsely inhabited hill regions of New York's estates could make for prosperous farms.[7]

Luckily for post-Revolutionary landlords, their estates lay directly in the path of migration. Soon after the restoration of peace, the owners of the surviving Hudson Valley estates began surveying the hilly areas in their domains and advertising for settlers. The owners of heretofore undeveloped lands in the Catskills and the Mohawk valley did the same. Most settlers bypassed leasehold estates for areas where they could buy their farms outright. But great numbers of migrants took advantage of the landlords' terms. Between 1779 and 1800, the number of tenant households on Rensselaerwyck tripled, from about 1,000 to about 3,000. Livingston Manor's population grew from 4,594 to 7,409 during the 1790s—an increase of 61 percent. And the principal leasehold towns of Delaware county, virtually uninhabited by whites in 1790, became home to 11,125 people by 1820.[8]

The new settlements dramatically expanded the geographic reach of the leasehold system. By 1807, when the economic slump following Jefferson's embargo on European trade ended further immigration, leasehold estates spanned 16 counties in eastern and central New York. In Albany, Rensselaer, and Columbia Counties, covering most of a 40-mile stretch of the Hudson River Valley and the nearby Tagkhanic and Helderberg Mountains, lay a core area of great manors. Here lay Rensselaerwyck, along with Claverack, 250,000 acres in the hands of Stephen's cousin, John Van Rensselaer. Here too lay 160,000 acres of Livingston land, divided between Livingston Manor and Clermont. To the south and west, in the foothills and valleys of Delaware, Schoharie, Ulster, Sullivan, and Greene Counties, lay a crazy quilt of small and medium-sized tracts owned by different landlords, leased under a variety of terms, and interspersed with areas of freehold farming. Finally, in the Mohawk and Susquehanna Valleys and in Dutchess County lay several isolated estates that ranged from 12,000 to 60,000 acres, islands in a sea of freehold farms.[9] In all three areas, landlords and migrants pursued their own visions of freedom and laid separate claim to the land.

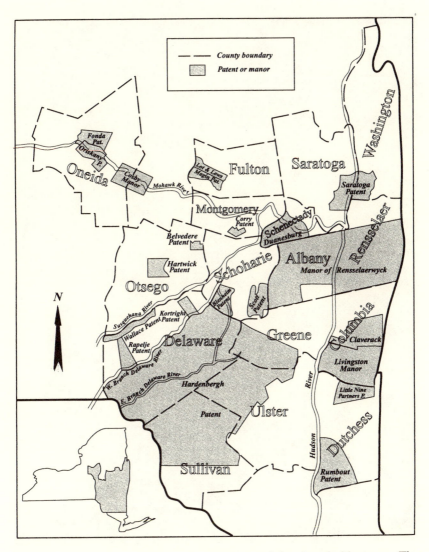

Figure 1.2. New York manors and patents containing leasehold estates. The manors of Rensselaerwyck, Claverack, and Livingston, as well as the Blenheim and Scott patents, consisted almost entirely of leasehold farms. Other patents were a mix of leasehold and owner-operated farms, usually with the latter in the majority. The county boundaries are those of 1840.

Aspirations

Leasehold proprietors were a varied lot. Towering above the others were the Livingstons and Van Rensselaers. Owners of the great estates of the core area as well as numerous tracts in the Catskills and Dutchess County, these families claimed over half the leased land in New York. Beneath these families

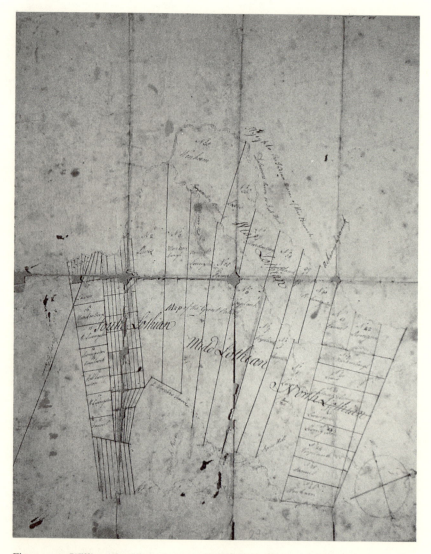

Figure 1.3. William Cockburn's map of the Hardenbergh Patent, probably from the 1780s or 1790s. The great manors of Rensselaerwyck, Claverack, and Livingston were undivided leasehold estates through the 1820s or beyond. The same was true of some patents, like the Scott patent and Blenheim patent in Schoharie County. Most patents, however, were divided among several proprietors, with much of the land being sold to independent farmers. Cockburn's map shows the million–acre Hardenbergh patent as divided into forty-two "great lots" and distributed among eight proprietors. Five of the proprietors leased their lands; the others sold them to settlers. Courtesy, New York State Library.

were a middling gentry: men like George Clarke and Goldsborough Banyar, descendants of the colonial elite whose estates, scattered across the Catskills and the Mohawk and Susquehanna Valleys, were often enormous (Clarke's was estimated to be worth a million dollars in 1812) but who fell short of the Livingstons and Van Rensselaers in wealth and renown. Lower still were small landlords like Isaac Hardenbergh, owners of a few thousand acres—gentlemen, indeed, but men who practiced their gentility on a small scale. In the early nineteenth century, these landowners were joined by individuals who, having made their fortunes in other areas, capped their achievements by becoming rentiers. John A. King, son of the Federalist leader Rufus King and a rising star in Empire State politics, bought the 17,000-acre Blenheim patent in the 1810s, complete with tenants, while Charles McEvers purchased leased land in Delaware County after having made a fortune in the insurance business.[10]

Despite their diversity, all landlords saw dominion over land as the key to attaining wealth and power, not for themselves as individuals, but for their family lineage. Their dominion derived from titles granted them by Dutch and English monarchs and confirmed by the New York legislature, or from the purchase of such titles. By granting part of their dominion to tenants, they expected to receive a handsome income. In 1804, Chancellor Robert R. Livingston, the proprietor of Clermont and a half million acres west of the Hudson, estimated that a gentleman wishing to live "*honnêtment*" in the United States required an income of at least $15,000. Almost all of this income would have to come from leased lands. Like other members of the post-Revolutionary gentry, landlords took a keen interest in the speculative schemes and new economic institutions of the early republic. Jeremiah Van Rensselaer, a Columbia County landlord, owned a glass factory and a woolen mill. Robert R. Livingston financed Samuel Fulton's development of the first steamboat and enjoyed, with Fulton, a monopoly of the Hudson River steamboat trade. And most proprietors invested in banks, insurance companies, urban real estate, and western lands. But their greatest wealth lay in their leasehold estates, and their other investments lost more money than they made. With few exceptions, the overwhelming proportion of landlords' incomes came from their tenants.[11]

Landlords sought symbolic as well as material tribute from their tenants. Like other members of the gentry, they subscribed to an organic and hierarchical worldview, in which every human being belonged to a clearly defined social rank, and in which people of different ranks were tied to one another through reciprocal obligations. Colonial proprietors like Sir William Johnson had taken pride in providing "sustenance to the poor and distressed" among their tenants; in his will Johnson beseeched his son to "sew lenity [lenience] to such of the Tenants as are poor." In return, they had received deference. Post-Revolutionary landlords made clear that they expected this relationship to continue. The day that Stephen Van Rensselaer inherited Rensselaerwyck, his valley tenants gathered at the Manor House to toast their new landlord,

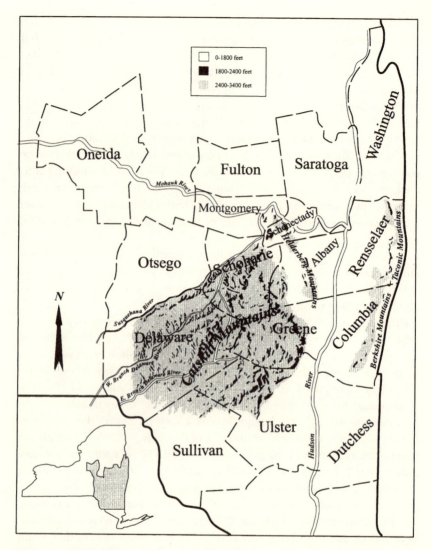

Figure 1.4. Hills and mountains of the leasehold district. Almost all of the towns that gave rise to a strong anti–rent movement in the 1840s were in the foothills or mountains.

eat his beef, and drink his ale and brandy. A friend of the patroon later recalled that the tenants "were not to be restrained from offering . . . the testimony of their joy, and their affection for his person." This was a ritual of benevolence and deference, in which Van Rensselaer exhibited his generosity and was repaid with a display of loyalty and affection. By sponsoring it, Van Rensselaer announced that he wished to manage his estate as a benevolent hierarchy and would require that tenants help maintain that vision.[12]

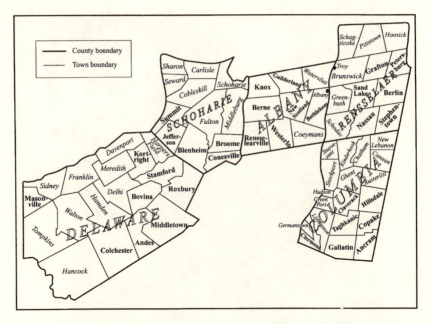

Figure 1.5. Towns in the five central anti–rent counties. Towns with a significant anti–rent movement are in bold. Town and county lines are those of 1840.

Landlords expected the income, the deference, and the votes they received from their tenants to underwrite a bid for genteel status and public power in the wider world. Rent income would provide the education, dress, homes, and furnishings demanded by the Atlantic cult of gentility, while deference would clinch landlords' status as great men. Gentility, along with the political support of loyal tenants, would guarantee power in civic life. Heirs to a tradition of civic humanism that stressed both the prerogative and the obligation of gentlemen to lead, they imbibed a profound sense of noblesse oblige and an equally profound sense that they were, as a young member of the Livingston clan put it, "candidates for glory."[13]

Unfortunately for landlords, these expectations rested on a foundation of sand. The titles to leasehold estates were notoriously weak. Some estates were founded in outright fraud. In 1684 and 1685, Robert Livingston applied for and received patents from the colonial government for two tracts of land totaling some 2,600 acres. Two years later, he received a confirmatory patent. Although the two parcels were miles apart, the new patent described them as adjacent; Livingston now claimed both tracts and everything in between, thereby creating the 160,000-acre Livingston Manor. Most estates contained ambiguous boundaries, which proprietors systematically interpreted to their advantage. The crown grant for the million-acre Hardenbergh patent, for example, described the western boundary of the patent as "the main branch of

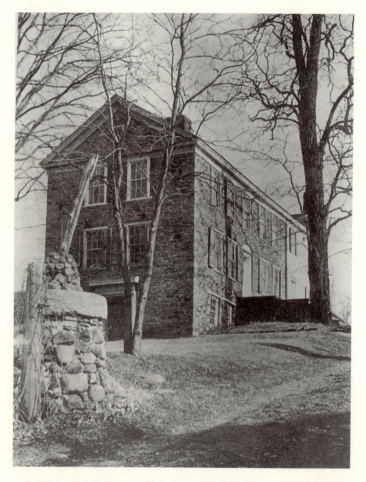

Figure 1.6. Lesser landlords sought to emulate the genteel performance of great proprietors, but did so on a smaller scale and in a simpler manner. Isaac Hardenbergh, a Delaware County landlord and land agent, had his "manor house" built between 1806 and 1812. For decades, it was the grandest house in the town of Roxbury. From Irma Mae Griffin, *History of the Town of Roxbury.* Courtesy, American Antiquarian Society.

the Fish-Kill or Delaware River." But the river had two branches of identical size, with hundreds of thousands of acres lying in between. The patent's proprietors, led by members of the Livingston family, placed the boundary at the western branch of the river, thus bringing the disputed territory into their estate. Other grants were technically void because their early proprietors had failed to pay quit-rents or settle the required number of families on their estates. The fraud and ambiguity of estate titles were a latent force in early republican New York, available to anyone seeking to challenge the landlords' power.[14]

Figure 1.7. Stephen Van Rensselaer in 1795, when he was 31 years old. Like other landlords, Van Rensselaer sought to make his body as well as his house an emblem of his power and gentility, through fine but restrained clothing and an erect but relaxed and graceful physical bearing. The clothing and the training necessary for this self–presentation were paid for with Van Rensselaer's rent income. *Stephen Van Rensselaer III,* 1795, by Gilbert Stuart. Courtesy of the Albany Institute of History and Art.

Where landlords wished to turn their estates into benevolent hierarchies that would provide them with income, deference, and a material basis for genteel performance, the families who settled the newly opened hill areas of those estates sought to recreate communities of autonomous, small-holding, patriarchal households. The majority of settlers came from rural New England, where such communities predominated. For Yankee emigrants, land was the material basis for establishing a productive household. It was also the basis for manhood and the independence, equality, and freedom they had fought for during the Revolution.[15]

The New Yorkers and Europeans who joined the Yankees shared their broad aspirations. "Yorkers" of Dutch, Huguenot, and Germanic ancestry aimed primarily at creating prosperous productive households which, one historian has observed, "rested . . . on secure property." The Germans also sought freedom from the taxation, forced labor, and "intrusion into their domestic happiness" that they had known in the old country. As with New Englanders, the Revolution had politicized this thirst for property. After 1776, large numbers of German-speaking Americans joined the Revolutionary armies inspired by an image of "the armed landowner who, shouldering his musket, would defend his property against the pretended claims of those who meant to tax them into submission." In Delaware and Schoharie counties, Yankees, Yorkers, and Germans were joined by former subtenants and resident laborers escaping the population growth, rising rents, and mass evictions of Highland Scottish estates. These migrants, too, sought the land that had been denied them at home.[16]

With the exception of the Scottish and some Yorkers, these migrants were strangers to tenancy. But they were familiar with the hierarchy and deference that landlords cherished. Most arrived on New York's leasehold estates at a moment when cultures of deference in their home communities were under attack but not destroyed. Yankees, Yorkers, and German-speaking immigrants had all been born into a world of ranks and orders, and many still expected that gentlemen would rule politically. But the Revolutionary struggle and attacks on religious authority convinced many that humble white men were equal to their supposed superiors in dignity, intelligence, and capacity to rule. Significantly, most Yankee settlers were Baptists and Methodists, who had a history of attacking established religious authority. Similarly, the "feudal notions, and attachment *to names*" that characterized pre-Revolutionary Scottish immigrants were eroded by mass evictions on Scotland's highland estates during the 1790s and by the destruction of the Scottish leadership class in America, the tackmen, during the Revolution.[17]

There was room enough for conflict between settlers and proprietors. Where the one's power rested on inequalities in landholding, the other's well-being depended on its widespread distribution. Where landlords sought princely incomes from those who worked the land, settlers wanted to devote the fruits of their labor to their own comfort and property. Where great men sought deference, the newcomers on their estates were learning to spurn groveling. But there was room for accommodation as well. If landlords could accommodate settlers' desire for secure property, and if tenants could make concessions to landlords' appetite for income, domination, and glory, perhaps the two groups could arrange a peace, however tenuous. The growth of the estates after the Revolution was built on such a peace.

Accommodation and Conflict *of W. C.*

Landlords faced a double challenge in expanding their estates. They had to establish control over hilly territory that they had heretofore ignored, and they had to attract loyal settlers. The earliest white migrants to the hill regions were squatters, many of whom claimed their farms as their own. Proprietors gave these squatters a simple choice: take a lease or get out. And they backed up this ultimatum with evictions.[18] Attracting settlers posed another set of challenges. Migrants wanted fertile land, and they wanted it free and clear. Landlords offered neither. Most were unwilling to sell their lands outright, and the majority of available land lay in the hills above the Hudson Valley and in the foothills of the Catskills, where soils were thinner and growing seasons shorter than on valley lands.

Proprietors overcame these handicaps in three ways. First, they offered men of substance large farms at bargain prices as an inducement to settle. Once in place, these prosperous settlers established sawmills, gristmills, and taverns, which encouraged further immigration.[19] Second, proprietors offered secure access to land for a low initial cost. Unimproved freehold lands cost between $1 and $3 per acre before 1810; at prevailing credit terms, a hundred-acre farm required a down payment of $25 to $100 and annual payments of up to $100. Federal lands cost a minimum of $1,280 before 1804 and at least $200 afterward. Such terms often overwhelmed the financial resources of migrants, who arrived in their new homes short of cash, equipment, and livestock.[20] Leasehold lands required a far lower initial investment. Aside from the large tracts they sold or leased to prosperous early settlers, both Stephen Van Rensselaer and the Delaware County landlord Morgan Lewis parceled their estates into 80- to 100-acre lots, thus preventing farmers from claiming more land than they could pay for. In order to maximize tenants' chances of surviving the early, difficult years of settlement, Van Rensselaer waived the initial seven years' rent. Afterward, he demanded 13 bushels of wheat for every hundred acres—equivalent to the average yield of a single upland acre—plus four fowls and one day's labor with a horse and cart. Lewis charged two bushels per acre. During the 1790s, the annual rent on a hundred-acre farm on Rensselaerwyck averaged $17.13; a similar farm on Lewis's estate cost $23.75 per annum.[21]

Nor did tenants sacrifice much long-term security. The largest group of tenants were granted perpetual leases, which made them the legal owners of their farms, subject to rents and other restrictions. As long as they paid their rents and abided by the other conditions in their leases, they enjoyed the same security as freehold farmers. A slightly smaller number signed leases in lives, which gave tenants rights to the land for as long as one, two, or three people named in the lease (usually the head of household and one or two children) survived. They enjoyed the same security as perpetual tenants, but for only one or two generations. Least common were leases in years, virtually all of which ran for 21 years or longer.

Finally, landlords offered tenants a wide variety of assistance during the early years of settlement. Stephen Van Rensselaer subsidized the building of community institutions on his estate by hiring schoolmasters, donating land and building materials to churches, and waiving the rent on ministers' farms. He also provided food to tenant communities in time of dearth. All landlords extended help to individual tenants—most frequently by offering abatements on the rent, but sometimes in more dramatic form. When the family of Justis Purdy of Bovina fell sick and lost their farm in the late 1810s, the landlord Janet Montgomery gave them 40 acres of land, without charge, enabling them "by the application of [their] bodily labor to gain a livelihood." Similarly, when Tobias Van Dyck of Woodstock fell ill and his family became paupers, 11 local men "prayed" to Robert L. Livingston, the son-in-law of the Chancellor, that he provide Van Dyck with a farm so that the settler could "help him Self to a Living." Livingston consented. Together with moderate rents, long leases, and the presence of early, prosperous settlers, landlords' assistance helped convince thousands of migrants to settle on the estates.[22]

Attracting settlers was one thing; getting them to pay was another. Landlords sought to profit from their estates in four ways: through rents; by preserving tracts for rent or sale at a later date when dense settlement had raised their value; by claiming a portion of tenants' improvements; and by profiting from mills and stores. In each of these areas, landlords and their agents treated tenants with gentle but insistent pressure. Tenants responded with equally gentle persistence. They wheedled, pleaded, dragged their feet, and ignored the rules that proprietors sought to enforce—all in an effort to minimize the costs and maximize the benefits of their relationship to their landlords.

Nowhere was this pattern of pressure and evasion more apparent than in the collection of rents. Soon after Stephen Van Rensselaer became patroon of Rensselaerwyck, he increased the wheat rents charged in new leases from 10 to 13 bushels per hundred acres. He also moved to make rent collection more systematic. Like most colonial landlords, his father's efforts to collect had been sporadic and ineffectual; three-fifths of his tenants had been chronically delinquent in their rents. Three months after he gained control of Rensselaerwyck, Stephen the younger had a notice posted throughout the estate, demanding that "some part" of the "arrears of rent which has long since been due" be paid within a month. Such payment, he warned, "will prevent a step which my ancestors have seldom been reduced to but which I shall be obliged to take if this demand is not complyed with." The "step" he proposed to take was to sue his delinquent tenants—a step so unprecedented that he could not bring himself to name it. Few tenants responded to this warning, and in early 1795 Van Rensselaer published another notice, this time stating his threats with clarity and confidence but also extending a new incentive to those who paid. Tenants who failed to pay their rents before spring, he warned, would have their accounts "put into the hands of an attorney to collect." Those who made a good-faith effort to pay, on the other hand, "will be generously dealt by." Van Rensselaer and his agents broadcast similar messages through the end of the decade.[23]

Van Rensselaer's threat of lawsuits, encouragement of partial payment, and promise of generous treatment placed rent collection on a new footing. Out of a sample of 22 tenants who had leased farms in the town of Rensselaerville during the 1780s and 1790s, all went to the manor office and settled their accounts in 1798 and 1799. In return, Van Rensselaer honored his promise of generosity. Seventeen fell short of paying their entire debt; Thomas Hun, the Patroon's agent, gave each of them an abatement for the remainder of what was owed.[24] Thereafter, Rensselaerville farmers made faithful if irregular efforts to pay their rent. Most occasionally let a year or two go by without a visit to the manor office, only to make several visits in one season, paying two or three years' rent in a short time. Though their rent was calculated in wheat, hens, and labor, no tenant paid more than half his yearly obligations in wheat, and none offered hens or labor. They made up the difference in rye, "sundries," promissory notes, and an occasional cash payment. With these sporadic and eclectic payments, Rensselaerville farmers kept more or less abreast of their obligations. Although by 1805 the majority owed some back rents, only four were behind by more than a year (see Appendix, figures 1 and 2).[25]

Van Rensselaer and Hun succeeded in exacting payment from hill tenants partly by making concessions to those tenants' ideas of proper economic behavior. The patroon and his agent operated in a world of commercial exchange where prompt, predictable payment of debts was the norm. But as Christopher Clark has shown, northeastern farmers "condemned undue pressure for the settlement of debts" as a threat to the economic security of debtors. Obligations were to be fulfilled not when a contract demanded it but when the circumstances of the debtor permitted it. Although leases on Rensselaerwyck required that each year's rent be paid on the first of January, Van Rensselaer and Hun allowed tenants to treat their rent obligations as they did their other debts—as obligations to be fulfilled at the convenience of the debtor. Just as significantly, they charged no interest on overdue rents.[26]

Regular payment also came at the price of patrician generosity. Between 1799 and 1805, Thomas Hun distributed 23 abatements, worth an average of £10 each, among 19 (83 percent) of 23 Rensselaerville farmers. Van Rensselaer and Hun used abatements to achieve three goals. First, they sought to help tenants out of difficult financial straits. Many abatements went to widows soon after their husbands' death; others went to tenants with little capital. They also sought to cultivate loyalty, especially among prosperous and influential hill residents. Above all, Van Rensselaer and Hun used lenience to encourage faithful payment of the rent. With the exception of abatements granted to widows, Hun gave subsidies only when the rent was paid. A disproportionate number of reductions accompanied very large payments, as a reward to tenants for catching up on their obligations. Van Rensselaer and

Hun thus used traditions of patrician benevolence as a hard-headed incentive for tenants to pay.[27]

Through a combination of threats and lenience, Van Rensselaer and Hun raised Rensselaerville farmers' rent payments to 80 percent of their obligations in the decade after 1796. They seem to have been equally successful among all of the manor's three thousand tenants, providing the patroon with an income of more than $40,000 a year. Having achieved this, however, Van Rensselaer and Hun curtailed their abatements, laying the groundwork for future crisis. Where they forgave 16 percent of their tenants' obligations between 1796 and 1803, they abated only 2 percent of those debts over the following decade. Tenants took up part of the slack, paying 88 percent of their obligations after 1805. But with Van Rensselaer unwilling to forgive the rest, their cumulative debt grew more than sixfold, from £115 in 1805 to £714 in 1819. In the latter year, Rensselaerville tenants owed an average of £31 each—the equivalent of two years' rent (see Appendix, figure 2).[28]

Great and middling landlords throughout the leasehold district followed Van Rensselaer's example in rationalizing rent collection and making shrewd use of lenience to encourage payment.[29] Smaller landlords could not afford such lenience, however. Isaac Hardenbergh, a Delaware County proprietor, conducted distress sales (legal procedures in which a tenant's personal property was auctioned off to pay for rent) against a few heavily indebted tenants, and he compelled several others to hand over their leases. Great and middling landowners, however, turned to such drastic measures only in the case of rebellion or outright refusal to pay. Such restraint accorded well with landlords' sense of themselves as benevolent gentlemen. More important, it helped retain tenants, maintain a steady flow of rent income, and avoid expensive legal proceedings. When Major Cochran, a subagent on Goldsbrow Banyar's Putnam County estate, began evicting a few heavily indebted tenants in 1809, he quickly ran up court costs of more than $200. Even worse, the seized farms remained uninhabited for another three years. Though Cochran was anxious to evict more tenants, Banyar's agent John Wigram counseled against it: "we have however to pay him the costs upon each suit, and . . . we shall find it difficult enough to get Tenants."[30]

If landlords' and their agents' efforts to increase their rent income resulted in negotiation and compromise, their efforts to augment their income in other ways met with more pervasive resistance and evasion. Nowhere was this more apparent than in disputes over the uses of the "landlord's commons" and the ownership of tenants' improvements. Tenants throughout New York's leasehold estates depended heavily on resources from unimproved estate lands for their livelihood. William Coventry, a farmer in the valley lands of Livingston Manor, hunted and fished for at least four days in 1798, catching between 50 and 60 shad a day and killing 18 pigeons "at one short" in April. During January and February he spent most days cutting and hauling firewood. And he peeled hemlock bark for four days. Finally, he set his hogs loose in the woods during the summer and fall, where they fed themselves on acorns and other mast. Tenants in the hill towns, where fish, game, and timber were more abundant and farms were less developed, made even more intensive use of common lands.[31]

Colonial landlords had acquiesced in these practices, allowing tenants to cut wood on the "landlord's commons." But as one observer noted, unrestricted cutting caused "the waste and destruction of . . . immense quantit[ies] of timber" and dramatically reduced the value of estate lands. After the Revolution, proprietors sought to end tenant timbering on the commons. Stephen Van Rensselaer and landlords in Delaware County forbade the practice entirely. Robert L. Livingston permitted Woodstock tenants to cut wood for their own use but outlawed commercial cutting from unoccupied lands. Whatever their specific policies, landlords deputized local subagents (usually prosperous men whom the landlords favored with large grants, low rents, and generous abatements) to guard timber stands and to prosecute unauthorized lumbermen. Their efforts failed miserably. Subagents occasionally caught and sued illicit timber cutters, but most lumbermen went about their business undisturbed.[32]

Quiet conflict also prevailed over conflicting claims to tenants' improvements. Legally, improvements that tenants made—cleared and plowed land, buildings, orchards, fences—ran with the land. Tenants with perpetual leases legally owned the land, with certain conditions, and thus owned the improvements as well. Squatters and tenants with leases in lives or years owned neither: since the land legally belonged to the landlord, so did the improvements on it. Yet all settlers claimed ownership of their improvements. In 1785, Daniel Moon settled on a farm in Rensselaerwyck that Harmon Best, a squatter, had occupied and begun to improve. Best returned and threatened to throw Moon out "Except I will give him one hundred dollars for his former possession." The following year, William Coventry looked over a life tenant's farm on Livingston Manor which, according to his cousin Alexander, "he talks of purchasing the improvements on." Whether they stayed put or sold out and moved on, creating improvements was the settlers' main avenue to accumulating property.[33]

Since the colonial era, landlords had respected tenants' claims to their improvements even when they were not legally required to do so, allowing them to sell their improvements to newcomers. But they sought to keep a portion of those improvements for themselves. Almost all leases also contained provisions known as the quarter sale, the sixth sale, etc., which required tenants who sold out to remit a portion of the sale price (usually a third, a quarter, a sixth, or a tenth) to the proprietor. Leases in lives or years also entitled the landlord to reenter when the lease expired, claiming all improvements as his or her own.[34] These claims on tenants' improvements produced deep discontent. During the 1790s, settlers on Rensselaerwyck voiced "doubts and uneasiness" over the quarter sale and asked Van Rensselaer to "obviate" these "obnoxious clauses." Van Rensselaer refused, and hill tenants responded by ignoring the requirement. For the next three generations, many tenants simply neglected to inform the manor office when they sold their farms. Settlers offered more overt resistance to leases in lives. John Wigram wrote to Goldsbrow Banyar in 1812 that squatters on Banyar's Delaware County lands "have for these several years been turbulent and much averse to taking three-life leases"; he predicted that he would have to evict several "before they will comply with our terms."[35]

Conflicts over improvements and timber rights gave voice to a deeper conflict over the nature of property. Landlords derived their claim to land from their legal title, and they believed that this title empowered them to set such terms on tenants' use of the land as they saw fit. In signing leases and paying rent, tenants legally recognized landlords' property in the land. But if they were to accumulate property of their own, they had to wrest it from the land with their own labor, in the form of crops, improvements, and timber. And they resisted when the landlords' claim to land interfered with their claim to the fruits of their labor. Many believed, as one tenant wrote in 1811, that land and the resources on it were "the common bounties of nature." When those resources were transformed into commodities, they became the property of the person whose labor had transformed them. Settlers claimed the value they added to the land in the form of cleared land, buildings, orchards, and fences as their property. In contrast, land that had not been transformed by human labor was open to use by all members of the community. The wood, fish, game, and mast taken from such land became the property of the person whose labor appropriated it.[36]

Negotiation and quiet conflict over rents, timber, and improvements gave expression to the tension between landlords' drive for income and tenants' desire for secure property. Yet through most of the leasehold district, this tension was expressed in wheedling, foot-dragging, threats, and reprimands, not in conflict at arms or at the ballot box. Most tenants and landlords fought over the *terms* of their relationship, not over the justice and propriety of the relationship itself. This was due largely to the landlords' restraint. As long as proprietors did nothing to endanger their tenants' access to productive property, tenants proved willing to struggle for advantage within the leasehold system, rather than against it.

Benevolence and Deference

Acceptance of the leasehold system meant more than an absence of overt resistance; it also meant participation in a theater of benevolence and deference. Landlords expected not just income from their estates, but confirmation of their status as great men. And as long as they acted with generosity and restraint, tenants were more than willing to provide that confirmation. When a minister in the mountains of Rensselaerwyck requested a site on which to build his house, he did so in a tone of abject servitude:

[If] it Please your Worship, patiently to hear me, As my Circumstances, [and the] Duty I owe to my family, Brings me to the [necessity?] of Sending your worship these lines, I hope your Worship Shall Not take Ill, patiently Considering, my boldness to your Worship, Coming from Necessity, and Ruin . . . I must Confess my Self, to be Below your Worship. . . .[37]

Tenants and landlords complemented such individual demonstrations of subordination with grander public rituals. In September 1788, Stephen Van Rensselaer and Thomas Hun visited a new settlement in the Helderberg Mountains of Rensselaerwyck. The visitors attended a town meeting where the settlers broke into a bitter dispute over where to build roads. The patroon offered to mediate and, according to Reuben Frisbee, a local doctor and merchant, soon brought the meeting to "perfect unanimity." In the evening, the settlers asked Van Rensselaer to "*christen*" their new community. The patroon agreed. But after a pause, he confessed that he could think of no appropriate name. Mr. Hun conferred briefly with him, and returned to the meeting to propose that the new town be called Rensselaerville, in honor of the great man. "The name being proposed to Mr. Van Rensselaer," Frisbee wrote, "he consented thereto with becoming readiness, which was received by the people with hearty attestations of joy and satisfaction."[38]

Rituals like these conveyed what James Scott calls the "public transcript" of landlord-tenant relations—a sanitized vision of those relations, presented for strategic purposes and intended for public consumption. The settlers' consent for Van Rensselaer to intervene in local disputes, their tractability in the face of his efforts at peacemaking—these allowed the patroon to play the benevolent patriarch and permitted tenants to act as favored, trusting dependents. The ritual of naming, the patroon's reluctance to name the new town, the joy of the inhabitants—all seem to marshal studied artifice to create the impression of spontaneously bestowing honor and affection on a reluctant recipient.[39]

Some tenants believed this happy vision. Reuben Frisbee, as a doctor and merchant, was the sort of settler whom Van Rensselaer tended to favor with free or discounted land, abatements, and other benefits; most likely he acted as the patroon's subagent in the town. He saw the ritual at Rensselaerville as the sincere outpouring of affection for a great man. We might well doubt other tenants' sincerity: there was too much to lose by withholding deference. But even when they were sincere, their fawning came with conditions. Manor residents usually depicted their deference as part of a reciprocal exchange— the reward for what Frisbee called "generous conduct." An 1801 meeting of Rensselaerville tenants praised Van Rensselaer as "a true friend to his tenants." The "favors and bounties" that he bestowed on "the unfortunate tenant whose crops have failed, the widow, the orphan," the meeting declared, proved beyond doubt "how worthy he is to possess property." Formulations like this left considerable doubt about whether such loyalty would be forth-coming if landlords' generosity waned.[40]

The Politics of Deference

Tenants on the great estates rewarded landlords' generosity not just with praise, but with their votes as well. In doing so, they assured landlords' po-litical power. This power, in turn, provided a second buttress to peace on New York's leasehold estates. If landlords' respect for tenants' economic se-curity rewarded tenant loyalty, their political power rendered overt resis-tance futile.

As Alan Taylor has observed, New Yorkers in the early republic conducted electoral politics through "interests"—hierarchical networks of influence, dominated by a wealthy individual and his "friends," which sought to control nominations and mobilize voters. In Albany County, Stephen Van Rensselaer and his father-in-law Philip Schuyler united their forces in a sin-gle "manor interest." In Columbia County, bitter rivalries between the Manor Livingstons, the Clermont Livingstons, and the Van Rensselaers of Claverack resulted in three competing manor interests. The Van Rensselaers threw their support to the Federalists, but that party's denial of high office to mem-bers of the Livingston clan drove both branches of that family into the arms of the Clintonians and the Republicans.[41]

Landlords and their allies controlled tenants' votes through a combina-tion of persuasion, pressure, and material rewards. At election time, propri-etors and their agents went among the tenantry, reminding them of the pro-prietor's generosity and of their outstanding debts to him, treating them at local taverns, and pressing ballots containing the names of the landlord's can-didates into their hands. To bypass New York's secret ballot law, they in-structed tenants to "fold up their ballots in a particular manner" or printed their ballots on special silklike paper, thus allowing observers to keep track of how individuals voted. The Van Rensselaer-Schuyler interest combined these methods of control with a tolerance for local autonomy, allowing Federalists in each town to nominate their own candidates for the state as-sembly.[42] These methods yielded overwhelming electoral majorities. From 1792 to 1801, between 85 and 94 percent of Rensselaerwyck residents in Albany County cast their votes for Federalist gubernatorial candidates. Voters in Albany and Coeymans, which lay outside the manor, gave a majority to Governor George Clinton in 1792 and voted 51 to 65 percent Federalist thereafter. Tenant votes were sufficient to carry the county with majorities of 77 to 83 percent in every election (see Appendix, figure 3).[43]

The Albany County opposition, led by Governor Clinton's loyalists and af-ter 1798 allied with Jefferson's Republican party, attacked landlords' politi-cal control of their tenants. In so doing, they provided the most trenchant public critique of the leasehold in the county. Landlords, they claimed, kept tenants "under a political cloud of darkness." When Stephen Van Rensselaer ran for lieutenant governor in 1795, the Albany Clintonian Abraham Yates insisted that his candidacy rested not on any abilities but on his "grand connections," his political "servitude" to Philip Schuyler, and his "command" over "a vast number of voters." "Talent and virtue, not birth and riches," Yates wrote, "should entitle a man to the suffrages of freemen." Such critiques meshed nicely with the Republicans' warnings that "REPUBLICAN GOVERNMENT is in danger of degenerating into ARISTOCRACY or MONARCHY, when the people unguardedly entrust the Administration to men who sigh after the MONOPOLY OF WEALTH which forms the basis of those systems."[44] For a brief moment in 1795, the Clintonians went beyond this attack on deferential politics. In a series of articles in the Republican *Albany Gazette,* "A Citizen" painstakingly reconstructed how the Van Rensselaers had obtained the grant for Rensselaerwyck by fraud and had violated the conditions of the grant. Because of these frauds and violations, the writer maintained, the Patroon "had no right" to the land he claimed.[45]

Most tenants publicly ignored the challenge to Van Rensselaer's title. And they responded with indignation to charges of political subordination, insisting that Van Rensselaer had *earned* their loyalty. In 1801, when Van Rensselaer ran for governor, a meeting of tenants' representatives made clear that their political loyalty to their landlord rested on his lenience and aid:

> We cannot speak too highly of his Benevolence. If any misfortune happens to any of his tenants, they are sure of indulgence. . . . We could, if we thought it necessary, mention instances, where the widow and orphan have received from him the greatest acts of kindness and generosity. He never fails to contribute to the support and maintenance of the clergy . . . In short, he is the friend of the poor and unfortunate—He is beloved by all— Our support of him is insured by our attachment to him.[46]

After 1801, however, Republican appeals won support from a growing minority of tenants. The Jeffersonians were aided by their party's control of the state Council of Appointment—and thus over county offices—in 1801. They were also helped by Van Rensselaer's cutback in abatements to tenants after 1803. In 1804, the Federalist vote dropped to 62 percent in the manor towns of the valley and to 66 percent in the Helderbergs. For their part, voters off the manor began returning modest majorities for the Republicans (see Appendix, figure 3). Despite these setbacks, the manor interest continued to win every election, with 60 to 63 percent of county voters, well into the 1820s.[47]

These majorities guaranteed that a large proportion of officials elected from Albany County would remain intimately connected to the landlords. During the 1780s and 1790s, Leonard Gansevoort, one of the "merchant princes" of Albany and the husband of Stephen Van Rensselaer's cousin Maria, served two terms as an assemblyman, another nine as state senator, a year as judge on the court of appeals, and a year on the powerful Council of Appointment. William North, himself a small landlord, served four terms in the assembly, two of them as speaker. And Thomas Hun, Stephen Van Rensselaer's estate agent, served two years in the assembly. Overall, 36 percent (34 of 94) of the terms served as congressmen, members of the state assembly, county sheriffs, or county judges between 1788 and 1799 were filled by landlords, their relatives, their lawyers or agents, their personal friends, or their close political allies. This proportion grew to 45 percent (54 out of 151) between 1800 and 1819.[48]

Numerous handicaps—divisions among landlords, a population of freehold farmers that outnumbered tenants, and a rebellious tenantry on the eastern fringes of their estates—kept Columbia County landlords from exercising Schuyler's and Van Rensselaer's kind of political power. Their greater vulnerability led to occasional, but significant, political challenges to the leasehold system by Republican politicians. But with a few lapses, Columbia County landlords remained firmly in control of their tenants' votes before 1820. In 1807, the Republican *Hudson Bee* complained that tenants "vote only on the proprietor's will, and are brought to the polls in posse comitatus to support federalism."[49]

Landlords enjoyed far less control over tenants' votes west of the Hudson river. Most proprietors lived elsewhere and exercised little personal authority over voters. In addition, leasehold land was broken up among numerous landlords who often supported opposing political parties. Both the Republican Morgan Lewis and the Federalist Verplanck family, for example, owned significant acreage in the Delaware County town of Middletown. Consequently, few landlords could control elections in any single town or county. Their agents and allies, on the other hand, enjoyed considerable influence. The Federalist landlords' agent Ebenezer Foote dominated local politics during Delaware County's first five years of existence, monopolizing both the county clerkship and the county's seat in the state senate.[50] The county's swing to the Republican camp in 1802 ended Foote's domination, but landlords retained a strong measure of influence. During the first two decades of the nineteenth century, proprietors' agents, lawyers, and relatives filled 16 percent (19 of 124) of the county's assembly and congressional seats and terms as sheriff and county judge. This influence far exceeded the political clout of tenants. Although the major leasehold towns contained 40 percent of the county's voters, residents of these towns served only 6 out of 52 terms in office (12 percent of the total) during the 1800s and 7 out of 54 terms (16 percent) during the 1810s.[51]

Tenants' exclusion from politics in Delaware County and their status as landlords' political clients in Albany and Columbia simultaneously extended landlords' power and limited settlers' independent access to the political system. But landlords' political control was never absolute. In important ways, the very survival of the leasehold system rested on this imperfect grasp on power. In the 30 years after the Revolution, settlers on the eastern frontier of the great manors offered numerous challenges to the leasehold system. The fate of their challenges was determined in the political arena.

Rebellion

The social peace forged between landlords and tenants did not go unchallenged. In four separate rebellions between 1751 and 1813, tenants and squatters in the eastern hill towns of Livingston Manor and Claverack and in Dutchess and Westchester Counties rejected the landlords' claim to the land and called for its distribution among the people who farmed it. Beginning in 1751–1757 as a movement of squatters from New England, these insurrections spread to established tenants as well. By 1811, most rebels were leaseholders. Regardless of their makeup, militants voiced ideals and pursued strategies that changed little over time.[52]

At the heart of every antiproprietor movement lay a set of beliefs about property that insurgents shared with frontier rebels throughout the new nation. Squatters and tenants carefully examined proprietors' titles, concluding that they were "not valid and without foundation." Although some rebels sought to establish their own right to the land with competing Indian titles, most appealed to an alternative tradition of property rights. Like other backcountry rebels of the Revolutionary era, they drew on a popular belief, dating back to the seventeenth-century frontier, that wilderness land rightfully belonged to those who "improved" it by clearing trees, breaking cropland, and constructing houses, fences, and barns. They believed that independent proprietorship was the natural status of free men, and that as long as unimproved land existed, everyone willing to improve it had a claim to a portion of it. Thus the Claverack insurgents of 1766 declared that "the land belongs to its bona fide tillers." Benjamin Birdsall, a leader of the Livingston Manor insurgents in 1811, agreed. "The people on the manor," he wrote, "live in a state of vassalage and servile dependence, incompatible with their rights and liberties as Americans." That dependence lay in the Livingstons' ability, through a fraudulent title, to cut tenants off from "the common bounties of nature." Here was an extended and radical version of loyal tenants' ideas. Where peaceful estate residents defended their property rights to the products of their labor in the form of improvements and timber from common lands, leasehold rebels claimed that the act of improvement gave them a claim to the land itself.[53]

Armed with these ideas, rebels petitioned colonial and state officials to overturn the proprietors' titles, while landlords lobbied for the vindication of their titles and the military suppression of the insurgents. At the same time, both sides struggled for control of the disputed territory. Rebel supporters, organized as Massachusetts militia units in the 1750s but later in crowds or informal paramilitary units, carried out a program of intimidation and violence against settlers loyal to the landlords. For their part, landlords commissioned lawmen to evict rebels and convinced state officials to send in the militia.[54]

The insurrections offered the greatest possible test of landlords' political power. The Livingstons and Van Rensselaers convinced provincial officials to crush the rebellion of the 1750s but suffered serious setbacks between the 1760s and 1780s. Unable to dislodge the insurgents from his estate and faced with a campaign by provincial and royal officials to revoke his title, John Van Rensselaer agreed to surrender some 66,000 acres of rebel territory in exchange for a patent confirming the rest of his estate. Loyalist landlords in Dutchess and Westchester counties also lost out when the new state government seized and sold their estates to their rebellious tenants. During the 1790s, however, landlords regained their former political power. Although they did not dominate either state party, they constituted a critical bloc within each. Only a handful of Republican officials offered support to the Livingston Manor rebels during the 1790s, and the Livingston family had little trouble convincing the legislature to ignore tenant petitions and send in the militia.[55]

During the 1810s, however, landlords' power to stem tenant challenges slipped again. Between 1801 and 1806, both branches of the Livingston family returned to the Federalist fold, effectively ending landlord influence in the ruling Republican party. In the wake of these defections, many Republicans began to appeal to tenant discontent. In 1811, numerous Jeffersonian legislators sought to enlist the state in support of tenants' efforts to overturn the title of George Clarke and to end legal enforcement of the quarter sale.[56] That same year, a 29-year-old lawyer named Martin Van Buren launched his electoral career by championing the cause of insurgent tenants on Livingston Manor. Van Buren took the case of the Livingston tenants, advising them that the patent to Livingston Manor was based on "fraudulent misrepresentation" and attacking the title in a series of letters to the *Hudson Advocate*. The following year, the state legislature directed Attorney General Thomas A. Emmet to sue for recovery of Livingston Manor. In the midst of this brewing conflict, Van Buren ran for state senate against Edward P. Livingston. After numerous public confrontations with the landlords, including one in which a surveyor for the Van Rensselaers challenged him to a duel, Van Buren won.[57]

Never before had political leaders shown such willingness to challenge the leasehold system. But the landlords still retained considerable political power, and their allies defeated every one of these challenges. The bills to overturn George Clarke's title and abrogate the quarter sale died in the legislature. Before the suit to recover Livingston Manor came to trial, the Council of Appointment replaced Emmet as attorney general with Abraham Van Vechten, Stephen Van Rensselaer's brother-in-law and private attorney. When Van Buren and Emmet (whom the tenants had hired upon his removal as attorney general) asked Van Vechten for a routine postponement of the case, the new attorney general refused. Unprepared and unwilling to go forward, Van Buren and Emmet refused to participate. Van Vechten halfheartedly tried the case, and lost. Thereafter, the legislature dropped all agitation on the leasehold issue, and Van Buren, now in the state senate and quickly assuming the leadership of the anti-Clinton Republicans, never again championed rebellious tenants in his home county. When the defeated Livingston tenants turned to violence, the state legislature sent in troops.[58] Once again, landlords' political power proved sufficient to quell any challenge to their dominion over the land.

With the exception of the Dutchess and Westchester uprisings in the 1760s, tenant and squatter rebellions remained on the eastern edge of the leasehold district. After the Revolution, only a tiny minority of tenants rose up against their landlords, and only the Manor Livingstons and the Van Rensselaers of Claverack faced insurgencies on their estates. Elsewhere, social peace prevailed. But the ideas that informed the rebellions were present on every manor and patent. Between 1790 and 1815, tenants, insurgent politicians, or rival claimants challenged the titles to every major estate in New York. Tenant insurgents' ideals of independent proprietorship survived among quiescent tenants as well. Many who signed leases on Rensselaerwyck appended the term "yeoman" after their names, thus asserting their status as independent proprietors while entering a relationship of dependency.[59] And the rebels' view that occupying improvement gave laborers a claim to the soil was only a short leap from the beliefs that led thousands of squatters and tenants to use the commons and to claim property in their improvements.

What separated loyal tenants from rebels was less their aspirations than their assessment of their interests and strategic situation. Most tenants remained loyal because their landlords rewarded loyalty and because proprietors' political power made rebellion foolhardy. Their aim was to get and keep property—a goal they shared both with Empire State rebels and with insurgent farmers throughout the early republic. But where tenant insurgents and other rural rebels sought property through collective resistance, most New York tenants believed that the most reliable way to acquire it was by cooperating with their landlords. In this respect, rebellions served as a warning to both landlords and tenants. Settlers saw in the reports of arrests, burned homes, destroyed crops and evictions the costs of open defiance. Landlords learned that tenants' loyalty was not guaranteed, and discerned the price of losing that loyalty in unpaid rents, deserted farmland, lobbying expenses, and court fees. Both learned that they could not act just as they wished; both learned to be circumspect in pressing for advantage.

The Revival of the Gentry

Outside the tumultuous eastern frontiers of Claverack and Livingston Manor, post-Revolutionary landlords and tenants proved willing to accommodate one another's needs and demands. In doing so, both were able to realize, with some qualifications, their central aim: the reproduction of their families and their modes of living across time. Landlords' success in populating the hill country on their estates with deferential, paying tenants allowed them to perpetuate themselves as an American gentry. Tenants' rents expanded their wealth, enabling them to display the "attributes of social superiority"—wealth, education, worldly experience, and refinement—which they believed qualified men to govern the economic, cultural, and political life of a republic. At Robert R. Livingston's home, the Polish nobleman Ursyn Niemcewicz "saw for the first time in America a European style of living, a magnificent carriage, superb horses, the servants in livery." Children grew up surrounded by books, Gobelin tapestries, and French furniture. Boys and girls began receiving private instruction at a very young age. For the boys, this instruction ended with attendance at college and a two- to five-year tour of Europe. Women refined their accomplishments in languages, literature, and music while keeping up with contemporary fashions in dress and coiffure; men cultivated learning and fashionableness but united these with a magisterial bearing.[60]

Where rents provided opportunities to cultivate refinement and genteel manners, tenant votes furnished a springboard to public power. Stephen Van Rensselaer served eight terms in the state legislature, two as lieutenant governor, and three as a member of the U.S. House of Representatives. Robert R. Livingston represented New York at the Second Continental Congress; helped draft the state's constitution in 1777; served as chancellor, the second most powerful office in the state, for decades; acted as the U.S. secretary of foreign affairs; and represented Thomas Jefferson's administration in France, where he helped negotiate the Louisiana Purchase. Members of a half-dozen proprietor clans occupied prominent places on the New York bench and in its legislature, constitutional conventions, and congressional delegations.[61]

These men saw political office as part of a broader mission of public service. Consumed by a faith that reason could unlock the secrets of nature and society, Robert R. Livingston published treatises on continental exploration, a national currency, the execution of monarchs, and the shortcomings of the postal service. He devoted his Clermont farm to agricultural experiments, publishing the results in a series of pamphlets. And he organized and funded numerous projects for agricultural and commercial "improvement": importing and promoting Merino sheep, attempting to manufacture paper from a local river weed known as "frog's spit," and developing Robert Fulton's steamboat. Van Rensselaer helped finance dozens of churches, moral reform societies, and orphanages and provided the cash to establish the Rensselaer School (later Rensselaer Polytechnic Institute), which quickly became the leading institution for scientific training in the New World. He also championed the cause of internal improvements, providing critical leadership in the building of the Erie Canal.[62] Through his efforts, Livingston hoped to contribute to the "happiness of man" by making discoveries "known into the common stock . . . by which the friends of the earth are increased." He also hoped

Figure 1.8. Robert R. Livingston in 1804. Painted while he was envoy to Paris ne-
gotiating the Louisiana Purchase, this portrait trumpets Livingston's mastery of
genteel ideals. His clothing establishes both his wealth and his refined taste, while
his relaxed but erect posture (as well as the extended right forefinger, ubiquitous
in portraits of gentlemen) provides evidence of a magisterial bearing. Beneath
his right hand is his "Plan for establishing an Academy of Fine Arts in New York,"
evidence of his application of his intelligence and education to the arts and to
public service. To the right is another tribute to his public service: a letter addressed to "Robt R. Livingston, Minister Plenipotentu[r]y from the United States
of America, Paris." *Robert R. Livingston*, 1804, by John Vanderlyn. © Collection of
the New-York Historical Society.

for an appropriate reward. The man who could introduce clover into general
use among farmers, he wrote, "will perhaps be better entitled to a Statue than
any other man in America . . . You will judge from my exertions that I am not
unambitious of the honor?"[63]

In their public activities, Livingston and Van Rensselaer pursued a vision
of progress that united enlightenment republicanism, patrician elitism, and

a faith in the ameliorative power of commerce. They wished to harness the power of reason to spread enlightenment and prosperity through every level of society. "It seems to comport better with the habits of our citizens and the genius of our government," Van Rensselaer wrote, "to place the advantages of useful improvement, equally within the reaches of all." To both men, such "improvement" was inseparable from commercial and industrial expansion. Their agricultural reform work focused on increasing farmers' commercial output and convincing them to adopt more entrepreneurial, market-sensitive practices. Van Rensselaer actively promoted manufacturing, which he "deem[ed] of vital importance to the independence of our country." His beloved Erie Canal and Livingston's steamboat aimed at tying such farmers to market towns and cities throughout the Empire State.[64]

Livingston and Van Rensselaer sought to transform Americans' living standards and culture, not their social relationships. They expected the extension of commerce, the expansion of agricultural production, and the growth of manufacturing to make American society more like their estates: benevolent hierarchies with themselves at the top. Decrying the "envy and ambitions of the unworthy" who sought to spread the belief that "education, experience, application, and genius [are] unnecessary in those who frame laws," Livingston insisted that only those who enjoyed "the competence [i.e., the estate] which affords leisure" were fit "to attend to the affairs of government." Landlords shared this belief with other members of the post-Revolutionary gentry, who celebrated a vision of commercial and industrial development guided by disinterested men of leisure.[65] As long as tenants remained loyal and paid their rents, this vision seemed achievable.

A Quasi-Yeomanry

The expansion of the leasehold system also allowed settlers to fulfill their primary aspiration: to recreate communities of independent, productive, patriarchal households in a new setting. Paradoxically, by acknowledging proprietors' dominion over the land and accepting political and social subordination to them, hill tenants were able to create communities marked by rough economic equality, household autonomy, and widespread access to natural resources.

Like their parents, tenants in the hill towns sought to create property and meet their material needs through a household-based system of labor. Children began to work as soon as they were able to perform limited chores; as they grew older, their parents assigned them tasks of increasing difficulty and responsibility. Males and females did the work assumed to be appropriate to their sex. Specific definitions of which tasks were "female" and which "male" shifted over time and varied from one ethnic group and family to another, but the notion that some tasks were masculine and others feminine remained constant.

Figure 1.9. Built on a 100,000–acre tract in western New York owned by a nephew of Stephen Van Rensselaer, this freehold settler's cabin resembled those built by post-Revolutionary settlers on New York's leasehold estates. The rail fences required a great deal of timber but relatively little labor. The stumps in the field often remained for years. The pig was not penned; rather, the fence surrounded crops and was designed to keep animals out. *First Cottage of Angelica*, 1808, by Baroness Hyde de Neuville. © Collection of the New–York Historical Society.

This system of production rested on patriarchal authority. Fathers had the power to regulate the labor, behavior, and morals of their wives and children. Their authority found sanction in the law, which denied children and wives a legal personality, preventing them from owning property, entering contracts, suing, or being sued. In the eyes of the law, civic rights—owning property, engaging in economic exchange, suing, voting—came to women and minors through their fathers or husbands. Patriarchal authority was also buttressed by inheritance practices, which kept land in the hands of men. Of the 13 fathers in the Helderberg mountains of Albany County who recorded wills between 1800 and 1815, 11 either gave twice as much land to sons as to daughters or reserved land for their male offspring, leaving daughters a cash bequest. Out of ten fathers with wills in the major leasehold towns of Delaware County, 7 did the same.[66]

In daily practice, however, husbands and wives took responsibility for different tasks, leaving one another free to fulfill those duties as they saw fit. William Coventry, a freehold farmer on the valley lands of Livingston Manor, carefully recorded his own work in growing crops, fishing, hunting, cutting timber, repairing buildings, and making tools. But he never mentioned the equally essential tasks performed by his wife—cooking, cleaning, growing vegetables, caring for their young children, sewing, making textiles. Beriah Holcom, a tenant in the hills of Rensselaer County, engaged in extensive trade with his neighbors in grain, apples, cider, hay, and meat. Although married, he never once recorded trading the textiles, eggs, milk, butter, and vegetables that farm women in central and eastern New York produced. Their wives controlled those tasks and exchanges.[67]

Tenants buttressed this coordination of tasks with an ethos of cooperation and submission. Fathers—and perhaps wives and children—believed that individuals should work for the good of the family and submit to the control of the male family head. Daniel Smith of Berne bequeathed all of his real and personal estate to his oldest son, Josiah. In return, he commanded Josiah to provide his mother and three underage brothers with "a comfortable and decent maintenance" and to "give Learning sufficient to transact any common business" to his brothers. For her part, Josiah's mother was to "do what shall be reasonable towards maintaining her own children," while Josiah's brothers were told to "be under his controle and assist in improving said farm for their common benefit." Smith's instructions represented a patriarch's effort to exercise his authority from beyond the grave. They also served to appoint a new patriarch to "controle" a young family. Testators like Smith saw patriarchal authority as ensuring that everyone worked for "the common benefit," and they instructed their heirs to use that authority to those ends.[68]

Tenant families supplemented their labor with help from other households. Those with few sons or daughters of working age took in young members of child-rich or distressed households. All families exchanged work with neighbors and organized "bees," inviting the entire neighborhood to help raise a barn, clear trees, or husk corn and providing the volunteers with ample food, drink, and music for dancing. By relying on family efforts and labor exchanges with neighbors, hill tenants minimized their expenditures—a critical consideration, given their shortage of funds and their need to augment their property. They made little use of slavery, which was expensive and morally repugnant to Yankee settlers.[69]

Wage work was more common but still scarce and expensive. Even a valley farmer like William Coventry, who lived in an area where cash and wage laborers were more plentiful than in the hill towns, wrote that he hoped his children would "never hire done what they Can doe themselves." Beriah Holcolm, who leased 60 acres in the hills of Rensselaerwyck, shared Coventry's sentiments. A total of eight males worked on Holcolm's farm between 1809 and 1815. Five were neighboring landowners who exchanged labor with Holcolm; they provided Holcolm with more produce than labor, and Holcolm repaid them in part with his own labor. Only three men worked in what seems to have been a wage relation, providing Holcolm with labor (and occasionally cash) in exchange for cash and produce. These men seem to have been the sons of local farmers, whose families could spare them only sporadically. Daniel Smith worked 10 days in 1811, but no one else worked for more than four days in a given year.[70]

Drawing primarily on family efforts and labor exchange between landed households, hill tenants divided their efforts among a stunning array of activities. Typically, women and girls raised vegetables, tended geese and chickens, and manufactured cloth, soap, candles, dyes, and beer.[71] Men grew diverse crops—wheat, corn, rye, buckwheat, potatoes, flax, apples—and raised hogs, cattle, and sheep. They also drew a substantial portion of their living from the woods. They cut wood for their own fuel, building materials, furniture, and tools, as well as procuring logs, hemlock bark (used by local tanners in curing leather), charcoal, wood ashes (made into potash by local merchants), shingles, and barrel staves for sale. Many followed secondary and tertiary occupations: William Coventry made shoes; Beriah Holcolm milled cider.[72]

This kaleidoscopic array of products served several purposes. They dispersed risk, allowing a family to withstand the failure of one or two crops without facing severe want. They spread labor requirements throughout the year, increasing the productive capacities of families.[73] They also kept down capital costs. The goods that tenants grew and manufactured required a relatively small investment: spades, axes, a plow, a yoke of oxen, a harrow, a hoe, a few scythes or cradles, two or three spinning wheels, a loom. These fell far short of the investment needed for commercial production of tobacco, butter, or cheese.[74]

Hill tenants' varied production also permitted them to strike a prudent balance between self-sufficiency and market production. Tenants met most of their consumption needs through their own efforts, thus conserving money and minimizing their vulnerability to shifts in commodity prices. They also produced goods for local exchange, which permitted them to acquire from their neighbors most of the necessities that they had failed to produce themselves. Beriah Holcolm's large orchards and cider mill allowed him to supply his neighbors with apples and cider and to receive grain, bricks, shoes, shingles, money, and work in exchange.[75]

Tenants also produced sizable surpluses for sale in long-distance markets. Men devoted their greatest efforts to wheat and timber products—precisely the goods that found the most ready markets. Cloth, the main commodity produced by women, also found a lively market. Marketing their products gave tenants access to some of the goods that they and their neighbors could not produce. In 1811, the customers at Lewis Hardenbergh's Roxbury store traded their ashes, shingles, hemlock bark, grain, and apples for luxuries like brandy, snuff, and tea and for necessities like metal pots, powder, shot, and tableware. Trade also provided a hedge against want—a critical consideration to families with little cleared land. During the winter and spring, when supplies ran short, Hardenbergh's customers bought large amounts of codfish, ham, and butter. Above all, long-distance trade allowed settlers to acquire funds with which to accumulate productive property. Poor roads, a paucity of merchants, and families' desire to feed and clothe themselves from their own farms set limits on hill tenants' ability to trade. But that trade proved critical to both family economies and the economy of the region.[76]

A final reason for tenants' diversified production was that it allowed them to supplement the produce of their small clearings with timber, game, fish, and livestock feed from the common lands of the estates. Use of the commons engendered conflict both with landlords, who strove to curtail tenants' timber cutting, and with other tenants, who objected to the damage done by free-ranging livestock. Unpenned rams attacked people and animals; roaming hogs broke through neighbors' fences and ate their crops; cattle dined on the hay in wagons and sleighs.[77] Incidents like these led to contentious town meetings in which farmers who worried about depredations on their crops battled the defenders of an open range. The first Rensselaer town meeting in 1795 declared that "Hogs may be permitted to go on the commons" provided they were outfitted with wooden yokes that prevented them from slipping through fence slats and rings that kept them from digging up crops. Rams, on the other hand, were to be penned between August and November. In 1804 the town prohibited all hogs and sheep on the commons but continued to tolerate roaming cattle. Two years later, the town reversed itself, declaring hogs "commoners" as long as they were yoked and ringed. In 1812, they reversed themselves again, prohibiting the roaming of horses, sheep, and hogs. In 1817, they again reversed course; hogs once again won the privilege to "run on the Commons." Roxbury residents applied no restrictions to livestock's use of the commons before 1809, when they outlawed the roaming of rams. The following year, they restricted the use of unenclosed land by hogs, rams, and horses during the summer and early fall (the time when crops were growing)—a practice that continued, with minor adjustments, into the 1820s.[78]

Rensselaerville's and Roxbury's actions attested to the conflict generated by the use of unenclosed land for pasture. But they also bespoke hill farmers' commitment to keeping unenclosed lands open to use by community members. Roxbury residents sought to regulate the use of the commons in ways that minimized livestock's depredations on crops, not to outlaw it. Even at their most restrictive, the people of Rensselaerville allowed cattle, which posed little threat to crops, to roam free most of the year. Neither town put restrictions on residents' timber cutting on common lands.

Together, landlords' policy of renting land in small lots and hill tenants' dependence on family labor, use of common lands, and modest production for market created a comparatively equal distribution of wealth. In the Albany County hill town of Rensselaerville, the wealthiest 10 percent of residents controlled 26 percent of the town's total wealth (including leased land) in 1800. The poorest half of taxpayers, in contrast, controlled 22 percent of the town's wealth. The richest tenth of Roxbury taxpayers in Delaware County held 30 percent of the town's wealth, while the bottom half claimed

25 percent. The gap between rich and poor, though real, was significantly milder than in the older agricultural settlements from which most tenants had come. [79] Inequalities in wealth largely paralleled those of age. Young men usually remained in their parents' households until their middle or late 20s, awaiting inheritance or accumulating the property they needed to farm with their own families.[80] Even after starting their own households, young men tended to be poorer than their older neighbors (see Appendix, table 1).[81] To a great extent, a lack of property was a matter of life stage; most younger, propertyless men could look forward to gaining property through inheritance or slow accumulation.

By the standards of their day, the largest property holders of the hill towns were men of modest wealth. The top tenth of Rensselaer's taxpayers owned estates worth between $1,383 and $4,222, making them about as rich as the middle third of New York City shoemakers or coopers. Roxbury's top 10 percent enjoyed an even scantier prosperity, with estates ranging in value from $563 to $2,160. Despite small fortunes, these men enjoyed an honored place in the leasehold hill towns. The merchants and millers among them provided essential services—milling grain, sawing logs, providing a market for farm and timber products, selling luxuries and necessities. Their businesses served as centers of community life, where men and women gathered, exchanged news, and conducted business. Taverns also served as centers for public business, housing both justice court and town meetings. The owners of these enterprises cultivated patron-client relationships with their poorer neighbors, acting as intermediaries with landlords and other powerful outsiders.[82]

Residents repaid these services with public honor. Just as they immortalized landlords in the names of towns and counties, tenants honored millers and manufacturers by naming the villages that sprung up around their businesses after them. Thus the village in Rensselaerville that grew alongside the mills owned by Uriah Hall came to be known as Hall's Mills; the village surrounding Samuel Jenkins's sawmill was named Jenkins's Mills; and the neighborhood of Peleg Peckham's tannery became known as Peckham's Hollow. Tenants also rewarded their leading men with prominent places in public life. Moses Smith, a Rensselaerville merchant and tavernkeeper, served four terms in the state legislature between 1804 and 1821. Johann Jost Deitz, a merchant in Bern, enjoyed "a marked influence" in the Dutch Reformed Church, served as a lieutenant in the local militia, acted as town supervisor for 12 years, and spent a dozen years in the state assembly. All assemblymen, sheriffs, and county judges who could be found in the 1800 tax list for Rensselaerville were among the top 10 percent of that town's property owners.[83]

If the men at the top of their town's economic ladder constituted a special group, so did those at the bottom. The number of hill town residents who had no access to landed property can only be estimated, but there were many of them. Of the 727 household heads who lived in Rensselaerville in 1800, 188 to 224—between 26 and 31 percent—did not own or lease land.

Between 124 and 174 (17 to 24 percent) controlled no property, real or personal, at all. Propertyless householders tended to be younger than their lease-holding counterparts.[84] Many of the landless were thus awaiting inheritance or accumulating the property with which to begin farming with their wives and children. Still, many of the landless were middle-aged or older. Some landless men were probably new arrivals, reconnoitering the area before leasing a farm; some doubtless had already passed their farms over to their children, while others probably left town between the tax assessor's and the census marshal's visit. And many were probably artisans and merchants—men who did not need land to prosper. But a small number of mature men had not yet—and might never—achieve a competence. Though the leasehold system provided a landed competence to most household heads, it did not provide it to all.

Despite inequalities, the economic dependence due to gender and generation was far more salient than class subordination in the hill towns. Extreme poverty usually resulted from old age, ill health, and bad luck, not from class-based deprivation. All of the Revolutionary War veterans who applied for government pensions between 1820 and 1826 from the major leasehold towns of Delaware County attributed their poverty to their and their family members' inability to work, due to illness, injury, or old age. Of 24 applicants, 12 listed their occupations as farmers, five were artisans, one was a miller, and one was a minister. Only three listed their occupations as day laborers or mentioned working for wages.[85]

The independence of the poor rested largely on the presence of the commons. The ability to hunt, fish, graze their livestock, strip bark, and cut timber on unimproved lands benefitted the prosperous and poor alike. But it had a special significance for the poor. It allowed them to meet a significant portion of their subsistence needs and to obtain money and credit with which to obtain land, livestock, and tools without depending on any particular person for employment. More than anything else, the presence of large tracts of common lands explains how a shortage of wage labor could exist amid a significant number of landless settlers.

By the late 1810s, landlords and most tenants had forged a tenuous peace. By yielding to proprietors' demands for rents and deference, tenants had won a secure hold on the land. By showing lenience and generosity, landlords were enjoying incomes and a degree of political power befitting their self-image as "candidates for glory." But beneath this peace lay ongoing conflicts of interest and aspirations. As long as landlords retained their political power and acted with restraint toward tenants, such conflicts could be contained. But if they failed to do either, peace on the estates might give way to open conflict.

Chapter 2

TOWARD CRISIS,

1819 – 1840

><+<+>-•-O-•-<+>-+<

Financial Troubles

When Robert Livingston, third proprietor of Livingston Manor, died in 1790, he divided the Manor among five sons. With this act, he abandoned family practice, rejected centuries of English and continental tradition, and endangered the economic power of the family line. Robert's father, Philip, and his father before him, had passed the estate to their eldest sons, bequeathing smaller parcels to their daughters and younger sons. Robert's grandfather had also entailed the estate, forbidding his heir from passing it to anyone but the "heirs male of ye name of Livingston" and enjoining him from selling it "to a Stranger." Other proprietors did the same, and for good reason. By preventing the division of their estates, they guaranteed the wealth and power of the lineage.[1]

But landlords who lived through and supported the Revolution came to see such practices as aristocratic and unfair to younger children. Leasehold proprietors were as anxious as their fellow patriots to eradicate hereditary aristocracy; the elite they wished to create was a "natural" one, based on merit, not birth. Doing so, they believed, meant abolishing a wide range of legal and familial practices—including primogeniture and entail. At the same time, they fell under the influence of new ideals of family life that emphasized the uniqueness of each child. Like Robert Livingston, they began to treat their children equally in their wills. When Johannes Van Rensselaer died in 1784, he divided Claverack among his five children. A few years later, Margaret Beekman Livingston distributed the 753,000-acre estate of her husband, Robert, equally among her 10 offspring. By the 1830s, only Rensselaerwyck and the lands of George C. Clarke remained in the hands of a single proprietor.[2]

To make matters worse, young landlords abandoned older practices of using marriage to buttress their families' wealth. Betrothals among colonial proprietors were rarely arranged; children chose their own mates, subject to the approval of their parents. But parents refused to sanction marriages unless they promised to augment the family estate.[3] After the Revolution, landlords joined other Americans in embracing a new, companionate ideal of marriage; dowries and the consolidation of fortunes gave way to a new emphasis on love and companionship. The 1770 marriage of Robert R. Livingston to Mary Stevens joined his Clermont and Hardenbergh Patent lands to the vast New Jersey tracts of the Stevens family. But the weddings of his younger sisters brought no such financial union. Gertrude married Morgan Lewis, a brilliant law student with a negligible inheritance; Margaret pledged herself to Thomas Tillotson, a man without family, talents, or patrimony. Catherine ran off with a Methodist circuit rider, while Alida wed John Armstrong, who described himself as "too poor to marry a woman without some fortune." By 1838, the improvidence of her relatives prompted Louise Livingston to conclude that "the Livingstons have none of them sufficient moral courage to·marry wealth."[4]

The result was inevitable. With the passing of each generation, the landed wealth of the proprietors was carved up like a carcass at a barbecue, and the betrothal of young heirs did nothing to fatten the portions. By the 1810s and 1820s, individual landlords were beginning to feel the pinch. Margaret Maria and Robert L. Livingston inherited half the estate of Margaret Maria's father, Chancellor Livingston, in 1813. This legacy—land in 20 towns, city lots in the metropolis, a share in the Hudson River steamboat trade—provided them with an income of $10,405 in 1817. Though princely by the standards of most New Yorkers, this revenue fell far short of the needs of men and women of their upbringing. In 1804, the Chancellor had concluded that no gentleman could live "*honnêtment*" on less than $15,000 a year. Robert and Margaret Maria might have found this estimate wanting, especially during the inflationary 1810s; they certainly failed to live within their more modest means. The couple had acquired cultivated tastes and sensibilities at an early age; as adults, they naturally indulged their passion for art, fine wines, and European travel. They conceived nine children, eight of whom survived the nursery and had to be provided with books, tutors, winters in New York City, and tours of the Continent. The couple was besieged with requests for aid from impecunious sisters and cousins, which they granted with reckless regularity. As a result, they faced a stack of debts that grew with each passing year.[5] Other proprietors faced similar troubles. Edward Livingston's debts totaled a quarter of a million dollars, leading his creditors to seize vast tracts of his Hardenbergh patent lands during the 1820s and 1830s. Although he enjoyed an undivided patrimony, Stephen Van Rensselaer's passion for funding schools, moral reform societies, and scientific experiments saddled him with $400,000 in debt.[6]

As their debts mounted, landlords increasingly abandoned their old commitment to patrician benevolence. Stephen Van Rensselaer continued to fund churches, schools, and agricultural reform societies until his death in 1839, but his children showed no intention of filling his shoes. Similarly, though some young Livingstons participated in home relief organizations in New York City, none took up the chancellor's mantle as a public-spirited man of letters. The heirs of these men displayed an understandable resentment of their fathers' willingness to squander their patrimony on the public weal. Shortly after Van Rensselaer's death, Joseph Eaton, director of the Rensselaer School, wrote the family to remind them of the patroon's promise of another $10,000. Stephen's son Alexander refused to convey the promised help. "It is quite absurd," he wrote, "to suppose that even should any such agreement . . . have been proposed, that at present it can be at all binding." Alexander's resort to the question of legal obligation shows how far he had departed from his father's sense of Christian duty. The family tradition of patrician benevolence was at an end.[7]

A New Economic Landscape

Tenants, too, faced new economic circumstances during the 1820s and 1830s. In the early decades of settlement, their acquisition of property had depended on cheap land, widespread use of the commons, and intensive use of family labor. After 1820, simultaneous and mutually reinforcing changes—population growth, environmental degradation, a switch from grain to livestock, and increasing access to markets—undermined these conditions, forcing tenants to devise new strategies for attaining property, security, and comfort. These strategies brought the hill towns more fully into an emerging capitalist economy. They changed many tenants' thinking. And they created new divisions and dependencies, raising some tenants to new levels of security and comfort while leaving a growing number landless, insecure, and poor.

The most visible change in the hill towns' economy was a switch from grain cultivation to livestock raising. Wheat, the main cash crop of the early settlers, had cost relatively little to grow and had yielded as many as 20 bushels per acre. But settlers cropped the same soil year after year, quickly exhausting its fertility. Winter frosts, smut, rust, and mildew devastated crops from the 1810s on; the wheat midge and Hessian fly wiped them out in the 1830s. In the meantime, the opening of the Erie Canal flooded local markets with cheap western wheat, ending all hope of making significant income with the crop.[8] Tenants continued to raise a wide variety of other crops and livestock, thus providing for family consumption, dispersing the risk of failed crops and low commodity prices, and spreading labor requirements throughout the year. But they replaced wheat with two new cash crops: wool and butter. With the explosive growth of the textile industry after 1815, Delaware county leasehold farmers' flocks grew by 13 percent between 1825 (the first year for which there are figures) and 1840; Helderberg flocks grew by 8 percent. At the same time, tenants in both counties began to specialize in the production of butter, which found ready markets in the region's cities and towns. Cattle

Stone House on the John More Farm—1829

Figure 2.1. During the 1820s and 1830s, widening access to markets and the improvements accumulated through decades of labor allowed many tenants to live in a degree of comfort unknown to their parents. Many replaced their smaller houses and log cabins with larger and more comfortable houses like this one, which John More, a prosperous Roxbury farmer, built in 1829. The new prosperity eluded landless estate residents, however. From Irma Mae Griffin, *History of the Town of Roxbury*. Courtesy, American Antiquarian Society.

herds in the Helderbergs grew by 18 percent between 1825 and 1840, while Delaware County tenants increased their cattle by 21 percent. (See Appendix, table 2). So critical was the new crop that a Delaware County poet hailed his home with the line: "O! Delaware, thou land of butter."[9]

Butter and wool were both worth singing about, for they offered farmers a way to earn cash and credit. But they drove up the costs of farming, placing new obstacles in the way of landless families seeking independence. A prosperous dairy required an expanded barn with room for wintering the herd and for storing winter hay, a dairy house for making butter or cheese, and an ice house for storage. It also required a butter churn or churning machine, a creaming dish, cooling racks, wooden ladles, and firkins for storing butter. Above all, it demanded money for livestock and land. Dairy cows cost between $20 and $25 a head in the 1840s, and each cow required an average of three acres of land. Thus the typical Delaware County herd (17 to 25 cattle) was worth between $340 and $625 and required between 51 and 75 acres of meadow and pasture, in addition to the land and tools needed to cultivate grains, root crops, and orchards. Sheep required less investment in buildings and cost only $2 per head. But they necessitated a proportionate investment in land, and declining prices from the mid-1820s on made them a poor source of income.[10]

Farmers also came to depend more on purchased seeds, fertilizers, and patented tools, all of which drove up their capital costs. Beginning in the 1820s, hill tenants replaced their old practice of weed fallowing with the cultivation of English meadow grasses like timothy and clover from purchased seed. They occasionally bought soil conditioners like plaster or lime and made increasing use of patented plows. And increasing numbers of them purchased blooded stock to interbreed with their native sheep. These innovations restored soil fertility and improved wool and milk production, but they also added to the costs of farming.[11]

The greatest hindrance to achieving economic independence, however, was a growing population. In the early decades of settlement, land had been available at no initial cost. But virtually all leasehold lands had been taken up by 1807; thereafter, young families could acquire a farm only by buying it from the present occupants, acquiring it from a landlord at a high rent, or inheriting it. The first option proved expensive: farmland in the Helderbergs sold for $10 to $20 an acre in 1820. The last promised the surest avenue to prosperity, but an increasing number of young men and women found it blocked. The number of inhabitants in the Helderbergs more than quadrupled between 1790 and 1820, leaving the area even more crowded than the New England towns that most early settlers had left. The leasehold towns of Delaware County grew more slowly, but lower population densities were partly offset by a more mountainous terrain, which left more land unsuitable for farming.[12] Early settlers had tried to accommodate their numerous offspring by dividing their farms among several sons. By 1840, this practice had left many farms too small to divide again. In the town of Westerlo, which had been carved out of Rensselaerville in 1825, 60 percent of farms (237 or 397) contained less than 100 acres, and a quarter (99) contained less than 50 (see Appendix, table 3). In response, the majority of fathers who registered wills passed their land on to only one child or dictated that the farm be sold and divided among their offspring. A smaller but growing number of Delaware farmers abandoned partible inheritance as well. As a result, increasing numbers of children received no landed inheritance.[13]

Diminishing legacies and increasing capital costs left leasehold farmers with a pressing need for cash. Tenants responded by dramatically increasing their production for market. George and Lucinda Holcolm, who rented 154 acres in the hills of Rensselaer County, practiced a diversified agriculture that in broad outlines differed little from that of George's father Beriah. With their two sons and three daughters, they raised at least 23 different crops and species of livestock in 1830, combining grains, vegetables, and orchard products with hay, sheep, hogs, and cattle. In addition, Lucinda and the girls made textiles, clothing, butter, and cheese. With this varied production, the Holcolms were able to satisfy most of their material wants from their own production. But George marketed far more of his crop than his father had ever done. Whenever weather permitted, he carted apples, onions, potatoes, cabbages, plums, and chestnuts to Troy, Pittstown, or Albany. In late November he sold 15 beef cattle, 3 calves, and 13 ewes, along with meat and hides from the fall slaughter. For her part, Lucinda produced a small amount of butter and cheese for sale and made occasional barrels of applesauce for George to haul to nearby cities and towns. In all, George made a total of 62 marketing trips in 1830, selling more than $500 worth of produce.[14]

Farmers like Holcolm were greatly aided by—and, in turn, helped create—a significant expansion in markets for their produce. After the War of 1812, the market towns of Albany, Troy, Catskill, Hudson, New York, and Philadelphia underwent phenomenal growth, and a burst of road, turnpike, and railway building improved tenants' access to them. The number of local merchants expanded as well, from 35 in 1820 to 104 in 1840 in the Helderbergs and from 17 to 79 in the main leasehold towns of Delaware County. The 1820s also witnessed the emergence of specialized commission merchants in wool, butter, and cheese, who made their living by collecting local farmers' produce and selling it on commission in New York.[15]

Tenants increased their market production both by working harder and by selectively shifting their efforts from consumption items to marketable commodities. Between 1825 and 1845, leasehold farmers cleared tens of thousands of new acres, increasing the number of improved acres per inhabitant by 20 percent in the Helderbergs and by 58 percent in the main Delaware County leasehold towns. And they cultivated each acre more intensively, adopting soil-preservation techniques like crop rotation, manuring, and fallowing with English grasses.[16] They also cut back dramatically on producing those subsistence items that were least remunerative or most easily replaced. Most tenants stopped producing wheat by the 1840s, and those that continued producing it did so only in small quantities. In an equally decisive shift, women transferred their labor from cloth production to cheese and butter making. Between 1830 and 1840, Lucinda Holcolm, her daughters, and her servant girls cut back on their spinning and weaving; the family's yearly purchases of factory cloth grew from 41 to 123 yards. At the same time, the value of the butter and cheese they sold grew from $20.28 to $119, bringing in over a third of the family's cash income. As was the case in much of the rural northeast, leasehold farmers' transition to a more market-centered agriculture rested largely on the transformation of women's work.[17]

Tenants also met their growing need for income by increasing their use of the commons. With a growing population and the rapid conversion of commons into improved farmland, a continuation of earlier levels of hunting, fishing, grazing, and timber cutting would have placed growing demands on an ever-diminishing supply of land. But tenants did not hold their use of the commons to old levels, for the market for forest products exploded at the very moment that they urgently needed money. Glass factories and village residents created a new demand for firewood. A growing army of tanners paid for the wholesale stripping of hemlock trees. Blacksmiths and metal works fueled a boom in charcoal production. Merchants advertised for boards, bark, shingles, barrels, ashes, and furs. Lumbermen along the Delaware River floated unprecedented numbers of logs to Philadelphia. By the end of the 1840s, extensive areas of Albany, Rensselaer, and Schoharie counties suffered from deforestation and soil erosion, the result of what David Ellis calls the "ruthless destruction" of upland forests.[18]

Population growth and the shift toward a more capital-intensive and commercial agriculture changed social and economic relationships as dramatically as they altered the upland ecology. One major change was a dramatic diversification of hill towns' economies. As young men faced new obstacles in acquiring farms, many sought out livelihoods in commerce, manufacturing, and the professions. Glass works, tanneries, metal works, and saddleries sprung up along roads and mill streams; villages became thriving centers of commerce and artisanal production. Between 1820 and 1840, the proportion of economically active Helderbergers who worked in commerce, manufacturing, and the professions grew from 15 to 17 percent; in the Delaware County leasehold towns, merchants, manufacturers and professionals grew from 11 to 19 percent of the population (see Appendix, table 4).[19]

This newly diverse economy meted out increasingly unequal rewards. In Westerlo, the distribution of wealth was moderately more unequal in 1840 than it had been in Rensselaerville in 1800. The wealthiest tenth of the population's share of the town's wealth increased from 26 to 30 percent, while the share owned by the poorest half fell from 22 to 20 percent. In Roxbury, the trend toward stratification was more dramatic: the wealthiest tenth of that town's population increased its share of total wealth from 27 percent in 1800 to 35 percent in 1840, while the holdings of the poorest half declined from 25 to 17 percent.[20] While the towns' wealthiest citizens attained new levels of prosperity, increasing numbers of young men and women found acquiring even modest property difficult. Although fewer heads of families in Rensselaerville/Westerlo were landless in 1840 than in 1800, increasing numbers of younger men remained in their fathers' or employers' households, continuing their struggle to acquire property into middle age. Where 12 percent of Rensselaerville men aged 26 to 44 had not yet established their own households in 1800, 21 percent in 1840 had failed to do so in that part of town that became Westerlo. The problem of landlessness and dependence was significantly greater in Roxbury. There, nearly a third of heads of family owned no land, and more than a quarter of the men aged 26 to 44 were dependents in the households of others (see Appendix, tables 1, 5, and 6).[21]

Those who failed to acquire land made their way through a patchwork family economy, providing for their material needs through a combination of wage labor and independent production. The Conklins, a poor family in Schoharie County, alternately rented land from prosperous neighbors and bought it on credit. Samuel and his two oldest sons farmed the home tract and hired out to neighbors, clearing land and doing other unsupervised work. Mary and her daughters spun and wove, earning, according to the youngest child, Henry, "over half of our living." The family also relied heavily on common lands. In the early spring, Samuel and the boys made maple sugar, a ready source of cash. As the weather warmed, the children caught trout and gathered wild leeks, cowslips, and adder tongues for the family table. In June and July, Mary and the younger children picked berries, which they dried for sale and winter supplies. With the return of cold weather, Henry and the older boys cut firewood for the family, drew logs, and made shingles for sale. Finally, as sons and daughters grew older, they hired out to other families, relieving the family of their support and earning money that could be added to the family coffers. This modified family economy allowed the Conklins to survive but not to achieve independent proprietorship. The Conklins never paid off a mortgage, instead selling out and moving on every few years.[22]

Poor families in the 1790s probably would have recognized most of the Conklins' strategies for survival. The only new element was the family's heavy dependence on working for wages and renting land from other farmers. By all indications, wage labor and subtenancy became increasingly common after 1820. Where Beriah Holcolm of Rensselaer County hired wage laborers for an average of three days per year between 1809 and 1815, his son George employed a hired girl and a hired boy for at least six months each in 1830, paid 11 others for a total of 78 days' work, and contracted with two neighbors to grow crops on shares. Henry Bull, the owner of a 101-acre farm in the hills of Schoharie County, employed workers for an average of 75 days per year between 1820 and 1845; in some years, his employees worked as many as 349 days. In 1850, 31 percent of all Westerlo farm households (121 out of 392) and 33 percent of Roxbury farm households (115 out of 350) contained at least one person over the age of 12 whose surname differed from that of the other household members; most of these were hired laborers or servants.[23]

Three changes contributed to the growing use of hired labor. First, dramatic increases in improved acreage per farm and the shift toward dairying increased farmers' need for labor. Dairy production required a steady supply of female labor from March through December, as well as tremendous bursts of men's work during the haying season. Households with both sons and daughters of working age could raise a substantial herd with family labor. But those with few working-age sons or daughters or with very large herds needed to hire.[24] Second, the relative shortage of available land and the increased capital costs of farming created a greater need for cash among the young and the land-poor. Finally, where once they could earn that cash exclusively through lumbering on common lands, the depletion of timber stands drove the young and land-poor in many areas to wage labor.

For many laborers, hiring out appears to have been a stage in the life cycle. Almost three quarters of the male laborers and landless farmers in Westerlo and Roxbury were younger than 30. In many cases, these young laborers enjoyed (or endured) a quasi-familial relationship with their employers that would have been familiar to an earlier generation. When George Holcolm hired Elisha Ingraham of Columbia County in 1830, he promised Elisha's father to "pay him 26 dols in clothing and cash and to school him three months." His wife, Lucinda, hired Esther Sheldon, a daughter of a sub-tenant of George's, as live-in help. The Holcolms also took in Quibe Lipp as a boarder so that Quibe could attend the local school. In return, Quibe was to "work two days each week" for George. As with apprenticeship arrange-ments, the Holcolms assumed the role of parents with their young charges. They were to provide for their material needs, instruct them, discipline them, and command their labor. Such relationships could often include genuine affection. When Ruth Conklin hired out to Tom Peaslee, a distant cousin whom she knew as "Uncle Tom," her employer accepted her as a member of the family, providing her with "a good place to work, plenty to wear, [and] plenty to eat." Four years later, she married Peaslee's son Nathan.[25] But for many, wage labor and subtenancy were becoming a long-term, even a per-manent status. Over a quarter of men in Westerlo aged 30 or older and more than a fifth of those 40 or older were laborers or landless farmers. In Roxbury, more than a quarter of the men in both age groups worked for others.[26]

These labor arrangements did not constitute a fully formed labor market. They bore the marks of an improvised local patchwork that, for both em-ployers and employees, merely supplemented family labor. Because of this, individual demand and supply of labor were extremely variable. To get the workers they needed, employers agreed to a wide variety of arrangements. The men who worked for Henry Bull and George Holcolm labored by the task, the afternoon, the day, the week, the month, and occasionally the year; they might labor every other day for a week, every other week for a month, or whenever they were needed and could get away from their other tasks. Some provided their employers not only with labor, but with small amounts of timber, farm produce, and textiles.[27] The poor of the leasehold hill towns, in other words, were not a rural proletariat; their access to productive prop-erty spared them that fate. But there was no denying their growing depen-dence on working for others, just as one could not deny that increased access to markets and superior access to land, livestock, tools, and credit enabled men like Bull and Holcolm to profit from their labor.

Prosperous farmers like Holcolm and Bull thus adopted numerous inno-vations: new crops, progressive farming techniques, an expanded commit-ment to market production, increased use of alienated labor. But they did so in the service of older goals: material comfort and propertied security for themselves and their children. Their strategy often worked. George and Lucinda Holcolm spent their early life together accumulating property. When Beriah Holcolm retired in 1824, he passed his 60-acre farm on to five children. George and his brother William bought their siblings' interest in the land and began farming together. Six years later, George bought William out and purchased a second, 93-acre tract. For the next 13 years, as their chil-dren grew old enough to work, George and Lucinda increased their income, plowing it back into tools, livestock, and money at interest. They also spent increasing amounts on consumer goods, achieving a level of consumption that their parents had never known. In 1840 alone, George bought two new stoves, a french bedstead, china table settings, ribbons, velvet, lace, kid gloves, silk handkerchiefs, straw hats, an ivory comb, and morocco shoes. The family partook of a varied diet, with coffee, tea, raisins, "sweet crackers," clams, sugar, and spices gracing their table. They enjoyed a two-horse pleasure wagon, books, trips to the circus, musical instruments, and singing lessons for the girls. As their sons grew older, George and Lucinda shifted their strategy back toward acquiring land. In 1853, when his son George P. turned 28, and 1855, when his second son, John, reached the same age, George bought two more farms. Like fathers for generations before him, he used his wealth to prepare a landed inheritance for his sons.[28]

Landless families like the Conklins found such security and comfort out of reach. Good seasons brought the rare treat of a barrel of flour, but most brought a steady diet of rye bread and johnny cake, whose monotony was interrupted in the spring and summer by trout, wild greens, and berries. The Conklin children went barefoot until the age of 12; Mary cooked in fireplaces until 1845, for the family could not afford a stove. Theirs was a precarious living, made on rented land and on mortgaged farms that never got paid off. Above all, it was a life marked by frequent movement. The family moved every year or two, prompting Henry to recall that they had "no place to lay our heads that we could call our own." Other landless people shared their footloose ways. Of the five men who worked for six or more days for George Holcolm in 1830, none bought land in Rensselaer County or were bequeathed anything in probated wills. Only 4 of the 15 men who worked for Henry Bull for more than six days in a single year between 1820 and 1845 bought land in Schoharie County or in nearby Albany County, and none inherited land in a probated will. The rest remained landless nearby or, more likely, moved on.[29]

New dependencies and economic pressures brought new conflicts in their wake. Poor families, and perhaps others, experienced significant conflict. Samuel Conklin's drinking and wanderlust proved a constant source of discontent among his wife and children, and his lack of property to pass on to his sons undermined his authority. Two of his three sons defied his and Mary's instructions and absconded from their employers; the third, who remained at home, tired of his father's scoldings and ran away as well. Sons could support themselves by their wages and were more likely to rebel than daughters or wives, but husbands in Delaware County occasionally announced in the local newspapers that their wives, and sometimes their entire families, had run away.[30]

Conflict also broke out between employers and employees. One of George Holcolm's workers stole; another "would not work nor mind to do what he was bid." Most conflicts ended with the employee quitting or being fired; young workers tied to their employers by long-term indentures simply ran away. Some workers went further, using anonymous violence to settle scores with their employers. In May 1841, Mr. McKee, a subtenant in the Helderbergs, settled a dispute with his farmer-landlord, Mr. Martin, by torching his two barns, corn house, and shed.[31] Although they testified to significant conflict between employers and employees, these disputes, like struggles within families, remained individual and based on personal grievances.

The weightiest conflict to appear on the new economic landscape was the struggle over the commons. Faced with the beginnings of deforestation and worsening conflicts over free-ranging livestock, many hill tenants sought to curb common rights to unimproved lands. After 1820, many farmers bought wood lots to assure themselves of an adequate supply of timber and firewood. These lots were, by definition, unimproved, and their legal owners came into persistent conflict with neighbors who wished to exercise their common right to the timber on those lots. In 1828, town meetings in both Roxbury and Rensselaerville outlawed the running of "hogs, horses, sheep, and horned cattle" on open lands. Unlike before, these votes were not reversed in subsequent years.[32]

These actions marked a milestone in the social and ideological development of the hill towns. Both the proliferation of timber lots and the new restrictions on livestock placed new limits on residents' ability to make a living from land that they did not legally own. Although they affected all residents, these restrictions particularly limited the ability of the landless to support themselves, deepening their dependence on wage labor and subtenancy. Just as important, they marked a turning point in upcountry tenants' social and economic commitments. Faced with chronic overuse of the commons and continuing conflict over timber and wayward livestock, increasing numbers of estate residents began to question older visions of property rights that emphasized the ability of all local residents to take natural resources from unimproved land. These tenants took a significant step toward a vision of property that constructed natural resources as subject to exclusive use by those who held paper title to them.

New economic circumstances thus compelled hill-country residents to rethink their economic and social values. Many estate residents sought to extend their integration into the broader capitalist economy. Because the price they received for wool depended on the health of the textile industry, hill farmers vigorously supported high tariffs on wool and cloth. They emphasized the interdependence of farming, commerce, and industry, insisting that the prosperity of all was dependent on robust, planned economic growth. A farmer-dominated tariff meeting in Rensselaer County declared that the solution to depressed farm prices and palsied commerce was the growth of "a *manufacturing population*" that would become "a body of consumers" for farmers, allowing them to specialize in "an article that will bring us profit" and that would "furnish our countrymen, as well as ourselves, with cheaper and better clothing." Such an economic transformation, they insisted, "requires the interposition of the legislative power of the nation," in the form of a tariff.[33] During the 1830s, Delaware County residents agitated ceaselessly for government help in building railroads and turnpikes through their county. They too sought to become fuller participants in the emerging regional and national economy.[34]

If tenants sought to be a part of a broader capitalist economy, most did not wish to become capitalists themselves. Like George Holcolm, most preferred to put economic innovation to conservative uses: they eschewed excessive risk, sought a competence rather than great wealth, and celebrated manual labor as the wellspring of economic equality and republican virtue. An 1838 article in the *Albany Cultivator* promised readers that a switch to dairying would provide farmers not with the means for "ostentation and extravagance" but with "substantial comfort . . . [and] equality." X. A. Willard, a New York dairy farmer, wrote that butter and cheese making "rests on no mere speculative basis—'up today, and down tomorrow,' but is permanent in its character and prospects and sure in its rewards." "A Broad Wheeler" warned that the "mercantile and commercial life" involved its practitioners in speculative risk, leaving each one sleepless "in devising the ways and meeting his engagements and sustaining his credit." He advised "our rising young men" to eschew such risky occupations, "put hand to hoe," and "learn to be content with such gains as economy and industry will always insure."[35]

Such sentiments rested on the labor theory of value. All hill-town residents agreed that "the labor of a country" constituted "the source of its wealth." Tenants distrusted the "speculation" they saw among merchants and other commercial men as an effort to create false wealth with no basis in labor. Hence the worries and instability of commercial life. And hence a recurring suspicion that merchants and other middlemen sought to cheat them out of the products of their toil. Popular lore and Democratic newspapers frequently depicted wool manufacturers, timber buyers, and butter brokers as working to drive down the prices of the articles they bought with deceptive reports of stagnant markets and collapsing prices.[36] Ever anxious to increase their exchange in a broader capitalist economy, estate farmers proved nonetheless highly suspicious of the men who linked them to that economy.

The new economic landscape did not change hill tenants' desire for land and the security and freedom that came with it. But it did change the conditions under which they sought it and their strategies for gaining it. Those conditions and strategies created new inequalities and dependencies in the hill towns. And they pressured increasing numbers of tenants into changing their definitions of property and the rules for gaining it. When conflict with landlords came, these new inequalities and ideas about property would set the terms of their challenge to the leasehold system.

A Revolution in Politics

Just as tenants played a part in creating a new economic landscape, they helped forge a new political order. This new order shifted the balance of power between landlords and tenants and transformed both groups' relationship to the centers of authority. Between 1820 and 1840, New Yorkers led the nation in redefining the rules of politics. The rules they instituted gradually eroded landlords' old claims to power. At the same time, they offered tenants new kinds of political experience and new lines of communication with political leaders. In the process, they shattered tenants' political dependency on landlords in the core manor counties, providing both with new and divergent ways of understanding politics and society.

New York politics went through three distinct phases between 1820 and 1840. In 1820 the Federalist party dissolved, opening a period of one-party Republican rule that lasted until 1827. Bitter competition between two rival Republican factions distinguished this period, as the followers of Governor De Witt Clinton vied for office with the Bucktails, led by Martin Van Buren. A second period lasted from 1827 until 1834, when the Anti–masonic and Workingmen's parties challenged the dominant Bucktails' hold on power. National politics complicated factional alignments during these early phases. As divisions over the presidency heated up after 1824, most Clintonians, Workingmen, and Anti-Masons threw their support to the National Republicans. The Bucktails, on the other hand, supported the Old Republicans, backing William Henry Crawford for president in 1824 and thereafter promoting Andrew Jackson. In 1828, the Clintonians made peace with the Bucktails, coalescing into a growing Jacksonian party. Factional chaos came to an end in 1834, when the National Republicans, Anti-Masons, and Workingmen united to form the Whig party. Thereafter, competition between Jacksonian Democrats and Whigs defined the contours of politics in New York and the rest of the nation.[37]

These realignments brought with them fundamental changes in political life. During the 1820s, popular demands for a widened suffrage, the popular election of presidential electors and judges, and the abolition of nominations by legislative caucuses emerged just as electoral competition reached a new level of intensity. In this context, both old factions and new political movements brought those demands into state politics. At the same time, these factions and movements experimented with new ways of mobilizing voters. In 1824, after the Bucktails blocked measures providing for universal white male suffrage and the popular selection of presidential electors, the Clintonians donned the mantle of "the People's Men," denounced their rivals as an aristocratic "Regency" at war with "the people's rights," and rode to power on a promise to democratize politics. The Anti-Masons extended the Clintonians' message and methods, building a political movement that combined intensive grass-roots organizing and a radical vision of absolute popular sovereignty. To defeat these challengers, the Bucktails emulated them, and the Whigs followed suit. By 1834, all political factions in New York were conducting a new kind of political campaign, based on grass-roots organizing and aggressive popular electioneering.[38]

One result was the creation of partisan organizations that drew unprecedented numbers of white men into the political process. Partisan conventions had been held on the leasehold estates since the late 1790s. But they had nominated candidates for a limited number of offices; their main job was to register support for candidates chosen by party insiders. During the 1820s and 1830s, People's Men, Anti-Masons, Jacksonians, and Whigs revived the convention and dramatically expanded its scope. By the early 1830s all nominations fell to a series of town, county, and state conventions.[39] To staff these meetings, party leaders recruited dozens of delegates from every leasehold town. Tenants also joined town-level committees of vigilance, which organized local campaigns under the guidance of county and state committees. Local activists tended to come from the wealthy and middling men of their towns, with Whigs recruiting more heavily than Democrats among the towns' merchants, manufacturers, and professionals. This expanded network of conventions and committees gave unprecedented numbers of prosperous tenants their first taste of organization building and political leadership. And where the leasehold activists of an earlier area owed their political allegiance to their landlord and his "interest," the loyalty of these leaders belonged to partisan organizations that their landlords did not control.[40]

Party organizations also brought humbler white men into the political process, teaching them to think in partisan ways. The number of partisan newspapers in the cities of the leasehold district increased rapidly after 1819, while rural counties like Delaware got their first party journals during the 1820s. The partisan press flooded its readers with reprints of legislative and congressional debates, speeches and proclamations by party leaders, reports on partisan meetings, and political commentary.[41] At the same time, local activists organized an endless round of rallies, parades, and dinners. Independence Day in 1834 found the Democrats of Delaware County marching to the Presbyterian Church in Franklin, where they listened to the Declaration of Independence and patriotic speeches from Jacksonian leaders. The participants then had dinner at Hollis's Hotel, where they offered 59 toasts to honorees like "Old Hickory" and "State Rights and the Literal Construction of the Constitution," accompanied by "the discharge of cannon, cheering, and music from the Walton Band." These occasions provided entertainment, and in so doing offered party leaders an opportunity to instruct the rank and file. Of equal importance, they allowed humble white men to act out their political convictions in marching, song, banners, and toasts and to see themselves as participants in national political affairs.[42]

This grass-roots mobilization created an unprecedented degree of popular engagement with politics. In 1840, rallies in the leasehold district regularly attracted between 1,000 and 4,000 participants. Voter participation in the Helderbergs skyrocketed, from a low of 36 percent in 1822 to over 90 percent after 1828. Turnout in the major leasehold towns of Delaware County jumped from 30 percent in 1820 to over 85 percent after 1838. Enthusiasm for partisan politics reached into every electoral contest: the selection of town supervisors, road commissioners, and fence viewers became occasions for fierce scuffling between Whigs and Democrats.[43]

During the 1820s, this new politics of organization building and popular mobilization coexisted with an older politics of "interest," allowing landlords to retain "immense influence" in state politics. Stephen Van Rensselaer and the Livingston family retained sufficient control over tenant votes for Martin Van Buren to attribute the 1828 victory of the National Republicans in Albany and Columbia Counties to "the Manor influence." With this power, proprietors continued to enjoy influence among Bucktail, Clintonian, and National Republican leaders. Van Rensselaer served as Albany County's congressman between 1822 and 1828; while in Washington, he boarded with Martin Van Buren and became an intimate of Henry Clay. Members of the Livingston clan and lesser proprietors like Gulian Verplanck and John A. King kept up a presence in the state legislature.[44]

But landlords had no stomach for the new style of politics. "Party mixes with every question," Van Rensselaer complained in 1824. "I absent myself when the battle commences—it is too disgusting for my Ear as I have ever kept good company. Vulgarity disgusts me." Such men could be of little use in forging political organizations or in winning votes outside their estates. Increasingly, control of state partisan organizations fell to self-made lawyers and editors—men like Martin Van Buren and Edwin Croswell among the Bucktails, Thurlow Weed and William Henry Seward among the Anti-Masons and Whigs. At the same time, the new network of conventions, newspapers, and electoral committees offered tenants direct lines of communication with party leaders, ending landlords' role as mediators between tenants and the centers of power.[45]

In the core manor counties, however, it was landlords themselves who dealt the final blow to the politics of "interest." Chronically indebted, landlords during the 1820s began to demand their back rents in full, and for the first time sued numerous tenants for recovery of their debts.[46] When Stephen Van Rensselaer abandoned his old policy of lenience, many tenants abandoned him at the ballot box. Support for the patroon's "interest" in the Helderbergs dropped from 60–70 percent during the 1810s to 56 percent in 1824 and 1828. After 1834, three out of five Helderberg towns consistently voted Democratic; Whigs, whom Van Rensselaer supported, won only 47 to 49 percent of hill tenants' votes. The manor towns of the valley and the city of Albany continued to vote for the Whigs, giving that party a slight majority in the county as a whole. But Van Rensselaer's loss of the towns traditionally most loyal to his interest made clear that the Whig's success depended more on organization building and grass-roots organizing than on his personal influence (see Appendix, figure 4).[47]

Helderberg tenants' new electoral independence transformed the makeup of officeholders. The patroon's family retained control over the county's seat in Congress through the 1820s, with Stephen Van Rensselaer serving four terms. But by 1828 Van Rensselaer had wearied of politics. He retired, vowing never "to appear again before the public in any other character than that of a Christian." His influence among the Whigs remained sufficient to guarantee Judge Ambrose Spencer, a relative and close political ally of the Livingston family, his seat. But the Democrats replaced Spencer in 1830 with the Albany gentleman Gerrit Y. Lansing, who had no connection to the patroon. In 1836, they elected the Helderberg-born lawyer Albert Gallup, who displayed active hostility to the landlord. Van Rensselaer's loss of influence was even more dramatic in elections to state and county offices. Where landlords and their allies served 45 percent (54 out of 121) of the county's terms as assemblyman, congressman, sheriff, and county judge between 1800 and 1819, they controlled only 26 percent (9 out of 34) during the 1820s and 5 percent (2 out of 40) between 1830 and 1840.[48] Landlords' allies lost political power in Delaware County as well. Their share of years in office dropped from 15 percent (10 of 64) during the 1800s to 1 percent (1 of 87) between 1830 and 1840.[49]

The declining political fortunes of landlords and their allies did not automatically shift power to humbler citizens, however. Instead, the coming of the second American party system gave unprecedented political power to lawyers. Attorneys had been prominent in politics since the adoption of the Constitution, filling at least 17 percent of offices for both Delaware and Albany counties in any decade. But they came to exercise a far more extensive dominance over the partisan politics of the 1820s and 1830s. Lawyers dominated the county cadre of party managers and stump speakers, and their share of elective offices expanded dramatically between the 1820s and the 1830s, from 20 to 50 percent in Albany County and from 36 to 64 percent in Delaware County.[50]

Whether lawyers or not, most officeholders did not pursue politics as a career. Party conventions typically nominated local partisan activists as a reward for years of work in the party cause. Officeholders who made the right alliances and showed a special talent could sometimes make a career out of politics. But in the majority of cases, both Whigs and Democrats declined to renominate officeholders after a term or two.[51]

If landlords enjoyed few public offices under the rule of party activists and lawyers, they continued to enjoy significant political influence. They and their agents served in county Whig and Democratic organizations through the 1840s, retaining considerable clout in local parties. They also held on to influence among state and national party leaders. Despite Stephen Van Rensselaer's Whig loyalties, Martin Van Buren assiduously courted his favor during the 1830s, affirming his "friendship" for the patroon and occasionally offering him government posts. Democratic leaders also courted the landlord John Armstrong, while Peter R. Livingston maintained a close relationship with the Whig leader and U.S. Postmaster General Francis Granger.[52] Proprietors' continuing political influence should not veil the enormity of the change, however. In less than 20 years, men used to acting as political patrons had become political clients.

For tenants, the change in political status proved equally decisive. Party organizations trained unprecedented numbers of estate residents as political activists, while drawing virtually the entire adult, white, male population into the business of elections. But the amount of direct political influence that tenants enjoyed varied from place to place. In Albany County, close competition between Whigs and Democrats compelled party leaders to keep their organizations open and responsive to a wide variety of constituencies. These leaders carefully distributed slots on each organization's ticket and central committee to assure representation by residents of the city of Albany, the valley towns, and the Helderbergs. As a result, Helderbergers' share of terms as sheriff, assemblyman, county judge, and congressman grew from 13 percent (13 out of 99) during the 1790s and 1800s to 44 percent (14 out of 32) between 1830 and 1840.[53]

In Delaware County, however, the Bucktails and Democrats won a majority of votes in every election between 1820 and 1840. Without the spur of competition, small, tightly knit cliques gained control of both party organizations. Every identifiable member of the Democratic "Delhi Regency" during the 1830s and early 1840s resided in the county seat of Delhi. Most were lawyers; almost all were members of St. John's Episcopal Church; and many were related to one another by blood or marriage. A similar group of intermarried Delhi Episcopalians ran the county Whig party. These cliques' control of party organizations increased the already disproportionate representation of Delhi residents among elected officials and intensified the exclusion of tenants from office. Delhi residents' proportion of years in office reached 47 percent (37 out of 79) between 1830 and 1840, while the share served by residents of the major leasehold towns dropped from 21 percent (12 out of 58) during the 1820s to 10 percent (8 out of 79) between 1830 and 1840.[54] The transformation of politics in the leasehold district severely weakened the landlords' political power and offered tenants critical political experience, but it did not automatically give the latter power.

The Politics of the Redeemer

Political change in the leasehold towns emerged from religious as well as partisan sources. When compared to the upheaval along the Erie Canal, the Second Great Awakening in the leasehold district seems a tame affair. Hilltown revivals tended to be small and sporadic. The Rensselaerville Presbyterian Church sponsored seven revivals between 1820 and 1840, each winning the church an average of 21 new members. Missionary work yielded equally modest results. Emissaries of the gospel occasionally encountered a schoolhouse packed with men and women "anxious for their souls' salvation," but most shared the assessment of a Delaware County missionary: "I cannot speak of any general awakening among the impenitent, or any revival in the hearts of the saints."[55]

Yet in towns of one or two thousand inhabitants, the cumulative affect of revivals could be impressive. Evangelicals became a significant presence in most leasehold towns, infusing their communities with the Work of the Redeemer. In the process, they brought about a second transformation in the public life of the leasehold district—an explosion of associational and reform politics. Beginning in the late 1820s, reformers in Delaware County established several voluntary associations: a Bible and prayer book society, a home missionary society, a Sunday school union, a temperance society, and an anti-slavery society. Activists elsewhere founded similar organizations after 1828.[56]

These associations pioneered a brand of politics very different from that practiced by partisan organizations. Evangelical reformers aimed not at attaining government power, but at transforming their culture and society by changing individual belief and behavior. They sought to do this through education, moral suasion, and the mobilization of community sentiment rather than through electoral combat. Temperance societies, the most successful of the reform associations, exemplify this style of politics. The first task of temperance advocates was to change their own life ways; they formalized their commitment to self-reform by publicly signing a temperance pledge. Society members supported one another's efforts—and rebuked and pressured backsliders—through vigilance committees. They also sought to educate the public by recruiting ministers, holding frequent meetings, disseminating newspapers and tracts, and visiting the homes of unredeemed neighbors. Education, mutual aid, and watchfulness were weapons in a battle for "public opinion"; reformers sought to make the consumption of distilled spirits a matter of public shame. Thus the secretary of the Bern society boasted that "Public opinion has undergone such a change, that even drunkards have become shy of being seen drinking the poison."[57]

Evangelical reformers sought to establish a utopia of assured salvation and social order. Saving souls was their central aim. But buffeted by economic dislocation, new tensions within and between families, and increasing geographic mobility, they linked this goal to a yearning for order and harmony. The officers of the Delaware County Domestic Missionary Society looked forward to the day when they could witness "the pleasing spectacle of communities well regulated, well instructed, and blessed with all the benign restraints and kindly influence of religious institutions, and enjoying in life and death, in time and eternity, the thousand nameless consolations of the religion of Jesus Christ." H. E. Bartlett of Delaware County described intemperance as subjecting the drinker's unlucky wife to "imprecations and brutal fury" while leaving "her form wasted with want and her heart breaking with anguish." Temperance, he insisted, would promote peaceful, affectionate, and well-ordered families.[58]

Just as important, temperance promised prosperity in an uncertain economy. Taverns, reformers declared, were "sepulchers of industry and prosperity"; "three fourths of all the pauperism in our land, is the result of intemperance." One Delaware County activist predicted that with the triumph of the temperance cause, the county's "hills and vales" would become "eminently productive . . . her poor-house might become solitary, her jail tenantless, and her multiplied population thrifty, peaceful, and happy."[59] In some cases, this promise of prosperity served the class interests of the new rural middle class. Temperance was not limited to prosperous estate residents, but employers often embraced the cause and imposed it on their laborers. In the process, they turned the movement into a tool of labor discipline. More than 50 Stephentown farmers and a number of Delaware County husbandmen "refused to admit ardent spirits to be used among their workmen." These employers discovered that laborers were "enabled to perform one-third *more* labor" without the use of ardent spirits. Along with the gradual adoption of "scientific" agricultural methods, the temperance movement intensified the exploitation of hired labor and nudged employing farmers in the leasehold district toward more rationalized, "businesslike" agricultural practices.[60]

Most evangelical movements remained limited in their appeal. As elsewhere, anti-slavery advocates remained a small band of dedicated radicals. The Delaware County Domestic Missionary Society tottered on the brink of bankruptcy through the 1820s and 1830s. But the temperance movement's promise of salvation, prosperity, restored health, and domestic harmony won widespread support. In 1833, temperance society membership represented a full third of Helderbergers over the age of 20; societies in the main leasehold towns of Delaware County enjoyed membership equivalent to 18 percent of their adult population.[61] The movement lost its power in the late 1830s, however, when advocates of "total abstinence" sought to end the consumption of wine and beer, which earlier temperance activists had tolerated, and abandoned the politics of education and community pressure for a campaign to outlaw the sale of alcohol. In 1837, Delaware County activists split between a Temperance Society and a Total Abstinence Society, while county residents held antitemperance meetings and flooded the local press with letters denouncing the movement. Support for both wings of the movement declined precipitously, robbing evangelical reform of its mass base.[62]

Though they failed to retain a central place in public life, evangelical reformers brought about permanent changes in the politics of the leasehold district. Like the Whigs and Democrats, they brought unprecedented numbers of estate residents into a political movement, providing them with skills in public speaking, running a meeting, recruiting members, and influencing public opinion. Evangelical movements tended to be more decentralized than political parties, allowing tenants to exercise these skills with greater freedom from outside direction. Most importantly, evangelical reformers learned a style of politics that differed significantly from partisan activities. The politics of education, agitation, and mobilizing community sentiment provided tenants with an expanded political arsenal whose impact would out-last the demise of the temperance crusade.

Partisan Messages
and Voter Loyalties

With the shattering of their old electoral alliance, landlords and tenants learned to think in divergent ways. Gradually during the early 1830s, and much more rapidly after 1837, Whig and Democratic leaders created coherent ideologies and programs. Through speeches, partisan rituals, and the press, white men on New York's estates imbibed these ideologies and learned to tie specific issues to a broad social and political philosophy. The leasehold Democrats' social vision centered on a celebration of the sovereign producer-citizen. The *Delaware Gazette* believed "the 'great mass'" of citizens to be "competent to judge of men and measures, and of such incorruptible integrity as not to suffer the principles of our government to be subverted." It believed that "no restraint or control" should be placed on the free exercise of the popular will "except their own unbiased judgement, and the lawful authorities which they themselves have constituted." While they acknowledged the duty of elected officials to set limits on ordinary citizens' exercise of power, Democrats paradoxically believed that those officials should reflexively carry out the will of the people they represented. No greater sin existed than for a representative to "vot[e] in opposition to the known will of his constituents."[63]

When Democrats invoked "the people" as the legitimate rulers in a republican society, they had a particular group in mind: white men who worked with their hands. Women, children, and men of color, they presumed, were incapable of a "manly" exercise of citizenship; and no white men exercised masculine political qualities as well as producers. Despite his local party's dominance by lawyers, a Delaware County Jacksonian offered a fourth of July toast to the "sturdy yeomanry and hard-fisted working-men, who are the only sure foundation of an independent government." A correspondent to the *Albany Argus* agreed. "The poor man," he wrote, "supports '*the main pillars of our country's liberty.*'"[64]

As self-styled champions of the producing majority, the lawyers and newspapermen who led the Democrats professed a deep suspicion of concentrated wealth. Directing old republican fears of concentrated power toward economic elites, they warned that, if unchecked, the wealthy would monopolize political power and fatten themselves on the products of poor men's labor. What allowed the rich to do so was artificial privilege bestowed by the government. In defending Andrew Jackson's war on the Bank of the United States, the *Argus* argued that the institution's danger lay not in its capital but in the fact that the government deposited its revenues there and exempted the bank from taxation. "The *people's* money enables this vampyre to suck their blood silently," thus "nourish[ing] the aristocracy, and furnish[ing] fat salaries for favorites." Such special privileges, "Putnam" concluded, created a *"privileged order"* and made "the rich richer and the poor poorer."[65] Just as dangerously, government-bestowed privilege created a corrupt alliance between wealthy men and cynical, office-seeking politicians that threatened republican government. Democrats attributed congressional and newspaper support for the Bank of the United States to *"Bank bribery."* The *Gazette* warned that "the aristocracy bring their money to bear upon the freedom of elections, and the political stock-jobbers barter away the suffrages of freemen. The citadel of liberty, the public press, and the ballot boxes, are invaded by a corrupt coalition."[66]

The solution to these dangers was minimal government, states' rights, and a strict construction of the constitution. Following the lead of Andrew Jackson, Delaware and Albany County Democrats called for government retrenchment at both the federal and state level and a limiting of government functions to those explicitly spelled out in the federal and state constitutions. Such a policy would prohibit a national bank and end the dangerous practice of public officials "arrogating to [themselves] powers that the constitution and laws of the Republic do not confer." With Jackson, they called for an end to government-granted "exclusive privileges." On the state level, they opposed the Whigs' program of deficit spending to expand the state's canal system.[67]

The Democrats' rhetorical defense of producers' rights and hostility to monopoly certainly appealed to many tenants' suspicion of speculation and artificial wealth. But it did not signal hostility to growing commerce or capitalist enterprise. "Mountain Boy," the Washington correspondent for the *Gazette*, saw "the prosecution of INDIVIDUAL ENTERPRISE" as a source of rising standards of living and greater national unity, as increased trade and rapid communication made the residents of the several states "in feeling and sentiment, as we are politically, one people." Nor did the Jacksonians' hostility to the Bank of the United States entail a hostility to the institutions of the new economic order. Democratic leaders invested heavily in local banks, while the Jacksonian press praised them as sound institutions. They wished to decentralize and regulate banking, not to abolish it.[68]

Their celebration of economic development and the particular economic interests of their constituents led many Democrats in the leasehold district to depart from their philosophy of minimal government. Leasehold farmers' dedication to wool-growing, which suffered greatly from foreign competition, led most leasehold Democrats to support a protective tariff. Similarly, Delaware County Democrats acceded to the demands of county merchants, manufacturers, and farmers for easier access to markets. Although they opposed the expansion of the Erie canal, these Democrats advocated state support for railroads and turnpikes connecting Delaware County to a variety of entrepôts. Such support, they reasoned, was only equitable, since their county's taxes had already underwritten the economic boom along the Erie canal.[69]

Though leasehold Democrats welcomed the integration of the leasehold district into a broader capitalist economy, they denounced efforts to spread the blessings of a capitalist labor system southward. In the late 1820s and early 1830s, Jacksonian newspapers had voiced opposition to slavery, publishing descriptions of the horrors of slavery and paternalistic accounts of African Americans' emancipation day celebrations. But starting in 1835, Democrats began a campaign to inoculate their readers from the abolitionist infection. Although he professed hatred for slavery, "Mountain Boy" argued that abolitionism was far more dangerous, for it threatened to "sever . . . the ties which bind these states together." The movement for emancipation also endangered social order and the rule of law. "We have laws which recognize slaves as property.—Laws which were made by the majority of the representatives of this nation, in solemn council assembled. *Must not those laws be obeyed?*"[70]

With statements like these, leasehold Democrats placed their attack on abolitionism on a foundation of unionism, social order, and the rule of law, not on the ground of white supremacy. Their defense of slavery revealed the double-edged quality of Democratic philosophy. On the one hand, the Jacksonians were the party of popular sovereignty, producers' rights, and unending economic progress. On the other, they were a party of states' rights, the rule of law, strict construction of the constitution, and vested rights—commitments that tended to undermine challenges to existing relationships of domination. In one moment, they could defend the rights of producers to the fruits of their labor. In another, they condemned efforts to defend those rights, *not* on the grounds that the laborers in question were racially inferior but because such efforts threatened social and political stability. Slavery was the first issue that caused the northern Democrats to run aground on this contradiction, but it would not be the only one.

On many fundamental issues, the Whigs of the leasehold district differed little from their Democratic rivals. In the late 1830s, the party fell under the reform influence of Governor William Seward, who had learned that opposing popular sovereignty to an audience of New York farmers was bad politics. They thus championed what the *Albany Evening Journal* called "a well regulated democracy." As Seward told a Delaware County audience, "the whole People err less often, in regard to their true interests, than any chosen few who may be charged with the responsibilities of government." Leasehold Whigs thus endorsed "an administration of the popular will through their chosen representatives."[71]

But where Democrats in theory tied such beliefs to a vision of limited government, the Whigs endorsed an activist state. Just as important, their vision of government activism vacillated between the democratic and the paternalistic. The Van Buren administration's failure to take dramatic relief measures during the depression of 1837–1842, Whigs argued, was evidence that the President saw "'the Government' as a power independent of the People. . . . The government which refuses to relieve the people under such circumstances, fails to fulfill its highest functions. For what purpose was Government instituted . . . but to secure for its constituency, protection and relief under all circumstances?" In formulations like these, calls for government to carry out the People's will turned into demands that the state act in the people's best interest. Whigs usually justified particular programs not because the People demanded them but because they were good for them.[72]

Armed with an alternately democratic and paternalistic vision of activist government, leasehold Whigs campaigned, with more consistency than Democrats, for government-sponsored capitalist development. Whigs enthusiastically endorsed a protective tariff; a national banking system and an ample supply of credit and paper money; and the use of state funds to expand New York's network of railroads and canals. In doing so, they emphasized the natural harmony of interest between classes. "The interests of labor and capital are coincident—not antagonistic," insisted one correspondent. Banking and credit were institutions by which "the *rich* man's capital" was mobilized to "stimulat[e] productive industry—creat[e] a demand for labor—and . . . enhanc[e] the wages of labor." Without them, "the *poor* . . . would be doomed to struggle through life in hopeless indigence." Similarly, Whigs endorsed a protective tariff as a means to ensure high wages for labor and high prices for farmers' produce.[73]

Thus Whigs, like Democrats, endorsed economic development based on private property and economic competition. But where the Democrats warned that government encouragement of such development could lead to class oppression, Whigs insisted that it would distribute benefits widely and strengthen the ties of mutual dependence among all classes. Thus, despite the similarities between their economic beliefs, Whigs and Democrats offered leasehold farmers different identities. Where Jacksonians depicted farmers as hardy, democratic yeomen locked in eternal struggle with an antidemocratic aristocracy, the Whigs of Westerlo described themselves as "a Business People."[74]

This identity was not narrowly economistic. Whig leaders taught that economic progress marched in tandem with moral and intellectual improvement. Thurlow Weed noted that the economic boom of the 1830s brought not only progress in "commerce and navigation" but diffused education and left the national territory "teem[ing] with an active and intelligent population." Another writer rhapsodized that "the pure sentiments of Whig Democracy" in Western New York spurred "agricultural, physical, and intellectual improvement in all you see." While the soil brought forth "teeming abundance," the people who cultivated it became "enlightened and independent."[75]

In the hands of its boldest advocates, economic and intellectual "improvement" became part of a broader project of social and moral regeneration. William Seward proclaimed that under the combined influences of democratic government, economic growth, and widening education, the "spirit" that drove Americans to accumulate property had become a revolutionary social and moral force. "It resists the inroads of aristocracy and demolishes all its defenses. It annihilates the distinctions, old as time, of rich and poor, masters and slaves. It banishes ignorance and lays the axe to the root of crime." Human nature itself was improving, as men's passions became "more equable and humane"; human energies, unleashed from ignorance and traditional fetters, were beginning to "break through the restraints of power and prejudice." This "democratic" spirit would ultimately result in "universal liberation"—an end to ancient prejudices, ignorance, and inequalities. With an enlightened government encouraging the self-liberating impulses of ordinary citizens, Seward promised, "our race is ordained to reach, on this continent, a higher standard of social perfection than it has ever yet attained; and . . . hence will proceed the spirit that shall renovate the world."[76]

Like other Americans, most leasehold tenants did not support one party over the other primarily because of its policies or ideology. Indeed, the reverse was more often true. Antebellum voters tended to follow the lead of their fathers and of community leaders in choosing which party to support. Once they were safely in a partisan camp, they learned how to think about public issues in Whig or Democratic ways.[77] Nonetheless, Whigs and Democrats each tended to appeal to communities with particular geographical, ethnic, religious, and economic profiles—possibly because community leaders followed ethnic, religious, and economic cues in their partisan choices.

In Albany county, the differences between Whigs and Democrats were simultaneously geographical, religious, and economic. All but one of the rural towns that cast a majority of its votes for the Democrats lay in the Helderbergs; all but one Whig town lay in the Hudson Valley or the foothills. This geographic division had a strong ethnic and religious dimension. Valley towns and the cities of Albany and Watervliet were an even mix of Yankee and Yorker, with a rough parity between evangelical denominations like the Baptists, Methodists, and Presbyterians and the religiously conservative Dutch Reformed, Episcopalian, and Lutheran Churches. The Helderbergs were ethnically mixed as well, but Yankees and evangelicals predominated there, and the temperance crusade found a remarkable degree of support. These New Englanders were religious outsiders in the county. The city of Albany, and hence the county, was dominated by a Whig establishment associated with the Dutch Reformed and Episcopalian Churches. Perhaps not coincidentally, hill residents tended to support the "outsider" party—the Democrats—as well. (see Appendix, table 7).[78]

Albany farmers' partisan loyalty was also related to their economic experience. The Whigs predominated in towns that experienced little dislocation in the transition to a more market-oriented agriculture, while Democrats dominated those towns where economic change brought significant social stress. Democratic towns were the most industrialized rural towns in the county, with the largest nonagricultural populations and the greatest investment in manufacturing per person. Farmers in these towns invested most heavily in dairy and wool farming, and thus were feeling most heavily the increased capital costs of those crops. These were the most marginal farmers in the county, working the least fertile land. They were thus the most likely to have suffered from the collapse of commodity prices and the contraction of credit after the panic of 1837. And they were probably the most receptive to the Democratic teaching that privileged elites were seeking to rob producers of the fruits of their labor through manipulation of commodity markets and the credit supply. (See Appendix, table 7.)[79]

Partisan loyalties in Delaware County had little to do with geography; Whig and Democratic majorities could be found in every corner of the county. Nor was religion heavily correlated with voting. Party loyalties ran more clearly along economic lines. Whig towns tended to be somewhat less industrialized than Democratic districts, with smaller nonagricultural populations and slightly less capital invested in manufacturing. Farmers in Whig towns raised fewer sheep and produced less wool, whose unstable market prices had been bedeviling husbandmen since the mid-1820s. But they raised more cattle and produced far more butter than their Democratic neighbors. In short, Whig farmers were meeting with more success in shifting to the new dairy economy than their neighbors (see Appendix, table 8).[80]

For all their partisan enthusiasm, citizens in the leasehold district harbored grave reservations about the political order they had helped create. Party activists and newspapers offered tenants two messages about their government. Those in power celebrated political leaders as carrying out the unmediated will of the people. Thus the *Argus* praised President Jackson during the Bank War for displaying "an upright and unfaltering devotion to the popular will . . . , regardless of . . . the efforts of a mighty monied power." The party in opposition, on the other hand, warned that those in power had betrayed the people. Drawing on democratic anxieties dating back to Tom Paine about the creation of a political class distinct from the people, opposition spokesmen depicted men in office as members of a privileged and corrupt class of "office holders" who "fattened upon the money of the people." The wealth and power these men enjoyed at public expense created social distance from their constituents, allowing them to forget and betray the public interest. "Van Buren," the *Journal* wrote, "has no interests or sympathies with or for the people. He is an Office-holder by trade, and has lived twenty-five years upon the Treasury. He *feels* none of the distress that he inflicts upon others. His interests are hostile to the general welfare." Worse still, office seekers stripped ordinary citizens of their republican independence, binding them to "a slavery more to be depreciated than European despotism." By demanding blind loyalty to party leaders and measures, politicians were able to "manufactur[e] public opinion," in the process stripping the people of their capacity for dissent and placing them in a position of "reckless subserviency to the good of a party."[81]

Whigs exploited fears of rule by a special class of office seekers far more than Democrats because they were out of power for most of the Jacksonian era. But whenever the Whigs won control of the state or federal government,

Democrats adopted the same rhetoric. Spokesmen for both parties doubtless exploited these fears cynically, as a ploy for winning voters. But these were shrewd leaders; since the rhetoric could easily be turned against them, they would not have used it if it did not speak to deep concerns among the electorate. Even as tenants established their loyalty to Whigs and Democrats and learned to think in partisan ways, they continued to harbor grave doubts about the new rules of politics.

Conservatism Transformed

Although loyal to the same parties as their tenants, proprietors shared few of their social and political beliefs. Where party leaders in the hill towns celebrated in different ways the promise of American life, landlords withdrew into bitter, snobbish insularity. By the late 1820s, they found themselves on the political sidelines and too broke to act on old ideals of noblesse oblige. So they redefined the characteristics that elevated them above the crowd. Refinement, worldliness, and accomplishment remained crucial to the landlords' identity. But where once they had pursued these attributes with their eyes turned outward, as a preparation for public service, they now sought them with an inward focus, for their own sake and as badges of status. Like his own father, Robert L. Livingston supplied his sons with private tutors and instruction in the arts. He wintered them in New York City to expose them to the cream of metropolitan society. He sent them to Geneva for advanced study, and, upon their graduation, financed two years' travel on the continent. But where his father had urged him to pursue glory as a public benefactor, Livingston urged his sons to become "accomplished and learned" young men, at home in "the best society."[82]

Landlords also reassured themselves of their special status by focusing on pedigree. Beginning in the 1810s, members of the great families began researching their family genealogies, with a new emphasis on the glories of their forbears. Peter Van Brugh Livingston made a long visit to his ancestral home near Callendar, Scotland, piecing together "the precise ancestor[s]" from which the New York Livingstons had come. Here too he spent long hours among the ruins of Livingston castle, where "my bosom heaved a sigh, at the sad contrast of the present with that of former days." Peter's relatives shared his nostalgia for better days and his newly insular sense of family glory. Intermarriage among the Livingstons, long an accepted practice, reached "epidemic proportions" after 1810. By 1841, Margaret Livingston could brag without embarrassment that of the 80 guests to her New Year's soiree, "nearly one half were Livingstons . . . . We had but two foreigners, not one parvenu or nouveau riche."[83]

Landlords also based their new sense of status on "breeding." James Fenimore Cooper, the patrician son of a New York landowner and a member of the Livingstons' inner circle, held up two models of deportment and refinement for his readers—one for gentlemen and ladies, the other for the mass. While the former cultivated "breeding," which connoted "refinement and polish," humbler men should strive for "a manly humanity, that shall not pretend to distinctions the party does not comprehend." Leasehold proprietors shared Cooper's obsession with breeding. When greeted by tenants, Stephen Van Rensselaer IV did not shake hands with them but extended his forefinger to be grasped. He also refused to acknowledge the presence of men of lesser status, even when traveling long distances with them. Margaret Astor, the daughter of the Delaware County landlord John Armstrong, forbade her children to laugh out loud or to wear bright colors; when bidding good night to their parents, they backed respectfully out of the room.[84]

Landlords complemented their exclusive, insular culture with an equally exclusive, insular politics. Many, like Stephen Van Rensselaer, lamented the "vulgarity" of the new political order. Others, like John Armstrong, voiced concern over corruption and "hocus pocus." For most landlords, these concerns fueled a deep hostility toward democracy. As early as 1815, Edward Livingston warned his son Lewis against the "false wit" that he had witnessed among fashionable men in New York. These men "ridicule democracy and republicanism," he wrote, "merely because they had imbibed a notion that it was not gentlemanlike to be a Republican." Thirty-one years later, Livingston's fears were still valid. Kosciouszko Armstrong, John's son, lamented the "mischievous increase of popular influence," which he feared would plunge the United States into "the slough of democracy." The young proprietor hoped for a civil war, which would replace unregulated democracy with "standing armies" and "the wholesome remedy of a firm, well regulated government, in which the people will have only such share, as they can use, without abusing."[85]

Landlords carried these sentiments into both major parties. Perhaps more than any other group, proprietors remained personalist in politics; their partisan loyalty depended less on principle and ideology (characteristics sorely lacking in all political alliances before the 1830s) than on personal loyalties and networks of clientage. The vast majority of leasehold proprietors, both Republican and Federalist, nursed an abiding hatred for De Witt Clinton. Thus when the Federalist party formally dissolved in 1820, former Federalists among the landlords joined their Republican fellow proprietors as Bucktails, the only faction left to oppose Clinton. During the early 1820s, only the Van Rensselaers remained outside the Van Buren/Bucktail political orbit. The political struggles of the 1820s and early 1830s drove additional landlords to the opposition. John A. King bolted in 1824 over the Bucktails' support for a soak-the-rich tax and for William Henry Crawford's presidential aspirations; he later rejoined the political fray as an Anti-Mason and National Republican. Peter R. Livingston joined the National Republicans when the Bucktails failed to renominate him for the state senate. And Stephen Van Rensselaer fell into the National Republican orbit after 1824. These deserters eventually became Whigs. But the majority of landlords remained true to their Bucktail allies, following them into the Democratic party. In doing so, they sustained a staunchly conservative and elitist wing of the Jacksonian movement.[86]

A reactionary wing of the Democratic party may seem surprising to contemporary readers. Marvin Meyers recognized the importance of this wing, but subsequent historians have ignored his insights, often painting the division between Democrats and Whigs as a division between producerists and elitists. But both parties were complex coalitions whose constituents and leaders did not choose their party primarily on the basis of policy or ideology. The Jacksonian coalition, in particular, was largely in place in many states (including New York) *before* it had any clear policies or ideology, and many stayed in that party despite deep philosophical differences with their fellow Democrats. Thus both parties contained activists who cherished a variety of political and social "persuasions"—including reactionary ones. Landlords were part of an important conservative movement in New York politics, one whose ideas crossed party lines. Allied with other members of the old gentry, many of whom were also facing economic ruin and political isolation, conservative spokesmen gave voice to the aspirations and resentments of a generation whose grasp on public honor and power had disappeared.[87]

One of the most important of these spokesmen was Daniel Dewey Barnard, a leading Albany County Whig and a lawyer and confidant to Stephen Van Rensselaer. Barnard gave eloquent voice to the gentry's discontent with democratization and the decline of deference. In doing so, he tied that discontent to a distinctly Whiggish vision of state activism, social harmony, and moral regeneration. Like his fellow Whigs, Barnard endorsed the pantheon of nineteenth-century liberal verities: government by the representatives of all male heads of household, the right to property, the sanctity of contracts, and a competitive economic order. But he sought to tie these verities to an organic vision of society that was drawn largely from Edmund Burke. Barnard chastised Democrats for their atomistic social vision and their emphasis on individual freedom. "Very little" of man's actual life, he wrote, was "really individual and isolate." Instead, "we are born into Society, and into the State, as we are born into the world." Human beings became human—acquired language and ideas, developed "Feelings and Affections," cultivated "Moral Sentiments"—in families, communities, and states. Like their other attributes, human beings' natural rights were acquired only in the "Social State," not against its demands.[88]

For Barnard, living in the Social State implied subordination. Individual reason was "not sufficient always " for individual self-control; the only alternative to a violent war of all against all was "Laws, which imply command and authority—a superior Will with the right to impose the laws, and enforce obedience to them." This political subordination was just one part of an organic web of hierarchies. "There must be orders in the society, and diversity of employment, and diversity of condition; and there must be a State, and the subjects of a state, somebody to command and somebody to obey." Obedience, he wrote, "must be practiced in the Family, . . . and in various social relations out of the family, and practiced in the State, and practiced before the Great Supreme."[89]

These relationships of subordination, according to Barnard, were not subject to human will. The state was "a historical or traditional power," descended from "the first Patriarchal state" and gradually developed according to each community's particular environment, needs, and historical experience. Its nature, power, and legitimacy were "ordained of God," and thus independent of "the people, or the individuals composing the nation." As such, it deserved absolute obedience. In the United States, of course, God and history had ordained governance by representatives of male heads of household in accordance with written constitutions. But even here, representative government could never abolish the need for subordination, which "exists by the will of God, and not by the will of man."[90]

As a frequent candidate for political office, Barnard could ill afford to specify which groups should rule and which should obey. But James Fenimore Cooper had no aspirations for office and could afford to be more specific. In 1838, he published the *American Democrat,* an extended brief for the social superiority of gentlemen. Even more than Barnard, Cooper rooted his elitism in a staunchly liberal political economy. Like his fellow Democrats, Cooper believed that a "natural" social order accorded all (white) men equal political and legal rights and equal economic opportunities, leaving them to compete for wealth and power. But where most Democrats believed that such a society would result in a rough equality among white men, Cooper argued that innate differences of talent and industry would result in widely different degrees of wealth, education, and cultivation. Under such a social order, "equality of condition is rendered impossible. One man must labor, while another may live luxuriously on his means; one has leisure and opportunity to cultivate his tastes, to increase his information, and to refine his habits, while another is compelled to toil, that he may live. One is reduced to serve, while another commands."[91]

This natural hierarchy was inevitable; the problem, as Cooper saw it, was that the lower orders displayed a "want of a proper deference for social station." The previous generation of gentlemen had based their claim to public honor largely on their actions as public benefactors, and Cooper knew that they could no longer sustain that role. So he lowered the criteria for greatness. The elite, he maintained, served as "the natural repository of the manners, tastes, tone, and to a certain extent, of the principles of a country." Their obligations were twofold. First, they were to act as "the guardians of the liberties of [their] fellow-citizens," using their superior education and intellect to maintain the "true principles of government" against the assaults of demagogues, theorists, and oligarchs. Second, they were to elevate the taste, "tone," and intellectual life of their communities. Gentlemen were to fulfill this latter obligation by consuming: their demand for luxury items raised the standards of skill among craftsmen, indirectly improving the consumption habits of the lowly. They also did so by example, as those around them learned that "that there are tastes more desirable than those of a mere animal." That was all. Where his father's generation had cherished a more rigorous definition of the obligations of gentlemen, Cooper warned against the "exaggerated notions, on the part of the publick, of the duties of the rich."[92]

The lowly were to express their gratitude for this service by extending deference and power to their superiors. "He who would honor learning, and taste, and sentiment, and refinement of every sort," Cooper maintained, "ought to respect its possessors, and in all things but those which affect rights, defer to their superior advantages." Nor was deference to stop at the courthouse lawn. Though political power rightfully rested in the people as a whole, good government required that the people delegate that power in the "intelligent and refined." Failure to do so would endanger republican government. "No political system can long continue in which this violence is done to the natural rights of a class so powerful," Cooper predicted. "Whenever the enlightened, wealthy, and spirited of an affluent and great country, seriously conspire to subvert democratical institutions, their leisure, money, intelligence and means of combining, will be found too powerful for the ill-directed and conflicting efforts of the mass." No statement better expressed the changed sentiments of the gentry. Once the proud custodians of the republican experiment, now they threatened to become its enemies.[93]

In their efforts to restore social, political, and cultural hierarchy, Cooper and Barnard offered a vision of capitalist development far different from those extended by their fellow Whigs and Democrats. Where Democratic spokesmen in the hill towns promoted a capitalism that would benefit farmers and petty entrepreneurs, and where hill-town Whigs espoused development that would uplift all classes and destroy ancient relations of subordination, the political allies of the landlords endorsed in principle what landlords and tenants had practiced until recently: a competitive, free-market order infused with hierarchy and deference. They shared this vision with other northern elites—notably large-scale manufacturers. Heirs to the Federalists' organicism and fear of disorder, these later paternalists tied their forbears' ideas to a firmer faith in economic competition and social mobility, and often to evangelical Protestantism. They sought to turn the institutions of a rapidly expanding capitalist economy into academies of order. Theirs was a distinctive, patrician vision of capitalist development, one that differed significantly from the more egalitarian vision espoused by entrepreneurial master artisans and small manufacturers.[94]

The defensiveness of Cooper's and Barnard's appeals reflected how dramatically landlords' fortunes had changed since the 1810s. Where leasehold proprietors once used ample and growing estates to further the public good and to win the grateful deference of subordinates, now solvency eluded them. Where they could once rely on the votes of their tenants and a large share of public honor, they now found themselves on the political sidelines, spurned by their subordinates at the polls. The America their fathers had celebrated in the 1780s was now dead, replaced by an insolent democracy. Proprietors withdrew from this foreign and threatening culture, comforting themselves with thoughts of the superiority of their pedigree, breeding, and sensibility.

Tenants greeted the political transformations of the 1820s and 1830s with far more enthusiasm than their landlords, for the new political order gave them political autonomy from their proprietors, a sense of political empowerment, and access to the corridors of power. Their response to economic change, on the other hand, was mixed and ambiguous. Many chipped away at old guarantees of access to natural resources, moving toward a more purely capitalist property regime. And many made increasing use of wage labor and subtenancy, joining elements of capitalist labor relations to those of family production. But even the most ardent entrepreneurs pursued innovation in the name of older goals, while those without sufficient resources saw the new economy narrow their opportunities to accumulate property and to realize comfort and security.

Whether dreaded or celebrated, the new political and economic order in the leasehold district undermined the post-Revolutionary peace between landlords and tenants. That peace had rested on two pillars: landlords' willingness to subsidize tenants' economic security and their overwhelming political power. After 1820, the proprietors' crisis of insolvency undermined their ability to practice lenience toward their tenants. And the transformation of public life shifted the political balance of power toward tenants. Now, with those pillars crumbling, the conflict of interests and aspirations that had always churned beneath the surface broke into public view.

what of earlier
anti-rent conflicts?

Chapter 3

THE FALL OF THE HOUSE
OF VAN RENSSELAER,
1819 – 1839

◦—⚹—◆◆❭—◦—⊖—◦—❬◆◆—⚹—◦

Sitting at his desk at Clermont in 1834, Robert L. Livingston con-
fided his worries to his diary. "My income being insufficient for
my establishment—and for my children—and poor Relatives," he wrote, "I
am busy employed in making my real estate more productive."[1] With this
plain notation, Livingston summarized a new dynamic in landlord-tenant relations, one that was eating away at the stability of the leasehold system.
Attempting to maintain old standards of living by depending on estates that
were getting smaller with each generation, landlords sought to squeeze more
income from their tenants. Their demands threatened the economic security
of numerous farmers, at the very moment that proprietors' political power
was in decline. Thus the twin buttresses to social peace on the estates—the
benevolence and the overwhelming political power of the landlords—began
to crumble at the same time. With their erosion, tenants began to grope toward a new way of dealing with their superiors. At first, they intensified old
strategies, turning individual wheedling and avoidance into outright obstructionism. But they haltingly began to abandon the habits that had worked
under the old regime; in growing numbers, they publicly challenged the proprietors' claim to the land.

The Crackdown

The panic of 1819 threw Stephen Van Rensselaer's finances into shambles.
In that year, he withdrew as the principal benefactor of the Rensselaer
School, and he began a new campaign to press tenants to pay their back rents.
His agents combed the estate, pressuring tenants to pay their debts, promis-
ing lenience if they paid, and threatening lawsuits if they did not.[2] Although
Van Rensselaer had made similar threats and promises of lenience since the
1790s, the context of his demands had changed. His campaign for payment
came during the depression of 1819–1823, when merchants and other cred-

itors were also pressing tenants to repay their debts. Worse still, it came when the terms of trade were against tenants. Estate farmers had accumulated their debts to the patroon during the 1810s, when wheat sold for between $1.50 and $2.25 per bushel. Douw Lansing, Van Rensselaer's agent, had converted the unpaid rent into cash. By 1821, the price of wheat had dropped to $0.75 per bushel, compelling most tenants to pay between two and three times the amount of produce that they had originally owed. Van Rensselaer's demands thus saddled the most indebted tenants with a crushing burden.[3]

In this new context, most tenants failed to respond as they had before. Between 1819 and 1823, only half of a sample of 24 Westerlo farmers eliminated their debt to the Patroon, reduced it to below ₤10, or remained debt-free; the arrears of a quarter increased. Moreover, most of those who significantly reduced or wiped out their back rents relapsed into debt in the following years. Although the farmers' total debt fell from ₤714 in 1819 to ₤455 in 1823, it crept back up to ₤561 in 1824 (see Appendix, figures 1 and 2).[4] In the face of this failure to pay, Van Rensselaer did what he had avoided doing for 39 years. In 1824 and again in the mid-1830s, he sued more than a hundred manor farmers for back rents. The suits were selective: for the most part, he prosecuted only prosperous tenants who owed more than $200. A few got the message. In 1825, another four Westerlo tenants visited the manor office and paid off their debts. This time, however, they received no abatements: the time for lenience had passed.[5]

Van Rensselaer's new severity extended to other issues as well. From the late 1810s on, he revived old conflicts over timber rights, mill privileges, and the quarter sale, abandoning the time-honored pattern of lenience, negotiation, and compromise. In 1818, his agents began to hire tenants to cut and haul timber on the manor's common lands. At the same time, they hauled tenants found cutting wood on the landlord's commons into court, charged them with trespass, and demanded restitution.[6] Farmers who had purchased their farms without notifying the landlord or paying the quarter sale faced an even worse fate. Since the Revolution, numerous tenants had shown their abhorrence for the quarter sale by neglecting to pay it; agents rarely sought out or prosecuted violators. But Van Rensselaer's leases made such sales void; if the quarter sale had not been paid, the land legally reverted to the patroon. In the early 1830s, Van Rensselaer began to exercise this right. He sued several illicit purchasers as squatters for damages and in at least one case had the purchaser evicted.[7] At the same time, he began to evict indebted millers when their leases expired, seizing their mills as compensation for their unpaid rents.[8]

Like his counterpart on Rensselaerwyck, Robert L. Livingston sought to overcome his financial woes by rigidly holding his tenants to the terms of their contracts. He began by trying to sell his lands. Many Clermont tenants accepted his offer, but Woodstock farmers suspected his title, and the few who agreed to buy their farms paid slowly and irregularly. In a few years, Livingston, again desperate for cash, wrote his agent, John Wigram, that "it is *most* necessary that my business at Woodstock should be prosecuted with energy, and that your undivided attention should be paid to see my instructions executed. . . . It has become absolutely necessary that the rents due should be collected." At the same time, the landlord escalated his long-standing battle against his tenants' timber cutting on the Woodstock commons, initiating a flurry of lawsuits against illicit loggers.[9]

Livingston's suits were part of an ambitious plan to transform lumbering on his estate from a cottage industry carried out by independent proprietors into a large-scale capitalist enterprise. He hoped to hire estate farmers to cut the timber throughout his Hardenbergh patent lands, raft the logs to his numerous sawmills, and saw the logs. These tenants could work for wages or use their labor to pay their back rents. In one bold step, Livingston hoped to cash in on his vast timber stands, reap more profit from his sawmills, and collect tenants' back rents. In 1833, he incorporated the Esopus Creek Navigation Company and oversaw the clearing of Esopus Creek and the Beaverkill for large-scale rafting. That summer, he ordered his agents to fan out across the estate, demanding "money or labour" and warning tenants that "this was the last call." Any tenants who failed to pay their back rents in cash, produce, or labor, he warned, would be taken to court.[10]

While landlords from the great families sought personal solvency by enforcing long-ignored rules and by bringing a new rigidity to the collection of rents, many lesser landlords introduced a far more fundamental change: a switch from long-term to annual leases. During his first two decades as a landlord in Delaware County, Isaac Hardenbergh offered perpetual leases, along with a few three-life agreements. In doing so, he offered tenants control over their work, security of tenure, and property rights in their improvements. But beginning in the 1810s, Hardenbergh (and, in later years, his sons) began buying back leased farms from tenants' widows and heirs, compelling tenants to return their farms in payment for their overdue rents, and suing delinquent farmers and snatching up their farms at sheriff's auction. He then re-leased the farms—often to the same tenant—for one to five years. Other landlords did the same. During the 1820s, lesser proprietors on the Goldsbrow and Rapelje patents and many owners of lands in Montgomery County replaced two- and three-life leases with yearly agreements.[11]

The switch to annual leases brought profound changes to landlord-tenant relations. Most importantly, tenants lost their former legal claim to the land. With it, they lost their economic security: landlords frequently rid themselves of troublesome tenants after 1820. Tenants also forfeited all claim to the improvements they created. Although some annual leases provided tenants with compensation for improvements made during their tenure, almost all made clear that new improvements would become the property of the landlord. With the introduction of annual leases, estate farmers were stripped of one of their most important claims to property and took a giant step toward the status of landless laborers.[12]

Some proprietors went further, designing leases that gave them control over both the labor and the crop of their tenants. Most yearly tenants continued to act as independent farmers, providing their own tools, seed, and livestock and controlling their work and their crop. But in the 1810s and 1820s, proprietors began to introduce share leases that did away with this independence. In 1813, Isaac Hardenbergh promised to provide William Sturges with a farm in Roxbury, a team of oxen, two cows, and six sheep. In return, Sturges promised to pay a third of all the grain and produce he grew, half the butter and cheese he made, half the calves and lambs born on the farm, and a pound of wool per sheep. The lease was to last during "the good will and pleasure of . . . Isaac Hardenbergh." Similar arrangements cropped up in abundance throughout Delaware and Montgomery counties after 1810.[13]

Leases like these spared tenants the need to assemble all the resources needed to run a farm—an enormous advantage to capital-poor farmers and to those who wished to expand operations cheaply. In exchange, however, they gave up control over their work and their product. By providing seed and livestock, the landlord determined what crops tenants would grow; many leases explicitly forbade lessees from raising livestock or growing crops not mentioned in the leases. Just as important, crops were no longer the property of tenants, but were jointly owned with the landlord until divided. We should not exaggerate the proletarian status of sharecroppers: Sturges and other sharecroppers still owned much of the equipment needed to run their farms, and they were probably free from day-to-day supervision by proprietors. But their status was a far cry from that of tenants on long-term leases. Share agreements provided a halfway house between long-term tenants' independent, proprietary status and the station of a wage laborer.[14]

The Tenants' Response (I)

In suing and evicting their tenants and in replacing long-term with annual leases, landlords dismantled one of the columns supporting peace on their estates: their promotion of tenants' economic security. Understandably, tenants opposed these innovations. There is no evidence that tenants overtly resisted the transition from long- to short-term leases. Most likely, their landlords' superior political influence discouraged them from offering open defiance. But they made the new regime as unmanageable as the old one. Both the Hardenberghs and Samuel A. Law, another Delaware County land owner and agent, used the coercive power of short-term leases to force tenants to pay their rent fully and promptly. Law evicted deadbeats, while Isaac Hardenbergh seized their personal property. Law charged interest on overdue payments, while Hardenbergh demanded that an unreliable tenant "give me security for the rent or give me up the place." But Law admitted to his employers that these tactics were no match for the poverty and obstructionism of the tenants. "I have thought, years agone, that times & difficulties of making and meeting payments, from the settlers, could scarce get worse," he wrote in 1830. Yet his adversities had gotten "rather worse, than better" over the years. All he could do was to make the best of the circumstances. "I shall thus endeavour, collecting, where can; compromising, where must, or do worse. . . ."[15]

On every front, tenants on annual leases resisted landlords' drive for increased control over their property and the productive process. Despite renewed prosecutions of illicit lumbering, tenants denuded local forests with increasing speed during the 1820s and 1830s. Nor did annual leases make evicting troublesome tenants easier. When Lewis Hardenbergh ordered a Roxbury sawyer named Days to leave, the tenant agreed but registered his dissatisfaction by announcing that he would take with him the wooden slabs that buttressed the Hardenberghs' mill and the running parts of a shingling machine. After two months of haggling, Hardenbergh decided to let the sawyer take the property. "For my Part it is Best and Get Some Rent . . . and have No Trouble about it hereafter . . . So that we can . . . begin a New." Hardenbergh's resignation, like that of Samuel Law, was a measure of just how limited the effective power of landlords was when dealing with determined tenants.[16]

Share tenants proved equally recalcitrant. In 1836, Samuel Law leased a farm to C. Simonson, providing him with six hundred sheep, two hogs, and eight hens. Simonson could keep a cow and a kitchen garden, but could grow no other crops without Law's permission. But rather than creating the commercial wool farm his landlord envisioned, Simonson used the land to pursue old-fashioned general farming. He neglected Law's sheep, spending his time in collecting hay and apples, making cider, growing potatoes, oats, and buckwheat, tending his kitchen garden, and raising his own livestock. Before the agreement was nine months old, Law decided to cut his losses. He drew up a new agreement, in which the business of raising sheep was "given up, wholly." The crops, "so far as Simonson has raised any," were divided between Law and his tenant. Angered and disgusted, Law repeatedly admonished himself and his tenant "to let the past go and be done with."[17]

Simonson's and other tenants' stubbornness marked a new stage in an old pattern of resistance. They abandoned their deferential habits in favor of open noncooperation. But their resistance remained individual and aimed at gaining specific advantages, not at challenging the leasehold system. They set strict limits on landlords' power, but did not threaten that power itself.

The same was true of much of the resistance to great proprietors' innovations. When Robert L. Livingston's agents demanded overdue rents, most Woodstock tenants put them off with token payments. When the landlord began suing unauthorized lumbermen and winning in court, his tenants intensified their assault on his timber stands. And when Livingston issued his "last call" for cash or labor, most tenants stayed home. Those who agreed to work proved to be unreliable. By spring 1834, workmen had finished clearing the Esopus Creek and the Beaverkill of obstructions. Livingston's superintendent, Henry Shultis, assembled a large force of tenants to cut logs and raft them downstream during the spring freshet. The men felled the trees without incident. In April the freshet came—an enormous one, capable of lifting mountains of timber and crowding them into Livingston's mill ponds. The tenants took one look at the swelled creeks, told Shultis that rafting in such high waters was dangerous, and went home. The logs remained on the riverbanks, and Livingston now faced his creditors with no new influx of cash.[18]

Rensselaerwyck tenants also avoided their landlord's attempts to force them to pay back rents. Though Van Rensselaer did convince his Westerlo farmers to pay more than half their debts between 1819 and 1825, he was not so successful over the long run. After a rush to pay in 1823 and 1825, tenants allowed their payments to fall off again. Between 1826 and 1830, rent payments plummeted to unprecedented lows; by 1829 their total indebtedness had grown to £832—more than the total in 1819 (see Appendix, figures 1 and 2). Those who were sued proved no more tractable. Although some settled, many more ignored the landlord's summons. When Van Rensselaer won a judgment by default, they ignored that too, forcing the patroon's lawyers to return to court to get the judgment enforced. And when Van Rensselaer began a second round of prosecutions in the mid-1830s, many farmers hired lawyers and challenged the patroon's arguments at every turn, dragging out the proceedings and forcing his lawyers to scramble for documentation of his claims. All of these strategies mired Van Rensselaer in court, draining his finances and dashing his hopes for a quick recovery of his rents.[19]

The Tenants' Response (II)

Tenants' obstructionism blocked the landlords' efforts to squeeze more money from them with remarkable effectiveness. But their resistance remained individual and defensive; it could create stalemate but could not resolve the growing crisis. In the mid-1820s, however, two developments pushed many tenants toward a new response. First, great proprietors began to sue their tenants. Lesser landlords' holdings were relatively small and surrounded by freehold farms or the lands of other leasehold proprietors. When these landlords began suing tenants and switching to annual leases in the 1810s, they dispossessed scattered families or clusters of families. When great proprietors turned to the courts, by contrast, they threatened the economic security of neighborhoods, entire towns, and, in the case of Rensselaerwyck, most of two counties. Under these circumstances, tenants shared a widespread sense of collective grievance and solidarity—and enjoyed the support of many of the prosperous and influential men of their towns. Second, great landlords' political power fell into steep decline, while tenants' own political experience grew. With this convergence of events, farmers on the estates of the great proprietors began to abandon individual for collective strategies. In doing so, they unearthed old memories of faulty titles, transforming a defensive effort into the beginning of a campaign to topple the proprietors from power.

The change on Rensselaerwyck began in the mid-1820s. Some time after 1824, Stephen Van Rensselaer sued Moses Winne, a Rensselaer County tenant, for cutting timber on unimproved land. Winne responded by challenging Van Rensselaer's title to the land in question. Several other manor residents came to his aid, offering financial support and filing countersuits.[20] At about the same time, a majority of Westerlo tenants began a rent boycott. Starting in 1827, 16 of 23 tenants—70 percent—failed to make even token payments at the manor office; they continued to withhold payments for periods ranging from 4 to 10 years (see Appendix, figure 1). In 1830, tenants from the hill towns of Albany county—Westerlo, Rensselaerville, Knox, Bern, and New Scotland—met to lay plans for a legal challenge to the patroon's title. They appointed Stephen Hungerford as their agent, instructing him to hire attorneys and obtain copies of the Dutch and English grants to the manor. And in 1835, tenants in both Albany and Rensselaer Counties mounted a petition campaign, demanding that the legislature tax leasehold rents and income from quarter sales.[21]

Elsewhere as well, individual resistance to landlords' new demands coalesced into a collective challenge to their rule. In 1827, tenants on the Scott Patent in Schoharie County organized to challenge their landlords' title in court. Three years later, Delaware County residents resurrected a fifty-year-old challenge to landlords' title to lands between the east and west branches of the Delaware river. And in 1839, tenants on Robert L. Livingston's land in the towns around Woodstock sued to overturn Livingston's title to land along the Woodstock-Olive line. They refused to pay rent and, when hauled into court for cutting timber on the landlords' commons, "pled title" as their defense.[22]

In embarking on these new forms of resistance, tenants got a taste of the limits and the possibilities of their influence in the new political order. Young lawyer-politicians like the Rensselaer County Anti-Mason and Whig Henry Z. Hayner proved willing to take their cases against their landlords, thus offering them allies in the parties. One legislator, Mr. Kemble of Rensselaer County, supported the tenants' petition campaign. But for the most part, the leaders of every party met the tenants' growing movement with silence. Although tenant resistance was strongest in the Democratic towns of Albany County, the Democratic *Argus* never reported on the farmers' campaign. Nor did the legislature act on the demands of the Albany and Rensselaer petitioners.[23]

More than any other event, Stephen Hungerford's efforts to find a lawyer to challenge Stephen Van Rensselaer's title revealed the political obstacles to his movement. Hungerford visited every prominent lawyer in Albany County, and each one informed him that he had already been retained by the patroon. "I can get no information from them," he complained. In desperation, he wrote to Martin Van Buren, Andrew Jackson's secretary of state. He asked Van Buren to help the tenants acquire a copy of the grant to Rensselaerwyck in London and to act as the tenants' attorney. After his youthful foray into antilandlord politics, Van Buren had devoted his adult life to building an electoral coalition that included both landlords and tenants. The controversy on Rensselaerwyck posed, on a state level, the same threat that the slavery question posed in national affairs—a splintering of the Democratic coalition. Accordingly, the Little Magician sought to discourage Hungerford's efforts. Claiming the press of official duties, he declined to act as the tenants' attorney. Reciprocating the tenants' claim of "friendship," he advised them not to challenge Van Rensselaer's title. He denied any knowledge of deficiencies in the title and warned that if they existed, "any attempt to invalidate it would be rendered unavailing by the passage of time and the acts of the parties." "I would not therefore advise any body, and particularly those who call themselves my friends," he concluded, "to embark in a controversy from which there is so little to hope and which must unavoidably be attended with great expense and trouble." Having disposed of Hungerford's request, Van Buren moved to protect himself from any accusation of having betrayed the patroon. He sent copies of Hungerford's letter and his own reply to Joel Sutherland, an Albany County judge and an ally of Van Rensselaer. He instructed Sutherland to show the letters to the patroon, thus clarifying his own role in the controversy, "if misrepresentation should make it desirable."[24]

Without the help of powerful political allies, the tenants' efforts collapsed. The Westerlo farmers' rent boycott faltered in the mid-1830s, when Van Rensselaer laid plans for a second round of lawsuits against his tenants. By 1833, nine of the sixteen tenants who had been withholding their rent had begun paying again, leaving only seven—30 percent—still refusing to pay. We do not know whether Hungerford found a lawyer or if he obtained a copy of the royal grant to Rensselaerwyck. If he did, his efforts, like the challenges to other landlords' titles, failed. Local and poorly coordinated, the tenants' efforts were no match for the political influence of the landlords, diminished though this was since the days of the Federalists.

Death of the Patroon

By 1839, New York's landlords and tenants had reached a stalemate. Proprietors' efforts to squeeze more money from their estates had failed everywhere, foiled by tenants' age-old tactics of foot-dragging, secret lumbering, and avoidance. Tenants, however, could hardly claim victory. Their campaign to overturn their landlords' titles had come to nothing. Increasingly burdened with rising capital costs, they had been forced to pay badly needed cash to their landlords. Worse still, increasing numbers of them were being hauled into court, subjected to ruinous judgments, and forced from the land.

At this juncture, the worst happened. On January 26, 1839, Stephen Van Rensselaer died at the Manor House in Watervliet. He left behind debts worth $400,000. On the other hand, his tenants' debts to him totaled the same amount. In his will, Van Rensselaer left to his executors a task that he had failed to accomplish: to save his patrimony by compelling his tenants to pay. He bequeathed Rensselaerwyck to two of his sons. Stephen IV, the only surviving son of the patroon's first marriage, was to receive the West Manor, which included all of his father's leasehold lands in Albany County. William Patterson Van Rensselaer, the oldest male issue of Stephen III's second marriage, got the East Manor, in Rensselaer County. The patroon's debts were to be paid by collecting the rents, notes, and mortgages owed to him by his tenants. If the amount the executors collected fell short, William and Stephen would have to assume the remaining debt. Van Rensselaer instructed his executors to show "all reasonable indulgence" toward the poor of the manor. But this last gesture toward benevolence could not mask the fact that the final crisis had arrived. Either tenants would come forth and pay unprecedented sums at the manor office, or his sons would face ruin.[25]

The news of Stephen Van Rensselaer's death brought forth a torrent of grief in the city of Albany. The state's senate and assembly devoted the morning to eulogies and voted to wear badges of mourning for 30 days. The Albany Common Council and the Albany Military Association also donned black ribbons. The Board of Canal Commissioners, the Albany Academy, the Albany Medical College, the Young Men's Association, and the Albany Institute all passed resolutions expressing sorrow at the patroon's passing. Even the children at the Albany Orphan Asylum wore badges of mourning. The next day, the state senate, assembly, and supreme court joined "a vast concourse of citizens" in a procession along North Market Street to the Dutch Reformed Church. There, the crowd spilled out of the church and into Clinton Square, standing silently while services were conducted.[26]

The tenants of Rensselaerwyck were absent from these proceedings. Few, if any, commemorated their landlord's passing. In Albany, Stephen Van Rensselaer was mourned as a pious and generous public benefactor; in the mountains above the city, gratitude and affection had given way to anger, worry, and a new spirit of resistance. When the news of the patroon's death reached the Helderbergs, some tenants worried "that the times would be worse" with the passing of the great man. Others, however, believed that "times would be better, for they wouldn't pay any rent."[27]

These sentiments bore witness to the growing crisis between landlords and tenants. The undivided patrimonies, generous incomes, and patrician politics that had provided the foundation for peace on the estates were gone. As a result, the central tension in the leasehold system—between tenants' drive for property and landlords' appetite for income—had come to a head, threatening to ruin both proprietors and farmers. But a resolution to the crisis remained elusive. Landlords' efforts to increase their incomes and tenants' bid to challenge the proprietors' claim to land had both failed. In the years that followed, landlords and tenants would each grope toward their own resolution to the crisis; in doing so, they would forever change politics and society in New York.

Chapter 4

ORIGINS OF THE ANTI-RENT
MOVEMENT, 1839 – 1844

➤━╎━◆❭━✦━◯━✦━❬◆━╎━◄

The Committee
and the Landlord

On May 22, 1839, twenty-five men, respectfully dressed in their Sunday best, met in the Hudson River town of Watervliet. When their horses and carriages had been stowed at Dunbar's tavern, they walked together to the manor office of Stephen Van Rensselaer IV, the new proprietor of the West Manor of Rensselaerwyck. They were expected. Earlier in the month, one of their members, Egbert Schoonmaker of Knox, had written to request a meeting with the young proprietor. Douw Lansing, Van Rensselaer's agent, had replied that this would be a convenient time for the patroon to meet.[1]

The men had come to negotiate a compromise in the looming crisis between Van Rensselaer and his tenants. They were from the five hill towns of the West Manor, where relations between the Van Rensselaers and their tenants were most volatile. In these towns, resistance to the Van Rensselaers had been most intense since 1820, and it was there that tenants' debts to the patroon were greatest.[2]

The death of Stephen Van Rensselaer III in January had shattered any hope that the growing conflict over back rents, quarter sales, and timber rights would subside. The patroon's will had saddled his heirs, William and Stephen IV, with $400,000 in debts. By year's end, Stephen raised $35,000 by mortgaging the manor house at Watervliet. With this money, he paid some of the most urgent debts of the estate but left a mass of creditors unsatisfied. William's finances tottered on the edge of collapse. Whenever one of his many notes fell due, he sent his agent, Casparus V. Pruyn, scurrying in search of a new loan to pay off the old one. When the property taxes on the East Manor came due in early 1839, Pruyn was forced to sell a hoard of gold to pay them, for no cash or credit could be found.[3]

The new loans merely bought William and Stephen time. The only way to end the cycle of indebtedness was to dun the tenants for their back rents—

the method set out in their father's will. On April 25, the brothers distributed a notice throughout the manor, commanding all tenants to call at the manor office and settle their accounts. The landlords' agents then combed the manors, threatening and cajoling tenants with a new fierceness. "To tell you all in a Letter," Pruyn wrote William, "would be too much, how uneasy I have had people, and how they have run about for money."[4]

These demands could hardly have come at a worse time. In early 1839, farm prices returned to normal after the panic of 1837 but collapsed again at the end of the year. As they had two decades before, manor farmers had failed to pay their rents, which were payable in wheat, when prices were high; manor agents had added the high cash value of their rents to their debts. Now the Van Rensselaers pressed them to repay those debts with produce that fetched depression-level prices. Moreover, the demand for back rents came at a moment when cash was scarce and when banks, merchants, and other creditors were pressing for repayment. Again and again, Casparus Pruyn answered William Van Rensselaer's demands for cash with the rejoinder that "the Farmers . . . have no money."[5]

William and Stephen Van Rensselaer handled the crisis in different ways, however. William, who had inherited the East Manor, showed a degree of patience toward his tenants. Pruyn warned his employer repeatedly against pressing his tenants too hard. "More than you think," he said, "now depends on . . . the Science of *Fishing*. . . . Beat the water and scare the Fish away, but a good [fisherman], carefully examines the bait, adjusts it & again, he catches them at last." Above all, he warned William against bringing his tenants to court. "Do not be persuaded by anyone to commence suits. . . . If what I have put in motion, does not bring in money—take my word for it, Suits will not." Reluctantly, Van Rensselaer followed his agent's advice.[6]

Stephen showed no such restraint. He allowed the executors of his father's estate to file suits against a handful of West Manor tenants—all of them, in the opinion of the executors, able to pay. He hoped that this action would pressure other tenants to settle their accounts. The suits had the opposite effect: they strengthened the discontent and the sense of collective purpose that had been growing for the past two decades.[7]

It was out of this renewed discontent that the 25 somberly dressed men assembled in Watervliet. In late April or early May, tenants in the five hill towns of the West Manor held meetings; each town chose five representatives to represent them in the growing conflict. Although many tenants were prepared to resist the demands of their new patroon, others feared a confrontation. The meetings instructed their representatives to meet with Van Rensselaer and to attempt to work out a compromise.[8]

The men chosen to do so were drawn from the organic leadership of their towns—prosperous, influential working farmers who had already demonstrated their capacity to lead their neighbors. Sixty-five percent had reached their fortieth year; only one was younger than 30. Most, if not all, headed their own households, and most made a living on the land. Of the 18 who could be found in the 1840 census, 16 were engaged in agriculture; one was a merchant; and another made his living as a tanner. These men were not uniformly wealthy, but all seem to have been prosperous property owners. Of the four representatives of Westerlo who could be found on that town's tax list for 1840, two were among the wealthiest tenth of the town's citizens, one belonged to the third-wealthiest tenth, and another fell into the fourth decile. Anecdotal evidence suggests that committee members from other towns held similar degrees of wealth. As substantial property holders and heads of families, tenant leaders were accustomed to commanding the labor of wives and children; many also controlled the labor of servants or leased their land to subtenants.[9]

In matters that were capable of dividing manor communities, tenants carefully chose leaders who represented all groups in their towns. Committee members represented all the major ethnic groups of the Helderbergs. Of the 23 committee members whose surnames had a clear national origin, 11 (48 percent) came from Yankee or English immigrant families, 5 (22 percent) traced their lineage to Holland, and 2 (9 percent) were of German stock. Men of Scottish, Irish, French, Huguenot, and Swiss origin also joined the committee. Whether or not the eighteenth-century rebellions on New York's estates were, as some historians claim, primarily ethnic conflicts between Yankee rebels and loyal Dutch-stock tenants, the tenants' movement that began in 1839 assuredly was not. In partisan loyalties, too, the committee drew from all segments of the manor towns. Of the 18 members whose political affiliations are known, 7 (39 percent) were Whigs and 11 (61 percent) followed the party of Jackson. This majority in favor of Democrats resembled partisan preferences in the Helderbergs.[10]

Most important of all, the majority of tenant leaders had crucial experience in leading their neighbors. At least 4 of the 25 served as deacons or elders in their churches; 8 or more had served in town offices. Most commonly, 14 members—47 percent—had served as county-level activists in the Whig and Democratic parties. Many more, no doubt, had been active on the town level. Here was a crucial, if unintended, consequence of the Jacksonian Revolution. In order to win the loyalty of ordinary voters, Whig and Democratic leaders had drawn unprecedented numbers of middling and wealthy citizens into party activities and taught them basic skills in education, agitation, and organization building. In doing so, those party leaders helped build a new group of local leaders, a group that could turn its skills to new purposes for which party leaders had no sympathy.[11]

As these farmers and traders approached the manor office, each quietly prepared himself to speak his part before the patroon. When they arrived, however, Van Rensselaer refused to meet with them. He passed through the front office as the committee stood waiting, but—as befitted a gentleman of his status—he refused to greet them, walking to his inner office without any gesture of acknowledgment. Moments later, his agent emerged to inform the committee that the patroon would not speak to them but required that they submit their grievances to him in writing.[12]

The committee retired to Dunbar's Tavern, where they drew up their grievances and requests for redress. Their message drew on a long-standing practice of appealing to the landlord's duty to look after tenants' economic security. The cash value of rents, the committee wrote, had risen enormously since the leases to Helderberg lands had been issued, even as those lands had become less productive. As a result, it was now "extremely difficult for many of the tenants to support their families and pay their rent, without involving themselves and posterity in extreme peril and hardship." In addition, the committee voiced the tenants' long-standing discontent with the quarter sales and with Van Rensselaer's exclusive control over mineral and manufacturing rights on the manor.[13]

To resolve these grievances, the committee asked that Van Rensselaer issue new leases to all tenants, in which rents in wheat, fowls, and labor would be commuted to a cash payment—at a rate considerably less than the current market price for those commodities. Tenants with poor land would be charged less than those with better soil. The quarter sale and the landlord's reservations on water and mineral rights would be expunged. In addition, committee members noted that many tenants carried an immense debt burden and asked the patroon to forgive the back rents of those whose debts exceeded the value of their personal property. Finally, they requested that all tenants be allowed to purchase their farms for a sum which, when lent out at interest, would earn the equivalent of the rent under the new leases.[14]

In their behavior toward the patroon and in their written statement, committee members maintained either a profound ambivalence or a painstaking deception. They carefully observed an old etiquette of deference (albeit a restrained version of it), but did so in the hope of fundamentally altering their relationship to their landlord. In requesting a meeting with Van Rensselaer, they carried on a time-honored practice, in which influential tenants represented the grievances of their humbler neighbors and attempted to work out a compromise. Their memorial did not challenge Van Rensselaer's title or question his authority to address the tenants' grievances as he saw fit. It demanded nothing, instead asserting the committee's "opinion" as to the proper redress. And it wisely neglected to mention that many tenants had accumulated their ruinous debts by boycotting their landlord. In making their requests, tenant leaders appealed to the landlord's duty to promote the economic security of his tenants. They "ask[ed]" that their grievances "be redressed in such a way as may be conducive to the future happiness and prosperity to ourselves and posterity."[15]

But where earlier tenants had demonstrated their loyalty to a powerful benefactor, the committee's requests amounted to a polite assault on Van Rensselaer's customary power and privilege. Committee members were the elected representatives of a growing movement—one in which many participants were prepared to resist the landlord outright. Their requests were to apply to all tenants, leaving no room for the landlord's traditional prerogative of granting favors on an individual basis. Moreover, they sought to abolish some of the patroon's long-standing economic privileges: the quarter sale, control over manufacturing, and the right to charge market prices for wheat rent. Most dramatically, they asked that all tenants have the privilege of severing their ties to Van Rensselaer by buying him out.

The committee dropped off their memorial and returned home that afternoon. Van Rensselaer responded a week later. Where the tenants' committee had appealed to his duty to look after tenants' material well-being, the young heir responded in the language of contract obligations and property rights. The tenants' forbears, he wrote, had signed their leases "with a full knowledge of the kind and amount of rent to be paid, and of the reservations and conditions to which the land was subject." Since he claimed nothing more than the original tenants had agreed to, the patroon said, any talk of burdens was irrelevant. The current rents, quarter sales, and reservations on manufacturing constituted "a part of my property"; any attempt to abrogate those lease provisions amounted to a request that he give them "a release of my interest in the land." He admitted that there might be some cases where the executors of his father's estate "will exercise a forbearance." But such lenience would be granted on a case-by-case basis, "without the interference or intervention of any third party, having no interest in the immediate matters." Van Rensselaer may have been talking to his attorneys; he spelled out his and his tenants' legal rights and obligations perfectly. But his response also reflected the patrician liberalism of conservative political spokesmen. He justified his unequal relationship to his tenants not in terms of benevolence but on the ground of the sanctity of property and contract.[16]

Nonetheless, the patroon was broke and ready to deal. He agreed to grant new leases in which wheat, service, and fowls were commuted to a cash payment. But where the tenants hoped to convert the wheat obligation at between $0.75 and $1.00 per bushel, Van Rensselaer proposed to do so at $1.42 per bushel—a rate that reflected the average market price for the grain over the past 47 years. He also agreed to sell his interest in the land to any Helderberg tenant, but at a much higher price than the committee had proposed. No one would get a new lease or a deed until he or she had paid off all back rents.[17]

The patroon's letter convinced most tenants active in the movement that polite appeals would yield nothing. On July 4, Helderberg residents held a mass rally in the town of Bern, where they gave formal reply. Their central complaint was that Van Rensselaer was endangering their hold on property, and thus their freedom. The landlord had "pretend[ed]," they declared, "that he . . . would make our condition easy and satisfactory to all; but when called upon by the committee for the purpose of trying his flint, he pecks it again and most wantonly aims a more deadly blow at our future prosperity and welfare." By refusing to meet the committee's terms and by continuing to take his tenants to court, he threatened to dispossess great numbers of leaseholders. In doing so, he endangered "that freedom which we have so freely inherited from our gallant ancestors, and which our innocent posterity have a right to . . . expect from us." The militants pledged to engage "our fortunes and our sacred honor even to the last extremity in protecting our rights *and our property* from being thus wantonly and unjustly forced from us." Thus they swore to resist their landlord for the same reason that earlier generations of tenants had remained loyal to his father: to ensure their hold on property.[18]

Now that Van Rensselaer had refused to meet their terms, the Helderbergers pointed out what they saw as the fatal flaw in his claim to power: his title was invalid. The landlord was no more than the "pretended proprietor" to the lands he claimed, and he must "establish . . . a good, sufficient, and valid paper title . . . for the . . . land we occupy" before tenants would reach a settlement. Like earlier generations of tenant insurgents, the Rensselaerwyck militants simultaneously denounced their landlord's relationship to them as a violation of republican liberty and sought to end that relationship by challenging his title.[19]

Nonetheless, the tenants still sought a compromise. If the patroon were to prove his title, commute wheat rents to cash at the rate of $1 per bushel, relinquish his claim to the quarter sale and other reservations, cease to collect the day's service and fat fowls, and agree to sell out to all tenants who wished to buy, they would come to terms.[20]

The Helderberg War

When they abandoned deference, Helderberg tenants adopted a combination of old and new strategies. Earlier insurgents on Livingston Manor and Claverack had combined local, defensive crowd actions with lawsuits and appeals to public officials. Rensselaerwyck militants had already tried the latter two strategies, only to be stymied by unsympathetic lawyers and Democratic leaders. Now they revived the tradition of crowd actions. At the same time, they drew on a newer tradition of voluntary association, which had reached the Helderbergs through temperance, moral reform, and anti-slavery societies. Emulating temperance methods, tenant leaders circulated a printed pledge obliging all signers to withhold all rent and to help prevent the sheriff from serving court papers in favor of Van Rensselaer. In addition, the insurgents threatened with violence anyone who dared to make an individual settlement with the patroon.[21]

Faced with this intransigence, Stephen Van Rensselaer again went to the law. In August, he commenced suits against another six tenants for nonpayment of rents. By fall, he had won several suits, but the tenants refused to pay the judgments. In mid-October, Van Rensselaer ordered the sheriff to collect those judgments by auctioning off the livestock, tools, and household goods of the defendants.[22] With this mutual hardening of positions, Van Rensselaer and his tenants turned their local dispute into a political crisis with statewide implications.

On August 27, undersheriff Amos Adams of Albany County rode west from the city of Albany with warrants made out against several Helderberg tenants. He stopped first at Isaac Hungerford's farm in Bern and served him with a warrant. Hungerford turned pale with anger. "I advise you as a friend to go no farther," he said. "You can't go thro' this part of the country and go to Albany a live man—we have determined to spill blood—we have made up our minds to die if necessary." Adams stayed the night at a local tavern; while he slept, someone crept into the stable, sheared the mane and tail of his horse, cut his harness, and damaged his carriage.[23]

The weapons that Hungerford and the nameless vandals used—threats and anonymous attacks on property—were well suited to their circumstances. The Helderbergers knew that the law was on the patroon's side; if they provoked a full-scale confrontation, they would be the losers. So they sought to drive Adams out of the mountains in ways that protected them from retribution. In doing so, they followed in a tradition shared by rural people throughout the pre-industrial world. For the moment, the scheme worked. On finding his wrecked carriage and denuded horse in the morning, Adams returned directly to Albany and refused to serve any more warrants.[24]

On September 15, another deputy, Daniel Leonard, began to deliver the warrants that Adams had failed to serve. Several tenants followed Leonard on his rounds, threatening to kill him and urging him to flee for his life. When the deputy paused at a local tavern, a band of 50 men dragged him outside. The men produced a tar barrel, set it ablaze, and ordered Leonard to throw his warrants into the flames. If he refused, they said, they would kill him. Leonard complied, and his tormentors forced him to buy a round of drinks. They then carried him in a wagon to the houses where he had served warrants. From mid morning until late afternoon, they bore the deputy through the neighborhood, compelling him to take back and burn the warrants he had served and forcing him to treat. All the while, they threatened him with a gruesome death, shouted huzzahs, and blew the tin dinner horns that they carried with them. At four o'clock, they informed him that he was free to go.[25]

During the following three months, these rites of intimidation gave way to large-scale confrontations. Between October and December, Albany County Sheriff Michael Artcher led three expeditions into the mountains, only to be turned back each time at Reidsville, a village at the crest of the Helderbergs. Each confrontation brought more participants on each side: by early December, Artcher was backed by a posse of 500 men, while the tenants mustered a force of some 1,500. By this time, the Helderbergers had assembled an impressive paramilitary organization. Sentries were posted on the road to Albany and ordered to warn of the sheriff's approach by blowing tin horns. Local farmers were organized into companies of 25, each with its own captain. At the same time, the tenants' leaders, who had condemned the elaborate abuse of Leonard, had convinced their troops to replace "rough music" with discipline and restraint. When Artcher and his posse found their path blocked at Reidsville by 1,500 men armed with clubs, the sheriff ordered his horsemen to ride into the crowd. The assembled farmers rushed forward with cries no more offensive than "stop them," grabbed the horses' reins, and turned them around. The horsemen came out of the scuffle without a scratch.[26]

These growing confrontations doomed the tenants' hope of limiting the conflict to their own turf. On December 4, Sheriff Artcher wrote to Governor William Seward, asking him to call out the state militia. After an all-night cabinet meeting, Seward instructed Artcher to attempt again to enforce the law without troops. Four days later, Artcher and a posse of 120 men were once again turned back at Reidsville, and the Sheriff renewed his request for troops. This time Seward complied, ordering militia units to reinforce the sheriff's posse.[27]

At the same time, the governor offered tenants a different avenue of struggle. In a proclamation distributed throughout the manor, he appealed to the tenants to remember that "the only security for the preservation of their rights consists in the complete ascendancy of the laws." The problem, he intimated, was not that the farmers' complaints were unfounded but that they were seeking redress in the wrong manner. Tenants' actions, Seward warned, carried the legal penalties for insurrection and might, if anyone were killed, expose them to charges of treason and murder. The proper way to remedy their grievances was by application to the courts and the legislature. If the tenants chose the latter course, Seward promised "every facility which the Executive Department can afford in bringing their complaints before the legislature."[28]

The tenants' entire strategy had depended on their ability to intimidate their enemies without a fight. With the militia mobilized, they had no choice but to concede to Seward's demands and accept his promises. A delegation of tenant leaders visited two Whig activists in Albany, Henry Wheaton and Azor Taber, and asked them to relay a message to Seward. They foreswore all further resistance to the sheriff and were ready to "cordially embrace the pacific offers" of Seward's proclamation. The crowd at Reidsville dispersed without offering a moment's resistance to the militia. Seward ordered all but one company of troops home while Artcher, backed only by a few men, delivered his warrants and made levies on several tenants' property. On December 15, their work done, he and the remaining soldiers returned to Albany.[29] In the meantime, the Helderbergers, buoyed by Seward's promise of help, prepared to fight in a new arena.

Expanding the Movement

From the start, tenants on the West Manor knew that their grievances were not theirs alone. As they blocked the way of Sheriff Artcher's posses, they sent emissaries to the neighboring counties of Schoharie and Rensselaer to orga-

Figure 4.1. William Seward in 1843, soon after leaving the governorship of New York. Although he called out the militia to suppress the Rensselaerwyck tenants' resistance to enforcement of their leases, Seward was the first political leader in New York to endorse the anti–renters' aims. His action initiated an alliance between anti–renters and Liberal Whigs that outlasted the Whig party. *William H. Seward*, 1843, by Henry Inman. Collection of the City of New York; Courtesy of the Art Commission of the City of New York.

nize among the tenants there. The organizers were only partly successful. On those estates where landlords' lenience had dissolved into unforgiving expropriation, the movement met with success. But where proprietors continued to soften their demands and extend rewards to loyal tenants, anti-rent emissaries made scant headway.

On the East Manor of Rensselaerwyck, Casparus Pruyn's lenience toward

Figure 4.2. Units of the New York militia march into the Helderbergs, ending the Helderberg War. *View of the Great Pass on the Helderberg Mountains, with the Lines of March in Service, December 1839,* 1840, by B. Brenell. Collections at Historic Cherry Hill, Albany, NY.

tenants enabled him to halt the spread of anti-rentism. In early November 1839 Pruyn learned that emissaries from "the infected district" had called a meeting in Sand Lake. Despite a bad cold and an injured arm, he rushed to the town, where he called on Mr. Butts, a loyal tenant. Butts attended the anti-rent meeting with several of his "friends," and they succeeded in convincing those attending to adjourn without setting a date for another meeting. Two weeks later, the anti-renters again called a meeting. Pruyn rode to the main road to Albany, where farmers were returning from market day. There, "I immediately urged such of the substantial farmers as passed to go & keep them down." In the following months, the agent kept close watch over the movement through his network of subagents and loyal tenants, mobilizing his "friends" wherever the anti-renters sought to organize.[30]

Pruyn strengthened the ranks of his supporters and weakened those of the militants with a judicious use of rewards and threats. "It will not do to abandon our Friends," he wrote Van Rensselaer in January. As for the anti-renters, Pruyn cautioned against revenge but urged that "we . . . show a proper self respect." When a partisan of the new movement called at the manor office, Pruyn, without making any accusations, offered a warning with bloodcurdling blandness: "Mr. VR is I think well appraised of what has been going on, any request for favor, will be duly considered by him—but any person that has or has *attempted* to form [a] combination against him, has no right to expect any." Pruyn's warning "had its effect before & after the meetings, it kept the bad ones away, while it encouraged our friends." By late December, the agent was confident that he had smothered resistance in the cradle. He was right, for a time. Though the Helderberg organizers did win converts, they could not create the kind of public, militant movement that had taken root on the West Manor.[31]

Anti-rent delegates fared better on the Scott patent, just over the Schoharie County line from the West Manor. Here, as on Stephen Van Rensselaer's estate, proprietors' indifference toward their tenants' hold on property paved the way for resistance. Before 1839, tenants on the patent had made faithful efforts to pay at least part of their rent. According to the agent for the estate, when their efforts fell short, they were "generally punctual [in] sending in excuses & soliciting indulgence." But the leases on the estate were all for two or three lives. In the late 1830s, the leases began to expire, and landlords claimed the tenants' fences, buildings, clearings, and orchards as their own, raising the rent to reflect the value of these improvements. This violated tenants' long-standing belief that their improvements were their own property, instantly turning them from property owners into comparatively poor families; Schoharie tenants had little to lose by publicly turning against their landlords. When emissaries from Rensselaerwyck began to call meetings in mid-1840, farmers flocked to the new organization. Between 1839 and 1842, the unpaid rents of the estate grew from $2,000 to $10,000.[32]

Once organized, the tenants of Albany and Schoharie counties pursued separate but nearly identical courses of action. On both estates, insurgents formed associations like the one adopted at Bern in 1839 and waged a two-front war. They organized a rent boycott, signing pledges and swearing oaths not to pay any rent until the landlords proved title. To ensure compliance, they canvassed extensively and held frequent meetings. They also assessed a tax (usually one-half cent per acre) on each member, using the funds to investigate their landlords' title and to defend tenants sued by the landlords. At the same time, they formed bands of armed and disguised men, known as "Indians," who intimidated landlords and agents who dared appear on the estates, prevented sheriffs from carrying out legal actions against tenants, and harassed local residents who opposed their movement.[33]

The boycott and the Indian bands were mere stopgaps. As hopes for a compromise waned, militants followed the advice that Governor Seward had offered them, petitioning the legislature for redress of their grievances. In 1840, the assembly alone received 20 petitions from the tenants of Albany and Schoharie Counties.[34] Inspired by Democratic assurances that the government was properly an extension of the will of a sovereign people and Whig visions of a democratic state that met the needs of the people, tenants placed their hopes for a final redress of their grievances in the legislature.

Tenants and Legislators

The Rensselaerwyck tenants' petitions in 1840 criticized their relationship to their landlords along three lines. First, they repeated the tenant committee's contention that because the land was no longer capable of growing wheat and the price of the grain had doubled since the leases were signed, wheat rents had become "onerous and oppressive." Second, they charged that their contracts had been fraudulently obtained. When the first settlers arrived in the mountains, the petitioners claimed, Stephen Van Rensselaer told each man to choose a farm and to cultivate it, rent-free, for seven years. At the end of this period, he promised leases that would require nothing but a nominal rent in wheat. But when the farmers returned to take their leases, they found that the agreements contained numerous "accursed" provisions: a quarter sale, rents in fowls and labor, and restrictions on mining and manufacturing. Many at first refused to sign. But the patroon's agent told them that the lease terms in question "were a mere matter of form, and never intended to be enforced." The settlers, the petitioners claimed, signed the leases under duress, for refusing to do so would mean losing their improvements. Finally, the tenants repeated their claim that Van Rensselaer's title was fraudulent. To redress these grievances, they asked that the legislature investigate Van Rensselaer's title and "abrogate" it if it found it to be invalid. Beyond this, they proposed no specific action, merely asking for "relief" from oppressive lease terms.[35]

Partisan doctrines of popular sovereignty and Governor Seward's promise of help raised tenants' hopes that the legislature would quickly redress their grievances. But Whig and Democratic representatives viewed the leasehold controversy within a framework of the constitution and existing law, and felt constrained from offering relief that would violate legal or constitutional prohibitions.[36] Just as important, they saw in the contest a series of issues that bore directly on the broad programmatic aims and strategic needs of their parties. Members of each party interpreted the issues raised by leasehold militants according to these aims, and each offered solutions that reflected their electoral and legislative strategies. As a result, tenants got not what they asked for, but what the leaders of each party thought they should have. The outcome was bitter disappointment.

Whig legislators forged a policy of rhetorical support and policy inaction. In 1839–1841 Governor Seward's liberal wing of the party had ample reason to take up the cause of the anti-renters. Though they held the governorship and a majority in the legislature, they were still a minority party in the electorate; their victories at the polls in 1838 and 1840 had resulted from public revulsion at the Democrats' handling of the economy in the wake of the panic of 1837. In an effort to turn this temporary victory into a permanent realignment and move the party toward a program of reform, Seward and his followers sought to win the support of groups like Irish Catholics, abolitionists, and anti-renters. Moreover, the state's landlords supported either the

Democrats or the conservative Whigs, with whom Seward's allies were beginning to feud. By striking a blow against the landlords, the liberal Whigs might weaken their political rivals.[37] Perhaps most importantly, Seward and his allies saw in the anti-renters' struggle an opportunity to advance their own campaign to free society from ancient obstacles to individual self-improvement, social mobility, and economic development.

When the Helderbergers submitted their petitions in 1840, the assembly voted to create a special committee, composed entirely of Whigs, to investigate the farmers' complaints. The committee endorsed the anti-renters' demand for legislative relief, but did so in ways that departed from the petitioners' reasoning. The report began by dismissing each of the tenants' major complaints on legal and constitutional grounds. The legislature was powerless to abrogate a title to real estate, while the Helderbergers' charge that the Van Rensselears had used fraud and coercion in compelling tenants to sign leases lay within the purview of the courts. Even if the courts could offer no relief, the legislature could do nothing, for "it is clearly improper to depart from general laws to legislate for these particular cases."[38]

With the tenants' grievances thus dismissed, the panel introduced its own interpretation of the leasehold system. The problem with patroonery was that it stood in the way of the Seward Whigs' vision of moral and economic progress. "It concerns the State," committee members wrote, "that the land within its limits should be made as productive as possible, all her natural resources developed, and her territory . . . occupied by an independent, industrious, and intelligent population." Conditions on Rensselaerwyck interfered with these aims by retarding the transfer of land. Quarter sales and a form of tenure that divided ownership between landlords and tenants prevented land from being bought and sold freely, thus serving as a roadblock to "the perfect use and complete development of [the land's] resources."[39]

The select committee's preoccupation with the alienability of land was hardly unique. Like liberal statesmen throughout the western world, committee members correctly saw the free transfer of land as essential to commercial, agricultural, and industrial development in the context of private property and an unregulated national market. Only when obstacles to the buying and selling of land were removed could the population be free to move wherever a rapidly developing economy required them. Only then could entrepreneurs with the capital needed to introduce new technology, techniques, and economies of scale be induced to invest in agriculture, thereby making it sufficiently productive to feed a burgeoning urban population.[40]

In order to remove this obstacle to capitalist development, committee members proposed a radical abridgement of the rights of property and a dramatic expansion of the power of the state. The legislature, they reasoned, held the power to seize an individual's property for public purposes. If tenures on Rensselaerwyck harmed the prosperity and moral progress of the people, it became the duty of the people's representatives to seize the estate, compensate its owners, and bestow full ownership on the tenants. With this report, the committee extended the Whigs' faith in a benevolent, activist state into new and dangerous territory. They endorsed a program that, if extended to all estates in New York, would expropriate a species of private property, abolish an entire set of class relations, and consign an elite to the dustbin of history. Such a proposal had not been espoused by the leaders of a major party since the northern emancipation acts of the 1780s.[41]

Committee members were aware of the radical nature of their proposal, and they backed away from endorsing immediate action. They recommended only that the legislature appoint commissioners who would attempt to mediate between Van Rensselaer and his tenants and would report to the legislature on "the agricultural improvement of the country and the enterprise and character of the population." In the meantime, they offered a nonbinding resolution that affirmed the power of the legislature to seize Rensselaerwyck through eminent domain. Although toothless, the principles endorsed by the committee stirred up partisan controversy and inspired opposition among conservative Whigs. Assembly Democrats united in opposition, while the Whigs split, 54 to 5. The bill thus passed and was quickly endorsed by the senate and Governor Seward.[42]

Where liberal Whigs raised the possibility of destroying the leasehold system with the aid of an activist state, the Democrats defended the institution behind a battlement of strict constitutionalism. The Jacksonians had ample reason to object to any assaults on the landlords' wealth and power. Most landlords, after all, were Democrats. Moreover, the same devotion to strict construction of the constitution that underlay their opposition to the Bank of the United States led them to frown on any legislative interference with contracts and property rights. These principles, when combined with a political alliance with slaveholders, had already led Democrats into an assault on the abolitionists; now, under pressure from landlord constituents, they informed an unswerving hostility to the anti-renters.[43]

Thus the Jacksonians drew on the Constitution, narrowly interpreted, to insist that the relation of landlord to tenant was a matter of private contracts. Any attempt to meddle, they believed, constituted an unconstitutional abrogation of contracts and an attack on the rights of property. Thus, when the 1841 elections gave the Democrats control over the legislature, the anti-renters lost the ineffective support they had previously enjoyed. The new legislature sent the tenants' petitions to the Democrat-dominated judiciary committee, which declared that the constitutional prohibition against laws that altered existing contracts "presents an insuperable barrier to the granting of the prayer of the petitioners."[44]

The anti-renters, however, were gaining strength on the ground. In 1843, William Van Rensselaer began to sue his tenants; they responded by flocking to the movement. With them came Smith Boughton, a charismatic doctor from the hill village of Alps. A native of Stephentown and a graduate of the medical branch of Middlebury College, Boughton had gone to New York City to help treat the victims of the cholera epidemic of 1831 and had fought in the Quebec Patriot Rebellion of 1837. Now his idealism and energy found an outlet in the tenants' cause. In the fall of 1843, a meeting of delegates from the three anti-rent counties chose him to lead their lobbying effort in Albany.[45]

Boughton took over the job at a seemingly auspicious moment. Since 1840, the anti-rent associations' attorneys had dug through records in Albany, New York City, Amsterdam, and London, and they believed that they had confirmed tenants' suspicions of their landlords' titles. Lawyers for the Rensselaerwyck tenants concluded that the original grant to the manor had never included a northern boundary—an omission that they claimed invalidated the grant. They also concluded that the English patent to the manor had never been properly executed; that the forbears of the current proprietors had usurped the manor from the rightful heirs; and that Stephen Van Rensselaer had fraudulently tripled the size of his holdings in the 1780s. Similarly, lawyers for farmers on the Scott patent concluded that the original patentees had failed to fulfill the terms of their grant, thereby invalidating it; and that John Livingston, from whom the current proprietors derived their title, had bought out the interest of only one of 78 original patentees, thereby gaining title to only 1,000 out of 78,000 acres.[46]

The common law, however, rendered this knowledge useless by barring tenants from challenging their landlords' titles as a defense when sued for nonpayment of rent. Just before Boughton began his lobbying campaign, anti-rent lawyers drafted "An Act Concerning Tenures," which promised to abrogate this rule while meeting Democratic legislators' rigorous standards of constitutionality. The bill provided that landlords who leased their land for terms longer than 20 years and who claimed title from the British government would have to prove title before he or she could enforce a lease in court. It also altered slightly the 1840 assembly committee's proposal: drawing on the eminent domain power of the state, it provided that leaseholders who held land in perpetuity could buy their landlords' interest in their farms at a rate decided on by three impartial parties.[47]

Heartened by the belief that they had overcome all constitutional objections to their demands, Boughton and his fellow anti-renters presented the legislature with more than 133 petitions asking for the passage of the law. Working against an intensive lobbying campaign by the Van Rensselaers, Boughton convinced legislators to appoint a committee to hear the anti-renters' case. That done, he shepherded a string of tenants and lawyers before the committee and solicited briefs from such Whig luminaries as Daniel Webster and Governor George M. Briggs of Massachusetts.[48]

These efforts were doomed from an early date. As Charles McCurdy has observed, although the Act Concerning Tenures met constitutional requirements at the time it was written, it was soon rendered unconstitutional. In 1843, the United States Supreme Court ruled that laws that significantly impaired anyone's ability to enforce a contract (such as the title-test provision of the Act Concerning Tenures) violated the contracts clause of the U.S. Constitution. That same year, the New York Supreme Court undermined the principle behind the law's eminent domain provision, ruling that the power of eminent domain did not empower governments to take one person's property in order to convey it to another.[49]

These decisions gave Democrats and conservative Whigs all the ammunition they desired. In 1844, the tenants' petitions went to a special committee composed of the all-Whig delegations from Albany and Rensselaer Counties, which endorsed in general terms the petitioners' eminent-domain scheme but once again proposed no specific legislation. The assembly quashed the committee's report and referred the petitions to the judiciary committee, a conservative panel composed of three Democrats and two Whigs. Armed with the recent decisions narrowing legislative powers to seize property and abridge the remedies on existing contracts, the report's drafters declared the Act Concerning Tenures unconstitutional. In doing so, they pushed Jacksonian political economy in a conservative direction and set the terms for future debates over leasehold tenures.[50]

The committee offered a fourfold argument. First, applying the Jacksonians' insistence on the narrowest construction of governmental power, it maintained that the tenants' demands went beyond the legitimate scope of any government. Second, by empowering the legislature to interfere in private matters of contract and in individual property rights, the Act Concerning Tenures threatened all property rights. Requiring landlords to prove their title before they could sue for back rents would make it harder for those landlords to enforce their contracts, thus impairing their right to enjoy their property. Empowering the legislature to seize entire estates was even more dangerous, for it would "vest in the Legislature full, complete, and arbitrary power over the property of the citizen."[51]

Behind this defense of limited government and property rights lay a third line of reasoning: that it was the government's job to protect vested rights—privileges, whether just or not, that were sanctioned by ancient usage. The antiquity of the manor title, the panel reasoned, should entitle it to extra protection from the legislature: "the policy of the law has ever been to shield and protect ancient titles followed by possession." Similarly, the ancient rule of law that forbade tenants from challenging their landlords' titles in court existed for "good reasons"; "those reasons and the policy of the law have been approved from time immemorial, and the committee would hesitate long before they would do aught to interfere with its operation."[52]

Finally, the legislators dismissed as fatuous the tenants' criticism of their lease terms and their landlords' titles. In 18 closely argued pages, they rebutted the anti-renters' challenge to the Van Rensselaers' title point by point. The claim that the lease terms were oppressive was equally groundless. Endorsing, with Stephen Van Rensselaer, the belief that contract terms that were agreed to by civic equals were by definition just, the committee argued that the quarter sales, the reservation of water and mineral rights, the fat fowls and day's service were all fairly bargained for. Furthermore, none of these requirements were exacted "in an oppressive manner, or to an unjustifiable extent." The "degradation and hardships" of which the militants complained, the committee concluded, "exist but in the imagination." The only solution for the tenants was to negotiate with their landlords. "The tenants can have all the relief to which they are, in justice and equity, entitled," the legislators maintained, "directly from the proprietors of the manor."[53]

The report was a devastating defeat for the anti-renters. The assembly as a whole adopted the committee's resolutions, thus officially endorsing the policy that the tenants must look to the landlords for redress. Both William and Stephen Van Rensselaer took quick advantage of their tenants' defeat by initiating a flurry of lawsuits.[54]

The Anti-Rent Phoenix

Leasehold militants responded to the Judiciary Committee report with outrage. Like most white men of their time, they enthusiastically supported the Whig and Democratic parties. But now they began to reassess old loyalties and to question their earlier faith in party leaders. As one Rensselaerwyck tenant wrote, they had "lost all hopes of redress from the proper authorities."[55] Burton A. Thomas, the corresponding secretary of the Rensselaer County Anti-Rent Association, was even more bitter:

> The Legislature has done us no good, but much injury. The select committee showed themselves to be fools, and perfectly dishonest. The Committee of the Judiciary . . . , by the Report, favoring Van Rensselaer as it does, had made a handsome sum of money out of the Van Rensselaers. They all being off this *manor,* and so situated that our votes would never reach them, have sacrificed us and our prayers on the altar of injustice.[56]

These were not cries of despair, but of renewed militancy. Failure in the legislature taught the tenants that relief could come only by more intensive cultivation of their own collective resources. Thomas made clear that despite the legislature's betrayal of them, the anti-renters were "determined to stand to our posts to the last." Meetings were being held "*all the time,*" and tenants were preparing to fight the landlords both in the courts and on the ground. More importantly, anti-rent leaders had become convinced of the need to expand and strengthen their movement. Only by doing so could they compel a corrupt and recalcitrant legislature to extend the aid they sought. In May 1844, delegations from Albany, Rensselaer, and Schoharie Counties met at John J. Gallup's home in Bern, where they agreed to send lecturers to every estate in New York.[57]

Tenant leaders lost little time in carrying this decision into effect. In May or June, John Mayham, a prosperous Schoharie County farmer and a leader of the Blenheim Hill Anti-Rent Association, traveled south into Delaware County. Starting on the lands of the Armstrong family, he called meetings in every neighborhood where leasehold tenures prevailed. Everywhere, he met with large and attentive crowds. Drawing on local memories of the Livingston family's fraudulent extension of the boundaries of the Hardenbergh patent, Mayham challenged the landlords' claim to the land between the two branches of the Delaware river. He urged his listeners to withhold rents and to adopt the dual organization that had evolved in Albany, Rensselaer, and Schoharie Counties. On the Hardenbergh and Kortright patents, a clear majority of tenants heeded his call. By August, a gentleman traveling through the county noted that "an agent dare hardly show his face in the infected district." By fall, he predicted, "every tenant will have joined the association."[58]

The story was much the same in Columbia County. In October, Smith Boughton and other Rensselaer County leaders went to Columbia, where the charismatic doctor drew enormous crowds. By November, tenants in several towns had stopped paying their rent, and bands of disguised anti-rent "Indians" were holding meetings throughout the hill districts of the manors. Less spectacular success greeted organizers' efforts in other parts of the region. By year's end, what were now called "anti-rent" associations had been formed in eleven counties.[59]

As lecturers fanned out across the region, anti-renters in several counties sought new strength in another area: electoral politics. Militants in the hill towns of Albany, Rensselaer, Schoharie, and Delaware Counties held independent conventions, where they nominated anti-rent candidates for the state assembly. The results were mixed. The entire anti-rent slate won in Schoharie County, but tenants in each of the other three counties saw only one of their three nominees win a seat in the legislature. Still, the outcome offered hope for the future. After a humiliating defeat at the hands of the judiciary committee only seven months before, the anti-renters felt the possibility that they might create a powerful, independent political movement with which to gain relief from the legislature.[60]

Indeed, anti-renters throughout the region felt a new sense of their own collective power. One sympathetic observer from Delaware County wrote that the new movement "wholly absorbs the attention of the *landless*" and had "given courage and confidence to those who were before without hope." This new hope was even more apparent in mid-January of 1845, when the anti-renters held their first state convention. For two days, 174 delegates from 11 counties met in the Lutheran Church at Bern, while some 1800 observers came to cheer on the proceedings. As one delegate wrote, the meeting went off "with all the *eclat* and brotherly love the vast importance of the meeting demanded. . . . It appeared as if the God of Heaven was with us . . . in the midst of the deliberations of a most glorious cause and meeting." When the convention was over, the delegates went home with a new sense of the promise and righteousness of their cause.[61]

By the beginning of 1845, the anti-rent movement had become a powerful force. With organizations in 11 counties, six of their own nominees in the state Assembly, and the beginnings of an effective political organization, anti-renters were now in a position to wield enormous influence in New York state. And with that influence, they injected their ideas about land and their distinctive vision of free labor into public life.

Chapter 5

LAND AND FREEDOM,
1844 – 1846

>—⊹—⟨⦾⟩—⟡—⊖—⟡—⟨⦿⟩—⊹—⟨

Every anti-renter knew that the leasehold system denied him his freedom. What a free society would be like was another matter. As anti-rent lecturers crisscrossed New York's leasehold estates in the fall of 1844, estate residents everywhere entered a long discussion about the kind of freedom they sought. They drew on ideas about property voiced by earlier tenant rebels and sustained by tenants' use of common lands. But their new economic circumstances led them to transform these traditions. By examining how these legacies changed, we can begin to understand the ways in which leasehold farmers' increasing integration into a capitalist economy shaped their social and political ideals.

Agrarian traditions and economic change were not the only forces to influence the anti-renters' notions of freedom. Whig and Democratic party activists were leasehold tenants' most influential teachers on social and political issues, and anti-renters drew heavily on their ideas and models of organizing. But the anti-renters proved critical and independent students, turning party teachings to new uses and combining them with ideals and practices drawn from other traditions. Their innovations reveal a great deal about a critical but understudied issue in antebellum politics: the ways in which the Jacksonian rank and file received, interpreted, and made their own the teachings of party leaders.

The Anti-Rent Associations:
Institutions and Leaders

By spring of 1845, the anti-rent movement had become a commanding force on New York's manors and patents. Anti-rent lecturers convinced tenants in 11 counties to form anti-rent associations and Indian bands, swelling the number of movement supporters to between 25,000 and 60,000. In the leasehold hill towns of Albany, Rensselaer, Delaware, Columbia, and

Schoharie Counties, where the movement was the strongest, a majority of estate residents embraced the cause, turning the anti-rent movement into a broad, multiclass coalition. A Rensselaer county activist wrote that the movement enjoyed the support of "all classes of our citizens, mechanics, laboring men, and professional men, as well as farmers." Anti-rent petitions, he said, were "signed by men of wealth and influence as well as by those occupying a more humble position in life."[1]

This new strength depended largely on institutions and practices that anti-rent leaders borrowed from political parties and reform associations. Modeled on temperance and other voluntary societies, the number of anti-rent associations exploded. In April 1845, the *Albany Freeholder*, the first movement journal addressed to citizens throughout the leasehold district, opened its doors. In its first year, the newspaper's readership jumped from 270 to 2,700. Three other anti-rent newspapers began publishing over the next 14 months. In establishing a movement press, the anti-renters followed the example of Whigs, Democrats, and evangelical reformers.[2] Drawing heavily on the rituals of the major parties, town and county leaders complemented the work of the anti-rent press with an endless round of meetings, dances, liberty pole-raisings, and rallies. Every Fourth of July between 1840 and 1847, hundreds of wagons, bedecked with banners, converged at a central location in each anti-rent county. On arriving, tenants joined a long procession, typically led by a brass band and followed by local Revolutionary War veterans, the officers of the day, 27 ladies dressed in white to represent the states of the Union, and the rest of the participants. The celebrants then heard the Declaration of Independence, listened to anti-rent speeches and songs, passed resolutions, and ate a picnic lunch. In the evening, they retired to a local inn for dinner, more music, and patriotic toasts. But for the special message of the speeches, songs, and toasts, these proceedings were identical to the Independence Day celebrations of the Democrats and Whigs.[3]

This creative borrowing from reform associations and political parties was just one part of an eclectic political style. Drawing on a varied set of political traditions, anti-renters built a movement with three distinct wings, each with its own leadership and message: the anti-rent associations, the "Indians," and the Anti-Rent/Equal Rights party. Leadership in the associations—and the power to shape their message—fell to male, property-owning, mature heads of household, many of whom had experience in party politics. Of 430 activists from the leasehold towns of Albany and Delaware counties, all were men. Of the 191 who could be found in the 1850 federal census, 96 percent headed their own households. Most were mature: by 1845, 61 percent of the activists had reached their fortieth year. As in 1839, the majority made their living on the soil, but now farmers were joined by a disproportionate number of doctors, lawyers, merchants, and manufacturers. Still, farmers predominated far more among the anti-renters than they did in the Whig and Democratic parties (see Appendix, table 9).[4]

Whatever their calling, anti-rent leaders were drawn most heavily from the

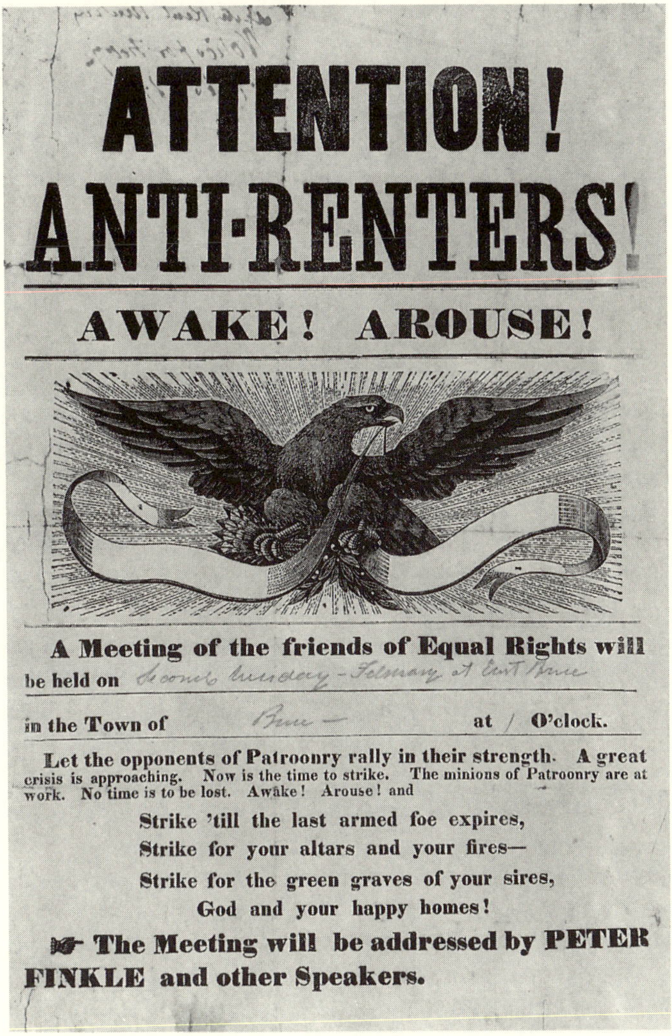

ATTENTION!
ANTI-RENTERS!

AWAKE! AROUSE!

A Meeting of the friends of Equal Rights will
be held on *Second Tuesday - February at East Berne*

in the **Town of** *Berne —* at / **O'clock.**

Let the opponents of **Patroonry** rally in their strength. A great crisis is approaching. Now is the time to strike. The minions of Patroonry are at work. No time is to be lost. Awake! Arouse! and

> Strike 'till the last armed foe expires,
> Strike for your altars and your fires—
> Strike for the green graves of your sires,
> God and your happy homes!

☞ **The Meeting will be addressed by PETER FINKLE and other Speakers.**

Figure 5.1. An Anti–rent broadside, probably from 1845. The screaming eagle, the rhetoric of wakefulness, and the call to defend homes—all appealing in martial tones to an implicitly masculine audience—were drawn from Democratic rhetoric and iconography. Courtesy, New York State Library.

prosperous property owners of their towns. Of the 33 anti-rent leaders who could be traced in the 1840 tax list for the town of Westerlo, 7 (21 percent) were among the top 20 percent of property holders in town, and another 13 (39 percent) fell into the second wealthiest fifth. Only two activists (6 percent) were among the second poorest fifth of property owners, and none fell into the bottom fifth. A small but significant number of landless men took up leadership of the Albany County movement, however. One leader listed his occupation as a laborer in 1850, and 13—12 percent—were farmers who lived in households in which no one owned any land. Thus anti-rent association leaders represented a far broader spectrum of wealth than did Whig and Democratic activists (see Appendix, table 10).[5]

As they had in 1839, many association leaders came from the ranks of Whig and Democratic activists. Sixty-four leaders (22 percent) had served as delegates to Democratic county conventions or had joined county committees of vigilance; another 37 had served as Whigs. In all, about 35 percent had experience as party activists on the county level. As in 1839, the leaders of the tenants' movement had learned how to build grass-roots organizations, convey a political message, and create a successful political culture from the Whigs and Democrats.[6]

In most ways, then, anti-rent leadership in 1845–1846 remained much like that of 1839. With slightly more inclusiveness, the anti-renters replicated the preexisting political leadership of the northern Jacksonian countryside, which fell to property-owning men accustomed to commanding the labor of the women, children, and servants in their own household, and who were presumed to represent the interests both of those dependents and of less prosperous neighbors. With a preponderance of substantial farmers, merchants, manufacturers, and professionals in their ranks, anti-rent leaders were far more likely to benefit from the new, more capital-intensive, wage-dependent, and market-oriented economy on the estates than were their followers. In addition, they had been trained in political leadership by the Whig and Democratic parties, and they had learned most of their political and social principles from party leaders. Through speeches, resolutions, and letters to the editor, these men, more than any other group, gave public voice to the grievances of the tenantry. To a significant extent, they shaped those grievances according to their special experience and political convictions.

Rank-and-file anti-renters were not entirely without influence over the message of their movement, however. Consent was one thing; enthusiastic support and the willingness to make personal sacrifices was another. To inspire the latter, anti-rent activists had to appeal to the values and yearnings of ordinary tenants. Moreover, such tenants held their leaders to strict standards of conduct. On two occasions, local officials elected on the anti-rent ticket violated community norms—one by buying land from his landlord, the other by compelling his neighbors to pay for water from a local stream to which he had mill rights. In both instances, townspeople began a campaign of rumor and innuendo against their leaders, causing such damage to the officials' reputations that they felt compelled to defend themselves in the movement press. Similarly, when an association officer in Columbia County used anti-rent principles to justify his refusal to pay the rent on a store he was leasing from a neighbor, local association members rebuked him, "telling him that that was not the principle on which they as an association acted." When the storekeeper then turned against the movement, his neighbors ostracized him, "letting him . . . work alone—eat alone—sleep alone—and drink alone."[7] Though leaders enjoyed significant latitude in shaping the anti-rent message, their followers provided the raw materials from which they would forge that message and set important limits on its final shape.

Agrarianism Transformed

In dialogue with rank-and-file anti-renters, association leaders forged a clear vision of the good society. In doing so, they simultaneously extended and narrowed the agrarian ideas of late eighteenth- and early nineteenth-century tenant rebels. Since the 1750s, insurgents on New York's leasehold estates had insisted that landownership was the only sure basis for human freedom. The anti-renters of the 1840s placed this idea at the center of their movement. Participants at a Grafton meeting put it most succinctly when they resolved, paraphrasing the words of the prophet Micah, "That it is for the manifest good of a republic that every farmer should be able to sit under his own vine and fig tree, with none to molest, or make him afraid."[8] But the anti-renters expanded on this idea. Since the early 1830s, Democratic leaders had attacked the special privileges that government bestowed on banks and other monopolies as a licence to expropriate the fruits of producers' labor and as the source of artificial disparities of wealth and power. These disparities, they argued, threatened republican government. Most tenants were Democrats, and they drew on their party's teachings to forge a full-scale attack on land monopoly.

In typical Democratic style, tenants traced landlords' monopoly over land to special privileges bestowed by the government. Landlords, they insisted, were "an aristocracy encouraged and protected by law" which "enjoy privileges denied to other men." Landlords' special privilege originated in the colonial-era "court gifts" of land that "exclude the poor and industrious from opportunities of labor except at the rich man's discretion." This privilege was wrongfully perpetuated when the revolutionary-era government confirmed the proprietors' titles "when all [were] convinced" that neither they nor their ancestors "ever had a shadow of a right to such land." And it continued to be protected by the present government. The anti-rent state convention of 1844 complained that a cluster of special privileges—the common-law rule that prohibited tenants from legally challenging their landlords' titles, the lease clause that allowed proprietors to seize tenants' personal property without a hearing, and the state's failure to tax rent income like income from mortgages—made the landlord "highly privileged above any other class of citizens" and subjected tenants to "feudal slavery . . . inconsistent with a code of equal laws."[9]

Once bestowed and protected by law, land monopoly empowered proprietors to "withhold from the people their dearest rights," the most important of which was the right to the fruits of their labor. The labor theory of value— the notion that labor creates all wealth—had been commonplace in American economic thought since the late eighteenth century and was implicit in the tenants' defense of their property in their improvements. Now, inspired by urban workers' use of the theory to attack economic inequality, the anti-renters harnessed it to their assault on patroonery. Joseph Hoag of Delaware County wrote that "the idea that a man must be compelled to toil, and still be under the stern necessity of remitting to another the effects of his labors to support him in opulence and luxury, is revolting to every principle of American liberty." From this principle, militants denounced not only rents but landlords' ability to seize tenants' improvements through eviction and the quarter sale. Association members believed that estate lands had been "literally worthless" before they were settled; tenants' labor in felling trees, building houses, barns, and fences, and breaking cropland had given the land its value. That wealth, militants reasoned, should remain in the hands of its producers.[10]

Anti-renters believed that proprietors' ability to strip others of the fruits of their labor gave them an unnatural degree of power, which threatened tenants' personal liberty. Proprietors subjected entire communities to their whim and stripped tenants of the personal dignity due them as laborers and as citizens of a republic:

> There are thousands in our midst denied all equality, and ground down by hirelings, below the dignity of serfs. Their farms, their hard earnings, their all, are held at the option of a man brought up in luxury, clothed in fine linen, whose hands were ne'er soiled by a day's labor. These laboring men scarce breathe in his presence; his mandates are those of a Dictator; and thousands must plod their way yearly with trembling steps and enter the halls of his lordship, bending and bowing . . . to solicit the favor of enjoying their property.[11]

Land monopoly also endangered republican government. Tenant-made wealth gave landlords inordinate influence in government, allowing them to corrupt officials and procure special legislation. Worse still, the proprietors' power over their tenants undermined the very foundation of republican government—an independent citizenry, free from the political will of others. "Juno, Jr." of Livingston Manor warned that the landlords' ability to eject tenants from their homes was "a powerful instrument in the hands of one man for bending his fellow man to his own will, and making him subserve his own selfish, political or mercenary purposes."[12]

These social evils—artificial concentrations of economic power, cultural subordination, corruption of the political process—were the very evils that radical Democrats attributed to monopolies. Anti-renters also added their own grievances to the list of monopoly's fruits. Foremost among these was economic insecurity. Landlords' power of eviction allowed them to strip tenants of the property accumulated over a lifetime and to subject them to a life of poverty and humiliation. It also threatened what tenants saw as their "right" to a home in a familiar place, connected to kin and community. Ejection from their homes, wrote "A Democrat, Old Style," robbed farmers of "their only means of subsistence and [left] them to become wandering vagrants in the country."[13] This theme of poverty and rootlessness echoed sadly throughout the speeches, letters, and songs of the tenants' movement. A poem about an ejected tenant family, read "with great effect" at a Fourth of July celebration in Delaware County, conveyed the depth of the tenants' fear of this fate:

> That for which we'd long been striving
> All our hopes for years to come,
> Torn away—our wives and children,
> Turned abroad without a home.
>
> Restless, wayworn, faint and weary
> Wanderers since that fated day,
> Often forced to change our dwellings;
> Thus we thread our cheerless way.[14]

In addition, anti-renters denounced landlords' restraints on their freedom to trade. They saw the right to enjoy the products of their labor as inseparable from the right to sell those products. They objected to the quarter sale precisely because it infringed on their right to sell their improvements. As one farmer put it, "the tenants have not the liberty to trade on their own earnings."[15] Similarly, the residents of Livingston Manor denounced as "unrepublican" the provisions in their leases that required them to sell their surplus at the proprietor's stores and to take their grain to the landlord's mills. The notion of commerce that many anti-renters defended seems not to have included trade in search of speculative advantage. Rather, they defended an older notion of trade as an exchange of equivalents between producers. A Columbia County anti-renter wrote to *Young America,* a journal of the New York working-class movement, that with the impending defeat of the landlords, "your mechanics in the cities might soon get village sites, where they could come among us and manufacture their articles, for which we would exchange our produce, saving between us the expenses of *rent* and *transportation.*"[16]

Thus the anti-renters claimed several "natural rights"—the enjoyment of the fruits of their labor, personal dignity, independence from the will of others, economic security, freedom to trade—and denounced the landlords' monopoly of the land for violating them. These rights, they insisted, could be realized only when every man held property in land. Universal landownership would place all who labored on an equal footing, freeing them from the personal humiliations that were the lot of the poor. It would guarantee independence, dignity, prosperity, and the freedom to trade, as one poet affirmed:

The farmer now delights to plow
A ray of hope is on his brow
He knows that soon his tasks and toil
Will be upon the RIGHT OF SOIL . . . .

Avaunt ye Tyrants! Then no more
Shall we keep wheat for thee in store;
But ev'ry grain raised by our toil
Shall be our own, by right of soil,
To eat, to save, to sell or sow,
Though Princely Lords say yes or no![17]

Universal landownership would also ensure the independence of the citizenry and, through them, guarantee the survival of republican government. "In all free governments," the Delaware County anti-renters resolved, "it is essential that the people themselves be free. They cannot be free unless independent. . . . To be completely sovereign, they must individually be the lords of the soil they occupy, and hold it freely, subject to no superior but the people themselves."[18] Finally, universal landownership would guarantee to all a home in a specific place, where they could be connected to previous and future generations. A Columbia County tenant declared: "We will defend the homes of our fathers, where (if any where) we and our children have a right to 'life, liberty, and the pursuit of happiness.'"[19]

The anti-renters' association of land and freedom was familiar to conventional Democrats. Drawing on a tradition that reached back to Thomas Jefferson, the followers of Jackson had long insisted that "a well educated, industrious and independent yeomanry are the safest repository of freedom and free institutions."[20] But with important constituencies among urban employers, workingmen, and landlords, few Democrats could safely argue, as the anti-renters did, that landless men were unfree. More concretely, the anti-renters' demand that the legislature abrogate the common-law rule barring them from challenging their landlords' titles in court flew in the face of the Jacksonians' reverence for vested rights and strict construction of the federal Constitution; the majority of Democrats considered the proposed law to be both unconstitutional and socially dangerous. Most importantly, the anti-renters directed the Jeffersonian tradition against existing concentrations of property, raising fears of an all-powerful state disturbing existing social relations and trampling on the rights of property. If successful, they might set a precedent that could be used against slave property; their movement thus posed a potential threat to intersectional harmony within both parties. Nor did it help that most landlords were Democrats.

While they took Democratic teachings in a new and threatening direction, most militants dropped the radical ideas of their agrarian forbears. Like the anti-renters of the 1840s, earlier insurgents had challenged landlords' titles and insisted that landownership was the only sure basis for individual freedom. But they had also offered their own definition of property rights, declaring that occupation and improvement conveyed ownership of land. This idea offered a powerful challenge to the existing distribution of property, providing a blueprint for ensuring that every white male who worked the land would own a piece of it. The Roxbury Anti-Rent Association embraced this idea in 1844: "The rentees hold that the land they occupy is their own, on account of what is called *legal* possession: that is, being actually on the land, and by enclosing it, while the Patroon's possession is by *proxy* only." But most anti-renters eschewed this line of reasoning. When Dr. John Cornell proposed placing the Roxbury insurgents' language in the platform of the Blenheim Hill Anti-Rent Association, his fellow activists rejected his motion. Instead, they, along with most other tenants, simply claimed that estate titles were fraudulent. To most tenants, passage of a law allowing them to "plead title" during prosecutions for rent was the key demand of the movement. This attack on landlords' titles posed a bold challenge to the leasehold system, but it could not protect tenants from having to buy their farms from the state if they succeeded. More importantly, it could not ensure universal access to land. Although anti-renters denounced the leasehold system for allowing a few men to expropriate the labor of thousands of producers, few challenged the definitions of property that made such landholdings possible. Thus "Clermont" of Columbia County stated that large landed estates "tend . . . to make the many . . . serfs and vassals of the few," but insisted that the tenants "do not ask for a division of the lands. They say if the lords do, in fact, *own* the lands as they claim, they alone have a right to dispose of them."[21]

The chasm between most anti-renters' social vision and their specific proposals grew out of their leaders' attempt to come to terms with agrarian traditions in the context of a changing economy. Amid endemic conflict between tenant owners of unimproved land and neighbors who saw that land as "the commons" and extracted resources from it, any suggestion that labor could establish a right to land risked dividing the movement. The spread of landlessness, wage labor, and subtenancy also rendered agrarian notions of property dangerous, for such ideas might spark conflict between the prosperous and the poor over the distribution of land. Instead of defending the right of the propertyless to land, leasehold activists looked upon them with fear and disdain. "Tossed about from place to place without any permanent local habitation," one insurgent wrote, the landless showed "a general selfishness, laxity of morals, and an indifference to the institutions and improvements of their neighborhood . . . and in fact the country at large."[22] This attitude helped legitimize an unbroken silence over the existence of the landless among leasehold militants; nowhere in the movement press was their existence acknowledged. Questions of whether they had a claim to land or whether their relationship to their employers undermined the independence, dignity, and equality due them as citizens went unasked.

Members of the anti-rent associations thus entered their conflict with landlords poised between older, agrarian ideals and newer realities. In remaining silent about common rights and the presence of the landless, most anti-renters gave mute assent to the existing distribution of land in their communities and to the practices that made some community members the employees of others. While they mobilized agrarian ideals against the landlords, they were unwilling to apply those ideals to themselves. Their social vision thus remained ambiguous, evasive, and contradictory.

The Face of the Savage

The anti-rent associations showed one face to the public; the anti-rent "Indians" displayed another. Where association members adapted the ideas and style of evangelical reform and the second party system, the Indians drew on an older tradition—that of anonymous violence and the charivari. Where the associations stressed the evils of patroonery as a system and strove to enact systemic remedies, the Indians voiced local concerns and aims, punished and rewarded individual behavior, and conducted a strategy of local defense. In so doing, they gave voice to a second side of the tenants' class identity and to a different conception of politics.

The Indians first appeared in public in early 1841. When the sheriff of Albany County tried to distrain (seize and sell) tenants' property to satisfy their rent obligations, bands of men, "disguised in skin and other grotesque dresses," "entirely frustrated" the lawman and sent him back to Albany. Anti-renters in Schoharie and Rensselaer Counties organized disguised bands in 1842 and 1843. When tenant leaders from these three counties began organizing throughout the leasehold district in 1844, they established Indian bands wherever they went. "We resolved to adopt the same kind of protection that was resorted to by the people of Boston when the tea was thrown overboard into the water of its bay," Smith Boughton later recalled. "We then raised in the various counties a large force of men completely disguised to prevent the landlord[s] from executing their threat." By early 1845, some 10,000 men had joined the Indians.[23]

The "tribes" that anti-rent lecturers helped create shared a distinctive organization. Each was neighborhood-based, banding together about a dozen neighbors. These bands were coordinated on a town, county, and regional level, with "chiefs" for each stage of organization. Each was a secret society, with each member's "paleface" identity known only to the members of his neighborhood tribe. Initiates took an oath to "support the constitution of the Anti-Rent Association and stand by each other as long as life lasts" and to "swear by the uplifted hand—and by the penalties of your life—that you will reveal no Indian secret whatsoever." Although association leaders helped found them, each tribe was independent and self-governing. Delaware County association officers administered the oath to initiates, bought calico and sheepskin for their disguises, and paid for their dinners. Everywhere else, association leaders eschewed all official connection with the tribes. Whether "paleface" activists associated with them or not, each tribe elected its own officers and "transact[ed] their own business according to their own laws."[24]

These ersatz aborigines also included a distinctive membership: young men. While the bulk of Delaware County association activists were in their 30s and 40s in 1845, 56 percent of that county's Indians were under the age of 30 (see Appendix, table 11).[25] Their youth placed them at the bottom of their communities' hierarchies of wealth and occupation. Only 11 of 73 Indians (15 percent) who were tried and convicted in the Delaware County courts were listed as farmers in their 1845 indictments, while 55 (75 percent) were listed as laborers. By 1850, many had come of age and chosen new occupations. A majority who remained in Delaware County until 1850 became farmers. Still, 29 percent remained as laborers in 1850, while no association activists held that occupation (see Appendix, table 12). Among those who became farmers, former Indians included far more land-poor husbandmen than did association activists (see Appendix, table 13).[26]

Although some Indians could count on overcoming their relative poverty as they grew older, the long-term economic prospects of many were significantly poorer than those of association activists. The vigilantes were foot soldiers, not leaders; they thus came from a broader spectrum of the leasehold towns than did association activists. More importantly, most came of age when land was becoming less plentiful and more expensive, the capital costs of farming were rising, and increasing numbers of mature men were turning to wage labor and subtenancy to survive. As a result, a substantial number of them remained poorer and pursued humbler callings than did association activists. Nonfarmers among association activists tended to follow high-status callings that were likely to prosper in the new economy: merchants, manufacturers, and professionals. Most Indian nonfarmers, on the other hand, made their living working for others, as laborers and journeymen artisans (see Appendix, table 12). While not statistically reliable, available information suggests that many Indians' low occupational status outlasted their youth. Half of the 10 Indian laborers in 1850 were 30 or older, and four headed their own households—an indication that their humble status was due to chronic landlessness rather than youth. Similarly, a third of the former Indians who headed their own households and who were listed as farmers owned no land, indicating that they, too, were joining the growing class of landless and land-poor. Even when they acquired farmland, many former Indians remained significantly poorer than land-holding association activists of roughly the same age (see Appendix, table 14).[27]

In short, the Indians drew heavily from two inextricably linked groups: young men and the landless and land-poor. A few had achieved a measure of prosperity, and many more would achieve it within a few years. A handful of others were older men whose prospects of achieving economic independence were already dim. But the majority were young men whose prospects were uncertain. These men suffered under a double handicap: the landlessness and dependence to which their youth temporarily subjected them, and the propertylessness and submission to which changing economic circumstances might condemn them permanently. Most Indians were unlucky enough to be present at the meeting of two systems of exploitation: an older (and still vigorous) one based on gender and age, and a newer one that was beginning to graft itself upon the old—that of class.[28] While association activists were drawn from those groups most likely to have been the beneficiaries of recent changes in commodity markets, the distribution of land, and labor practices, the Indians included those who most keenly felt the dislocations and insecurities brought about by those changes.

Despite their special social makeup, the anti-rent braves represented the views and aspirations of a broad segment of leasehold residents. When the Albany County Indians tarred and feathered deputy sheriff Chauncey Rider in 1841, a crowd of about 100 undisguised tenants attended. Upon discovering that the Indians had forgotten to bring feathers, one observer ran home to get some. Similarly, when the Columbia County Indians stopped Sheriff Henry Miller from serving process in late 1844, some 500 observers cheered them on. Non-Indians also celebrated the braves on newspaper mastheads, on banners and transparencies, and in songs.[29]

The popularity of the natives resulted partly from their adherence to a tradition with deep roots in the hill towns of the estates. The Indians were an extension of the charivari—or, as it was called in the leasehold district, the "skimeton." This was a ritual crowd action, practiced widely throughout rural Europe and North America, and universally carried out by boys and young men. Sometimes, as Bryan Palmer suggests, they served as "ritualized methods of enforcing community standards and morality." Men and women who violated the unwritten moral code of their communities—especially those who breached sexual and marital norms—were visited by crews of grotesquely disguised young men and treated to the intimidating "music" of kettles, pans, horse fiddles, sea shells, cow bells, tin horns, and "rather low songs." Frequently, offenders found their property destroyed or were subjected to a complex ritual of threats, physical intimidation, and assault. More often, skimetons were elaborate pranks played on newlyweds. Brides and grooms were "saluted" with strange spectacles and raucous noise until the groom agreed to treat the crowd to liquor.[30] In their membership, their rituals of intimidation, and their disguises, the Indians were identical to the bands of young men who "serenaded" newlyweds and wrongdoers.

Perhaps even more than charivari revelers, about whose inner life we know little, the anti-rent Indians created a fantastic ritual world. Upon being sworn in, each brave created a new identity for himself, taking on an "Indian" name like "Rainbow" or "Pompey." Each learned to speak in a "native" dialect, which one observer described as "our common vernacular, mouthed with a strange intonation, with an occasional sprinkling of Dutch." Each was initiated into the rites of his tribe—dramatic entrances into public gatherings with war whoops and gunfire; dramatic and dangerous displays of horsemanship; an exotic, winding frolic known as the "snake dance." And each

Figure 5.2. Costumes of the anti–rent Indians. This photograph was probably taken at an anti–rent reunion or reenactment during the 1870s or 1880s; the costumes are consistent with descriptions and graphic depictions of Indian disguises from the 1840s. From David Murray, ed., *Delaware County, New York: History of the Century.* Courtesy, American Antiquarian Society.

crafted a costume that conveyed both membership in a tribe and an individual "Indian" identity. The basic design of the costume was standard: a long hunting shirt or a calico gown and pantaloons; masks of leather or glazed muslin with holes for the eyes, ears, and mouth and with peaks, like animal ears or devil's horns, at the corners. Each brave embellished this uniform according to his individual style with brightly colored paint, false whiskers made from horses' tails, brass rings, strings of beads, and "parti-colored patches [and] furs." A farcical oversupply of weapons completed the outfit. An observer at a gathering of the Rensselaer County tribes in 1844 saw "some carrying swords, knives, bits of scythes, and threatening looking cheese knives, others clubs and muskets, while all had pistols in their belts."[31]

Unlike charivari revelers, however, the main purpose of the Indians was political. Like the Democratic Callumpthian bands of New York City and Baltimore, the Molly Maguires of Ireland and Pennsylvania's coal fields, and the Ku Klux Klan of the Reconstruction South, these masked bands turned charivari into a weapon of social conflict. In this struggle, the Indians served several strategic purposes. Most importantly, they prevented landlords from collecting rent and lawmen from evicting tenants or conducting distress sales. When landlords or their agents appeared on the estates, local Indians chased them away, put their homes to the torch, and "besmeared" their carriages "with human filth." Lawmen who sought to serve distress warrants or eviction notices were taken captive and forced to surrender their legal papers. In confronting sheriffs and their deputies, the natives were careful to distinguish between friend and foe. They knew that even sympathetic sheriffs had to serve process to avoid charges of official negligence, and they treated such lawmen to a jovial ceremony. When Columbia County Sheriff Henry Miller arrived in Copake Flats to serve distress warrants, he was met by some 200 Indians who escorted him, to the accompaniment of a marching band, to the farm where he was to serve his first warrant. There the braves brandished their weapons and threatened violence to Miller, publicly forcing him to give up his legal documents. They then marched him back to the local tavern and treated him to brandy. Raising his cup to the sheriff, the chief Big Thunder told the assembled natives that Miller "was as good an anti-renter as any of them." The natives gave him a rousing three cheers, bought him dinner, and sent him home.[32]

Lawmen who earnestly sought to evict tenants or seize their property experienced no such delights. When Sheriff Batterman of Albany County tried to serve process on delinquent Helderberg tenants in the summer of 1844, the Indians, rather than providing him with dinner and applause, shot his horse. When he returned with three deputies two weeks later, the vigilantes seized him, tied him up, and told him that they would let him go if he promised to return to Albany immediately. Batterman refused. The braves then tore his clothes, seized his pistol and papers, clubbed him in the face, and treated him to a dose of tar and feathers. Then they turned to Batterman's terrified deputies, promising them the same treatment unless they shouted "Down with the Rent!" and carried the sheriff back to Albany with his feathers intact. The deputies gave the required oath and, with their humiliated employer in tow, beat a hasty retreat.[33]

As the Albany County braves' treatment of Batterman attests, the Indians were ready to use violence if lawmen refused to surrender their papers and leave the area. But they were careful to keep their violence within strict bounds. They knew that the death or serious injury of a lawman might bring troops to the hill towns. They accordingly depended more heavily on threats, indignities, and ruses than on physical assault. Batterman's battering was exceptional; the braves usually accomplished their purposes without laying a hand on lawmen. The vigilantes often assembled before a scheduled distress sale and carried away the tenant's livestock before it could be sold. At other times, they intimidated potential purchasers—or entered the bidding themselves, driving up the price of a single item until nightfall forced the sheriff to call off the sale. Whatever their tactics, the braves' opposition to lawmen protected community members from dispossession and, in doing so, minimized outside pressure to abandon the rent strike.[34]

Just as important was the Indians' second tactical aim: to ensure local support for the anti-rent movement. Tenants who violated the ban on doing business with the landlords were subjected to harsh punishment. When Abraham Decker of Schoharie County leased a timber lot from his landlord in the spring of 1841, local braves stripped the lot of its best timber, mutilated Decker's horses, damaged his barn, pulled down his fences, and tarred and feathered him. The vigilantes meted out similar punishments to landlords' local subagents, tenants who aided lawmen, and community members who sympathized with their landlords.[35]

With these methods, the Indians silenced the opponents of the anti-renters, creating the appearance of unanimity in support of the movement. They ended payment of rents and prevented the dispossession of tenants with equal success. "An agent dare hardly show his face in the infected district," according to one observer. John O'Brien, a landlord's agent on Scott's patent, complained that "it would be in vain to attempt to Collect Rents within our Patent so long as disguised men were allowed with impunity to resist all sales . . . the resistors have uniformly succeeded in preventing the sales."[36]

In addition to their strategic service, the Indians served a critical ideological function. Nowhere was this more clear in their claim to be "Indians." On the one hand, this claim reinforced their tactical aims. By taking on this disguise, estate youths protected themselves from identification and arrest. Just as important, they drew upon the racist myth of the bloodthirsty savage, pervasive in literature, folklore, and Democratic rhetoric, to terrify their enemies and keep waverers in line. Their elaborate displays of weaponry, their violent public rituals, and their grotesque disguises reinforced this savage image. At the same time, they helped perpetuate the fiction of white tenants' respectability by projecting responsibility for their lawlessness and savagery onto another race.[37]

On the other hand, the "Indian" identity reinforced, in the grotesque language of the charivari, the associations' celebration of independent, patriarchal, commodity-producing households. The braves claimed to be the aboriginal inhabitants of estate lands, who had long since given way to white settlement by moving to new lands beyond the Rocky Mountains. The landlords' fraudulent monopolization of their former domains, they insisted, compelled them to return and re-establish their title. Shortly after forming anti-rent associations, Delaware County insurgents "issued a Proclamation" that "as the land did not belong to the landlords they having no title" and since the state would not challenge the proprietors' claims, the land "must of course belong to the Indians." The tenants then "proceeded at once to clothe and equip the Indians in great masses." Lawrence Van Deusen, editor of the *Guardian of the Soil*, confirmed that the Indians were claiming title to their ancient home. "Leaving the question of *title* to be settled between the *Lords* and the '*Indians*,'" he wrote, "the farmers will pay rent, if they *must* pay rent, to the successful party." But the Indians did not wish to remain permanently on their eastern domains; rather, they wished only to rid them of the landlords and once again vanish to make room for legitimate white settlers: "It is presumed, however, that if the 'Indians' succeed in establishing *their* title, they will immediately retire to their home beyond the Rocky Mountains—or somewhere else."[38]

By claiming title through an appropriated "Indian" identity, anti-renters underscored the fraudulence of the landlords' titles and made a better claim to the land than any white person could make. Just as important, they appealed to a second and equally ubiquitous image—that of the "vanishing Indian," noble but doomed to extinction in the face of a superior white civilization—to underscore the superiority of freehold farming to landlord rule. In countless antebellum novels and plays, white audiences learned to think of Indians as noble savages, blessed by simple virtue and primitive wisdom. These attributes did not make Indians equal to whites; indeed, fictional aborigines nobly accepted their ultimate extinction, "forecasting," as Robert Berkhofer argues, "the wonders and virtues of the civilization that was to supersede the simplicity and naturalness of aboriginal life." The myth of the happily displaced aborigine legitimated white expansion (including the treaty violations and violence that made it possible) by identifying white civilization with "progress."[39] The anti-renters turned this myth to their own purposes. By contending that the "Indians" wished to liberate their ancient home from landlord rule, they made clear that communities of freehold farmers were the genuine embodiment of American progress and the true heirs to the red man's donation.

While serving the strategic and ideological aims of the anti-renters, the Indians gave voice to aspirations and a style of politics that were silenced elsewhere in the movement. The anti-rent associations and electoral organizations spoke in a language of natural rights; they sought to create a republic of freeholders by enacting impersonal, universally applicable laws. The Indians, too, embraced the doctrine of natural rights and affirmed the primacy of electoral and legislative politics. But they simultaneously acted on a locally oriented, corporate tradition in which each community enforced its own unwritten code of conduct. The braves drew on the belief, sustained by gossip, ostracism, church discipline, and charivaris, that each community had a right to defend itself against those who violated its moral code. In attacking landlords, lawmen, and up-rent tenants, they simultaneously enforced their communities' moral code and redefined that code to outlaw behavior that aided the landlords or weakened the anti-rent movement. As the huge crowds of paleface supporters attested, many community members endorsed the Indians as the legitimate enforcers of community norms.

Just as important, the Indians continued to give voice to a personalist and particularist worldview that their associations and electoral organizations had abandoned. Where paleface leaders spoke of universal principles and a vision of justice that applied indiscriminately to all white men, the Indians sought to protect the specific kin and neighbors who made up their communities. The prophet of the Rensselaer County tribes assured his "white brethren" that the Indians "were not contending for their own rights merely, but for the benefit of their neighbors also; that they were blood connexions of many who stood around them." They enforced a conception of justice that took into account the individual character and standing of the individuals with whom they dealt. They nursed abiding grudges against particular lawmen and treated them with special harshness. One such lawman was Bill

Snyder, an Albany County deputy sheriff notorious for his abusive language and bearing toward tenants. When the Helderberg Indians captured Snyder and gave him a thrashing in September 1841, a Helderberger immortalized the fight in a song, "Big Bill Snyder," that was sung throughout the leasehold district. Anonymous letters bore witness to similar grudges. One threatened a landlord's agent with "TAR AND FEATHER" and "A DOSE OF PISTLS PILS" and closed with the telling line: "THE PUBLIC FEELING IS AGAINST YOU."[40]

The braves also served the special needs of the young, landless men who joined their ranks. Above all, participation in the tribes was fun. H. Scott recruited Barbour Stafford to his local tribe by telling Stafford that "it was nothing but fun & almost every boy was joining it." Only after establishing this did Scott add that "it was a good cause." The tribes provided farm boys with an opportunity to fraternize with other boys, to vent aggression, and to engage in an exotic and fun ritual. They also afforded occasion for feasting and drinking. As with skimetons, Indian ritual demanded that outsiders treat the braves to food and liquor. The landlord Anthony Livingston convinced a tribe that had cornered him to let him leave town by "furnishing refreshments." The Earle family of Andes set out "wheat bread and butter, . . . veal, pork," and an entire calf "cooked in pieces" for the tribes that came to stop a distress sale on their farm.[41]

On a deeper level, the Indians helped their members cope with their subordinate and insecure status in their communities. As we have seen, many farmers and artisans were adopting a new ethic of temperance and self-restraint, new forms of time-discipline, and new "businesslike" methods—and imposing these new habits on their (mostly young) hired laborers. The opportunity to take on an "Indian" identity permitted these same laborers to abandon this regimentation and self-restraint: to feast and drink; to dance, run, and ride their horses with abandon; to vent anger—in short, to act like savages. And it allowed them to do so without calling into question their own (white) respectability, for they projected their uncivilized behavior onto a distant race.[42]

"Indian" identity also permitted young laborers to affirm their manhood at a time when it was in question. Lacking the usual badges of manhood—property, dominion over wives and children, the vote—the natives claimed their manhood in different ways. Their overwhelmingly martial tone—their fantastic display of weapons, their war whoops, their elaborate threats, their feats of horsemanship—flaunted their manhood. So too did their stance as selfless protectors of their (implicitly female) communities, as a song penned in their honor affirmed:

From rocky mountains we are come,
To free our lands from slavery,
Never again to see our home
Till we execute our bravery.

Your pleasant homes you shall enjoy,
We boldly have avowed it,
Your peace the tyrants would destroy,
But we will not allow it.

Our tawny arm is stretched out still,
To shield you and protect you,
Our dearest blood we'll freely spill
We never will neglect you.[43]

The benefits of "Indian" identity went even further, allowing those who appropriated it to reverse the usual channels of subordination and receive "marked deference" from their superiors. When a Rensselaer County brave died in 1844, some 2,500 undisguised men, women, and children attended his funeral. The procession to the ceremony conformed to the Indians' hierarchy of honor and authority. Five chiefs rode in front, 96 braves followed on horseback, and the palefaces brought up the rear. Upon arriving, the war chief gave the order to dismount, crying out, "Let some of the white men tie your horses." Several spectators "seized the horses with great alacrity." When ordered to be silent, the crowd hushed. Even the officiating ministers obeyed the command of the braves. The Indians' ritual world could serve the same function as an early modern carnival, allowing those near the bottom of the social scale to overturn their subordination and, for a moment, lord it over their superiors.[44]

In one respect, the natives upheld the economic interests of the young and landless: by defending the right of community members to take resources from common lands. When a subagent for Robert L. Livingston confiscated the timber that trespassers had cut from the "landlord's commons" in Woodstock, a band of Indians tarred and feathered him and threw him from a low ridge. Similarly, the Rensselaer County Indians assaulted a tenant who tried to haul away the timber that trespassers had cut on a timber lot he owned. In doing so, they defended a practice that allowed all community members, even those without land, access to natural resources.[45]

The Indians did nothing to pit their interests against those of their older and more prosperous neighbors, however. Although they were the objects of exploitation in two overlapping systems of labor and authority—the family and wage labor—they never challenged, or even pointed out, that exploitation. Rather, they sought to protect the former system and to affirm their own masculine worthiness within it. Their defense of common rights was not a challenge to the inequalities prevalent in leasehold communities but an attempt to preserve a practice that helped young men to acquire the money needed to become full members in those communities. Like the antirent associations, the Indians sought to defend an idealized version of household production; they asserted their special needs and interests *within* that system of production, not against it.

Exclusions

For all its egalitarianism, the anti-renters' social vision was highly exclusive and hierarchical. Male insurgents defined themselves in universalist terms: as producers and as republican citizens. Their movement, they insisted, was in essence a struggle for the right of all producers to the fruits of their labor and for the right of all citizens to dignity, independence, and political power. But not everyone qualified as a citizen or a producer. Male association members sustained a myth that they alone did the work of the farm or workshop in order to provide for dependent, nonproducing women and children. "Why is it," asked Joseph Hoag, "that while their father labors assiduously from early morn till late at night . . . he cannot have the satisfaction of seeing his family benefitted by his constant toil . . . ?"[46] Similarly, when male anti-renters spoke of "citizens," they meant men. At a Fourth of July celebration in Kortright, Erastus Root proposed a toast to this "large and respectable convocation of my fellow citizens." He then continued: "The ladies, too, add grace and dignity to the meeting." For such men, the moral attributes held to be the foundation of republican government—virtue, independence, and patriotic courage—were distinctly masculine. One movement leader warned his readers that if they failed to defend the republic from land monopoly, "you are *not* acting either a *just* or a *manly* part toward those countless millions whose bondage or freedom . . . is staked upon the momentous issue. Meet the necessity like a man. Come to the rescue of our institutions while there is still time."[47] To the anti-renters, the capacity and the duty to sustain the republic through engagement in public life rested in men alone.

Male activists did, however, accord women a role in redeeming the republic. A movement song expressed it best:

Come join the anti-renters,
Ye young men bold and strong,
And with a warm and cheerful zeal,
Come help the cause along.

Oh, that will be joyful, joyful, joyful
When Patroonery is no more!

Come join the anti-renters!
Ye men of riper years,
And save your wives and children dear
From grief and bitter tears.

Oh, it will be joyful, joyful, joyful
When Patroonery is no more!

Come join the anti-renters!
Ye dames and maidens fair,

And breathe around us in our path
Affections hallowed air.

Oh, it will be joyful, joyful, joyful,
When women cheer us on.[48]

Just as male anti-renters depicted men's economic labors as support for
the women and children in their families, so too did they see men's public
labors—including the anti-rent movement itself—as protection to dependent women and children. But women did have a role: to cheer their men
on. Drawing from notions of republican womanhood and newer ideas from
the cult of domesticity, men in the movement believed that women were to
do so primarily as wives and mothers. The anti-renters of Schoharie county
noted that anti-rent women were "too proud to nurse a slave" and proclaimed
that since they were to be "the mothers of the coming generation, we have
faith . . . that under their tuition, a sentiment will go forth that will sweep the
last vestiges of Patroonery from the land." Similarly, an anti-rent speaker told
the young ladies at a Delaware county meeting to "discard all who are not
friendly to equal rights." To the married women in the audience, he recommended that if their husbands' efforts on behalf of the cause flagged, they
"crowd so close to their heels that they will be compelled to go ahead."
Women were to inspire moral restraint as well as patriotism in their men. One
anti-rent speaker noted with pleasure the presence of so many ladies in the
audience, for "their presence will aid me in preserving that order and deco-
rum so necessary in all public assemblies."[49]

Just as they expected females to play an auxiliary and indirect role in public life, male insurgents did not expect women to enjoy directly the rights for
which they fought. Land, the cornerstone of the anti-renters' good society,
was out of the reach of the vast majority of farm women, and no anti-renter
challenged the inheritance practices and property laws that kept the soil out
of female hands. Similarly, militant tenants did not think women deserved
the equality and self-determination for which men fought. Nor did anti-rent
men imagine that women had a claim to the fruits of their labor superior to
that of their fathers or husbands. In the eyes of male tenants, women were
not autonomous social actors; they were subordinate members of their fathers' and husbands' households. The rights for which the anti-renters fought
were to rest in men, as the representatives of households; women would enjoy the benefits of these rights *through* their men.[50]

Despite their exclusion from the rights anti-renters sought to secure, tenant women had an enormous stake in the movement's success. The money
they earned by making butter, cheese, and eggs, as well as the money they
saved by gardening, sewing, canning, spinning, and weaving, accounted for
a significant portion of the property that the anti-rent movement sought to
defend. Overdue rents and landlords' demands for repayment threatened
their security, prosperity, and place in a stable community as much as men's.

Thus women participated in the movement and, like their men, usually did so in ways that reflected broader gender conventions. Occasionally, they brought their domestic skills to the aid of the movement, as when the ladies of Berne presented a banner to the Albany County association, "most chastely and beautifully decorated with roses, and inscribed 'A Free Soil—Bern is Coming.'" Similarly, women took oaths as Indians—"not indeed," one male activist said, "that they might be permitted to wear calico and bear arms in this crusade against their foes, but that they might be the honored dress makers and ornamenters of masks for their husbands, sons or lovers, the brave heroes." More frequently, women performed an ornamental role. Anti-rent Fourth of July processions often included 27 ladies dressed in white to represent the states of the Union. When Ira Harris, an immensely popular anti-rent leader, toured Delaware county, "the ladies" greeted him at several towns, "waving their white handkerchiefs to greet him onward in the great work he has just begun."[51]

Still, a significant number of leasehold women acted less like cheerleaders for activist men than like independent actors in a collective effort. In the process, they sometimes violated the gender conventions celebrated by the anti-rent movement. When posses poured through Columbia, Schoharie, and Delaware Counties in search of Indians in 1845, tenant women acted as sentinels, blowing tin dinner horns to warn the braves when lawmen approached. They also hid the fugitives and ran their farms when husbands had to flee. In many places, they took over the tasks their "Indian" brothers and sons had performed. In Columbia County, women "behaved very rudely" toward the posses, "hooting and following most abusively at them." In New Scotland, they destroyed the wagon of a deputy who conducted a distress sale.[52]

Many female anti-renters saw in the movement an opportunity to extend their sphere of public action and to voice their own grievances with the leasehold system. In 1845, women began writing to the anti-rent newspapers, passing their own resolutions at anti-rent meetings, and separately petitioning public officials. Most correspondents noted that it was unusual for women to address the public on political matters, and many denied that they wished to intrude upon male prerogatives. But, they said, the leasehold system and the actions of its defenders had so endangered the well-being of their households and their communities that they felt compelled to speak. A "Farmer's Daughter" asked, "how long shall our children go unfed, unclothed, uneducated,—how long shall we be required to live in log cabins—how long deprived of churches . . . ? As long as Patroonery is permitted to exist." In May of 1845, when *posses comitatus* were sweeping through Delaware county to arrest anti-rent Indians, several women from the county petitioned a member of the state assembly to ask for an end to martial law. "We know that legislation is not woman's province," they wrote, but martial law had subjected "the female part of the community" to "unparalleled indignities."

Our husbands are driven from their homes . . . ; our defenseless houses are broken open in the dead of night and ransacked at will. Even the paraphernalia of female apparel has been rudely rummaged over, for the amusement of unprincipled young men. . . . It is intolerable, indeed, to see our floors and carpets trampled over by the dirty feet of the sheriff and his posse. . . . Women have been dragged from their beds in some instances, and otherwise grossly insulted.[53]

Here was a version of anti-rentism that purported to grow organically from women's duties as wives and mothers. Female anti-renters aimed not at changing those duties but at fulfilling them; doing so required that they intervene in public life.[54] But they affirmed only those responsibilities that were celebrated in male anti-renters' mythology. They emphasized their duties as housekeepers and nurturers of children rather than their production of commodities: gardening, spinning, weaving, and dairying. Along with other antebellum white Americans, male and female anti-renters rendered women's productive work invisible.[55] Similarly, even as women acted as sentinels and harassed lawmen, they echoed their husbands' depiction of them as defenseless, passive females who needed the protection of men. Nor did they challenge the assumption that land, independence, equality, and the full fruits of their labor were to benefit women only through their men, as subordinate members of male-headed households.

Women were not the only group in leasehold society to be excluded from the community of producers. Anti-rent activists never acknowledged the presence of landless and land-poor men in the hill towns, nor did they address their right to property. A similar disdainful silence hung over the rights of the handful of African Americans who lived in the leasehold towns. Anti-renters paid scant attention to these residents; when they did mention their black neighbors, they used them as a dusky mirror by which to measure their own degradation. Like white antebellum wage earners, the anti-renters saw black people as "anti-citizens"—objects who represented all the dangers of servility and degradation in a republican society. One militant wrote that, after 25 years of petty humiliations at the hand of his landlord, he finally understood the degrading nature of the leasehold system when he was forced into the company of African Americans. While attempting to speak to his landlord, he was sent to the basement to eat with the house servants: "I had the blushing honor to eat with the negroes!" It is doubtful that many anti-renters saw such people as candidates for membership in their society of freeholders.[56]

Ironically, it was the Indians who made the racial exclusions of the movement most clear. The natives' promise to withdraw to their home beyond the Rocky Mountains affirmed the inevitability of Indian removal and the settlement of American lands by exclusively white communities. And it perpetuated the myth that the Indians cheerfully accepted their fate. Behind this myth lay the belief that "progress" was an exclusively white affair, one that required the disappearance of aboriginal peoples. Like most antebellum white men, the anti-renters did not listen to actual native peoples or to African Americans; rather, they created an image of racial others that served their own purposes. In doing so, they gave voice to a class identity that was unmistakably white. In promoting their egalitarian class agenda, the anti-renters simultaneously helped advance the multiclass cause of white supremacy and Indian removal.[57]

The anti-renters thus offered a clear vision of freedom. To them, a "free" society was one of independent proprietors, where male producers commanded family labor and met one another as equals in the marketplace and in politics. In such a society, every adult white man would enjoy the fruits of his labor, independence, political and cultural equality, economic security, free trade, and a secure place in a stable community. Beneath this equality lay numerous inequalities and exclusions. The anti-renters sought to abolish "unnatural" class hierarchies and to retain those based on the "natural" distinctions of gender, age, and race. Just as important, as landlessness, wage labor, and conflicts over the commons escalated, most militants abandoned those conceptions of property rights that provided a way to achieve their vision of freedom, embracing instead ideas about property that implicitly buttressed land monopoly.

Anti-renters articulated their vision of freedom with two voices: one that spoke the universalist language of natural rights, popular sovereignty, and party politics; one fluent in the local, corporate language of the skimmeton. These two voices should remind us that politics for the antebellum producing classes was not simply a matter of partisan enthusiasm and voting. Instead, people who worked with their hands engaged in several kinds of "politics" at once, with each strategy and style displaying a distinct political identity and serving a particular set of material and strategic needs.[58]

This is not to say that the anti-renters or other members of the producing classes eschewed electoral politics. They fervently believed in the redemptive power of the ballot box and the petition, and they looked to them for the final solution to the leasehold crisis. It was in the arena of electoral and legislative politics that the fate of the anti-renters' vision of freedom would be determined.

Chapter 6

THE PARTIES
AND "THE PEOPLE,"
1844 – 1846

Articulating a vision of freedom was one thing; achieving it was another. Since 1840, the anti-renters had known that winning freedom required access to the power of the state. Although their early attempts to enlist the government in their cause had failed, their newfound strength after 1844 gave them a far better chance at success. Their renewed efforts to win political power reveal a relationship with political leaders that was far more complex than historians of Jacksonian politics have suggested. Party leaders and tenants belonged to distinct but overlapping political subcultures, with different social ideals, conflicting political practices, and incompatible definitions of "democracy." Whig and Democratic activists did not simply represent tenants' views, nor did they simply coopt and silence them. Instead, their relationship with militants was a dialectical one, marked by conflict and reciprocal influence. This relationship, moreover, contained the seeds of change. Between 1845 and 1846, anti-renters, Whigs, and Democrats began a process that would transform both popular politics on the estates and party politics throughout New York.

"The People Rule"

Whether they participated in the rent boycott, donned the "Indian" garb, or voted for anti-rent candidates, leasehold militants acted on a conception of democracy that they had learned from the Democrats and adapted to their own purposes: the unqualified sovereignty of the people. Insurgents believed that a single popular will existed, separate from and above the clash of personal, group, or local interests. This will, when not distorted by corrupt influences, always pointed to the best interests of a community. From this point of view, government appeared as nothing more than an extension of the will of the citizenry. George W. Lewis of Sand Lake summarized this view well: "The people rule in this country, and they can make any laws they are a mind to, . . . and it is a libel and an insult, upon the patriotism of the sons of '76, to tell them that they can't do the work."[1]

For most anti-renters, popular sovereignty implied the right of the people to overthrow any laws or institutions that injured the common good—including the federal and state constitutions. They thus ridiculed the Democrats and Conservative Whigs who had opposed their demands on constitutional grounds. According to "Socrates," anyone who sought to "protect and defend the constitution of the State, however . . . shamefully it may encroach upon the constitution of the people" was "only fit to be the servile drudge of Patroonery." The only just course of action lay in "consulting the best interests of the people" and making the constitution and laws "harmonize" with those interests. For many, popular sovereignty also implied the right—indeed, the duty—to break laws that violated natural law, defied the will of God, or offended the sensibilities of a sovereign People. L. H. Vermilia warned that the laws that enforced farm leases "never can, they never will, hereafter be enforced."

> It is useless to lay so much stress upon law and order, when injustice is so palpable as to be seen and felt in every man's household. That law and order ceases to become binding when the main feature of all law, equality, and the right of the people to govern themselves is broken down in a manner that would disgrace many a nabob of older countries.[2]

As they had done with the Democrats' social vision, the anti-renters adapted the Jacksonians' ideals of popular sovereignty and put them to new uses. With this adaptation, leasehold militants turned the teachings against the teacher. They also drew on a long tradition of popular belief. Although the Federalists of the 1780s, and later the leaders of the Whig and Democratic parties, recognized multiple legitimate interests in society, less learned citizens often rejected their leaders' pluralist assumptions. Public meetings and voluntary associations clung to earlier notions of a unitary people's will, and they claimed to speak for "the People," despite their obvious minority status. The anti-renters carried forward this tradition: theirs were not the demands of a minority (albeit a very large one), but of the People themselves.[3]

After their humiliating defeat in the legislature of 1844, the anti-renters believed that the only way to make the government defer to the People's will was to create an independent electoral organization. Their state convention resolved in 1844 to support only "nominations made as ANTI-RENT, laying aside all old party lines." Earlier that year, militants in four counties had met before the Whig and Democratic conventions were held and nominated their own candidates for the state assembly. They left open the possibility of an electoral alliance with the major parties, however. Every anti-rent candidate was a Whig or Democratic activist; if they chose to, local Whig and Democratic organizations could endorse the militants' choice and harness the anti-rent vote in November. In Delaware and Schoharie Counties, where lopsided

Democratic majorities had long permitted party organizations to ignore out-lying towns, both parties scorned the anti-rent nominees. But in Albany and Rensselaer Counties, where politics were highly competitive, the Whigs sought out a partial alliance with the tenants. Eleven anti-rent activists attended the Albany County Whig convention and helped place Ira Harris, one of the anti-renters' Whig nominees, on their ticket. The Rensselaer Whigs acted similarly, nominating the anti-rent candidate for Congress and one of the three anti-rent nominees for assembly.[4]

The election results offered a different lesson for anti-renters in each county. In Delaware, where militants had fielded independent candidates, one out of three anti-rent candidates won a seat in the legislature. In Schoharie, the entire independent ticket triumphed. Albany County militants, however, found that they needed to cooperate with the major parties. The anti-rent ticket swept the hill towns of Albany County, where the movement was the strongest, by a margin of more than three to one. But voters in Albany city, which held 49 percent of the county's electors, continued to vote straight party tickets. So did the manor towns of the valley, where a modest anti-rent movement had taken root. As a result, the Whigs won the election, helping send Harris to the legislature but defeating the other anti-rent candidates by wide margins. Still, hill tenants proved a formidable electoral bloc, giving Harris 2,000 more votes than his fellow Whig nominees. In Rensselaer County, too, the Whigs won the election by wide margins, helping the anti-renters they had nominated into office but rudely dispatching the movement's independent candidates to private life.[5]

No single lesson emerged from the election. In Albany County, the anti-renters had the power to swing elections, but not to win them on their own. In Schoharie and Delaware, on the other hand, alliances with the Whigs or Democrats proved both impossible and unnecessary.

Fragmented Parties and Popular Insurgencies

For all their disappointment with the Whigs and Democrats, the anti-renters needed their help. The men who led the anti-rent associations possessed the authority and organizational abilities necessary to build strong local movements. But linking such movements into a statewide effort, electing men to the state government, writing laws, and winning concessions from the legislature required the skills of lawyers, lobbyists, and seasoned politicians—talents that were in short supply in the leasehold towns. Luckily for the anti-renters, many party activists were receptive to initiatives from the political margins. Electoral competition was fierce: between 1840 and 1846, no successful candidate for governor won as much as 53 percent of the statewide vote.[6] Thus party leaders had an enormous incentive to win new constituencies over to their parties. This incentive grew after 1842, when both major parties slipped into bitter factional bickering. From its beginning in 1834, the New York Whig party had united conservatives like Daniel Dewey Barnard, who espoused an organic, paternalist view of society; and former anti-Masons like William Seward, who embraced a democracy of white men and sought to free society from ancient forms of bondage. When Seward and his allies sought the support of abolitionists, Catholics, and anti-renters by opposing slavery, endorsing state support of parochial schools, and promoting the abolition of the leasehold system, Conservatives were horrified. By 1842, infighting between Liberals and Conservatives became so fierce that Seward refused to be considered for renomination as governor, fearing his candidacy would "divide my party in convention."[7]

Beginning in 1843, the Democrats, too, broke into warring camps. Radicals who remained devoted to the party's program of laissez-faire economics and limited government found themselves in battle with Conservatives anxious to promote economic development through government-sponsored roads, canals, and corporate charters. These divisions worsened in 1844 and 1845 when the Democratic national convention dumped Martin Van Buren as its presidential nominee and the Polk administration embraced the annexation of Texas. Radicals, who came to be known as "Barnburners," feared that a southern "slave power" had captured the national party; these partisans endorsed the Wilmot Proviso in late 1845. Conservatives, who took the epithet of "Hunkers," supported the administration's pro-Texas stance.[8]

These disputes created important openings for popular movements like the anti-renters. Factional competition within parties gave partisan activists an added incentive to win new supporters, for such allies could help them not only win elections but wrest control of the party from their factional rivals as well. More importantly, factionalism made such alliances less costly by setting the potential supporters and opponents of popular movements into warring camps. All Whig landlords sided with the Conservatives, leaving the Liberals free to offer cautious support to the anti-renters. Though their specific legislative proposals changed over time, before 1846 Liberal state leaders looked upon leasehold militants with a mixture of condescension, hostility toward the leasehold system, and electoral pragmatism. Horace Greeley summarized these attitudes well:

> As to anti-rent, the matter is very simple. The Landlords are nearly all Loco-Focos, and mean at that. They have brought on this trouble by their selfishness. The tenants are poor, ignorant, some of them reckless and criminal, but have a good deal of right on their side. The quarrel must at last be settled by compromise, and can't be permanently settled in any other way. Now shall we abuse the Tenants altogether, and throw the votes of a dozen Counties solid against us? Or shall we treat with both parties fairly and try to bring them to a compromise, and so hold at least to *our own* votes?[9]

Similarly, while Barnburners maintained their party's hostility to the anti-renters after 1843, Democratic landlords' loyalty to the Radicals allowed Hunkers to forge an alliance with the tenants' cause. The Hunkers found significant support among farmers in those counties that lay near existing or proposed canals—counties that included Albany, Rensselaer, and Schoharie. Just as important, they had begun to abandon their party's devotion to limited government and strict construction of the Constitution. Thus, when tenants in these counties began to demand legislative action on the leasehold issue, they found ready, though vacillating, allies among upstate Hunkers.

William C. Bouck, the leader of the Conservatives, began courting anti-rent votes while governor in 1843 and 1844. He kept up a friendly correspondence with anti-rent leaders, offering to mediate between landlords and tenants. He also steadfastly ignored a flood of requests from lawmen and private citizens that he call up the militia against the Indians.[10]

Contracts, Property, and the Defense of the Leasehold

While the anti-renters forged alliances with Liberal Whig and Hunker activists, their landlords mounted a political campaign of their own. In late 1844, a meeting of 20 leasehold proprietors founded the "Freeholders' Committee of Safety." Funded by contributions assessed upon every landlord in the state, the organization began an intensive lobbying campaign to defeat the anti-renters' legislative initiative and suppress the Indians.[11] At the same time, the landlords' allies embarked on a war for public opinion. In doing so, they extended their defense of a patrician, hierarchical capitalism and offered a distinct alternative to the anti-renters' vision of freedom. In December 1845, Daniel Dewey Barnard, the Conservative Whig leader and executor of Stephen Van Rensselaer's estate, published "The 'Anti-Rent' Movement and Outbreak in New York" in the *American Review*, a national Whig journal. That same year, James Fenimore Cooper began *The Littlepage Manuscripts*, a three-volume family chronicle that recounted the history of the leasehold system from colonial settlement through the present. In these works, Barnard and Cooper both turned their patrician vision of capitalist development explicitly to the defense of the leasehold system.[12]

To different degrees, both writers defended the leasehold system as a beneficent institution. Although Barnard admitted that perpetual rents posed a "serious inconvenience" to progressive, entrepreneurial farmers, he depicted the system as promoting prosperity and republican equality. By expanding Rensselaerwyck after the Revolution, Barnard argued, Stephen Van Rensselaer "created a body of substantial freeholders, three thousand in number . . . every one of whom was as good a voter as himself." Cooper was even more enthusiastic about the social and political benefits of the leasehold. The novelist rejected as "Utopian" the anti-renters' notion that "every husbandman is to be a freeholder"; "the column of society," he wrote, "must have its capital as well as its base." The relationship between landlords and tenants was "entirely natural and salutary," for it promoted the prosperity of poor farmers, advanced the "civilization" of the country, and encouraged progress in agriculture. Just as important, the inequality embedded in the leasehold permitted landlords to resist a pernicious trend toward crass materialism and unprincipled democracy in American culture.[13]

The heart of Cooper's and Barnard's defense of the leasehold lay not in their praise for its social utility, however, but in their depiction of anti-rent attacks on it as a threat to contracts and property rights. According to Barnard, the leasehold system rested on simple real estate transactions that bestowed no special privileges on landlords. Stephen Van Rensselaer's title "was just such a title as every man in the State has who hold by deed." Similarly, leasehold agreements were "mutual contracts" that established no special relationship "except what the mutual obligations of the contracts established."[14] The anti-renters' efforts to abolish the leasehold were nothing but an attempt to abolish "property, existing in the form of rents"; any failure to uphold property in that form would endanger "private property . . . in any form." For his part, Cooper insisted that "the state is bound to make all classes of men respect its laws, and in nothing more so than in the fulfillment of their legal contracts."[15]

In defending leasehold contracts and landlords' property, Barnard and Cooper articulated a vision of free labor far different from that offered by the anti-renters. These men affirmed the legal equality of the laborer while allowing for authoritarian relations between classes. Echoing employment-law doctrines recently formulated in the courts, they held that any labor relationship entered into voluntarily was both free and binding. Behind this reasoning lay a distinct notion: that freedom amounted to the formal equality between parties to a contract. As Barnard observed, "Both parties stood upon their contracts, and, as contracting parties, they stood before the law of the land upon a footing of perfect civil equality." Liberty was to be measured not by the conditions of labor or the degree of personal autonomy enjoyed by the laborer, but by the ability of an individual to enter into an agreement without coercion.[16]

Cooper and Barnard also articulated a political vision at odds with that of the anti-renters. Both embraced a kind of political Calvinism, which insisted on the innate depravity of the vulgar mass and on the need for elites to check their corrupt impulses. To them, the anti-rent movement represented a breakdown of elite restraint, as demagogues encouraged and empowered the selfish delusions of the hoi polloi. According to Cooper, anti-rentism resulted from "men mistaking their own cupidity for the workings of a love of liberty." This selfishness was mobilized by "demagogues" who proclaimed it to be the voice of progress. Similarly, Barnard argued that by giving "countenance and support" to the anti-renters' "licentiousness," political leaders "aggravated a merely local and temporary ebullition of popular heat and impatience . . . into a popular commotion which shakes the pillars of the state." If unchecked, the corrupt alliance between deluded plebs and demagogues would lead to "the utter overthrow of all social order, and the ruin of the whole social fabric."[17]

Cooper and Barnard offered slightly different solutions to the dangers of anti-rentism. Cooper called on men of property and principle to exert their proper influence to discountenance the anti-renters' cupidity. Their influence, he believed, would be sufficient to reclaim public opinion and political leadership from the cause of agrarianism and anarchy. Barnard, on the other hand, called on *political* leaders, as the representatives of the state, to firmly suppress the anti-renters. Despite their differences, both men looked to elites to restrain a deluded people.

Transforming the Message

Cooper's and Barnard's fear of a corrupt alliance of demagogues and deluded plebs had a certain basis in reality. The structure of Jacksonian politics created opportunities for popular movements to win allies and, perhaps, reshape the political landscape. Political outsiders seeking entry to the corridors of power were everywhere in Jacksonian America. The emergence of mass-based, partisan politics had flooded the towns and cities of the nation with what Horace Greeley called "a large class of young lawyers and aspirants" who were "more anxious to be on the winning than on the right side, and whose gaze is fascinated and fixed by the prospect of judgeships, seats in the legislature, &c.&c." The anti-renters found allies among precisely these outsiders. They came from two overlapping groups: party activists allied with the Liberal Whigs or the Conservative Democrats, and reformers from the abolitionist and land reform movements. Many of the tenants' supporters were ambitious young lawyers and editors just embarking on political careers. Others, particularly those from the Whig party, were mature and accomplished lawyers whose political prospects had been compromised by their support for the anti-slavery cause. Still others came from the National Reform Association, a land-reform organization based in the journeymen's movement of New York City. For many leaders in all three groups, the leasehold conflict provided an opportunity to serve a cause that they believed in deeply. For all, the movement presented an occasion to advance their careers and to win a new constituency to their organizations. The anti-renters offered a well-organized cadre of activists and several thousand votes—considerations that might secure a nomination, swing an election, and breathe life into a stalled political career.[18]

These leaders played an essential role in the tenants' movement. They brought skills as lawyers, editors, and lobbyists to the cause. They also brought their own ideas about political economy and political expediency, and they fought to bring tenants to their way of thinking. These allies served as ideological middlemen between the anti-renters and the political parties or reform organizations to which they belonged. They sought to reshape the tenants' thinking to conform with the broad programs and ideologies of their organizations. At the same time, they struggled to convince their organizations to champion the anti-renters' cause. In the process, they opened up bitter debates about leasehold farmers' place in the broader economic and political order.

One such leader was Thomas A. Devyr. The son of an Irish baker, Devyr was a paragon of that nineteenth-century character, the Reformer as globetrotting moral adventurer. He was active in nationalist and anti-landlord movements as a youth, publishing *Our Natural Rights,* a pamphlet calling for reform of the Irish land system, in 1838. During the 1830s he moved to England, where he edited the *Liberator* of Newcastle-Upon-Tyne and helped lead the Newcastle Chartists in their attempt to overthrow the British government in 1840. When the Chartists' conspiracy was uncovered, Devyr fled to Williamsburg, near Brooklyn, where he served briefly as a Democratic editor. But his relationship with the Jacksonians quickly soured and, in 1844, he helped found the National Reform Association, an organization led and supported by New York City craftsmen and dedicated to land reform. Beginning in 1842, Devyr served as an occasional speaker and writer for the anti-renters; in April 1845, he signed on as editor of the *Albany Freeholder,* the central organ of the statewide movement.[19]

Throughout his service as an anti-rent leader, Devyr worked to tie the tenants' hopes for a nation of freeholders to the National Reform Association's attack on one of the cornerstones of the capitalist order: private, alienable property in land. Drawing on the Enlightenment beliefs of the Anglo-American radical tradition and echoing his former Jacksonian colleagues, Devyr argued that society was regulated by laws as immutable and understandable as the law of gravity. Social harmony and prosperity were possible only if society was organized according to those laws. And "the Law of Nature and Nature's God" bequeathed to "every man who comes into this world . . . an equal right to the soil."[20]

Land, Devyr believed, was not a commodity but part of the common inheritance of humanity, to be used, but never owned, by its cultivators. To demonstrate this truth, he drew on two sources that tenants understood well: the labor theory of value and the Bible. The source of all rightful property, he argued, was labor. Anything created by human labor belonged to the laborer who created it and could be used, sold, or given away as he saw fit. Land, on the other hand, was created by God; no human being had a right to buy it, sell it, or claim it as his own. Biblical precedent confirmed this insight. Devyr reminded his readers that the ancient Israelites had provided land for each family and had prohibited anyone from selling that land for more than 50 years. Though a family in the Holy Land might lose its property through sale or debt for a time, the land would be returned on the Day of Jubilee.[21]

Treating land as a commodity broke a link in nature's "circular chain of harmonies," creating endless human misery. Like the Democrats, Devyr subscribed to Adam Smith's belief that an unregulated market was the best arbiter of relations among producers. "The law of demand and supply," he insisted, "is a most harmonious *and regulating* law, provided man has the option of 'supplying' his wants from the soil." Private property in land made a mockery of this promise of social harmony, for it inevitably led to land monopoly, from which sprang all the evils to which humanity was heir. Those who worked the land were compelled to pay tribute to its nominal owners, supporting those proprietors in idleness and luxury while they themselves lived in poverty and ignorance. Destitution and overwork inevitably took its toll in crime, immorality, and insanity. Other members of the propertyless class flocked to the cities, where they flooded labor markets, driving wages to starvation levels. These emigrants, too, lived lives "much more toilsome and joyless than those of the lower animals"; they too paid the price in crime, debauchery, and mental illness. Such degradation endangered republican government by creating a servile and ignorant citizenry. At the same time, the power, wealth, and superior learning of the great landowners gave them excessive influence in government, resulting in "*monopoly of Legislation*." To Devyr, the experience of England and the Continent warned Americans of the impending consequences of land monopoly in their own country:

> What has raised the accursed thrones of the old world? . . . Monopoly of the Soil sustains . . . Aristocracy . . . Monarchy is the central head of that monster . . . *all* the anarchy, *all* the wars, all the hunger, nakedness, and desolation of heart—*all* the sterility of human intellect—*all* the social crime that has, up to this day, turned God's fair earth into a human hell, *all*, *all* had their deep rank root in Land Monopoly.[22]

Restoring humanity to its natural right to land, Devyr predicted, would usher in a new utopia. Nature's bounty would ensure that every family lived in "cleanliness and comfort." With the means of production available to all, the law of supply and demand would be "freed of the Anti-human influences that are at work upon it"; market exchange would turn society into "one vast system of cooperation" from which all producers would benefit. Universal access to land would create a new race of free and independent yeomen who would "guarantee the power—the prosperity—and the undying stability of the Republic." And it would free all people from incessant toil, providing producers with the leisure they needed to free themselves from ignorance. The result would be an era of unprecedented progress and enlightenment.[23]

Devyr thus revived in a new and more radical form what most anti-renters had quietly dropped: a challenge to prevailing definitions of property as derived from paper title. In so doing, he offered them a mechanism by which to realize their vision of universal landownership. But he gave them mixed messages about whether their natural right to land should be enforced on

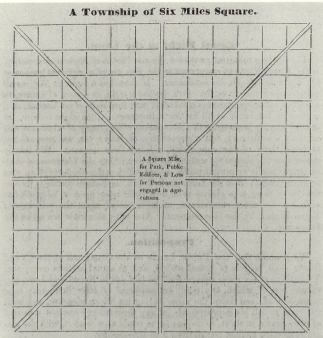

A Township of Six Miles Square.

A Square Mile,
for Park, Public
Edifices, & Lots
for Persons not
engaged in Agri-
culture.

The above plan of a township makes provision for 140 families of
farmers, and 60 or more of other occupations, say 200 families or 1000
individuals in a township. There would be some waste land or water,
and there would be some individuals working for others in order to get
means to go into business for themselves, so that there would probably
be at least 1000 individuals in a township when fully settled; and then,
if we consider the capabilities of improving the land, and the advantages of co-operation, we can easily imagine how a township might support four or even eight thousand individuals, by families to the third or
fourth generation voluntarily remaining on the *homestead.*
    In the centre square mile represented in our diagram, might be laid
out a Public Park, of about thirty acres, in which might be situated the
Town Hall and other Public Edifices, around which might be laid out

Figure 6.1. The National Reformers' utopia. This sketch illustrates the reformers' plan for the public lands: a township of inalienable 160–acre farms and one-
acre town lots, all given to landless settlers by the government. Courtesy of the
Astor, Lenox, and Tilden Collections, New York Public Library.

New York's estates. At times, he explicitly disavowed any wish "to disturb . . .
the *present* ownership of land." At others, he proclaimed that "degradation,
crime, and human agony must continue, and grow more intense . . . or the
rights of property must be invaded." In his specific proposals, he remained
loyal to the National Reformers' demand for a legal limit on all future accumulation of land and for distribution of the nation's public lands in small, inalienable lots to settlers, free of charge.[24]
    Where Devyr sought to tie the anti-renters' dream of universal propri-
etorship to an explicitly agrarian political economy, Liberal Whigs and

Conservative Democrats worked to convince tenants that widespread land-ownership would be the natural outcome of economic competition, social mobility, and the laws of the market. Ira Harris, the most beloved anti-rent leader, had known leasehold tenancy from an early age. His father Frederick had grown up on Rensselaerwyck; during Ira's first six years, Frederick had farmed a tract that he leased from George Clarke. Frederick prospered as a tenant, and when Ira was six he moved the family to a 400-acre freehold farm in Cortland County. There the family prospered sufficiently to send their son to Homer Academy and Union College. At 22, Ira began to study law in the office of Ambrose Spencer, a former state Supreme Court justice, leading National Republican, and veteran of the anti-leasehold conflict of the 1810s. As a commissioner to revise the state's laws in 1812, Spencer had recommended that the legislature abrogate the quarter sale.[25]

In 1826, Harris moved to Albany and opened his own law office. There he acquired a lucrative practice and a gleaming reputation for clarity of mind, simplicity and power of expression, and knowledge of the law. He also became a leader in the cause of evangelical reform, serving as an officer in the American Baptist Missionary Union, the New York State Temperance Society, and the New York Anti-Slavery Society. In politics, he cast his lot first with the Anti-Masons, then with the Liberal Whigs. Through all his public activities, Harris embraced the reformers' and Seward Whigs' dedication to liberating humanity from ancient forms of bondage. Probably because his abolitionism assured his defeat at the polls, he eschewed a prominent role in party politics. He served only once as a delegate to an Anti-Masonic county convention, never receiving a nomination for office before he joined the anti-rent cause. Harris first began working with the anti-renters in 1844, advising them in their efforts to lobby the legislature. In that year, he won a seat in the state assembly on the Whig and anti-rent tickets.[26]

Harris's counterpart in Albany County was Robert Watson, a young lawyer who moved to Albany in 1839. Watson quickly threw himself into local politics, serving as a Democratic functionary in the tenth ward, a secretary to the city's Young Men's Democratic Association, and an election-time stump speaker in the rural towns around the capital. He also lent his support to local causes like the Irish Repeal Association, thereby building a network of support for both the party and his own career. Watson began to provide this kind of support for the anti-renters in 1840, collecting affidavits from the surviving pioneers of the Helderbergs and speaking at anti-rent meetings. In 1845, he won a seat in the state assembly on both the anti-rent and the Democratic tickets.[27]

Despite their different party loyalties, Harris and Watson offered the anti-renters identical social visions. Like Devyr, they endorsed militants' desire to control the fruits of their labor. But they argued that private property in land, far from foiling this desire, fulfilled it. Land was not a common inheritance of all humanity, but, as Harris put it, "the reward to successful industry." The problem with the leasehold system was that it prevented farmers from turn-

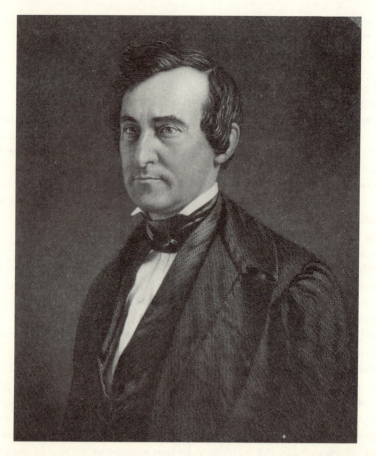

Figure 6.2. The two faces of Whiggism, part 1. Daniel Dewey Barnard, an intimate of Stephen Van Rensselaer III and executor of his will, led the Conservative Whigs' attack on the anti–renters. © Collection of the New–York Historical Society.

ing their labor into private property. According to Watson, short leases and the quarter sale allowed landlords to seize their tenants' improvements, thus tending to "fatten the rich man's field with the sweat of the poor man's brow." As a consequence, leasehold tenures destroyed the natural tendency of people to promote the public good by pursuing private gain. Rather than enriching their soil with manure and careful cultivation, tenants "taxed it to the uppermost. . . . No works of utility, improvement and of elegance will be constructed with an idea of being enlarged hereafter." Worst of all, the quarter sale restricted commerce in land. Land, according to Harris, was "an article of the market"; the opportunity to accumulate it became an incentive to industry and a spur to economic development. By placing restrictions on the alienation of land, the leasehold system proved "a blight upon the prosperity of those counties where such tenures prevail."[28]

Figure 6.3. The two faces of Whiggism, part 2. Ira Harris, an abolitionist and a partisan of William Henry Seward's reform wing of the party, became the insurgents' most popular and successful political leader. Courtesy of the Albany Institute of History and Art.

Both Harris and Watson insisted that the three demands adopted by the Anti-Rent State Convention of 1845—abolition of distress, taxation of rent income, and abrogation of the common-law rule that barred tenants from challenging their landlords' titles—were the only legitimate remedies to the evils of the leasehold system. To Watson, these laws would end landlords' special legal privileges and thereby destroy all that was oppressive in the leasehold system. He thus sought to win the anti-renters back to a narrow, orthodox version of antimonopoly thought and to quiet those who wanted not just equality before the law, but laws that would promote equality as well. Harris, by contrast, saw these demands through the prism of the Liberal Whigs' state-centered utilitarianism—as a legitimate use of the state to "destroy a system which has so long crippled the energies of so great a proportion of our community."[29]

With the leasehold system weakened or destroyed, both men believed, individual enterprise and the free flow of land and labor to their most efficient uses would best ensure a widespread distribution of land. According to Watson, young, landless men would work as laborers to accumulate the capital with which to begin farming on their own. These early years would instill industry, economy, and temperance in a young man, for "every dollar he can spare will go to pay for his farm." Once he purchased a homestead, security of property would spur his energies: "the young freeholder is constantly . . . making improvements upon his farm, for he knows he is providing a happy home for himself and his children." This same energy would infuse all of society; estate residents would soon "see a class of men with buoyant spirits urging on their own fortunes and the public prosperity. We should see these streams . . . dotted with flourishing villages, and see the farms improve in an incalculable manner." Harris, too, saw social mobility in a market economy as the best guarantor of a widespread distribution of land. But he did not promise land to all. Rather, he wished only to "enact such laws as *in their tendency,* would distribute land *as equally as possible,* among all classes of the community." Indeed his insistence on a free market in land ensured that there would be inequalities in land ownership. "The real estate of a country," he said, "should be left free to center, where it sooner or later will, if competition and enterprise are left free to operate unobstructed, in the hands of the industrious and prudent. Every attempt to interrupt this natural course of things is contrary to the true interests of a *republican* community."[30]

Watson's and Harris's message honored the primary concerns of tenants—control over the fruits of their labor, economic security, dignity, personal autonomy, and political independence. But Harris and Watson subordinated these aspirations to the larger objectives of economic competition, social mobility, and free enterprise. Thus they transformed the anti-renters' conception of freedom as land, security, equality, and exchange into the freedom to compete and prosper in a buoyant capitalist economy. In their vision, nothing was guaranteed but the freedom then being endorsed by the courts and by economic elites: self-ownership and control over one's body and labor.[31] They thus placed the anti-renters' vision of free labor on the narrowest possible foundation.

This limited conception of freedom also contained an expanded vision of capitalist development. Watson and Harris sought to make individual landholding as widespread as possible, and insisted that unbridled capitalism best served that aim, rather than concentrating the soil in a few hands. Through this formulation, they and their Whig and Democratic colleagues wedded the anti-renters' desire for a society of freeholders to the belief that social mobility would end economic inequality. They sought to link popular defenses of producers' rights to a conviction that equality, prosperity, and republican government would best be preserved by the emerging capitalist economy. This was not a new synthesis; the Jeffersonian Republicans espoused an early version of it during the 1790s.[32] But it continued to be re-created in social

and ideological conflict as entrepreneurs and political leaders justified capitalist social relations to audiences championing producers' rights. Such conflicts were common in the years before the Civil War. Only a decade before,
urban master artisans had forged a similar synthesis to defend their new
workshop practices from the challenges of an emerging labor movement.
These ideas provided a powerful challenge to Conservatives' celebration of
hierarchy, and would soon become the ideological centerpiece of the new
Republican party—their ideology of free labor.[38]

Narrowing the Boundaries
of the Political

Just as they worked to tie the anti-renters' social vision to their own ideas
about political economy, so too did Whigs, Democrats, and National Reformers seek to reshape tenants' conception and practice of politics. For his part,
Devyr endorsed militants' vision of absolute popular sovereignty. But he
battled what he saw as their parochialism and their preoccupation with limited, defensive measures. He filled the *Freeholder* with reports on the condition of the peasants of Europe and reprints from Chartist and National
Reform newspapers; his editorials ceaselessly reminded leasehold farmers
that their movement was "not a mere local, selfish movement. . . . It is the *advance guard* of that great reform movement which is destined to disenchain
the entire people of the Republic, and their entire posterity." The Irishman
hoped to create an electoral alliance among anti-renters, urban workers, reformers, and western farmers. The Indians' violent resistance to unjust laws,
he wrote, was justified but inexpedient; such resistance merely "kick[ed]" the
laws aside "for a moment." A permanent solution to the problems of patroonery and land monopoly could be arranged only "by a match of rifle-
shooting at the ballot boxes."[34]

For their part, Whig and Democratic activists served as missionaries from
the party Church. They strove to replace the anti-renters' syncretic political
culture with a strict adherence to the rules of the parties. Men like Watson
and Harris sought to convince anti-renters that democracy was not a process
by which the People enforced their will unimpeded, but a cosmopolitan
process of coalition-building, of linking local movements and issues to state
and national platforms, and of brokering between constituencies. Samuel
Gordon, a Democratic supporter of the Delaware County militants, con-
tended that the anti-proprietor struggle was "too narrow a platform to erect
a political party on"; it was properly "a single ingredient in the democratic
cauldron, in which the great and conservative elements of eternal right, truth
and justice, are mingled to compound the greatest good to the greatest number."[35]

This conception of politics required a strict adherence to the constitution
and the rule of law. Watson, Harris, and their colleagues suffered frequent

attacks from members of their own parties for their alliance with "lawless agrarians." They knew all too well the political costs of Indian violence and the tenants' disdain for constitutional guarantees to contracts and property. They sought to contain these costs by silencing such ideas and activities. Robert Watson strove to convince his tenant supporters that the success of their cause depended on winning the support of "public opinion" and of state legislators; both required that they disband the Indians, show strict regard for the constitution, and disavow the "agrarian" ideas of the National Reformers.

> We wish the legislature to understand distinctly, that we ask them to pass no law that will violate the constitution—that will rob a single individual of his rights, or that will in any manner impair the sacred rights of property. Let what will come, we feel that the laws and constitution of our country must be maintained.[36]

A single phrase—"let what will come"—spoke volumes. It revealed that for Watson, as for Whig anti-rent leaders, commitment to constitutionalism and the rule of law came before commitment to the aims of the anti-renters. Watson and Harris repeatedly affirmed their belief in the constitutionality of the anti-renters' demand for laws abolishing the right of distress, taxing landlords' rent income, and permitting tenants to "plead title" when sued for rent. Theirs was a minority opinion, however; most judges and lawmakers held the title-test bill to be unconstitutional. Thus Harris's statement that he would support all anti-rent demands that were consistent with "fair and constitutional legislation" begged the critical question: what if those measures were unconstitutional? Similarly, Watson made clear that if the anti-renters were forced to choose between existing property rights and their desire for "the homes of our fathers," they must choose the former: "If the landlords have title to this land, let them keep it." Most critically, party activists' demand that the Indians disband threatened to undermine the rent boycott and subject thousands of tenants to eviction. Whig and Democratic anti-rent leaders thus affirmed the justice of the anti-renters' wish to destroy the leasehold system and win ownership of their farms, but they also entreated them to be ready to give up those aims if they could not be won by legislative and constitutional means. Alexander Johnson, a Rensselaer County Whig, encouraged anti-renters to "imagine . . . a better state of society," but insisted that "we must for the time being—submit" to landlord rule.[37]

The Defeat of the Indians

The debate over the boundaries of legitimate political action were decided in conflict on the ground. Although the Indians enjoyed ardent support among many anti-renters, "men of wealth and influence" in the leasehold towns shared Watson's and Harris's distaste for them, fearing that they would alienate support among the state's political leaders. Two events brought this conflict into the open. On Wednesday, December 18, 1844, the anti-renters of Columbia County held a rally at Smokey Hollow. More than one hundred Indians made a spectacular entrance, rushing into the village square while they whooped, yelled, and fired their pistols into the air. A stray shot killed William Riffenburg, a young farm hand who had come to see the spectacle. The next day, 50 Indians from Grafton, Rensselaer County, attacked five men who were hauling timber from a lot that one of the men had purchased from William Van Rensselaer. Elijah Smith resisted the attack, rushing upon his assailants with an axe. One brave aimed a pistol at Smith, warning him that "if you advance any further, I will blow you through." Smith continued to advance. As one vigilante grabbed Smith and jerked him away, the other fired his pistol, striking Smith in the back. Smith died soon thereafter.[38]

These incidents frightened the allies and emboldened the enemies of the anti-renters throughout the state. Whig and Democratic editors vilified the movement as an "insurrection." Ministers condemned the anti-renters as a threat to social order and republican government; two Delaware County churches excommunicated militants. In Columbia, Delaware, Schoharie, and Ulster Counties, where Democratic cliques controlled local politics, lawmen assembled *posses comitatus* and marched on the anti-rent towns, where their men searched tenants' homes, harassed inhabitants, arrested suspects, and served landlords' writs. At the request of the Columbia County sheriff, William Bouck, the outgoing governor, called out the militia. The new Barnburner governor, Silas Wright, refused to address the tenants' grievances until their "lawless and passionate proceedings" ceased. Until that happened, he wrote, his sole responsibility was to enforce the laws "with vigilance and firmness." He therefore promised all necessary aid to lawmen in suppressing the Indians and called on the legislature to make the act of appearing armed and in disguise a felony. The legislature quickly complied.[39]

At this juncture, those anti-renters who opposed the Indians took action. Leading men in the anti-rent towns called meetings that condemned the "*violent attacks* and RIOTOUS PROCEEDINGS" of the vigilantes and called on all anti-renters to help the civil authorities "in bringing these *violators* of law . . . to punishment." In Columbia County, anti-renters gathered for public burnings of masks and calico. The state anti-rent convention followed suit, disavowing all connection with "lawless and reckless desperadoes."[40]

These anti-renters endorsed much of the reasoning of their Whig and Democratic allies. In part, they focused on the requirements of legislative strategy. "If such depredations are persisted in," a Sand Lake meeting warned, "we can expect no redress of our grievances. . . . With what grace and confidence *can* the friends of the tenants in the legislature present and advocate their claims?" On a deeper level, they denied the Indians' claim to represent "the People" and rejected their neighbors' faith in unfettered popular action. Genuine popular sovereignty, they declared, was possible only *within* the limits set by the constitution and the rule of law:

> Our government is a government of laws, constituted and emanating from the people, the legitimate source of delegated power and constitutional law; that law so made is the sovereign and supreme will of the land, and no individual or number of individuals have a right for their own purposes to resist or obstruct its execution—such obstruction with impunity establishes precedents for further violations, being dangerous in the extreme, and effecting in their consequences anarchy and the establishment of arbitrary and despotic power.[41]

The Indians rejected these calls to disband. As long as posses roamed their neighborhoods, they remained demobilized or appeared only at a safe distance from the lawmen. But as soon as the sheriffs sent their deputies home, the Indians reappeared, preventing evictions and distress sales, rescuing their arrested comrades, and punishing neighbors who cooperated with the landlords. Public support remained high. The work of the Schoharie county braves, one correspondent reported, "has been openly exulted in, and approved by many in this part of the county."[42]

The conflict over the Indians was rooted in conflicting notions of politics. To Indians and their supporters, existing laws were not the embodiment of the People's will but the product of a conspiracy between landlords and politicians to perpetuate the former's unnatural power over tenants. The eagerness of county and state officials to crush the anti-rent movement demonstrated that this conspiracy extended to the suppression of civil liberties:

> Freemen, arouse! These impish lords have caused
> The guardians of your rights, to stain your laws,
> (Which should be free and equal unto all,)
> With *damning blots,* of special legislation—
> 'To hold fair justice' scales with partial hand,
> And make it a *crime,* for you, to *speak* your wrongs,
> Or nobly to repel them![43]

Under such circumstances, many argued, the Indians were the natural heirs to the Sons of Liberty—defenders of the People's liberty and "a natural, and necessary consequence of the wrong perpetuated upon the farmers, and attempted to be enforced by law."[44]

Most importantly, the braves refused to disband because the anti-renters' legislative strategy alone could not achieve their most cherished goal: the protection of specific kin and neighbors. A band of Rensselaer County vigilantes "declared in the most violent manner that they should . . . prevent any arrests of their friends from being made until such time as the Legislature shall act in the matter. . . . The Indians swear that they will not allow their friends to be 'picked off.'" Similarly, Yellow Jacket, an Albany County chief, affirmed his tribe's "determination to watch over and protect the people of these counties, . . . *penal laws to the contrary notwithstanding.*" Their determination marked the final confrontation between the parliamentary, legalist, and universalist tradition embodied in the party system and the defensive, localist, and personalist tradition of crowd actions and the skimeton.[45]

The braves could not win. The support of the governor and of an outraged citizenry outside the estates emboldened lawmen in Columbia and Delaware Counties to serve legal process and pursue Indians with increasing vigor. These lawmen learned that, for all their threats, the braves carefully avoided bloodshed. Where once they had given up their legal papers and gone home or had allowed themselves to be tarred and feathered, now they fought back. In response, the Delaware and Columbia County Indians assembled in larger groups and began using their rifles. Most fired over the heads of their enemies or into the ground before their feet, but some were less restrained. At an eviction in Tagkhanic, Columbia County braves peppered Deputy Sheriff Sedgwick and Hudson Constable John Travers with buckshot, ripping Sedgwick's clothing and wounding Travers in the head and arm. Each confrontation contained increasing danger of a lethal outcome.[46]

That outcome arrived on August 7, when Delaware County Sheriff More and a handful of deputies conducted a distress sale at the Andes farm of Moses Earle. Between 100 and 200 Indians attended. The sheriff tried to move Earle's cattle into a clearing to begin the sale, but the Indians surrounded the cattle and blocked the gate to Earle's farm, preventing prospective bidders from entering. On earlier occasions this resistance would have convinced the sheriff to call off the sale. But deputy sheriff Osman Steele decided to call the Indians' bluff. On horseback, he and Delhi constable Erastus Edgerton jumped the gates to Earle's farm and rode into the midst of the tribe, guns leveled at the braves. A chief ordered his men to shoot the horses, and the braves fired two volleys. Their bullets killed the horses. Intentionally or not, three shots also hit Steele. The deputy died that evening.[47]

The repression that followed the killing of Steele quickly outstripped anything that had preceded it. Sheriff More called together a posse of 500 men and went in search of those responsible for Steele's death. "Indignation meetings" were held throughout the county, and Democratic editors throughout the state called for the execution of Steele's killers. On August 27, Governor Wright declared Delaware, Columbia, and Schoharie Counties in a state of rebellion. Troops and posses combed the anti-rent towns for suspects, using information from local spies to track down their quarry. In the process, they adopted something like the Indians' tactics of intimidation. They broke into houses and barns, harassed and shot at local anti-rent sympathizers, and broke down the fences and destroyed the crops of association members.

Figure 6.4. The death of Deputy Sheriff Osman Steele at the hands of the anti-rent "Indians." This print was based on the testimony of "up–rent" witnesses. Steele is on the rearing horse, center right. Steele's killing led Governor Wright to declare three anti–rent counties in a state of rebellion; the arrests and intimidation that followed led to the permanent demobilization of the Indians. Courtesy of the New York State Museum, Albany, NY.

Many of those arrested were promised a death sentence and, under pressure from the sheriff, the district attorney, and their own lawyers, pled guilty and named other braves. In Delaware County alone, almost 250 were indicted for murder, robbery, riot, or appearing armed and disguised; 84 were convicted. Twelve men pled guilty to manslaughter and received life sentences. Two chiefs, John Van Steenberg and Edward O'Connor, were convicted of murder and sentenced to hang.[48]

The effect on the leasehold towns of Delaware County was devastating; the impact on the Indians, permanent. "Whole neighborhoods" were stripped of their young men, as those who were not arrested went into hiding or fled across the Pennsylvania border. "The farms are abandoned, . . . the ordinary intercourse of business and society broken up." Landlords quickly began dunning tenants, issuing eviction notices, and holding sheriff's sales. Once again, the anti-rent associations called for the disbandment of the Indians. This time they succeeded; the Indians never regrouped. Crowd actions ceased to be part of the anti-renters' political arsenal.[49]

"The People" against
the Parties

While it ended open resistance to the laws, the repression of the Indians convinced a growing number of anti-renters that their political system was in crisis. As they saw it, the People had awakened to a galling wrong in their society and had demanded redress of that wrong; the People's representatives, rather than bowing to their masters' will, "refused to give them any aid" and "thrust them into prison." The reason was simple: wealthy landlords and mercenary politicians had forged a corrupt alliance. As "C" saw it, "*money* is felt at the ballot box . . . . Officers, whose business it is to watch over the liberties of their constituents, will not dare to act contrary to the will of the landed aristocracy, for fear its influence, will not *return* them, to their cherished place of office." These specific grievances led to a more systemic and wide-ranging attack on the Jacksonian political system. All anti-renters celebrated and wished to extend one of the accomplishments of the Jacksonian Revolution—the opening of the electoral process to mass participation by white males. But many saw its other innovations as hindrances to genuine popular sovereignty. The most important of these was the domination of public life by a special class of political leaders. A Delaware county correspondent wrote that "the people" had long been held "in bondage" by "office-holding aristocrats"; he hoped that an anti-rent political victory would cast these politicians from power, allowing the people to "govern themselves."[50]

In voicing this complaint, leasehold militants overlooked the frequent rotation in office that marked the Jacksonian political order. While misdiagnosed, their concern with a political "aristocracy" spoke to real grievances. One such grievance was the disproportionate political influence of wealthy men, and especially of lawyers. Men of wealth, many tenants worried, had come to dominate legislative halls, allowing them "to control and rule us" and to "make laws to suit themselves." So too had lawyers come to monopolize positions of political power, allowing them to draft "abstruse, dark, blind, and unintelligible" laws in order to force people to depend on their expertise. Current lawmaking, many anti-renters believed, was little short of a conspiracy among lawyers to "relieve" the farmer "of his purse."[51]

Another grievance was the power of party leaders to hoodwink voters and stifle democratic discussion, a power that anti-renters traced to partisan enthusiasm and party discipline. "When a few mercenary demagogues, who, having the advantage . . . of a press, have raised the name of an individual for office, and declared him to be an honest, patriotic, intelligent democrat, or whig," S. Ingraham wrote, "the people have always shouted amen to *their* choice." Once in office, these leaders "deceived and misrepresented" the people. Blinded by partisan passion and pinioned by their leaders' insistence on party discipline, the people had allowed those leaders to "act over and over again . . . the same infamous farce of deception."[52]

In borrowing the Whigs' and Democrats' anti-incumbent rhetoric, some militants probably emulated their teachers' cynical use of that rhetoric. But for many, the attack on "office-holding aristocrats" seems to have been genuine. While Whigs and Democrats often cast about for the flimsiest examples of "aristocratic" behavior on the part of their opponents, the political abuses of which the anti-renters complained were directly tied to the central concerns of their movement. Moreover, leasehold militants called for ending these evils not only by bringing their own party to power, but also by enacting a number of reforms: limits on the number of terms an individual could serve in office, abolition of patronage posts, enforcement of binding instructions between constituents and representatives, and elevating plain farmers and mechanics to office. Finally, many insurgents sought to put their rhetoric into action and, in the face of formidable political odds, sought to cut their ties to the major parties. Anti-renters expressed an almost millennial faith that their movement might purify politics, winning in practice the sovereignty and equal laws that party leaders had promised them.[53]

The spring elections of 1845 convinced many that this goal was achievable. Anti-renters in Albany, Schoharie, and Rensselaer Counties fielded independent slates for every post, from fence viewer to town supervisor, and won in a landslide. The victory extended to the valley municipalities of Albany and Rensselaer counties, where voters had repudiated anti-rent candidates only five months before. In most localities, the Democrats and Whigs, overwhelmed by the outburst of anti-rent enthusiasm and by the defection of their usual activists to insurgents' ranks, declined to nominate any candidates at all. This victory convinced many insurgents that they were on the verge of a seismic change in politics. Surveying the results of the Rensselaer County elections, Thomas Devyr exulted, "The terms 'Democratic' and 'Whig' are . . . passing into the dead languages. . . . Patroonery is virtually dead, and it only remains for the good and wise of all parties to becomingly compose its limbs and give it a decent sepulcher."[54]

Along with the repression of the Indians, this victory convinced many anti-renters that cutting their ties to the major parties was both necessary and possible. As the fall campaign approached, the advocates of third-party politics came into conflict with insurgents who wished to strengthen their alliances with the Hunkers and Liberal Whigs. In Albany County, the anti-renters struck a compact with the Hunkers. Breaking with the previous year's practice, the county executive committee voted to hold its nominating convention three days *after* that of the Democrats, which would allow them to choose from among the Democratic nominees. Meanwhile, Democratic anti-renters in Bern and Rensselaerville appointed delegations to the party's convention. When the Jacksonians' meeting was held, the new Hunker anti-rent coalition controlled the floor and pushed through the nomination of Robert Watson and Thomas L. Shafer, a Bethlehem anti-rent activist.

This new arrangement proved controversial in both the Democratic and anti-rent camps. The anti-rent towns of Knox and Westerlo boycotted the

Democratic convention, while the Barnburners called a separate meeting, where they dropped Watson from the ticket and replaced him with Dudley Burwell, a Barnburner and an opponent of the anti-renters. Despite this opposition, the anti-rent convention placed Watson and Shafer on their ticket. The convention then unanimously renominated Ira Harris, who had proved loyal to the tenants' legislative program and was sure to win a place on the Whigs' ticket.[55]

Despite Barnburner opposition and divisions in their own ranks, the Albany militants' new strategy proved a major success. In the Helderbergs, the anti-rent nominees beat their nearest competitor by a margin of twenty to one, while residents of the valley manor towns gave the ticket two-thirds of their votes. Even in Albany city, the anti-renters won hundreds of votes, weakening the major parties' lock on the city electorate.[56] By choosing among the candidates of the major parties, the Albany insurgents guaranteed their success and opened the possibility of a fundamental shift in electoral allegiances in their county. But their success came at a cost: Albany militants limited themselves to candidates who were acceptable to party leaders and non-anti-rent voters—and who consequently fought to contain some of the militants' demands and political practice.

Rensselaer County insurgents rejected such a compromising alliance with the parties. The anti-renters of Sand Lake declared that "the existing parties" had refused "to act successfully upon the causes that have so long agitated this country, and now gnaws like a canker-worm, at the root of the tree of liberty." In doing so, they "have already forfeited all claims upon a free and independent people." Sentiments like these prevailed at the county nominating convention, where delegates refused to renominate Henry Z. Hayner, a tenants' lawyer, for the assembly on the grounds that he had been "previously nominated by the whig party." Rensselaer County militants marched into the fall campaign with a fully independent ticket—and lost. The entire Whig slate prevailed in November; not a single anti-rent candidate won office.[57]

In Delaware County, too, anti-renters sought not to make alliances with the existing party organizations, but to crush them. But here they were successful. Ironically, the repression of the Indians strengthened the anti-rent political movement. Increasing numbers of estate residents came to agree that "there is at Delhi, a base clique of godless and corrupting politicians, . . . who are striving to make political capital out of the death of Steele, to attain their own sordid and damnable ends."[58] To topple this clique, they needed to win the support of nontenants, many of whom feared and hated the anti-renters as outlaws. Their opportunity came in October. As in most other counties, Delaware County Democrats divided the slots on their electoral slate between the county seat and outlying towns. Normally, delegates from Delhi and the towns caucused separately to fill their slots on the ticket; the choice of these caucuses was then ratified by the full convention. In their determination to destroy the tenants' movement, however, Barnburner leaders in Delhi secretly drew up a slate of "law and order" candidates from every town and rammed it through the county convention.[59]

This action sparked the rural delegates' long-simmering resentment of the Delhi Regency's control of county politics. Anti-rent sympathizers immediately bolted the meeting, called an "Equal Rights" convention, and began organizing support in the freehold towns for an independent political campaign. On October 16, delegates from 13 of the county's 18 towns met, including all of the anti-rent towns and 6 of the 11 towns where no strong movement existed. The delegates made clear that their main aim was to topple the Delhi Regency, not to abolish the leasehold system. The recent Democratic convention, they declared, had "violated every principle of democracy" by "totally disregarding the popular will of the county, and treading under foot the rights of the towns." As "citizens of independent towns in the county," they felt honor bound to "oppose this aristocratic distinction" and drive the clique from office. They remained silent regarding the anti-renters' conflict with the county's landlords.[60]

November brought what Delaware County residents had thought they would never see: a humiliating defeat for the Democrats. The county Whig and Democratic leadership "united in hostility to the 'Equal Rights' ticket," only to be swept aside. The anti-renters and their allies won by over 1,100 votes, carrying 12 of the county's 18 towns. Despite their party's silence on the leasehold issue, the result elated Delaware anti-renters. Their movement, they believed, would soon revolutionize politics, bestowing power upon a sovereign people. One activist predicted that once the Equal Rights party consolidated its victory, "Old Delaware will stand forth unchained and untrammeled by Law and Order office-holding Aristocrats, and the people who have been so long in bondage, will govern themselves."[61]

The anti-renters had good reason to celebrate: they had demonstrated formidable electoral power. They had won control over the governments of three counties and a significant voice in the legislature. But the disparate routes they had taken to achieve that power left their relationship to the parties unresolved. As a consequence, the ends to which they might use their power remained unsettled as well.

Tenants and Legislators, Again

The anti-renters' new political power and the limits to that power became apparent in the 1846 legislature. After the insurgents' victory in the 1845 elections, a majority of legislators proved willing to address their demands. But they once again shifted the terms of debate that the tenants had established, eschewing their unconstitutional demands and drawing out the latent individualist and entrepreneurial themes in their thinking. Their achievements, rather than eliciting euphoria from the tenants, brought forth anger and fears of betrayal.

The number of anti-rent legislators who entered the assembly and senate in January 1846 had grown from five to seven, and numerous other anti-rent activists claimed seats on the basis of Whig or Democratic nominations. More importantly, as Charles McCurdy has found, the recent election convinced Governor Wright that his reelection and the political survival of the "true Democracy" required that the Barnburners end their hostility to the anti-renters. In his annual message, he called on the legislature to enact two of the militants' long-standing demands: abolition of landlords' right of distress and taxation of landlords' rent income. He did not endorse the anti-renters' most cherished reform—a law allowing tenants to challenge their landlords' titles when prosecuted for rent—because it was unconstitutional. But on the advice of Martin Van Buren, he instructed Van Buren's son, Attorney General John Van Buren, to draft a bill that would allow tenants to buy their landlords' interest in their farms after the current proprietors died. On January 12, Bishop Perkins, Wright's spokesman in the assembly, introduced a series of resolutions that outlined the plan.[62]

A month later, the assembly appointed a committee to report on the issue. The committee included five Barnburners, including Samuel Tilden as chair; Ira Harris and his Whig ally John Young; and Reuben Lewis, a Delaware County anti-renter. The committee's report turned Harris's and Watson's fear that patroonery obstructed capitalist development into an article of bi-partisan consensus. "Industry and frugality," it declared, were stimulated by "a desire to escape incumbrance and attain independence"; by making the farms of tenants forever encumbered, the leasehold system smothered these virtues in the cradle. Worse still, lease restrictions on alienation obstructed "a free exchange of the lands"; they thus "tend to restrain labor from seek-ing, through shifting employments, its most advantageous application, and to repress the disposition, the habit, and the opportunities of enterprise."[63]

With the support of the Liberal Whigs and both factions of the Democrats, the committee submitted bills to abolish the right of distress and to tax land-lords' rent income. But, like Governor Wright, it rejected the demand for a law allowing tenants to challenge their landlords' titles in court. Over Harris's objections, a majority of committee members declared that the bill would place an onerous burden of proof on leasehold proprietors. After hundreds of years of quiet possession, in which witnesses had died, original grants had turned to dust, and lines of succession had become obscured, few landowners would be able to meet the evidentiary standards of the law. "If this require-ment were applied to all landowners in the state," the committee wrote, "it may well be doubted whether many [titles] . . . could be sustained." In place of this law, the committee submitted Silas Wright's devise-and-descent bill. The legislation proposed to allow tenants, upon the death of their landlord, to buy the reservations on their farms for an amount which, at interest, would yield the value of the rent and services provided for in the lease. In addition, the law prohibited future agricultural leases whose terms exceeded 10 years.[64]

The committee's proposals decisively shifted the terms of debate that the tenants had established. The bills to amend the statutes of inheritance and to tax landlords' rent income applied only to lands leased for a period of more than 10 years. In defending this limitation, committee members argued that oppression lay not in the expropriation of the fruits of another's labor but in making the expropriation permanent. "The most objectionable feature" of the relations between landlord and tenant, they wrote, was that "they are perpetual." Short-term leases and sharecropping arrangements, on the other hand, were "more analogous to the management of an estate . . . through hired agents or assistants"; as such, the owner's supervision ensured that the land would be improved. More importantly, short leases were adapted "to the peculiar and temporary circumstances of the parties"; as such, they "no doubt exist beneficially." The relationship of landlord and tenant, employer and employee, was not in itself oppressive; what saved it from being so was the promise of social mobility.[65]

Backed by the electoral power of the anti-renters and the support of both parties' leadership, all three bills passed the assembly. The senate concurred in the distress and taxation bills, and Governor Wright signed them both. But the devise-and-descent bill died in committee. This partial victory demonstrated the broad bipartisan support that the anti-renters had won. But it also revealed the tension that their movement was stirring up in both parties. Although the distress and tax bills met with little opposition in the assembly, a fifth of the Democrats and a third of the Whigs in the lower house opposed the buyout bill. In the senate, 2 out of 5 Whigs and 8 out of 21 Democrats opposed the distress and buyout bills.[66]

Here was evidence of how far the anti-renters had come since 1844—and an indication of the corrosive impact of their success on both parties. Only two years before, the legislature had brusquely rebuffed the tenants' demands for government action in the leasehold conflict. Now it put the government into action on their behalf, outlawing one of the landlords' most hated practices and taxing their rent income. In addition, a majority of both parties in the assembly had endorsed a far more momentous use of the state: the outright abolition of the leasehold system.

Leasehold militants, however, were less inclined to marvel at the power they had won than to bemoan the legislature's failure to meet their demands in full. The laws to tax rents and to abolish distress accomplished their least urgent goals. Nor were they encouraged by the assembly's passage of Wright's buyout scheme. Since 1840, anti-renters everywhere had made clear that they would buy their farms only after the landlords had proven title. They believed that both houses' refusal to allow such a test to take place only proved their corruption. The Tilden committee's defense of laws barring challenges to ancient titles, one local leader wrote, was "a specimen of honesty and morals that should make the critic blush." The farmers, he wrote, "hold that morals and honesty consists in doing right, and disapproving of every thing that is wrong; and wherever wrong exists, that it should be always corrected. The doctrines taught and approved by *some of the readers of Blackstone now filling high places* that fraud, corruption, sin and iniquity should become venerable on account of its age, and acknowledged to be the law of the land, finds no response in an American bosom."[67]

Some anti-renters also objected to the legislature's decision to limit the application of its tax law to leases of more than 10 years' duration. John Bowdish, writing "on behalf of the tenants of Montgomery," complained that lands leased for one or a few years were more, not less, onerous than those held under long leases. In his county, rents were "enormous" and continued to rise every time a contract expired. As a result, the wealth created by "the labor of those who reside here" was drawn off to enrich men in distant parts of the state. "Those communities which suffer the most by paying enormous rents," he argued, "should at least be benefitted by the advantages to be derived from the tax assessed on the landlord." Although Bowdish simply asked for equity in a specific law, his reasoning challenged the Tilden committee's assertion that class subordination was oppressive only when permanent.[68]

Nothing, however, matched the anti-renters' anger at the distress bill. Distress was not the only remedy at landlords' disposal when dealing with recalcitrant tenants; all leases gave proprietors the right to eject those tenants who failed to perform their part of the bargain. To win the support of undecided legislators, the Tilden committee had included a clause confirming the right of reentry in its distress bill. The senate later added an amendment that simplified the procedure by which the landlords could reenter, and the assembly agreed. With this amendment, the bill actually tipped the balance of legal power slightly toward the landlords. Kosciuszko Armstrong, heir to leasehold lands in Dutchess and Delaware Counties, told his brother that he was not bothered by the abolition of distress; the bill, he wrote, "simplifies the proceedings, and so far, is of benefit to the landlords."[69]

That an ostensibly anti-rent law should end up helping the landlords was bad enough. Alexander Johnson, a Whig who had recently cast his lot with the anti-renters, made matters worse. In an editorial in the *Albany Freeholder*, Johnson mistakenly declared that the new law did away with the requirement that the landlords prove nonpayment of rent; now, he said, landlords could eject tenants without going to court. Moreover, he declared that landlords were preparing to take quick advantage of the law. "A shower of notices," he predicted, "will fall upon the whole Anti-Rent district." Despite this imminent threat to their security, Johnson, like his Whig and Democratic colleagues in the movement, urged the tenants to maintain "peace and good order and a quiet submission to the laws."[70]

The new law and Johnson's inflammatory editorial created "panic" in the leasehold district. Tenants, having learned to distrust men loyal to the major parties, began to feel that their own leaders had betrayed them. One found it "exceedingly singular" that "this very objectionable section" had been examined for so long by anti-rent legislators "without being objected to as a section entirely unasked for by the tenants!" Thomas Devyr, who was now openly feuding with Whig and Democratic anti-renters, sharpened this discontent:

"This, it strikes me, is helping one's friends with a vengeance! And where, let me ask, was the bravery, acumen, and watchful jealousy of a Van Schoonhaven, a Harris, a Hayner, a Watson, a Smith, and the sundry other valiant gentlemen who so affected to have the interests of the Manor tenants at heart?" To quiet the anti-renters' outrage, Ira Harris began an emergency speaking tour of the anti-rent towns, telling audiences that "*all the provisions* of said law are wise and salutary" and that "the tenants have nothing to fear from the operation of the law."[71]

Harris's efforts had their intended effect: the immediate panic of most tenants was allayed. But the deeper problem remained. The legislature failed to act as the tenants expected it to—as an extension of their collective will. As long as this was the case, anti-renters would continue to look upon the actions of their political leaders with deep distrust.

Reforming Organic Law

Anti-renters had another chance to reform the state's land system: the constitutional convention of 1846. Here, their options were more extensive than in the legislature. The convention could not allow tenants to challenge their landlords' titles in court, for that was barred by the federal courts. But it could empower the government to seize leasehold estates through eminent domain. Perhaps because the recent defeat of Silas Wright's devise-and-descent bill convinced them that any form of state expropriation of landlords' estates was doomed to defeat, however, the anti-renters' Whig and Democratic allies made no plans to present a land-reform program to the convention.[72]

Thomas Devyr, however, saw in the upcoming convention an opportunity both to engraft land reform on the state's organic law and to cement an electoral alliance between the anti-renters and the National Reformers. In May 1845, shortly after voters had approved a convention, he called for constitutional reform aimed at "regulating LAND MONOPOLY—of moderating down land ownership to a scale that will prevent it from being able to eat up and exterminate the liberties of the country." To ensure that this reform be properly advocated, he urged anti-renters to elect National Reformers as delegates. A month later, George Henry Evans published a detailed proposal for constitutional reform in *Young America,* the National Reformer's official journal. Evans called for limiting all future acquisitions of land to 160 acres or one city lot; prohibiting the sale of land to anyone who already owned land; and requiring that corporations divest themselves of all land except the lots occupied by their businesses. In addition, he proposed a special commission to oversee the breakup of leasehold estates, determining "on principles of *equity,* what (or whether any) compensation shall be paid to the claimant in full extinguishment of his claim." With Evans's proposals in mind, Devyr called for a new monthly convention of anti-renters to determine their strategy for "final emancipation."[73]

Devyr's efforts were a direct challenge to the tenants' Whig and Democratic allies, and they opened the way to bitter factional conflict.[74] Hoping to head off anti-rent endorsement of Devyr's "agrarian" program, Harris, Watson, and their allies sought to prevent the anti-renters from nominating delegates or advocating specific constitutional provisions. But militants in five counties held conventions, nominated delegates, and proposed reforms. Columbia County tenants demanded that the convention "annihilate feudal tenures," while Montgomery County insurgents called for the annulment of all existing leases and the transfer of ownership to the current occupants of the land. A handful of individuals and local meetings publicly endorsed the National Reformers' call for a constitutional limit on individual landholdings. So did Horace Greeley, the Whig editor of the *New York Tribune* and a recent convert to National Reform.[75]

Leasehold militants sent eleven delegates to the constitutional convention, most of them indifferent to Evans's agenda for constitutional reform. But Horace Willard, an anti-rent delegate from Albany County, proposed "forbidding all future accumulation of the soil to exceed 320 acres per man; and to provide some equitable mode for the gradual reduction of the present landed monopolies." With a growing clamor for action from the leasehold district, the anti-renters' Whig and Democratic allies abandoned their efforts to keep land reform out of the convention. But with hostility to confiscation schemes growing in both parties and with their devotion to private property intact, there was little they were willing to do. The Committee on the Creation and Division of Estates in Land, which included Ira Harris and George Clyde, a Columbia County Democratic anti-renter, ignored Willard's proposal. Its report instead recommended the abolition of "all feudal tenures . . . with all their incidents." Since leasehold tenures were not legally feudal, the provision was an empty gesture. Harris explained that it would outlaw "certain incidents" to leases, like distress, which had already been abolished, and fealty, which no lease required. The committee also proposed to prohibit future leases lasting more than 10 years and to ban future restraints upon alienation in leases. Amendments quickly exempted present leases from the abolition of feudal tenures and extended the permissible length of leases to 12 years. The convention inserted the amended proposals into the new constitution.[76]

The *Albany Freeholder,* now under the editorship of Alexander Johnson, a Rensselaer County Whig, greeted the committee's report with enthusiasm. "This report places the whole subject in a nutshell," Johnson wrote. The proposed amendments "present all the anti-renters claim for." But the amendments were all prospective; they did nothing to address the grievances of current tenants. Indeed, the real accomplishment of the new provisions was ideological, not legal: they encoded into the state's organic law a new consensus that leasehold tenures had no place in a republic. Ira Harris admitted that "his only object . . . was to obtain for this body and the people a formal prohibition of this system, and to secure against it the moral influence of such a declaration, that the system was not congenial with our institutions, and ought to be eradicated from among us." Ambrose Jordan, a Whig and anti-rent delegate from Columbia County, agreed. "So far as these tenures could be brought into disrepute and yet preserve the faith of the state . . . and private rights, it should be done." Caught between the federal Constitution, their own dedication to private property in land, and many legislators' opposition to expropriation of leasehold lands, on the one hand, and the demands of their constituents, on the other, anti-rent leaders were left with little to do but make symbolic gestures.[77]

Devyr and his supporters excoriated what they saw as their representatives' timidity. "Vox Populi, Vox Dei" of Rensselaerville wrote that he expected "the sordid, the base, and the time-serving; the office holding, office seeking, and aristocratic" to deny the "'RIGHTS' *of each 'to his share of the raw materials God has created for the sustenance of our race'*"; but he claimed surprise that the anti-rent delegates, men of "supposed liberality of sentiment, patriotism, and discernment, can hesitate one moment to set about these reforms." Devyr ridiculed the liberal assumptions of the anti-rent delegates. Commenting on the convention's ban on future leases lasting more than 12 years, he directly challenged Whig and Democratic leaders' insistence that temporary class subordination was beneficent:

> Abolish this feudal tenure to-morrow, and substitute short tenures at the option of the landlord. Do this, and things will very quickly find themselves in a plight worse, by a thousand times, than they ever were. We . . . have seen the workings of the short lease, and . . . year-to-year systems in the old country. The negro slave is not in a position one quarter as bad as are those men who are ground down and enslaved by the short lease, or no lease system.[78]

These complaints had little impact on the outcome of the convention. In its land-reform provisions, the new constitution wrote the Whigs' and Democrats' liberal assumptions into organic law. Henceforth, the state's land policy would promote short leases, social mobility, and a free market in land. The constitution's broader political reforms did even more to promote a liberal economic order. Ironically, it did so largely by granting the popular democratic demands like those of the anti-renters. The document made virtually all administrators and judges subject to popular election. It also placed dramatic new curbs on the legislature's power to incur debt and pass special incorporations, thus fulfilling widespread demands for ending "special legislation." But it placed these reforms within a wider project of curbing the power of the state government to intervene in the economy. The result, worked out by legislatures over the next decade, was a newly liberal, laissez-faire order. As L. Ray Gunn writes, government intervention in the economy, once extensive and geared toward serving legislators' notions of the public good, became "a passive, supervisory, formalized system whose chief function was to provide a stable and predictable arena for the resolution of social and economic issues." In the process, power to shape the economy was transferred to private hands.[79] This new constitutional order greatly diminished insurgents' chances for winning new concessions from the legislature.

The anti-renters' first two years in electoral politics proved a paradox. Once the militants had proven their electoral clout, members of both political parties endorsed their vision of a society of freeholders and passed laws that at least nominally met their demands. But the tenants' political influence was heavily mediated. They were simultaneously unclear and divided concerning the implications of their social vision for property rights and the distribution of land, and their political leaders resolved that ambiguity in favor of their own constitutional scruples and commitment to the fundamentals of capitalist political economy. Just as dramatically, political leaders rejected the militants' definition of democracy, forcing them to replace their eclectic political practices with a strictly electoral and legislative approach. And in the electoral and legislative arenas, they laid the anti-renters' demands on a bed of Procrustean constitutionalism.

These triumphs and disappointments left the anti-renters more divided than when they had started. Although the conflict over the Indians was resolved, the questions about the proper limits to popular sovereignty that underlay that conflict were not. These divisions now surfaced in debates about the movement's relationship to the major parties. Moreover, the deep ideological and programmatic differences between the National Reformers and Whig and Democratic anti-renters remained unsettled. As the anti-renters sought to make sense out of their electoral victories, the demise of the Indians, and the fate of their demands in the legislature, these conflicts came to the forefront of the movement.

Chapter 7

"A RIGHT TO THE SOIL"

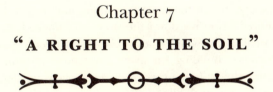

In May 1845, as Indians confronted posses and anti-renters began to prepare for the fall elections, Thomas Devyr broke into open conflict with the Whig and Hunker allies of the anti-renters. At stake in the struggle was the very meaning of the movement. The breach between Devyr and his opponents brought two unresolved disputes into the open: the proper basis of property in land (and thus the distribution of the soil) and the anti-renters' relationship to the major parties. The outcome of the conflict would determine whether the anti-renters would endorse the rules of capitalist political economy and the second party system, or seek to transform them. This conflict reinforced the lessons learned in the battle over the "Indians" and in the anti-renters' efforts in the legislature and the constitutional convention. Leasehold militants had learned that well-organized popular movements could win a measure of political power and could change policy and political discourse, but could do so only by being transformed themselves. The growing struggle over politics and property rights replicated that dialectic, changing both the anti-rent movement and the ideology and policies of the tenants' allies.

A Break in the Ranks

Thomas Devyr's campaign for land reform at the state constitutional convention and his open efforts to forge an electoral alliance between anti-renters and National Reformers ended his cooperation with the tenants' Whig and Democratic allies. Two months after he began his campaign, Robert Watson warned an audience of anti-renters against "agrarian, leveling doctrines." "The success of your cause . . . depends on the character of the papers that are your organs, and upon the men that you send to the legislative halls. . . . If either your papers or the organs of your sentiments assume extravagant, indefensible, unreasonable grounds, your cause is incalculably injured." Later that month, Charles F. Bouton, the Conservative Democratic publisher of the *Albany Freeholder,* fired Devyr as the paper's editor.[1]

Bouton's action sparked outrage in the anti-rent towns. Association leaders called a special convention, at which they protested the sacking of the Irishman and sought to buy the paper from Bouton. Bouton refused. For his part, Devyr moved his office down the street and opened the *Anti-Renter,* a newspaper dedicated to the tenants' cause and openly allied with the National Reformers. Building on many insurgents' growing distrust of the major parties, the Irishman carried on a vitriolic campaign against the "Freeholder gents"—a small clique of "political quacks" who, he warned, sought to take over the anti-rent movement and turn it into a vehicle to advance their careers. At the same time, the New York City National Reformers sent Alvan Bovay on a lecture tour of the leasehold district. Bovay addressed more than 5,000 anti-renters in four counties, winning enthusiastic support for the National Reform program wherever he went. For their part, Harris, Watson, and their allies worked to discredit Devyr and the National Reformers and to limit the anti-renters' energies to "abolishing legally and justly all feudal tenures."[2]

The controversy between Devyr and his rivals sparked extensive debates among local anti-rent leaders and the rank and file. "A.D.C.," a National Reform sympathizer from Delaware County, wrote in mid-1846 that "land monopoly is the all absorbing topic of discussion in almost all of our private and public assemblies." Jonathan Allaben, a Delaware County anti-rent assemblyman; John Evans, editor of Columbia County's *Equal Rights Advocate;* Calvin Pepper, the Albany County insurgents' lawyer; and Smith Boughton, the former Big Thunder and one of the most revered leaders of the movement, declared their allegiance to the cause of National Reform. So did scores of activists in the town and county anti-rent associations. These leaders proved critical in winning the rank and file over to the reformers' cause. Hundreds, perhaps thousands, of ordinary tenants became converts to National Reform. Devyr's new newspaper enjoyed a circulation of 2,000. Scores of letters poured into the offices of the *Anti-Renter* and *Young America,* endorsing the notion that each citizen had a natural right to land. Over a dozen local anti-rent associations held meetings to support the *Anti-Renter* and call for the freedom of the public lands. In the hill towns of Albany County, anti-rent activists created chapters of a new organization called the National Reform and Anti-Rent Vanguard Association, which merged the two movements into one.[3]

Other insurgents denounced their neighbors' attempts to meddle with existing property rights. Some followed Harris's and Watson's belief that property in land was the reward to successful labor. According to "William Tell" of Rensselaer County, the majority of anti-renters supported the right of a man to hold any amount of property "accumulated through his own honest industry." Most, however, gave no theoretical defense of their beliefs and saw no reason to do so. That land was a commodity was simply common sense; to challenge this belief was outside the bounds of civilized discourse. Thus "Clermont" of Columbia County insisted that although large landed estates "tend . . . to make the many . . . serfs and vassals of the few," the tenants "do not ask for a division of the lands. They say if the lords do, in fact, *own* the lands they claim, they alone have a right to dispose of them."[4]

This defense of private property did not result from the Whigs' and Democrats' success in winning the hearts and minds of tenants. Not a single rank-and-file anti-renter or local leader publicly endorsed Harris's and Watson's belief that economic competition and social mobility would guarantee widespread access to land—despite the fact that this belief reflected many tenants' own experience. Indeed, many insurgents ignored the arguments of Whigs, Democrats, and National Reformers alike and defended their own notions of property. Estate lands, all tenants agreed, owed all their value to the improvements created by tenants. Many argued that if the landlords' titles were legally valid, the tenants should buy them out, but should pay only the value of the lands in their unimproved state.[5] The vast majority of anti-renters, however, refused to enter into this divisive debate. Instead, they insisted only that the landlords' titles were fraudulent and should be investigated. In doing so, they implicitly endorsed existing definitions of property.[6]

Embedded in the polemics over the nature of property rights was another, equally important dispute—one over how to ensure equality. No anti-renter advocated an absolute equality of wealth, even among male householders. All knew from experience that some producers were more talented and industrious than others. All wished to create a society in which "equal chances" prevailed—in which each man reaped the full, and unequal, fruits of his own exertion and ingenuity, along with the unacknowledged proceeds of his wife's and children's work. Tenants like "William Tell" believed that equal chances were best served by treating land as a commodity; if land were accumulated only through "honest industry," its distribution would accurately reflect the differences in talent and industriousness within each community. Supporters of the National Reformers, on the other hand, insisted that property in land destroyed equality of opportunity. "Experience" of Columbia County argued that while equal laws "allow all, by their own honest exertion, to acquire as much wealth as they can, from the products of labor, they should not allow the more wealthy to seize and draw to themselves the main sources of such products. Land is the life blood of the community, and therefore, is the natural inheritance of every individual." By defending the "natural right" of all to the "use" of the land, government would "make the success of the *rich,* as well as of the poor, depend upon their own exertions, and not upon partial and unjust laws."[7]

Devyr and the National Reformers found support wherever the anti-rent movement was strong and the radicals had won the backing of local leaders. Support was strong in the hill towns of four counties: Albany, Rensselaer, Delaware, and Columbia. These were four of the five counties where the movement was most powerful; in each of these counties, prominent leaders cast their lot with Devyr and his allies. In Schoharie county, where the anti-renters were strong but local leaders opposed the radicals, the campaign to unite the two movements made little headway. Areas of lukewarm anti-rentism displayed a similar lack of enthusiasm for Devyr and his allies. Support was greatest in Albany and Rensselaer Counties, where Devyr had cultivated a close relationship with tenants and where the majority of the subscribers to the *Albany Freeholder* resided.[8]

No community was unanimous in supporting the National Reformers, however. Where radicals gained a foothold, their warfare with Whig and Democratic spokesmen split the anti-rent leadership and placed members of the same class in opposing camps. Most Albany County anti-rent activists who sided with Devyr and the National Reformers were drawn from the regular leadership of the anti-rent associations. Of the 33 supporters who could be identified, 26, or 79 percent, had played a leading role in at least one regular association meeting. Over half had done so more than once, and at least a quarter served as officers in their local anti-rent associations. These men did not differ significantly in occupation, age, or landed wealth from those who opposed them. Like their rivals, they were mature, prosperous, property-owning heads of household. National Reform supporters tended to draw more heavily from the doctors and lawyers of the hill towns than did their adversaries, while Devyr's opponents appealed more to manufacturers. But the overall differences in the occupational makeup, wealth, and age of the two factions were statistically insignificant. (See Appendix, tables 15 and 16.) Rather than pitting class against class, the conflict over the nature of property and the distribution of land split the rural middle class and may have divided other classes as well.[9]

These divisions reveal much about the place that members of the rural middle class sought in the broader capitalist order. Leasehold residents had for 20 years or more sought to increase their market production, and many, if not all, celebrated their integration into a broader, diversified economy. But they divided bitterly over whether the rules of capitalist political economy should apply to the distribution of land. A majority believed that the rules of the market, when fairly applied, rewarded labor fairly; or they instinctively accepted those rules as common sense. A significant minority, however, challenged those rules. These radicals rejected neither markets nor diversified economic development; instead, they embraced a vision of development in which independent proprietorship was guaranteed as a natural right, not subject to the laws of the market. They revived, in a new form, the beliefs and aspirations of their frontier agrarian forbears.

If their relationship to the means of production did not influence anti-renters' factional loyalties, their partisan commitments probably did. The partisan makeup of those Albany County activists who did not support the National Reformers roughly matched that of their communities, with 60 percent supporting the Democrats. But 9 out of 10 who supported the National Reformers hailed from the party of Jackson (see Appendix, table 17). Because of the low number of National Reformers whose partisan loyalties are known, these figures should be interpreted with caution. But they accord with what we know about the National Reformers. As John Ashworth and Jonathan Earle have demonstrated, the National Reformers were heretical Democrats. They shared the radical Jacksonians' language and concern for producers' rights; most had at one point been loyal Democrats; and the majority supported the Barnburners' policies on banks, internal improvements, public debt, and government power. Moreover, many Democratic anti-renters blamed the campaign against Devyr on Ira Harris and the Whigs; they were convinced that their efforts were part of a Whig campaign to control the anti-rent movement. Most probably, the factional disputes among anti-renters marked not only a split in the rural middle class but among leasehold Democrats as well.[10]

Most anti-rent activists, however, refused to take sides in the struggle between Devyr and his rivals. L. W. Ryckman, a National Reform lecturer, wrote from a tour of Albany and Rensselaer counties that "I find no opposition to our principles, except from the Old Hunkers, and Commercial and Land speculators." Still, he found "a great unwillingness to agitate or discuss any thing outside of their local affairs." When broad principles and alliances threatened to divide their movement, most anti-renters stuck to immediate, unifying demands. And they fought their leaders' attempts to force them to choose sides. The anti-renters of North Blenheim made this clear when they declared that God had created the land for all humanity, then passed a resolution praising Ira Harris for his service to the anti-rent cause. From late 1845 on, anti-rent associations throughout the leasehold district called unity meetings, in which they forced their quarreling leaders to share the podium.[11]

In their political strategy, too, most tenants refused to accept the terms of debate proposed by their feuding leaders. Many National Reform sympathizers remained devoted to Ira Harris, ignoring Devyr's call to purge "political quacks" from the movement. Just as important, supporters of an alliance with the Whigs and Hunkers rejected their leaders' belief that anti-rent demands should be but one of many elements in the platforms of the major parties. No less than their National Reform rivals, these militants sought allies who would help create a new politics of the people, built on the ashes of the existing parties. In January 1846, "H.M.S.," a long-time Democratic activist and one of the architects of the Albany militants' alliance with the Hunkers, rose in the county Democratic convention to denounce his fellow Jacksonians' attempts to reunite the Conservative and Radical factions of "that old rotten party." He saw no point, he roared, in trying "to unite the pure, vital, virtuous Democracy of old Rensselaerville with that poisonous party, so deeply stained with modern aristocracy, to wit, the Barnburners of the city of Albany." The only hope for the republic, he argued, was to destroy both parties and unite the progressive elements of both. "I am sure the spirit of Seventy-Six still lives; and it only remains for our two great political parties to be sifted, and the virtuous part of both parties to unite their efforts to secure to ourselves equal rights, and to posterity a free soil."[12] Most anti-renters wanted to create a new kind of politics, but they wanted to control the content of that politics. And they wanted their leaders—Whigs, Hunkers, and National Reformers together—to lead them to it.

The Election of 1846

The three-way conflict among National Reformers, Whig and Hunker activists, and insurgent tenants reached crisis proportions in mid-1846, as all three groups prepared for the gubernatorial election. That spring and summer, local anti-rent meetings called for an early nominating convention and proclaimed their desire to nominate Ira Harris as the anti-rent candidate for governor. In this way, they hoped to retain an independent political organization, choose their own candidates, and have Harris lead their independent effort. For their part, Devyr and George Henry Evans published a call for a state convention of land reformers to make an independent nomination for governor. Through this convention, they hoped to turn their support among anti-renters into a formal political alliance.[13]

The tenants' Whig and Democratic allies discouraged both of these strategies. The proposed land reform ticket could destroy their alliance with the anti-renters, while an anti-rent nomination of Harris would exacerbate divisions among the Whigs. Although many Liberal Whigs wished to make Harris their standard-bearer, downstate Conservatives "raise[d] a mad-dog cry" over the prospect of his nomination. Horace Greeley predicted that Harris "could be elected out of sight if the *Whigs* would vote for him, but they won't. He would lose thousands all about, on account of the terrors of anti-rent." To avoid these dangers, the Whig and Democratic allies of the anti-renters urged their constituents to hold their conventions after those of the Whigs and Democrats and to choose their candidates from among the parties' nominees. "No party," Alexander Johnson warned his readers, "can be long sustained in this country, with but one idea for its basis; and but one measure for its object. But a body of men, comparatively few in numbers, may engraft a favorite measure upon one, or the other, of the two parties into which the people are inevitably divided . . . , and thus secure success for their cause."[14]

The National Reformers' overture and their rivals' response deepened the divisions in the movement. While many anti-renters wished to unite with the National Reformers, others feared that such an alliance would divide the rank and file and force their Whig and Democratic allies to abandon the movement. When John Evans, editor of the Columbia County *Equal Rights Advocate* and an enthusiastic National Reformer, discussed the proposed land reform convention with local militants, he found opinion hopelessly divided. He reluctantly concluded that an endorsement of the National Reformers should be avoided. Just as important, even the staunchest supporters of union were unwilling to subordinate their movement to that of the New York City reformers. When the land reform convention was held in August, some thirteen delegates from the manor towns of Albany County attended. These delegates endorsed the National Reform platform but angrily rebuffed the city men's efforts to nominate a ticket composed entirely of National Reformers. The convention adjourned without making a nomination.[15]

Despite this rejection of coalition, many were determined to bypass the Whig and Democratic organizations and name their own candidates. Antirenters in Rensselaer, Delaware and Columbia Counties held their county conventions before those of the Whig and Democratic parties and nominated independent slates. In Albany, too, where anti-renters had long cooperated with Hunkers and Liberal Whigs, leasehold militants called an early convention. But here, conflict between the advocates of continued cooperation and those who wished to cut their ties to the parties erupted into open conflict. The advocates of cooperation won control of the meeting and nominated a slate made up of the likely Whig and Democratic nominees. Once these nominations were made, the convention adjourned and most delegates left, expecting that the delegates to the state convention would be selected by meetings in the individual towns. The allies of Ira Harris, however, reconvened the meeting and named supporters of cooperation with the major parties as the county's delegates to the state convention.[16] This ruse outraged so many tenants that the county committee called a public meeting to reopen the nominations. That meeting was so chaotic that Calvin Pepper, a National Reform sympathizer, could not tell whether it had confirmed or set aside the nominations. Although he deplored the "abuses" that had taken place at the original convention, he urged his fellow anti-renters to support its delegates. Any efforts to appoint a new delegation, he warned, would "destroy the anti-rent party in this locality."[17]

Pepper's hopes for a return to unity were dashed at the anti-rent state convention. Under pressure from Harris, the state central committee called the convention after the Whigs and Democrats had made their nominations. The Democrats had renominated Silas Wright, whom most anti-renters still hated for his part in the repression of the Indians. The Whigs had passed over Ira Harris in favor of John Young, a Liberal member of the assembly from Livingston County. Young's record on anti-rent issues was mixed. In 1845, he had served on a legislative committee that had killed the bill to abolish distress for rent. But in 1846, he had served on the Tilden Committee, endorsing that committee's tax, distress, and devise-and-descent bills. Still, he remained opposed to allowing a court challenge to the landlords' titles. Thus the major candidates held exactly the same position on the leasehold controversy; both supported the tenants' least controversial demands and wished to destroy the leasehold system, but opposed doing so on the anti-renters' terms.[18]

When the anti-rent state convention gathered on October 6, a number of delegates arrived determined to nominate Ira Harris. But Harris had instructed an ally in the Albany delegation to inform the delegates that, if selected for governor, he would refuse the nomination. R.G. Dorr, a Columbia County Barnburner who had allied with the anti-renters, offered a resolution to make no nomination. Since neither party had nominated anyone satisfactory to the anti-renters, he argued, choosing either candidate would "have a direct tendency to separate and destroy the anti-rent organization, and divide its members into their former political and party associations." After extensive debate, Dorr's resolution was voted down. Another delegate proposed making any nomination provisional on the nominee's endorsing the anti-renters' legislative demands in writing; that too was defeated. After four hours of wrangling, the delegates voted for their nominee. Some National Reformers pressed for Henry Bradley, a Liberty party activist, who had promised to support the association's platform; several delegates endorsed Burton A. Thomas, president of the Rensselaer County association. Neither candidate had the votes. On the second ballot, the delegates selected John Young as the anti-rent standard-bearer. Immediately, 7 of the 36 delegates, all of them National Reformers or Barnburners, walked out.[19]

Sixteen days later, these bolters, now joined by several anti-renters, National Reformers, and Liberty Party activists, assembled at the Albany City Hall. National Reform leaders had long sought the support of political abolitionists. Over the years, they had won the endorsement of Gerrit Smith, a leading light in the Liberty Party, as well as of less prominent antislavery men like Calvin Pepper, the Albany County anti-renters' lawyer. Reformers in both camps saw such alliances as a way to expand the influence of their movements. Abolitionists like Smith and Pepper were also convinced by the National Reformers' contention that access to land was a natural right; they endorsed the NRA's program as an essential part of their struggle for human liberation. Now, land reformers, land-hungry farmers, and abolitionists forged their first political alliance—one that would be repeated in the following decade and a half.[20]

Once assembled, this new coalition dubbed itself the Free Soil party and forged a platform that appealed to the anti-renters' hopes of destroying both the leasehold system and the rule of professional politicians. At the same time, it sought to link these aims to broader land and labor reform. The delegates offered resolutions calling for the abrogation of all leasehold contracts, a homestead act, and an equalization of the rewards to labor. Calling on all honest patriots to reject the "humbuggery, conservatism, and demagoguism" of the Whigs and Democrats, the delegates nominated Lewis Masquerier, a New York City National Reformer, for governor and William Chaplin, an abolitionist, for lieutenant governor. Thomas Devyr and two long-time anti-rent activists, Thomas Shaffer and John J. Gallup, won the convention's nominations for the state legislature.[21]

The anti-renters' nomination of Young generated nearly as much dissension among the Whigs as it did among anti-renters. J. Watson Webb, editor of the New York *Courier and Enquirer*, denounced Young's support for the anti-rent bills during the previous legislative session as "the most bare-faced at-tempt at LEGISLATIVE ROBBERY—the most manifest outrage on vested rights, that has ever been brought forward in any civilized community." The anti-rent nomination, he exclaimed, was the result of a cabal among Liberals, who had long been conspiring to take over the party and ally it with various move-ments for radical reform. Worse still, this cabal had betrayed its party in the process. It had ensured that Hamilton Fish, a conservative, received the Whig nomination for lieutenant governor, knowing that he would be replaced by the Democratic candidate at the anti-rent convention. The Liberals, Webb charged, set Fish up as a "stool pigeon for John Young." With the support of the city's other Conservative journal, the *Express,* Webb pledged to lead New York City Whigs in a revolt against Young's nomination. A month before the election, Horace Greeley estimated that some 5,000 Whigs now opposed Young because of his alliance with the anti-renters.[22]

If National Reformers and Conservative Whigs were unhappy with elec-toral developments in 1846, leasehold militants had even less reason to cel-ebrate. Far from providing a vehicle for achieving political renewal, the Free-Soil party promised only to divide their movement further. Only 12 days remained between the convention and election day, and Devyr and his allies had precious little money or organization with which to campaign. Nor did they try very hard. The Irishman held only three public meetings before the election, and the *Anti-Renter* did not seriously promote the Free-Soil ticket. Instead, Devyr concentrated on wrecking the chances of the regular anti-rent nominees. Reiterating his charge that a clique of office-seekers was taking over the anti-rent movement for partisan purposes, he urged his readers to "'choke off' the Junto by killing off every man on its 'slate' at the ballot box." He also published letters and reports that openly supported Silas Wright and the Barnburner slate.[23]

If the Free-Soilers offered little hope for political renewal, the regular anti-rent slate did no better. With Conservatives outraged at his nomination by the anti-rent convention, John Young approached the leasehold issue with trepidation. Harris and other Whigs toured the estates, reading a written pledge from the nominee to pardon the convicted Delaware County Indians. But Young himself ignored all questions regarding his stance on the anti-renters' legislative demands. Addison Gardiner, the anti-rent nominee for lieutenant governor, kept even more distance from the militants. Although he described leasehold tenures as "inconsistent with the habits of our people and the spirit of our institutions," he did not accept the anti-rent nomination or promise support for the tenants' demands. The Democratic creed, he said, was sufficiently "catholic" to "embrace every reform demanded by the public good"; thus, he could not "consistently recognize the necessity of another and distinct political organization."[24]

Faced with this unhappy choice, most militants voted for the regular anti-rent nominees. In Albany, Columbia, Delaware, Rensselaer, and Schoharie Counties, Young and Gardiner won in a landslide, garnering between 56 and

86 percent of each county's vote. Between 1,000 and 3,000 voters in each of these counties—from 19 to 51 percent of the electorate—abandoned the tickets of the major parties, giving the anti-rent nominees enormous margins over their Whig and Democratic running mates. Voters in an additional four counties gave the ticket more modest majorities. These votes were sufficient to ensure a statewide victory for both Young and Gardiner. With the help of some 2,000 disgruntled Hunkers who abandoned Silas Wright for John Young, the anti-renters swept their ticket into office by over 11,000 votes. No less important, they sent 11 of their nominees to the assembly.[25]

In important ways, this was an enormous victory for the anti-renters. Militants could look forward to a serious and respectful hearing in the legislature and the governor's mansion. "We shall no longer be regarded as banditti," the *Freeholder* exulted. "We shall not be turned out of the halls of the Legislature by . . . some lickspittle of the landlords. . . . We shall have a patient and respectful hearing."[26]

But the victors had decisively defeated many anti-renters' efforts to revolutionize politics. Inspired just months before by the expectation that they could dictate the Whig nominee for governor, militants now admitted that their movement had become an appendage of the Whigs. Moreover, the only widely popular leader to endorse their desire for transforming politics suffered a humiliating defeat. The Free-Soil vote was so small that it was left out of the statewide tally; in Albany County, where support for the National Reformers was as strong as anywhere, the ticket garnered fewer than one hundred votes. In early December, Devyr, despairing and indebted, closed the doors of the *Anti-Renter* and returned to his former home in Williamsburg.[27]

Toward a Homestead Act

If the conflicts of 1845 and 1846 transformed the political landscape in which ordinary tenants acted, so too did they change the terrain on which their Whig and Democratic allies stood. For all their success in defeating Devyr in convention and at the polls, Watson, Harris, and their allies could not contain the growing appeal of his ideas. To win the support of tenants who had been convinced that they had a natural right to land, they began to adopt the National Reformers' rhetoric and part of their program. In December 1845, Alexander Johnson published a Devyr-like denunciation of land monopoly as "the fruitful cause of most of the inequalities and one-half at least of the crimes of society." The concentration of landownership, he wrote, created vast inequalities of power that would result in "aristocracy, . . . a national faith, . . . a theocracy, . . . and . . . monarchy." To avoid this fate, Johnson proposed a modified version of the National Reformers' central demand: a homestead act. He called for the public lands to be distributed in small lots to actual settlers, at a price that would cover the costs of surveying. By focusing exclusively on the public lands, he avoided the implications of his condemnation of land monopoly for lands that were already owned. Instead, he endorsed a truncated version of the National Reformers' creed: that "man has a certain 'inalienable right,' not only to 'life, liberty, and the pursuit of happiness,' but also to a sufficiency of the common elements, by God created *and not already appropriated* to render the first inalienable right, operative and palpable."[28]

Other Whig and Democratic allies soon followed Johnson's example. Joseph Babcock, who, like Johnson, had replaced an anti-rent editor fired for his National Reform sympathies, began his career at the *Equal Rights Advocate* of Columbia County with no interest in the National Reformers' program. But within a month of his taking the editor's chair, he, too, declared that "no man should possess . . . more of the surface [of the earth] than is requisite, by the application of his labor, to satisfy his own and his dependents' real and substantial wants." Like Johnson, Babcock ignored the implications of his new philosophy, disavowing any support for "a direct division of property." Instead, he called for distributing the public lands to actual settlers, at graduated rates that would permit poor husbandmen to receive free farms. In late 1845 and 1846, this line of reasoning swept through the ranks of Whig and Democratic anti-rent leaders. Robert Watson, Ira Harris, and several others embraced the policy of free (or nearly free) distribution of the public lands, in limited quantities, to actual settlers.[29]

Here was a brilliant innovation. In a short period, men like Johnson, Harris, and Babcock endorsed many tenants' commitment to the principle that each man had "a natural right to land" and made it safe for vested rights and for capitalism. They did so by placing the existing distribution of land out of the bounds of discussion and by focusing their constituents' attention on the public lands. Dividing these lands among working farmers would infringe upon nobody's property rights—except for those of Indians, who, as every anti-renter knew, were destined to disappear at the approach of white settlers. Thus a cross-class racist consensus allowed innovative politicians to use the myth of an "open" West to redirect and contain producers' radicalism. Whig and Democratic leaders also abandoned the National Reformers' insistence that the plots given to settlers be made inalienable and that no settler on the public lands be allowed to own more than 160 acres. The "Democracy of freeholders" that Johnson and his allies envisioned had room for the unlimited accumulation of land.[30]

Men like Johnson and Harris also made critical concessions to their constituents' faith in popular sovereignty and a higher law. They did so not by endorsing autonomous popular action, but by stressing the right and duty of the government to serve the public interest. Where once he had cautioned the tenants that the legislature could not abrogate contracts or disturb the rights of property, now Alexander Johnson denounced as "absurd and preposterous" the notion that "the Legislature is bound to enforce strictly all contracts between individuals, however contrary to the spirit of our institutions, or injurious to the public interests." The editor now endorsed a vision of a powerful, utilitarian state, guided by the interests and sensibilities of the people. "It is contrary to the interests of any commonwealth, to protect or cherish a system that disparages, wrongs, or ignominiously offends, any class of its citizens," he wrote. In order to remedy these wrongs, "the legislative power of any state may proceed to repeal any law, or annul any contract, which is contrary to the spirit and object of its institutions and government."[31]

Such a vision was not entirely new. The Whig legislators of 1840 had endorsed the notion that the legislature could destroy systems of property and labor that violated public policy. But unlike those legislators, Johnson called for state action to enact the demands explicitly made by the anti-renters. And he counted among the wrongs which such a state should remedy an "offense" to the sensibilities of its citizens. William Van Schoonhaven, a Whig anti-rent state senator, implicitly endorsed Johnson's reasoning. After the Tilden committee rejected the anti-renter's title-test bill because it would abrogate vested rights and legal precedents, he endorsed the tenants' belief that "neither equity nor morality would justify" a failure to pass such a law, "whatever may be said about expediency, established theory, or 'settled principles of law.'" In the face of their constituents' insistence that the government should be the extension of the will of the people, Johnson and Schoonhaven began to abandon their party's paternalist notion of the state. In the process, they began to explore the possibility that the government might serve as a powerful agent of the expressed will of the people.[32]

Johnson's and Schoonhaven's thinking revealed both the constraints and the creative power embedded in the relationship between party activists and their constituents. Both men had played a part in defeating the anti-renters' efforts to forge an independent political presence; their efforts ensured that to the extent that the voices of the anti-renters would be heard in the corridors of power, they would be heard in muted and distorted tones. But these men and their confederates became more radical in the process. They helped forge a new vision of free labor. They helped pioneer a new land policy that reflected (but could not fully enact) the anti-renters' dream of universal landownership and the National Reformers' belief that every citizen had a natural right to land. At the same time, they began to cobble together a new conception of a powerful state, responsive to the expressed will of the citizenry. Such ideas were embraced only by a minority in 1846. But they contained the seeds of broader change.

Chapter 8

FAST-FISH AND THE TEMPLE
OF THE PHILISTINES

These two laws touching Fast-Fish and Loose-Fish, I say, will, on
reflection, be found the fundamentals of all human jurisprudence;
for notwithstanding its complicated tracery of scripture, the
Temple of the Law, like the Temple of the Philistines, has but two
props to stand on.

Is it not a saying in everyone's mouth, Possession is half of the
law; that is, regardless of how the thing came into possession? But
often possession is the whole of the law. What are the sinews and
souls of Russian serfs and Republican slaves but Fast-Fish, whereof
possession is the whole of the law? What to the rapacious landlord
is the widow's last mite but a Fast-Fish? What is yonder undetected
villain's marble mansion with a door-plate for a waif; what is that
but a Fast-Fish?

Herman Melville, Moby-Dick (1851)

With these words, Herman Melville offered a painful insight
into the political economy of his era. The passage was first
published in 1851, shortly after the Compromise of 1850 ended a protracted
struggle over slavery and preserved a political climate in which the claim to
human property was insulated from political challenge. Regarding property
in human beings, the law of fast-fish was inviolable.[1]

Nor was Melville referring only to slavery. When he referred to "the rapacious landlord," he may have had the leasehold estates of his native New York
in mind, for it was upon the law of fast-fish that the tenants' movement finally
foundered. Between 1847 and the publication of *Moby Dick*, anti-renters
learned with dramatic finality the limits to popular power under the second
party system. For all their electoral power, they could not compel their government to abrogate the tangle of laws and legal rules that made landlords'

property inviolable. This failure bred profound disillusion with the political order. In combination with broader economic and cultural changes, it encouraged many to reexamine both their commitment to the anti-rent cause and their place in the emerging capitalist economy. From 1846 on, economic recovery and cultural change began to create new opportunities to resolve the leasehold conflict on an individual basis. In the face of political defeat, most tenants seized these opportunities. In the process, they simultaneously ended their movement and made their peace with the rules of capitalist political economy.

In defeat, however, the anti-renters transformed the world around them. In seeking individual solutions to the crisis, they ended not only the anti-rent movement, but the leasehold system as well. Just as important, they helped transform New York's political order. Melville's passage contained not just a description, but also a portent of change: like the Temple of the Philistines, a structure with only two props cannot stand. It was not the law that was at risk, however, but the party system through which lawmakers were chosen and organized. Here, again, the author doubtless referred to the slavery controversy, but perhaps not to that alone. Alongside abolitionists, antislavery politicians, and land reformers, New York's anti-renters and landlords helped undermine the stability of the second party system and assisted in laying the groundwork for a new political order.

A Radical Minority

The legislature of 1847 proved paradoxical for the anti-renters. On the one hand, their elected representatives proved more attentive to their demands and ideals than any previous spokesmen. On the other, those not directly elected by the anti-renters found their demands increasingly troubling. In the new laissez-faire political climate ushered in by the constitution of 1846, legislators were unwilling to sanction government action to abolish a system of class relations. The tenants' demand that the state facilitate their challenge to the landlords' titles ran afoul of one of the legislators' central aims: providing a stable and predictable environment for economic activity. Just as important, escalating political battles over slavery brought long-standing divisions in both parties to a point of crisis.[2] In their efforts to maintain unity, party leaders sought to silence the leasehold controversy. In this new context, the anti-rent movement became a political orphan.

Once in office, John Young showed no inclination to address the anti-renters' demands. He publicly denied having promised to pardon the jailed anti-rent "Indians," and his annual message to the legislature ignored demands for a law allowing tenants to test their landlords' titles.[3] The militants' representatives in the legislature, by contrast, campaigned vigorously to turn their constituents' demands into law. Early in the 1847 legislative session, anti-rent assemblymen reintroduced the title-test bill. They also offered four new measures that sought to allow tenants to buy out their landlords and to compel landlords to pay ejected tenants for their improvements. In doing so, they continued to grope toward a social vision that united the anti-renters' desire for universal landownership with a faith in a competitive market economy. And less than six months after the political demise of Thomas Devyr, they linked this effort not just to a campaign against the leasehold system, but to an attack on land monopoly. The bills were sent to the select committee on leasehold estates, which included five anti-rent legislators (one Democrat, four Whigs), and quickly won approval. The committee's report began with a broad attack on land monopoly. "Large tracts of land in a few hands," it wrote, were "a public evil," for they made "the cultivators of the earth" into "serfs or slaves" and caused "famine and oppression" throughout the world. Committee members sought to ensure a widespread distribution of land in a way that preserved individual property rights, upheld the constitution, and encouraged individual enterprise. "That surely is the wisest political economy," they wrote, "which interposes the fewest checks and hindrances to individual enterprise, but which directly promotes a wide and equable diffusion of property." Along with Whigs like Horace Greeley, urban "workie" Democrats like Mike Walsh and George Wilkes, and western politicians like Andrew Johnson, these legislators sought to appeal to agrarian radicals and land-hungry farmers. At the same time, they sought to use those radicals' critique of land monopoly to create a political economy that reconciled economic equality to the needs of a competitive market economy. And they did so in a bipartisan fashion: like earlier anti-rent legislators, they were creating a social vision that cut across party lines.[4]

The committee also made significant new concessions to anti-renters' desire for absolute popular sovereignty. Like the Whigs of the 1840 legislature and the bipartisan majority of the 1846 assembly, it confirmed the power of the state to abolish social relations that injured the public weal.[5] In doing so, the panel abandoned earlier Whig legislators' paternalist conception of the state in favor of a more democratic vision. Extending the ideas of Whig anti-renters like Alexander Johnson and William Van Schoonhaven, it linked its predecessors' state-centered utilitarianism to a new belief that policy should reflect the popular will. Committee members did not adopt the reasoning of the anti-renters. Instead, they argued that, whether valid or not, popular conceptions of justice should direct the action of the government, lest popular discontent create disorder. "A man unskilled in the deep and subtle reasoning upon which the principles of the common law . . . are based . . . cannot perceive why, if it can be shown that a grantor has really no title to give, and that his deed actually conveys none, the grantee should not be allowed to withhold the consideration." "In view of the present excitement," the committee argued, the "technical impediments" of the common law must give way to the anti-renters' sense of justice. In barring tenants' evidence against his title, "the landlord exercises a legal, abstract right; but circumstances affecting the public interests and peace, may render such exercise unwise and impolitic." In other words, ancient legal protections to vested rights must give way before popular conceptions of justice. In this formulation, the public good was no longer defined according to natural rights or transcendent justice, but according to a democratic, utilitarian calculus—the self-defined interests of the many.

> We have evidence that this leasehold tenure is felt as a grievance, by at least one-twelfth part of the population of this State. The tenants being by far the more numerous class, in whose well-being that of the community is more immediately concerned, their interests ought in this particular to preponderate over those of the landlords.
>
> It is a salutary rule, without which society and government could not exist, that the interests of the few must yield to the public interest. A private evil must be sustained, rather than a public injury.[6]

The committee's report represented both unprecedented deference to tenants' ideals and a portent of future ideological developments. In its synthesis of the Whigs' utilitarian conception of the state and the Democrats' vision of the government as a direct representative of the popular will, it embraced something like the rank-and-file anti-renters' belief that vested rights and arcane rules should give way before the demands of the people and the good of the community. In its economic and social thinking, it endorsed the anti-renters' hostility to land monopoly and hope for a nation of freeholders—but sought to make them compatible with the requirements for growth in a competitive market economy. The committee's thinking was hardly the same as that of rank-and-file anti-renters; but, more than any previous statement by political leaders, it took into account the thinking of ordinary tenants. In the process, it helped to refine a new ideology of free labor and an expansive, democratic, and utilitarian conception of the state—both of which would become hallmarks of the radical wing of the Republican party.[7]

For the moment, however, the report represented a marginal body of thought. Of the five anti-rent bills introduced in the assembly, four died on the speaker's table. Only one, the measure allowing tenants to challenge their landlords' titles in court, made it to the floor, and there it was defeated. Like earlier anti-rent measures, the bill divided both parties.[8]

Stalemate

With their defeat in the 1847 legislature, the anti-renters reached the limits of their political power. The nomination and election of John Young had opened up bitter disputes between Whig and Democratic anti-renters, severely weakening the movement. Democratic anti-rent activists in Delaware County had supported Ira Harris for governor in 1846. But the nomination of John Young and a local convention that gave the "lion's share" of nominations to Whigs led these leaders to feel that they had become pawns of the Whig party and to "regret that they have allowed themselves to be so strongly committed against Governor Wright." In December 1846, Jonathan Allaben, a newly elected anti-rent assemblyman, approached N. K. Wheeler, a leader of the Delaware County Barnburners, for help in battling the Whig leaders of the movement. Allaben "insists that he will not be a *Whig*" and was determined "to prevent the body of the anti- renters from joining the Whigs." Democratic anti-rent leaders elsewhere struck similar alliances. Building on Silas Wright's support for anti-rent measures in 1846, they created several county-level alliances with the Barnburners, displacing the Hunkers as the insurgents' main Democratic allies.[9]

These partisan jealousies severely weakened the movement. Activists throughout the leasehold district complained that "disorganizers" had "assumed the name of Whig or Democratic anti-renters" and were seeking to nominate tickets composed entirely of Whigs or Democrats. Departing from a long tradition of dividing nominations evenly between Democrats and Whigs, the 1847 anti-rent state convention offered 8 of its 12 nominations to Whigs. In response, four Democratic anti-rent leaders bolted, condemning the meeting as a convocation of "political hacks" and complaining that the nominations were "brought about by the existence of foul play, and the most damnable hypocrisy and pipe-laying." Perhaps because of similar conflicts, the anti- renters of Rensselaer and Delaware counties failed to make any nominations for the legislature. When the votes were counted, the anti-renters retained control of most county governments in the leasehold district but lost most of their independent presence in the legislature. Only one of the five anti-rent nominees to the state assembly won office; the militants' sole nominee for the state senate lost. These divisions, along with the stalemate in the legislature and a vigorous campaign of legal prosecutions by landlords, led many tenants to abandon the movement. By the end of 1847, associations in movement strongholds like Rensselaerville, Sand Lake, and Kortright had ceased their activities. The Delaware County *Voice of the People* lamented that "the People have become lukewarm . . . their zeal has subsided, and we as a party are retrograding to the dark and blinded days of partyism."[10]

As anti-rent electoral strength dissolved into partisan bickering, party leaders began to distance themselves from the movement. These leaders had long been aware of the capacity of the leasehold controversy to divide their parties. As the slavery controversy threatened both parties with open factional warfare after 1845, Democratic and Whig commandants sought to silence the controversies that threatened to divide their organizations. No one understood the costs of tangling with the anti-rent issue better than Governor John Young. Soon after taking office, he disavowed any intent to pardon the jailed anti-rent "Indians." After anti-rent newspapers denounced his delay and militants sent petitions bearing 11,000 signatures, however, he issued the pardons. This action failed to placate his erstwhile allies, who remained incensed at his failure to address their legislative agenda. But the pardons did win him the abiding enmity of conservative Whigs, who began a campaign to dump him from their party's ticket in the November elections.[11]

Thus when the anti-renters' electoral collapse created an opportunity to silence the leasehold controversy, Young seized the initiative. In his annual message to the legislature, he expressed his support for legislators' refusal to pass the title-test law. Any attempt to change the rules that protected property, he argued, would undermine all property rights. Still, the legislature had a "high duty" to "seek out and remove any causes of discontent that may exist among its people." One way to allay popular discontent "without offending . . . the laws that govern the rights of property," he suggested, was for the state to consider challenging proprietors' titles. In studiously vague language, he suggested that if the legislature were to order the attorney general to commence suits of ejectment against such owners of leasehold estates "as you in your wisdom prescribe," it "will have discharged a duty which . . . it owes to the importance of the subject and to the interest as well of the landlords as . . . of tenants."[12]

Young's proposal was brilliant. By circumventing the objections of conservatives, he promised to achieve the tenants' central legislative demand—a court challenge to the landlords' titles. More importantly, the measure would move the anti-rent issue from electoral politics to the courts. There was just one problem: it could never overturn the landlords' titles. New York law allowed land owners to claim title by possession through their tenants, and its statute of limitations confirmed all titles, fraudulent or not, for land claimed and held peaceably for more than 20 years. As long as legislators were unwilling to abrogate these rules, the state could legally recover unoccupied lands, but not lands occupied by tenants. Young's proposal did not aim at winning relief for the state's tenants; it aimed at *appearing* to do so. It was a cynical attempt to quiet a politically destabilizing movement.[13]

Legislators seized on Young's proposal with enthusiasm. Conservatives from both parties denounced the plan as an attack on vested rights that would force citizens to "litigate with the power that should protect them," but both the assembly and the senate endorsed the plan. Like Young, the plan's supporters knew that the statute of limitations would prevent wholesale recovery of the estates, and opted to pass responsibility on to the attorney general. The joint resolution "instructed" the attorney general "carefully to inquire" whether there were a "just doubt" to any estate titles and whether the state could legally lay claim to any part of estate lands. If he found that the state could claim such land, the legislature ordered him to "take such measures . . . as will test the validity of such titles or claims." As with earlier anti-rent bills, the vote reduced old partisan allegiances to rubble. In the assembly, the Democrats split 16–6, while Whigs divided 47–25. Senate Whigs and Democrats were similarly divided.[14]

Such divisiveness would soon become a thing of the past. With this vote, party leaders and most legislators forged a new policy on the leasehold conflict: silence. At the 1848 Whig convention, Conservatives unceremoniously dumped John Young from the state ticket. That done, Liberals and Conservatives arrived at a tacit agreement on the anti-rent question. When the delegates elected Joshua Spencer, a Conservative ally of the Van Rensselaers, as a presidential elector, the allies of the anti-renters convinced their fellow delegates to rescind the nomination. Anti-rent Whigs then proposed Ambrose Jordan, the anti-rent candidate for attorney general, only to be met by bitter opposition from Conservatives. James Brooks of New York City warned the assembly that the anti-rent excitement "was a two-edged sword, and it would cut whoever touched it." He urged his fellow delegates to nominate another candidate. Above all, he demanded that Whigs cease all agitation over the anti-rent issue: "This discussion must stop, if we would have harmony." Brooks's remarks were greeted with "loud applause," and his recommendations were adopted unanimously. His proposal soon became unofficial policy among both Whigs and Democrats. From 1848 on, few state officials or candidates for state office would raise the leasehold issue, either to support or condemn the anti-renters.[15]

Portents of Political Revolution

Despite the growing silence in the legislature over the leasehold issue, political leaders were powerless to stop the conflict from dividing their parties. Beginning in 1847, many anti-renters renewed their search for political openings, extending their alliance with the National Reformers and creating a new coalition with the political anti-slavery movement. In the process, they helped create a coalition that accelerated the destruction of the second party system in New York.

The legislative defeat of 1847 deepened militants' discontent with the second party system. "B," a former Columbia County tenant, argued that the legislators knew all too well that the estate titles were fraudulent; their "unnatural quibbling" about constitutional issues was the result of landlords' bribes. Their failure to defend the natural rights of the tenants, he argued, shattered the social contract and restored to the anti-renters the right of revolution. Tenants were no longer bound by the constitution and the laws, but were "thrown upon the laws of God and nature. If there is no other remedy for self-preservation, physical force must be employed." The tenants of Tagkhanic agreed. Since the legislature had "spurn[ed] the source of its origin," the power of the people, once delegated to representatives, "reverts to the source which gave it, REVERTS to the People; and it is THEIR right, and it is *their duty,* to exercise that power *themselves,* and in their *own way,* to accomplish the objects for which it was given."[16]

Most anti-renters' faith in the political process was briefly restored when the legislature authorized Attorney General Ambrose Jordan to sue for recovery of leasehold lands. The resolution gave new life to the movement, as tenants' committees visited Jordan in Albany, demanding legal action against their landlords and offering to hire assistants and gather documentary evidence for trial. The besieged officer announced in September that he would begin suits against Stephen Van Rensselaer and the owners of the Hardenbergh patent. By early 1850, he had initiated 11 suits for the recovery of leasehold lands in nine counties, including Livingston Manor, Rensselaerwyck, the Hardenbergh patent, and the holdings of George Clarke. But militants remained distrustful of Jordan for his early delay in initiating suits, and rumors that he was conducting the suits in bad faith began circulating throughout the leasehold towns. Every delay brought forth new claims that the suits were in "crisis" and demands for an explanation of the "unwarrantable delay[s]."[17]

In this climate of pervasive distrust, militants sought new avenues for gaining power in politics. A significant minority of anti-renters began renewing their ties to the National Reform Association in late 1847. Declaring that "National Reform and anti-rent *principles*" were "one and the same, and *with us inseparable,*" local associations in Bern and Rensselaerville officially merged with the land reformers. Other associations placed National Reformers in leadership positions, and some leaders found a new enthusiasm for the reformers' principles. The Albany *Freeholder* proclaimed that "every anti-renter *from principle* must be a National Land Reformer" and called for a political alliance between the two movements.[18]

Even more important was the anti-renters' alliance with the burgeoning political movement against the expansion of slavery. In New York as elsewhere, national conflicts over the spread of slavery brought divisions in both parties to the breaking point. In 1847, the Barnburners walked out of the Democratic state convention after Hunker delegates voted down a plank in favor of the Wilmot Proviso. The following year, they led a secession from the national party and helped create the Free-Soil party, a coalition of anti-slavery Whigs, Wilmot Democrats, and members of the Liberty party. The New York Whigs avoided an open breach, but they too experienced growing tensions over slavery. In 1846, William Seward openly dedicated himself to the gradual abolition of slavery in the South; his allies Horace Greeley and Ira Harris did the same, while scores of other Liberal Whigs campaigned to end the spread of slavery into new territories. Their stance outraged Conservative Whigs; when party leaders pressed for Seward's election to the U.S. Senate in early 1849, Conservative opposition briefly threatened to create an open breach in the party.[19]

Most anti-renters became quick converts to the politics of antislavery. Beginning in 1847, both the *Albany Freeholder* and the Columbia County *Equal Rights Advocate* established a free-soil editorial policy. Most anti-rent associations did the same, adopting resolutions like that of the Scott patent association: "We love a free soil, and will not compromise our principles for the extension of slave territory." Just as important, militants sought to forge a coalition with anti-slavery forces. In 1847, the tenants of Columbia County hired William Seward, undisputed leader of the anti-slavery Whigs, to represent them in their court challenge of the Livingston title. In early 1849, when they won permission to hire an assistant to help Attorney General Jordan in his challenge to estate titles throughout the state, movement leaders again chose Seward. The enthusiasm of anti-renters for anti-slavery politics led Horace Greeley to urge Thurlow Weed to abandon his strategy of closing ranks against divisive reform causes. "You don't seem yet to understand that the men who enjoy most of the hatred of the Aristocracy are the very men whose names will go best before the People . . . I wish you would let us try it." A national ticket in 1848 with Seward as the candidate for Vice President and "any body . . . but Webster or a slaveholder" for president, Greeley promised, would "regain the Anti-Rent vote . . . and carry the State."[20]

Many anti-rent leaders placed greater hope in an alliance with the Free-Soil party. Building on their deepening ties to the Barnburners, these leaders saw in the Free-Soil rebellion an opportunity to end the political quarantine of the anti-rent movement. In 1847, Columbia County militants engineered an alliance with local anti-slavery Democrats, adopting a platform dedicated to combating both land monopoly and the spread of slavery. Despite the strong opposition of Whig tenants, the anti-rent nominating convention endorsed the Democrats' nominees for three of four county offices. When the Barnburners formed the Free-Soil party in 1848, the anti-renters went with them, nominating all but one of the new party's candidates. The county Free-Soil newspaper, the *Freeman's Advocate,* established an editorial policy that militantly supported the anti-renters.[21]

Encouraged by the national Free-Soil convention's endorsement of a homestead act, anti-rent activists in other counties sought alliances with the new party in 1848. The Delaware County anti-renters joined forces with the Free Soilers, endorsing their entire ticket. Militants in Albany County comprised at least a quarter of the delegates who formed the local Free-Soil organization, but conflict between anti-slavery men, Whigs, and Hunkers prevented the county anti-rent association from making any nominations. Free-Soil supporters triumphed at the state anti-rent convention, however. Affirming their conviction "that no more land should be held by any person than can be actually cultivated," the delegates nominated John Dix, the Free-Soil candidate for governor, as their standard-bearer.[22]

The alliance between leasehold militants and anti-slavery politicians was part of an emerging national alliance that encompassed abolitionists, anti-slavery politicians, land reformers, and land-hungry farmers—one that would color the politics of the late 1840s and 1850s throughout the North. Historians are just beginning to study this alliance, but the experience of New York's leasehold district offers some preliminary insights.[23]

First, in binding together the causes of land reform and anti-slavery, the alliance won important new constituencies to each cause. But it did so in a way that dulled the threat that the radical wings of both movements posed to constitutionalism and the rights of property. The Free-Soilers' and anti-slavery Whigs' pledge to keep slavery out of the territories deflected the threat to property rights implicit in the abolitionists' immediatism. In the same way, both groups' call for a homestead act channeled land reformers' and anti-renters' belief in a natural right to the soil into policies that would disturb no white man's property rights. They thus contained the radical implications of some constituents' demands in the same way: by applying it exclusively to the federal territories, where white men's property rights in land and human beings had not been established. In addition, both anti-slavery Whigs and Free-Soilers left constitutionalism unchallenged (Seward's "Higher Law" speech notwithstanding) by keeping the Garrisonians' Christian anarchism out of politics and by ignoring the anti-renters' and National Reformers' own versions of "higher law" thought.[24]

Just as important, the anti-renters' alliance with anti-slavery politicians united different constituencies that were dedicated to using the power of the state to promote "free" and "democratic" systems of social relations. As such, they opposed prevailing political winds, which blew toward limiting the government's role in social and economic policy to establishing a stable legal framework for economic activity.

Finally, the new alliance helped create a distinctly producer-friendly and agrarian strain of anti-slavery ideology. Although Martin Van Buren, the Free-Soilers' standard-bearer, deflected both anti-renters' and National Reformers' efforts to get him to endorse their cause, local Free-Soil activists sought to win the support of tenants by convincing them that their struggle against the leasehold system involved the same principles as the national struggle against slavery. In the process, they helped disseminate the expansive, producerist definitions of "slavery" and "freedom" embraced by earlier anti-rent politicians. An Albany County Free-Soil meeting warned that slavery and land monopoly were both "combinations of wealth against the liberties of the masses" and demanded that the public lands be used "to secure the interest and uphold the rights of the free laboring classes" by reserving them "to provide homes for the free emigrant." Andrew Colvin, an Albany County Free-Soil activist, explicitly endorsed the anti-rent movement, promising that tenants would soon "rejoice in a free soil and freedom from the rent," with each producer free to "recline under his own vine and fig tree, with none to molest or make him afraid." The campaign against slavery in the territories, he insisted, was part of the same struggle. Slavery forced free white laborers to "work side by side with the slave" and concentrated available land into large plantations, thus denying white laborers both the dignity and the land due to them as white men and as producers. Emphasizing his party's promise of a homestead act and revising its slogan to include the struggle of the anti-renters, he predicted that the combined efforts of the two movements would soon usher in a new era of freedom:

> Free soil, a free home, free tenure, and one hundred and sixty acres for each free man in the west, are becoming the rallying cry of the mighty hosts of the North. Your action has contributed to set these hosts in motion. And

they will triumph and you will triumph, and then indeed the proud boast may go out from our beloved land—we are free, we are a happy people—we are the Model Republic.[25]

Most anti-rent activists heartily embraced this synthesis of anti-slavery and anti-rent aims. Hiram Grant, who became editor of the Albany *Freeholder* in late 1848, declared chattel slavery and patroonery merely to be "slavery in different forms." Similarly, Calvin Pepper urged militants to devote themselves to a broader struggle against all forms of servitude. Just as "a man cannot be a friend of freedom and not be an Anti-Renter," he wrote, so too a defender of chattel slavery "cannot be a true or consistent Anti-Renter." At the same time, anti-renters strove to expose what they saw as the Free-Soilers' hypocrisy in remaining silent on the leasehold issue. "I heartily wish that those who talk so loudly about *'Free Soil' a great distance off,* would say a word or two about *'Free Soil'* in the Empire State," wrote Elijah Hammond of Schoharie County. Similarly, Hiram Grant ridiculed many anti-slavery advocates' definition of freedom as self-ownership and equality before the law; no man would be free, he argued, without access to land.[26] Far more than they had endorsed the liberal political economy of Robert Watson and Ira Harris, the anti-renters enthusiastically endorsed the expansive notion of freedom espoused by their anti-slavery allies. And they pressed those allies to live up to their ideals.

In this they failed. For all its innovation, the anti-renters' alliance with the Free-Soilers and anti-slavery Whigs did nothing to help them achieve their local aims. The linking of anti-slavery with the challenge to the leasehold system took place on the margins of anti-slavery politics; it was never articulated in state or national anti-slavery forums. There, only the demand for a homestead act served to represent the anti-renters' and other agrarian reformers' aspirations. Free-Soil and Liberal Whig legislators were unwilling or unable to break their parties' silence on the leasehold issue. Politicians like William Seward and Andrew Colvin endorsed the anti-renters' challenge to their landlords' titles without proposing a law that would make that challenge legally effective. A political resolution to the leasehold conflict was as distant in 1848 as it had been in 1844.[27]

Nor did the anti-renters offer much help to the Free-Soilers. Endorsing their ideas was one thing; voting for them was another. The anti-rent–Free-Soil ticket swept the anti-rent towns of Delaware county, but elsewhere divisions between Whig and Democratic anti-renters led most tenants to eschew the alliance. Only one anti-rent town each in Albany and Columbia counties gave a majority to the Free-Soilers; no towns did so in Schoharie and Rensselaer counties.[28] These paltry results combined with the new party's defeat at the national level to make the alliance short-lived. Most Free-Soil leaders returned to the Democratic fold in time for the 1850 elections. Nor did many Whigs share Horace Greeley's enthusiasm for an anti-"aristocratic" ticket that could unite anti-slavery and anti-rent votes. The anti-renters' alliance with the anti-slavery Whigs remained an arrangement with individual politicians, not a movement. But it outlasted the 1840s and would bear fruit in later years.

Landlords, Conservatives, and Silver-Grays

Like their tenants, New York's leasehold proprietors sensed a crisis after 1848 and responded by seeking to extend their political alliances. In doing so, they increased the political cost of supporting tenants' demands, reinforcing the deadlock in the legislature. Just as important, they, like the anti-renters, helped weaken party loyalties and linked the slavery controversy to social and political conflicts in the Empire State.

In the wake of the legislature's resolution empowering the attorney general to investigate leasehold titles, the Freeholders' Committee of Safety expanded its efforts to defeat the anti-rent movement. In addition to subjecting proprietors to ruinous court costs, this measure confirmed their fears that amoral demagogues in the service of selfish popular majorities controlled the politics of the state. James W. Beekman, a member of the Freeholders' Committee, wrote that "this whole agitation is the vilest humbug—and the movers in it are if intelligent wholly insincere. . . . if we permit much further tampering with Manorial affairs, all property will be in danger, and agrarian laws will, as we say here, come next in order."[29]

The landlords' counterattack took several forms. They established a coordinated defense strategy against possible suits for recovery of their estates.[30] They also escalated their lobbying campaign. In early 1850, the Freeholders' Committee hired Duncan Pell, the landlord George Clarke's brother-in-law, as their agent in Albany. With the help of Campbell White, a Hunker assemblyman from New York City and himself the owner of leased land, Pell forged an informal coalition dedicated to forcing "both the great parties" to "throw off Anti Rent" and grant "some good *affirmative* action *in favor of the landlords.*" Pell targeted potential allies in the legislature, bombarding them with up-rent speeches, editorials, and articles; recruiting White and other allies to lobby them; and "procuring letters" from influential constituents, demanding action against anti-rent legislation. With an increasing number of lawmakers on board, Pell mapped out a legislative strategy. He wrote bills and amendments for his allies to present in the legislature, drafted plans to stall anti-rent bills in committee, and coordinated floor efforts to vote down anti-rent initiatives.[31]

Pell buttressed his legislative efforts with a vigorous propaganda campaign. He sought to "back . . . up" his allies by publishing their speeches and by sending laudatory articles and editorials to newspapers throughout the state. In this way, he hoped to create a new climate, hostile to anti-rent, in both parties. He had a great deal of help. During the early 1850s, conservatives founded several journals dedicated to battling the forces of anti-slavery, anti-rent, Fourierism, National Reform, and other movements that, they believed, threatened to destroy the Constitution and organic social relations. These journals were only too happy to publish Pell's editorials and the speeches of his collaborators. Pell, in turn, used these journals to create a new climate of opinion in the leasehold towns, recruiting landlords to buy subscriptions for the influential men on their estates.[32]

Finally, Pell coordinated the efforts of local Whig and Democratic activists, primarily landlords' lawyers and agents, to ensure the nomination of candidates hostile to anti-rent. Thomas Machin, an agent for the landlord George Clarke, asked his employer to inform Pell that "I will do all I can for him & can git him two or three Delegats that will vote for him in the convention if he wishes them."[33]

Pell failed to win the "*affirmative* action" he had hoped for—a bill discontinuing the attorney general's suits and confirming proprietors' titles. But he did help turn public opinion against the anti-renters. His efforts insured that any legislative support for the insurgents would create a backlash in the press and in the conservative wings of both parties. When a bill passed the senate postponing court proceedings against tenants until the state's suits for recovery of leasehold estates were decided, Pell coordinated a successful campaign to block passage in the assembly. His allies also steered a bill to allow tenants to buy out their landlords to the judiciary committee, where four confederates promised that there would be "no hurry with the report." By early April 1850, Pell could brag that "the Anti-Renters are dead" and that "we have effectually used up Anti-Rent." He did not exaggerate. After the rout of 1850, the anti-renters lost all support in the capital; for the remainder of the 1850s, not a single piece of anti-rent legislation was introduced.[34]

New York's landlords supplemented their legal and legislative strategy with a "flood of prosecutions" against debtor tenants. Unlike previous efforts to collect the rent, the proprietors' campaign included no offers of lenience. The assignees of William Van Rensselaer, who had handed over his lands to creditors in 1848, warned the tenants of Rensselaer County that "our duty will prevent the exercise of the lenity and forbearance, which as individuals, and in our own concerns, we should be glad to indulge." In addition to their back rents, Albany and Rensselaer County tenants had to pay the costs of the lawyers and agents who prosecuted them. Worst of all, the Van Rensselaers and their assignees ceased suing tenants for breach of contract, instead applying to the courts to have them evicted. Tenants faced an even harsher situation in Columbia, Schoharie, Montgomery, Otsego, Oswego, and Sullivan Counties, where many of the area's two- and three-life leases expired in the late 1840s. Landlords there seized the land, evicting tenants or selling them their farms at a price that reflected the value of their improvements. After two generations of work to improve their farms, the *Freeholder* complained, tenants "find themselves compelled to leave, or purchase at a high rate, the farms whose chief, indeed almost entire, value, is owing to their own labor."[35]

The landlords' counterattack placed enormous strain on the second party system. Pell's coalition of legislators included Democrats like Campbell White, Senator Charles A. Mann, and Assemblyman Elijah Ford, as well as Whigs like Senator George R. Babcock, Senator E.D. Morgan, and Assemblyman Joel Nott. Like the anti-renters, the landlords were creating a coalition that shattered party lines. And as they did with the anti-renters, leaders in both parties sought to end the conservatives' efforts. "You can have no idea of the exertions made here to keep Mann & Babcock quiet by Dems to Mann & Whigs to Babcock," Pell wrote to White in 1850. "They tell them that their course on this matter will defeat their party."[36]

Pell's campaign was part of a broader reactionary movement that gained strength during the sectional crisis. While it worsened divisions in both parties, this movement inflicted especially heavy damage on the Whigs. Since 1840, Conservative Whigs had despised William Seward and his allies for their opposition to slavery, their support for public funding of Catholic parochial schools, and their encouragement of the anti-renters. The leasehold movement's nomination of John Young, Young's pardon of the anti-rent "Indians," Seward's national leadership among anti-slavery Whigs, and Horace Greeley's embrace of Fourierism and National Reform deepened their animosity. By 1850, Conservatives were openly calling for the party to divest itself of "Sewardism."[37]

Leasehold proprietors and their collaborators were at the center of this broader movement. In 1850 the *Albany State Register* opened its doors and quickly became the key journal of the anti-Seward movement. With the explicit aim of replacing Thurlow Weed's *Albany Evening Journal* as the central organ of New York Whiggery, the *Register* dedicated itself to "purg[ing]" the party "of abolitionism, antirentism, fourierism, and agrarianism, which were slowly but surely sapping its foundations." According to Pell, the new journal was planned and advised by some of the landlords' closest political allies: "[Daniel Dewey] Barnard [John] Spencer [Guilian] Verplanck & all that set." Its chief financial backers included the landlord George Clarke and the Van Rensselaer brothers; Pell predicted that other leasehold proprietors "should contribute handsomely."[38]

To conservatives throughout New York, "abolitionism, antirentism, fourierism, and agrarianism" were inextricably linked. Assuming, like Barnard and James Fenimore Cooper, that all humans were depraved by nature, the *State Register* declared that these movements encouraged citizens to follow the dictates of their debased consciences rather than deferring to the restraints of tradition, law, and the Constitution. The anti-renters, the *Register* claimed, were attempting to abrogate legal contracts in the name of a flawed and selfish sense of justice; in the process, they threatened to "overrid[e] the constitution of the United States." Similarly, the New York *Commercial Advertiser* denounced abolitionists' resistance to the Fugitive Slave Law as an abrogation of the Constitution. Such attacks on fundamental law threatened to dissolve all social bonds. "Government cannot exist, nor social order be maintained," the *State Register* warned, "if any set of men, may construe the constitution and laws as they understand them to suit their own purposes." Such selective obedience to the law would inevitably "dissolve the Union of the States," "prostrate all law and order in the dust," and end in "the resolution of society into its original elements."[39]

With fears so drastic, it is no wonder that Conservative Whigs were willing to divide their party. Duncan Pell informed White that the founding of the *State Register* "splits up the party and defeats it next fall. This is certain." When the 1850 Whig state convention endorsed Seward's outspoken opposition to the Compromise of 1850 in the U.S. Senate, the Conservatives walked out. Most Silver-Grays, as the bolters came to be called, limited their protest to Seward's continued agitation of the slavery issue and the resulting threat to the Union. For the most strident reactionaries, however, the anti-rent issue never lay far below the surface. When New York City Silver-Grays adopted a joint ticket with the Hunkers, their central committee flooded the state with a handbill that presented the slate as the "Anti-Disunion Ticket. Anti–Abolition, Anti-Seward, Anti-Weed, Anti-Anti-Rent, Anti-Demagoguism." Most Silver-Grays remained loyal to the Whig state ticket in 1850, and the two factions restored a semblance of harmony at the 1851 convention. But the party was weakened beyond recovery. In 1854, most Silver-Grays abandoned the party for the Know-Nothings; a year later, the remaining Whigs, now representing a minority of New York's voters, officially merged with the new Republican party.[40]

The Whigs and Democrats failed to resolve the leasehold conflict to either tenants' or landlords' satisfaction. And they failed to contain that issue. As a result, the discontent of both landlords and tenants helped destroy one of those parties. The leasehold controversy was not the most important issue to divide the Whigs and Democrats; slavery was. But to many New Yorkers, the two problems were not separable. Both threatened property rights and the constitution. Both led citizens and their leaders to explore the possibility that their government might have the power to alter or abolish existing systems of class relations. And both pitted the advocates of a democratic, activist state against the defenders of an organic social order. By helping bring these issues home dramatically to New Yorkers, the anti-renters and their landlords helped lay the groundwork for the political transformation of the 1850s.

Prosperity and Uplift

The stalemate in the legislature and the anti-renters' declining power at the polls dashed tenants' hopes for political redress of their grievances. At the same time, economic and cultural change created new possibilities for resolving the leasehold crisis. After 1845, the hill towns of New York's leasehold estates began to recover from the depression that had begun in 1837. Spurred by growing demand for manufactured goods and by landlords' willingness to sell mill sites, manufacturers invested heavily on the estates, creating a manufacturing boom in a handful of towns. In 1846, the Erie Railroad connected Delaware County to the Erie Canal and the Hudson River. Manufacturing and commerce revived in the region's cities and market towns as well. All of these developments increased demand for the products of leasehold farms. After falling steadily since the late 1830s, commodity prices in New York City began to improve in late 1844; they continued to rise for the rest of the decade and for the first eight years of the 1850s. By 1846, butter making had become so remunerative that Delaware County grazing lands were selling at a premium.[41]

The improving economy was accompanied by important cultural changes. After a long period of quiescence, temperance advocates rebuilt their movement, now dedicated to total abstinence from alcohol. In doing so, they revived the message that prosperity and security could be won through individual hard work and self-restraint. Temperance lecturers began to tour the anti-rent district in 1846, convincing thousands of tenants to take the pledge of total abstinence. The cold-water men quickly turned to political action, beginning a campaign in Albany and Rensselaer Counties to ban the sale of liquor. In the spring elections of 1846, the leasehold towns of both counties voted "no licence" by heavy margins.[42]

Tenants' enthusiasm for temperance did not mark a retreat into individualism. The movement drew heavily from mutualist traditions; temperance societies offered camaraderie and mutual support to the teetotaler. The effort to enact and enforce the local ban on liquor was a collective one as well. But the point of the movement was to reform individual morality and habits, and temperance advocates insisted that doing so would end poverty and social misery. In New Scotland, cold-water men declared that tippling was "a precursor of the combined evils of indigence, pauperism, and crime." An Albany County Fourth of July toast saluted "The temperance ship—full sails and no breakers: may she land all her passengers in the haven of plenty."[43]

Tenants strove in numerous ways to take advantage of the improving economy. In 1846, advertisements for new agricultural machinery like power threshers and corn stalk cutters began appearing in the local press, and many leasehold farmers presumably bought them. Farmers also began a vigorous campaign for improved transportation to market. Local meetings promoting railroad construction sprang up throughout the estates. The movement for plank roads proved even more popular. Beginning in the late 1840s, farmers and urban residents throughout New York created a veritable craze for toll roads surfaced with boards. Such roads held out numerous advantages. They were cheaper to construct than roads built with macadam, the alternative hard surface. And unlike dirt roads, they promised smooth, year-round travel. By 1857, the state had chartered 352 plank road companies.[44]

A large number of those companies were founded in the leasehold district. There, the early impetus to build came from urban centers at the terminus of the proposed roads. The movement for the Albany and Schoharie plank road, for example, began in Albany. Success, however, required the support of tenants, both for investment capital (some $60,000 was needed for the Albany-Schoharie road) and for permission to lay the road through their fields.[45] Although some tenants opposed the proposed roads, they were outnumbered by enthusiasts.[46] In 1849 and 1850, scores of meetings were held throughout the leasehold district. Tenants bought stock, joined committees to survey routes, and volunteered to serve on boards of directors. In many cases, farmers proposed their own roads and elected committees to drum up support in the cities and market towns along the proposed routes. Helderberg farmers so wanted a road from Albany to Gallupville in Schoharie County that several promised to donate the land needed for the road to the company that would build it, free of charge.[47]

Tenants' enthusiasm for reformed habits and improved access to markets were not new. They had long sought markets and celebrated their growing integration into a dynamic, diversified economy. And they had always appreciated the role that individual effort and habits played in achieving prosperity. But the movements for temperance, railroads, and plank roads placed exclusive focus on markets and on individual character and efforts; they promoted a road to prosperity that depended, in the end, on the efforts of individual families. On a practical level, these movements and the everyday effort to take advantage of expanding markets involved an enormous investment of time and energy, one that might otherwise have been devoted to the anti-rent cause. Along with farmers' widening access to cash and credit, the new emphasis on self-improvement and creating opportunities for economic self-advancement made it easier for prosperous farmers to seek out an individual resolution to the leasehold crisis.

Such a resolution was made more attractive by the legislature's silence on the leasehold conflict and by the declining political clout of the anti-rent movement. It was made imperative by the landlords' vigorous prosecution of uncooperative tenants. In Woodstock, anti-renters had never developed an independent electoral organization. Instead, they had depended on the Indians to defend them from lawmen. When the Indians disbanded in 1845, resistance collapsed and farmers "flooded" Robert L. Livingston's heirs with requests to purchase their farms. A decade later, over half of the farms in town had been purchased; by 1862, only 20 families remained as tenants. Other tenants followed suit. By 1864, only 23 percent (83 out of 359) of Roxbury farms remained under lease, while three-fourths or more of the valley farmers in Rensselaerwyck had purchased their landlords' interest in their farms. In early 1847, the officers of the Blenheim Hill Anti-Rent Association in Schoharie County drew up a plan for tenants to buy the Blenheim patent from their landlord, John King. King agreed. The anti-renters of Tagkhanic tried to negotiate a collective buyout with the Livingston family in 1847. Wherever buyouts became common, the anti-rent movement came to an end. Only in the hill towns of Albany and Rensselaer Counties and on the Montgomery and Otsego county estates of George Clarke did resistance continue past 1860.[48]

By buying their landlords' claims to their farms, leasehold farmers acquiesced in the rules of capitalist political economy. They abandoned in practice the arguments of some tenants that occupation and improvement provided a superior claim to land than a paper title; they surrendered as well the National Reformers' belief that land was not individual property but a common inheritance to which every citizen had a claim. Whatever their private belief, they publicly assented to the proposition that land was a commodity and could be claimed only by those who had acquired, through purchase or inheritance, paper title. With a greater or lesser degree of willingness, the people who made up the family economy of the leasehold towns accommodated themselves to the emerging capitalist order around them.

Not all estate residents could afford to purchase the landlords' claims to their farms, along with the livestock, equipment, and buildings needed to succeed in the new farm economy.[49] Many opted for a second solution to the leasehold crisis: emigration. Since the late 1830s, newspapers in the leasehold district had been publishing accounts of the cheap and fertile lands of the West. Young men who emigrated to western lands could buy their own farms, the *Albany Freeholder* promised, "unshackled by perpetual leases and unburdened by an everlasting rent charge."[50] Thousands of estate residents departed, leaving most leasehold towns with a shrinking population. With one exception, the hill towns of Albany county lost between 16 and 26 percent of their inhabitants between 1840 and 1865. Most principal leasehold towns of Delaware county lost population as well. (See Appendix, tables 18 and 19.)[51] Like the tenants' buyout of the landlords, emigration substituted individual for collective solutions to the leasehold crisis. Together they helped put an end to the anti-rent movement.

A Whimper, Not a Bang

The anti-rent movement had taken seven years to build; it took another six to die. Spurred by political frustration, factionalism, buyouts of the landlords, and emigration, the movement was in collapse by the late 1840s. In mid-1848, a visitor to Delaware County wrote that "order and quiet have regained possession of the valley. . . . The disaffected appear to have submitted to the law of necessity and right; the rents, I am told, were never better paid." Tenants who remained active in the movement found their energies consumed in factional disputes. In 1849, the state executive committee refused to call a state convention, so Albany County activists nominated a state ticket on their own and called a state convention to confirm the nominations. Though poorly attended, the meeting managed to split into two rival assemblies, and anti-rent leaders and newspapers spent the rest of the election season attacking one another's candidates. The following year brought still more rival conventions, competing tickets, and attempted takeovers.[52]

The resolution of the attorney general's suits to recover leasehold estates further weakened the movement. In 1851, the courts dismissed the state's suits, signaling the final victory of vested rights. Justice Cady of the state supreme court dismissed the state's case against George Clarke with bitter sarcasm. "In the days of Methuselah," he wrote, "witnesses might have been found to testify in relation to a fraud one hundred and twelve years after it was committed; but it would now be idle to attempt to find such witnesses." If the courts were to countenance the state's action, "no man holding under a colonial grant can have perfect confidence in his title." The statute of limitations and the numerous acts passed by the post-Revolutionary legislature to confirm pre-Revolutionary grants of land, he wrote, barred the state from recovering the patent. The state's effort to do so was an oppressive act, taken in bad faith.[53] Justice Wright, rendering a decision in the state's suit to recover lands in Livingston Manor, sided with Cady. Wright fully endorsed the now-prevailing belief that leasehold tenures were "antagonistical to free institutions." The system of landlord and tenant, he wrote, "retards the accumulation of property" among tenants, "paralyzes their energies," and "weakens an innate sense of independence" among the citizenry. But these evils were nothing compared to the dangers posed by tampering with vested rights and settled rules of law.

> Under no circumstances, should the influence of popular convulsion be permitted to invade the Courts, or control, in the slightest measure, the administration of the law. Individual rights would be insecure; titles afloat and at hazard, without an enlightened, firm and rigid adherence by the Courts to the rules of the Statute and Common Law affecting Real Property. Those rules have been sanctioned by experience and illuminated by the wisdom of the past, and their object and end is personal protection and security. For a Court in a single case to falter in the application of known and fixed principles of law relating to real property, might be, in effect, to unsettle and throw into utter confusion and uncertainty all titles to lands. Consequences like these would be infinitely more to be deplored than the continuance for a season of the relic of feudalism.[54]

These decisions, and a similar one in the suit against William Van Rensselaer, ended the state's alliance, however deceitful, with the anti-renters. Breathing a sigh of relief, the attorney general conceded defeat and dropped the suits that were still pending.

Defeat in the courts ended anti-rent as a regional movement. In June 1851, the *Albany Freeholder* closed its doors, leaving militants without a single newspaper. That fall, the anti-rent electoral apparatus was felled by a landlord's scheme. In September, agents hired by George Clarke won seats at the anti-rent state convention. According to a jubilant letter from Clarke to Campbell White, they "had control of the meeting" and got the convention to "adopt the entire democratic ticket." Clarke predicted that this event would "succeed in drawing the lines between the tenants and get them quarreling among themselves, which ends in breaking them up." He was not disappointed. Whig *Pogo* supporters bolted the convention and called their own meeting, where they named a rival anti-rent slate, made up entirely of Whig nominees. For the remainder of the election season, supporters of both tickets toured the leasehold district, battling for votes of farmers.[55]

In the wake of this split, what was left of the state anti-rent organization collapsed. The state executive committee ceased to meet; when the 1852 elections came around, they issued no call for a convention. Most local and county organizations also folded. Albany, Rensselaer, Montgomery, and Otsego County militants, though constantly diminishing in number, maintained their rent boycott and kept up a program of legal challenges to the landlords into the 1880s. But these were isolated, local movements. Henceforth, the only effective weapon against patroonery would be the mortgage.

After thirteen years, the anti-renters failed to achieve their central aim: overturning their landlords' titles. The court decisions of 1851 made clear that the rights of property were inviolable, "regardless," as Melville observed that same year, "of how the thing came into possession." For their part, most anti-renters ended their challenge, buying from their landlords the claims to land that they believed to be their own. They failed, too, to break party politicians' exclusive hold on political power or to abrogate the limits that those politicians placed on the exercise of popular sovereignty. Instead, they suffered the final humiliation of watching what was left of their movement shattered by a handful of landlord's agents. With this twin defeat, all hope of establishing their right to the soil or absolute popular sovereignty died.

Failure to enforce their social and political vision was not the failure to effect change, however. The anti-renters brought about a dramatic transformation in New York society and politics. By buying out their landlords, they destroyed an entire system of class relations and consigned a critical part of their state's elite to the dustbin of history. They transformed the social thought of legislators and party leaders, sparking widespread revulsion at "feudal" inequalities and forcing conservatives to back away from defending social relations that seemed to discourage social mobility and the free transfer of property. They transformed party ideologies, compelling a significant group of party activists to articulate a new definition of freedom and a new conception of the state. In the process, they helped divide both parties and helped create a new political alliance. The full impact of these changes could barely be felt in 1852. But in the coming decade, they would prove to be decisive.

N y Populism

Chapter 9

FREE LABOR

A Class Destroyed

In 1895, a small army of carpenters and teamsters converged upon the Van Rensselaer Manor House at Watervliet, dismantled it, and carted it off. One group took the great entrance hall, with its hand-painted wallpaper from the eighteenth century, to the new Metropolitan Museum of Art in New York City. Another hauled the main body of the house over the Tagkhanic mountains to Williams College, where it became the new home of the Sigma Phi fraternity.[1] The workmen left the wings standing on the grounds, for they were no longer inhabitable.

No Van Rensselaer was present to see the house dismantled. Once the architectural embodiment of their wealth and power, the house had been uninhabited for more than 15 years. In the meantime, its former glories had been surpassed by financiers' and manufacturers' homes in Albany and Troy. The fading grandeur of the house mirrored the declining fortunes of the owners. By the time that the Court of Appeals vindicated his title to the West Manor in 1852, Stephen Van Rensselaer was already near bankruptcy. Together, the anti-renters' 13-year boycott and the state's suits to recover the manor had brought him to the brink of ruin. His brother William's fortunes were even more hopeless. By 1848 his debts totaled half a million dollars, and he was forced to sign his lands, his manor house at Bath, and his yet-to-be-completed game park over to trustees.[2]

To make matters worse, the anti-renters continued to hound the Van Rensselaers in court, foiling their hope to wrest more income from their estates. Worse still, they won a decision which significantly diminished the value of the brothers' property. In 1852, tenants' lawyers began to argue that, since all lands in the state were allodial, perpetual "leases" were not leases at all but grants of land. The original settlers and their successors were not "tenants" at all, but the owners of the land, subject to rents and reservations. Thus, the lawyers argued, the quarter sale was "repugnant to the estate in fee granted" and legally inoperative. In October 1852, the Court of Appeals agreed. Although it upheld the Van Rensselaers' legal claim to rents, the court declared the quarter sale to be "void in law." Buoyed by this victory, militants began fighting to extend the decision, arguing before the courts that the nature of leasehold grants voided not only the quarter sale, but landlords' right to rents as well.[3]

Into this disaster stepped Walter S. Church, a speculator with contacts in the state and county Democratic parties. Ten months after the Court of Appeals voided the quarter sale, Church bought all of Stephen Van Rensselaer's interest in Rensselaerwyck for 50 to 60 cents on the dollar. Five years later, he bought out William's interest in the East Manor, which had been returned to him by the assignees the previous year. To finance his deals, Church brought on partners. He also leveraged his assets, agreeing to pay the Van Rensselaers over a long period and borrowing $30,000, with the yet-to-be-collected rents as collateral, for his down payment. Church wagered that his claim to rent would be upheld by the courts. In this, he may have been helped by his friend, Democratic Supreme Court Justice George Gould. As state legislators and anti-rent pamphleteers often suggested, Gould may have told Church that the tenants' arguments would be rejected long before the court's ruling was made public.[4]

In short, Church was a well-connected, high-risk speculator. If the Van Rensselaers had abandoned most of the noblesse oblige that had been their father's pride, Church never had any such attributes to relinquish. Nor could he wait for the courts to rule on his right to collect rent. During the spring and fall of 1855, he distributed notices and addressed crowds throughout Albany County, demanding that tenants pay their back rents and buy their farms within a month. To every tenant who paid his debts, he offered to sell for a sum that at 6 percent interest would yield the equivalent to the present rent. To those who were willing to abide by these terms, he promised the possibility of abatements and generous terms of credit. To those who failed to settle, he vowed to "immediately and indiscriminately sue." Uncooperative tenants would be charged interest on all back rents and compelled to pay a 25 percent premium for the purchase of their farms.[5] Twenty-four Westerlo tenants complied, settling their accounts and purchasing their farms in 1855 and 1856. Church reneged on his implied promise to them, offering no abatements and requiring each purchaser to pay the interest on his back rents. By 1860, however, only 21 percent of Westerlo farmers had purchased their lands, and anti-renters throughout Albany County continued to meet, resist Church in court, and observe the rent boycott.[6]

Their resistance bore little fruit. In 1858, the Supreme Court and Court of Appeals rejected Rensselaerwyck tenants' claim that the nature of their contracts voided Church's claim to rents. Every justice agreed with the original ruling that a relation of landlord and tenant did not exist on Rensselaerwyck and that the farmers of the estate owned their farms in fee. But each decided that Church *did* have a right to collect rents and services and to eject

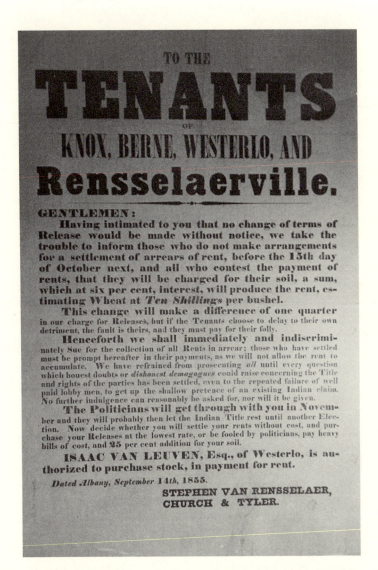

TO THE

TENANTS

OF

KNOX, BERNE, WESTERLO, AND

Rensselaerville.

GENTLEMEN:

Having intimated to you that no change of terms of Release would be made without notice, we take the trouble to inform those who do not make arrangements for a settlement of arrears of rent, before the **15th** day of October next, and all who contest the payment of rents, that they will be charged for their soil, a sum, which at six per cent, interest, will produce the rent, estimating Wheat at *Ten Shillings* per bushel.

This change will make a difference of one quarter in our charge for Releases, but if the Tenants choose to delay to their own detriment, the fault is theirs, and they must pay for their folly.

Henceforth we shall immediately and indiscriminately Sue for the collection of all Rents in arrear; those who have settled must be prompt hereafter in their payments, as we will not allow the rent to accumulate. We have refrained from prosecuting *all* until every question which honest doubts or *dishonest demagogues* could raise concerning the Title and rights of the parties has been settled, even to the repeated failure of well paid lobby men, to get up the shallow pretence of an existing Indian claim. No further indulgence can reasonably be asked for, nor will it be given.

The Politicians will get through with you in November and they will probably then let the Indian Title rest until another Election. Now decide whether you will settle your rents without cost, and purchase your Releases at the lowest rate, or be fooled by politicians, pay heavy bills of cost, and **25** per cent addition for your soil.

ISAAC VAN LEUVEN, Esq., of Westerlo, is authorized to purchase stock, in payment for rent.

Dated Albany, September 14th, 1855.

**STEPHEN VAN RENSSELAER,
CHURCH & TYLER.**

Figure 9.1. Walter Church's announcement, issued with Stephen Van Rensselaer and Church's business partner Oscar Tyler, demanding immediate settlement from the tenants of the hill towns of the West Manor of Rensselaerwyck. In these towns, anti–renters continued to organize and withhold rent long after the collapse of the regional movement in 1852. Countesy, New York State Library.

tenants who failed to fulfill the requirements of the leases, and they invented a series of new terms—an "entity assignable equivalent to a reversion," a "quality assignable, or vendible character," a "*pro hac vice* equivalent to a reversion"— to describe Church's legal claim to the land. Armed with these decisions, Church fulfilled his promise for wholesale prosecutions. On February 17, 1860, on his own authority as a colonel in the New York State National Guard, he led the twenty-fifth regiment into the Helderbergs and, in the midst of a blizzard, ejected the family of Peter Ball. For the remainder of the decade, posses and militia companies made frequent junkets into the anti-rent towns, while gangs of Helderberg youths hired by Church served summons and intimidated anti-rent supporters.[7]

Under this combination of legal, doubtfully legal, and illegal pressure, the last remnant of the anti-rent movement faded away. Anti-renters kept up a lively public presence until at least 1877, and individual families and groups of neighbors resisted Church's demands for rent and purchase money well into the 1880s. But these resisters gradually lost the support of their neighbors. Tenants in the valley towns, their fortunes buoyed by high commodity prices throughout the 1850s, were the first to comply with Church. By 1860, virtually all of the farmers in Watervliet had purchased the fee to their farms; about three fourths of their counterparts in Guilderland did the same. Buyouts in the Helderbergs came more slowly, but there, too, the majority of tenants ended their resistance and purchased the land they had long considered their own. By 1870, well over half of the farmers of Westerlo had purchased their farms. By 1900, only a few leasehold farms remained, and the Anti-Rent Wars were a distant memory.[8]

His victory against the anti-renters did not make Walter Church a rich man, however. As one observer noted, breaking the mountain farmers' resistance required "a pack of hounds in the shape of hungry attorneys, who have beggared him by their fees and advice." Just as distressing, dozens of would-be landlords appeared to claim Rensselaerwyck as their own. By 1863, twenty-one parties had filed suit to win ownership of the East Manor alone. Long after the courts had affirmed Church's right to collect rents, enough lawsuits were still pending "to bankrupt a good many patroons." Because of these expenses, Church asked for and received a more advantageous deal from William Van Rensselaer in 1859. Two years later he defaulted; Van Rensselaer annulled the contract and sold the East Manor to one of Church's partners. Church retained the West Manor, but he does not seem to have achieved great wealth from it. We do not know what became of him. He seems to have slipped unnoticed from the public eye, and his death went unnoted in the Albany and New York press.[9]

For their part, William and Stephen Van Rensselaer retreated into genteel obscurity. Stephen spent his days in religious study and devotion, in the service of his church, and in dispensing "elegant and refined hospitality" at the Manor House. William moved to Rye in 1852, never returning to Rensselaerwyck. Both benefitted from industrialization and population growth in Watervliet, Albany, Troy, and New York, which increased the income from their urban properties. Stephen died at the Manor House in 1868, at the age of 79. His widow remained there for another decade but eventually moved to an apartment in Albany, leaving their ancestral home in the care of a groundskeeper. William expired in 1872. With their landed estate reduced to a handful of valuable urban lots, neither branch of the Van Rensselaers suffered from penury, but neither enjoyed the honor and power that their father had accepted as natural. As one contemporary wrote, they had long since "sunk . . . into indistinguishable obscurity."[10]

Few members of the landlord class escaped this fate. When Robert L. Livingston died in 1843, his estate amounted to nothing more than the old Chancellor's house, now in a scandalous state of disrepair; a few adjoining acres; and an unimproved riverfront lot to the south of the house. His son Eugene had foreseen this state of affairs and, in the wake of the panic of 1837, had married an heiress. His other son, Montgomery, married a fashionable but penniless maiden and pursued a career as a painter, from which he derived great satisfaction but no money. When Montgomery died in 1855, his entire savings was stowed in an old top hat. His debts were so extensive that the executor was forced to sell the Chancellor's house at auction. His widow was left without a legacy.[11]

Of all the great and middling landlords, only George Clarke, who enjoyed the rare privilege of an undivided inheritance and a weak anti-rent movement on his estates, retained extensive leasehold lands into the 1880s. But Clarke became overextended in hops production and land speculation during the late 1870s; hops and land prices collapsed during the 1880s, just as renewed tenant resistance imposed new court costs and lawyers' fees on the landlord. In 1886 he declared bankruptcy, and his creditors broke up and sold off his lands. With his bankruptcy, the last member of New York's landlord class faded into obscurity.[12]

One outcome of the Anti-Rent Wars, then, was the annihilation of the leasehold system and, with it, New York's landlord class. But although the tenants' movement provided the *occasion* for the destruction of the system and the class, they were not the sole *cause*. With the exception of George Clarke and Stephen Van Rensselaer, every major landlord in the state had begun selling his or her lands before the beginning of the tenants' movement in 1839. With these two exceptions, the end of patroonery was assured by the landlords' own abandonment of primogeniture and arranged marriages after the Revolution and by their failure to live within their diminishing means. In the case of Van Rensselaer, the tenants could take more credit; but even there, the proprietor had offered to sell shortly after the tenant committee's visit in 1839. The central issue on Rensselaerwyck and elsewhere was not whether the leasehold system would be destroyed, but upon what terms. Most anti-renters had claimed the land as theirs because of the landlords' fraudulent titles and their own occupation and improvement. Others had demanded it as a natural right. None desired to buy it without a court test of the landlords' titles. Buying the landlords' interest in the land thus marked the anti-renters' defeat, not their victory. The rent boycott, the laws taxing rents and abolishing distress, and the attorney general's suits to recover leasehold lands led many landlords to lower their asking prices. But most landlords required tenants to pay back rents, interest, and legal costs before they could buy their farms. These costs frequently exceeded the price of the farms, wiping out any price advantage won through struggle. With the government unwilling to abrogate property rights and constitutional rules in carrying out the people's will, this defeat was inevitable.

The anti-renters could take credit for a fundamental change, however: the destruction of the ideological defenses of the leasehold system, and with them, the last vestiges of public support for contractual social relations marked by deference and hierarchy. The conservatives' vision of free labor as authoritarianism sanctioned by contracts remained the centerpiece of labor law for the rest of the century, a product of the courts' application of the English law of master and servant to American labor relations. But this ideal would enjoy no support in the political parties or public debate, and it would find no realization in lived class relations. With the demise of the landlords, class relations based on patrician ideals would disappear from New York—and from the North as a whole. The Anti-Rent Wars were thus part of a broad regional transformation: the abolition of "unfree" relations of labor. Along with the elimination of slavery, indentured servitude, and other forms of coerced labor—a process that began during the Revolutionary era and ended with the adoption of the thirteenth amendment—the anti-renters helped turn the northern United States into a society based on an ideology and practice of "free labor."[13]

Yeomen in a Capitalist Order

Destroying unfree systems of labor was one thing; defining the freedom that would replace them was another. On this issue, the anti-renters had been clear about what they wanted. They had fought for a society of freeholders, in which universal white male access to land put an end to class inequality and guaranteed to every white, male producer the full fruits of his and his family's labor, freedom from deference, and political independence. The only hierarchies that would remain were the "natural" ones of gender, age, and race. The anti-rent "Indians" had also fought to preserve particular communities and to defend the land and security of the individuals who lived in them.

Leasehold militants succeeded in perpetuating the independent, patriarchal, commodity-producing households that they had championed. With the buyout of the landlords, tenants everywhere except on the estates of George Clarke and in the hill towns of Rensselaerwyck had been replaced by freehold farmers by 1865. By the end of the century, leasehold tenancy had completely disappeared as a system; only a few leased farms remained as a legacy of the estates. The farms that now rested in the hands of resident owners continued to be organized as household systems of labor. The work of each household continued to be organized by sex and age, with husbands and fathers retaining final control over productive and marketing decisions and over the disposition of property.[14]

Farm households continued to practice general farming, meeting many of their subsistence needs through their own production. Families in the hill towns of Albany and Delaware Counties produced small amounts of wheat, peas, and beans in 1864—crops that were unprofitable as market commodities but which they needed for their own consumption. In addition, farm women continued to produce considerable, albeit declining, amounts of textiles. But far more than in 1840, farmers geared their efforts toward the production of crops for market. And, far more than before, they specialized in a single commodity. The former anti-rent towns of Delaware and Albany counties saw a dramatic drop in the production of two crops aimed at home consumption, wheat and hogs, as well as declines in some cash crops. Helderberg farmers raised fewer cattle and planted less rye and potatoes; Delaware county husbandmen devoted less effort to wool, grain, and tuber production. In place of these products, Helderbergers nearly doubled their production of wool, whose price had skyrocketed due to wartime demand. Former tenants in Delaware County increasingly specialized in dairying, more than doubling their output of butter between 1840 and 1864. These increases were made possible by the widespread adoption of improved stock, better feed, and progressive methods of livestock management. The number of cattle in Delaware County increased only slightly, while Helderberg farmers' increased wool production came despite a small decline in the number of sheep. Farming on the former estates was becoming more market-sensitive, more "businesslike," and far more capital-intensive. (See Appendix, table 20.)[15]

Farmers in both counties, in other words, were now specialists in livestock raising. Helderberg farmers now devoted at least 74 percent of their improved land to pasture and fodder crops, while former tenants in Delaware County devoted 93 percent of their improved land to such uses. Still, this was not a monocrop economy, with the fortunes of farm families tied to the fluctuating price of a single commodity. In addition to providing many of their subsistence needs at home, families in both counties grew several market crops, thereby lessening their dependence on a single, volatile market. Most Helderberg farmers produced moderate amounts of butter, poultry, and eggs; Delaware County husbandmen supplemented their dairy production with wool, eggs, and fowl. (see Appendix, table 20).[16]

For those who obtained land and capital, worked hard, got out of debt, and enjoyed tolerable health and luck, this increasingly commercialized economy offered a degree of comfort and security unknown to earlier generations. But the young and landless found it harder than ever before to join the ranks of property owners. The transition from tenant to freehold farming required a lot of cash. So did the land, blooded stock, tools, fertilizer, and specialized buildings needed to mount a successful livestock operation.[17]

Young, landless, and land-poor farmers were also hurt by shortages of timber in the eastern areas of the leasehold district and by residents' abandonment of the tradition of common right. Albany, Rensselaer, and Columbia

Counties suffered from severe deforestation during the late 1840s and 1850s. Even in those areas in which forests were still extensive, local authorities limited or abrogated residents' ability to take resources from open lands. Town meetings throughout the leasehold district outlawed the running of swine and cattle on the commons, while county boards of supervisors restricted hunting and fishing. The Delaware County ordinance aimed only at preserving game and fish for county residents, requiring nonresidents to apply for a license to hunt or fish in the county. Albany County, however, established hunting seasons for various species of game, assessing stiff fines against those who hunted out of season. It also outlawed large-scale fishing with poisons or nets. This law, and others like it, was essential to conserving game and fish. But it put strict limits on the extent to which residents could accumulate property without selling their labor power.[18]

Thus the transition to a free labor economy on the former leasehold estates was a process fraught with risk and uncertainty. Nowhere was this more clear than in tenants' efforts to purchase their farms. When Walter Church brought eviction proceedings against James Bishop of Westerlo in 1855, Bishop owed hundreds of dollars in back rent and $105 in interest and court costs. Luckily, Bishop had taken advantage of the booming farm economy and, perhaps, had the help of prosperous kin. He immediately paid his debt to Church and, six months later, bought Church's interest in the farm for another $334.42. He also bought a small lot held by a neighbor who could not pay his back rents, expanding his farm from 85 to 122 acres.[19]

David Willsie's transition to freehold farming was less smooth. He began farming Lot number 314 in Westerlo in 1853, making frequent payments to Church during his first four years. But he stopped paying after 1857. In 1865, Church began eviction proceedings, to which Willsie responded by paying half his rent, interest, and costs, worth $300. To cover the other half of his debt, he brought in his brother Hiram, who paid another $300 and apparently began to farm with him. The brothers did not make another payment until 1882, when David Ball, Hiram's father-in-law, paid off $695 in back rents and interest and bought Church's interest in the land for another $545.[20]

Peter Van Leuven was not so lucky. A Westerlo tenant since the 1830s or before, Van Leuven, like most of his neighbors, did not pay any rent between 1840 and 1851. In the latter year, he remitted $207.54 of his back rents, leaving a balance of $126.15. He did not appear at the manor office again until 1871, and Church served him notice of eviction. Unlike Bishop and Willsie, Van Leuven had neither cash, credit, nor prosperous kin to help him through this crisis. In an effort to show his good faith, he paid $51.20, but Church evicted him nonetheless. His farm, along with that of two neighbors, was taken over by A.S. Green. Green remained a tenant until 1879, when he paid $751.82 in back rent and bought his expanded farm for $577.[21]

These stories were multiplied many times over, but their main features remained the same. For virtually all farmers with back rents, usually buying out their landlords was very expensive, exceeding the value of the landlord's interest in the land. Not everyone succeeded in doing so; many, like Van Leuven, were evicted and compelled to move on. Indeed, most Westerlo tenants left rather than buying their own farms; those who did buy them were newcomers or prosperous neighbors expanding their holdings. Of the 66 people who bought Westerlo farms from Stephen Van Rensselaer or Walter Church between 1840 and 1899 and whose length of stay on their farms before purchase could be determined, 28—42 percent—had resided on their purchases for less than a year. Another 12 percent had lived on the farms they bought for one or two years. Only 19—less than a third—had worked their farms for 10 years or more. Many who became full owners of farms could, like David and Hiram Wiltsie, attribute their success to the financial help of nearby kin. A large portion of those who made the transition to freehold farming expanded their holdings in the process, taking over the farms of their less successful neighbors.[22]

The difficulties of accumulating the property needed for successful farming meant that landlessness, wage labor, and subtenancy remained prominent in the postleasehold economy. In Westerlo, which had suffered from declining soil fertility and diminishing farm size since the 1820s, the proportion of heads of family who were laborers or landless farmers grew from 18 to 25 percent between 1850 and 1860. The proportion of men aged 35 or older who were laborers or farmers without land grew from 23 to 26 percent. In Roxbury, however, a booming dairy economy, larger farms, and massive emigration allowed the level of landlessness to decrease. There, the proportion of family heads who were laborers or landless farmers dropped from 24 to 18 percent during the 1850s, while the proportion of men aged 35 and older in those occupations declined from 25 to 19 percent.[23]

While many of the landless remained in the hill towns as laborers and subtenants, a greater number left.[24] Doubtless, many of those who emigrated stayed close to home, moving to an adjacent town or a nearby county. Others, however, went very far indeed, making several unsuccessful attempts before achieving a competence. Harvey M. Seaman was born in Delhi, Delaware County, in 1829, the son of a farmer. Seaman's parents had 11 children and could not provide them all with land. They sent Harvey to learn the retail trade from his uncle, H. R. Millard, a Delhi merchant. Seaman lived with Millard for six years, serving him as a clerk. At the expiration of his clerkship, he went to work on his parents' new farm in Pennsylvania. After another three years, he got a job as a clerk in New York City, but quit after a few months. He again returned to his parents' home, teaching school rather than working for his father. After three terms, he became a peddlar—an occupation at which he failed miserably. Casting about for a new occupation, Seaman settled on carpentry. He remained at the trade for only one and a half years. Hearing of the wealth to be gained in the gold fields, he set out for California in 1851. In partnership with his brother Amasa, he became a dealer in mining claims and the manager of a local ferry. In these occupations, the brothers finally met with success. In five years, they acquired enough property to return home. In

1856, when Harvey was 27, he and Amasa settled in Hamden, Delaware County, near two of their brothers. There they bought a tannery together, and there Harvey remained. He bought his brother's interest in the tannery three years later and added a feed mill, a grist mill, and a sawmill. In 1869, at the age of 40, he married Isabel Goodrich, with whom he raised four children.[25]

Seaman's story is hardly typical, but it does contain many elements that others shared. Most parents could not afford to provide all their sons with land; instead, they strove to provide them with cultural capital—with training for another calling. Like Seaman, many who failed to acquire property responded by moving on, searching out new careers and opportunities in unfamiliar locales. And as with Seaman, family connections were at the center of many people's search for a competence. Support from family members was critical in gaining property, and, for many, property afforded them the privilege of settling among kin.

In another way, Seaman's experience was not typical. Not all young men from the former leasehold estates succeeded in acquiring property, and the lives of those who did not were less likely to be recorded for posterity. Any of the reverses in Seaman's career could have been permanent. Poor parents, without helpful kin, might not have been able to provide their son with training as a clerk—training that probably contributed substantially to Seaman's ultimate success. Without a father's farm to return to, Seaman might have remained a merchant's clerk—an occupation that was becoming a less promising avenue to independence in the mid-nineteenth century. Without family support, he might not have been able to scrape together the passage to California or the capital needed to set up a business there. Undoubtedly, many emigrants—and many who stayed close to home—remained in dead-end situations, as unapprenticed and sweated craftsmen, salaried clerks, undercapitalized farmers, wage earners, and tenants.[26]

In the end, the society that the anti-renters helped create fulfilled much of their vision of freedom. Postleasehold society remained grounded in patriarchal, productive households, in which inequalities of power fell primarily along the lines of gender and age, not those of class. Most male heads of families owned land and, with it, enjoyed considerable freedom from control by others. Merchants and creditors continued to prosper from the fruits of farmers' labor, but neither had sufficient power to extract a large proportion of the farmers' surplus, to compel deference, or to control their economic destiny. Landowning farmers, artisans, and shopkeepers did not develop a critique of the credit system or of wage labor in the leasehold towns. Now, with patroonery destroyed, they saw themselves as keeping the full fruits of their labor and as rising or falling by their own efforts. They were now free, as the anti-renters had hoped, "to eat, to save, to sell or sow—Though Princely lords say yes or no!"[27]

But this society fulfilled only one version of the anti-renters' utopia. All anti-renters had hoped for a society in which every adult, white, male head of household had access to land. A substantial minority had sought to do so by limiting the size of landholdings and establishing legal recognition for every man's right to a portion of the soil. Another, overlapping group, probably representing the majority of anti-renters, had sought to preserve their communities and to guarantee the property and security of every community member. These hopes failed to materialize with the disappearance of patroonery. Instead, Ira Harris's and Robert Watson's vision of society triumphed. In the postleasehold order, men were not assured land but were guaranteed the opportunity to acquire it through labor, market exchange, and capital accumulation. Social mobility rather than equal access to natural resources served as the guarantor of equality, and individual initiative—the drive to acquire property and achieve prosperity for one's own family— served as an the engine of economic growth. In this society, social mobility required geographical movement; rather than promoting stability in community membership, the rules of the new order intensified the problem of transience.

Farmers in the leasehold district thus emerged from the Anti-Rent Wars as a yeoman class within a capitalist order. Postleasehold society was not a capitalist society, in which production was controlled by the owners of productive property and carried out by the waged labor of the propertyless. Instead, the economy on the former estates remained primarily dependent on family labor and on hierarchies of age and sex. But the place of that society in the broader capitalist economy was now assured, and its inhabitants now offered no sustained challenge to the rules underlying that economy.

This process of class re-formation, and the consolidation of an industrial capitalist order of which it was a part, hinged both on changes in economic practice and on political and cultural conflicts. Leasehold farmers played a complex role in these struggles. Neither "capitalist" nor "anti-capitalist" in outlook, they selectively appropriated some elements of the capitalist order while remaining ambivalent and divided about others. Most had always embraced with enthusiasm one element of the new order: the expansion of markets for their produce. Although they depended increasingly on alienated labor after 1820, they attempted neither to justify nor condemn this practice or the growing class divisions in their towns. Instead, they celebrated a vision of universal landownership that denied the existence of the landless and, in doing so, excluded them from the benefits of land reform. Just as important, virtually all anti-renters challenged a central element of the emerging capitalist order: the sanctity of contracts agreed to by legal equals. They did not dispute the need for enforceable bargains. Rather, they sought to establish a contract regime that did not recognize bargains that originated in economic coercion or infringed upon the right of each white man to personal dignity and the fruits of his labor. Most importantly, leasehold insurgents divided bitterly over the legitimacy of a cornerstone of the capitalist order: private property and a free market in land.

Such eclecticism, evasion, and division would have been difficult to translate into economic reality, even if political leaders had been receptive. But it is nonetheless of momentous importance that leaders were not receptive. The federal and state constitutions protected private property, the sanctity of contracts, and vested rights. And the guardians of state power in the early nineteenth century—the courts and the political parties—were unanimous in their support for liberalism. Despite deep policy differences, from the mid-1840s on both Whigs and Democrats supported private property in land, economic competition, the unlimited accumulation of property, and the sanctity of contracts entered into by legal equals. Because of their monopoly over elected and appointed offices and their near-complete control of the press, Whig and Democratic activists limited the tenants' access to the state and to broader public opinion. They sought to exclude from public discussion all elements of the anti-renters' ideology and program that challenged either the constitution or the needs of an expanding capitalist economy. Leasehold militants sought to challenge these activists' control over the political process, but they failed. If they were to harness the power of the state in their efforts to destroy patroonery, they would have to do so through the parties—and according to the parties' rules.

Still, the anti-renters' acquiescence in the new economic order was a choice. Perfectionist evangelicals, segments of the emerging working class, and a multiclass reform coalition that would later be known as "labor reformers" all withstood the cultural and political power of the parties, keeping alive their own, sometimes anti-capitalist, visions of "free labor."[28] The anti-renters' abandonment of their oppositional culture, with its challenges to some of the tenets of the emerging capitalist order, grew out of their advantageous position in the new order. Leasehold farmers had always celebrated two important elements of the capitalist economy: ready markets for their produce and the opportunity to accumulate property. The new economy allowed them to take advantage of both in ways that urban journeymen and postbellum southern family farmers found impossible. As general farmers, they met many of their own subsistence needs and produced a variety of crops for sale. Thus, neither their subsistence nor their status as landowners was at the mercy of the fluctuating world price of a single commodity. In addition, where capitalist development created new, superior classes to expropriate the labor of journeymen, southern upcountry farmers, and western corn and wheat growers, most New York tenants found no such new class of oppressors. Instead, the development of a national market with capitalist enterprise at its center provided them with resources to buy their way out of class subordination. As a result, those elements of the new order that violated estate residents' ideals and aims—growing landlessness, increasing use of wage labor and subtenancy, rigid enforcement of all contracts—left them ambivalent rather than outraged at the new order.[29] Just as important, those most likely to be injured by that order offered little opposition because they were the most likely to leave. Much of the potential discontent of the local poor was carried to the west and the cities or absorbed in the ceaseless effort to acquire property.

Figure 9.2. Prosperous residents of the former leasehold estates identified themselves both as laborers and as substantial property owners. This 1880 illustration
of the Storie homestead in Bovina idealizes both agricultural labor and its outcome: a productive, well–ordered farm. The Stories owned two farms—possibly
an outcome of the consolidation of farm ownership that came with the buyout of
the landlords. Mrs. Storie is depicted as co-proprietor of the farm, but only men's
work is in evidence. From *History of Delaware County, New York*. Courtesy, American
Antiquarian Society.

The absence of a sustained challenge to the capitalist order does not mean
that former tenants thought or acted like "pure" capitalists. As household
producers, they continued to occupy an ambiguous place in the capitalist
economy, conforming outwardly to the rules of the market but ruled inter-
nally by a logic entirely different from that governing capitalist enterprises.[30]
Their identity remained dualistic: landowning farmers were both propertied
"business people" and laborers. And their thinking reflected this dualism.
Residents of the former estates in the 1870s and 1880s cherished a distinctly
producerist version of capitalist social thought—one that had first been introduced by Whig and Democratic anti-rent leaders like Ira Harris and
Robert Watson. Smith Boughton, the former "Indian" chief and leader of the
Rensselaer County anti-renters, credited the tenants' movement with having
ushered in a free-labor utopia. The anti-renters, he recalled in the 1880s,
"stripped" the landlords "of their feudal privileges." Forgetting that he and

many of his followers had claimed the soil by natural right, he boasted that the movement had allowed tenants to buy their farms "in fee absolute." Thus each tenant "could sit under his own vine and fig tree of his own planting with no one to make him afraid of being disturbed or driven off." To Boughton, this victory for producers' rights was inseparable from the opening of the former estates to industrial enterprise. With the tenants' victory over the landlords, manufacturers "have erected many hydraulic works which are doing an immense business." "Therefore," he concluded, "great good has arisen from our struggle to overthrow the tyranny that hung over us."[31]

Harriet Jenkins Washbon, a resident of Rensselaerville, dissented bitterly from Boughton's assessment of the anti-renters' accomplishments but shared his enthusiasm for the capitalist economy that had solidified after 1846. Under such an economy, she believed, financial success depended only on the individual industry of each producer. Washbon blamed the relative poverty that her town suffered during the depression of the early 1870s on the previous generation's failure to seize upon the opportunities offered by an expanding market economy. The leasehold conflict, she complained in 1873, had "put our country back" because it had "cost, in time and money, enough to cross and re-cross our town with railroads." The memory of that conflict, she wrote, would remain "painful and humiliating . . . till the energy and industry of our young men has made up, in some measure, for the years of worse than idleness of a portion of our inhabitants."[32]

Farmers' faith in a capitalist order could be double-edged. Nowhere was this more clear than in the Patrons of Husbandry, which rural producers on the former estates joined in droves between 1874 and 1900. The New York Grange never offered a political or ideological challenge to the capitalist economy. Indeed, much of local chapters' efforts were devoted to helping members thrive in that economy by teaching them progressive farming, marketing practices, and habits of industry and sobriety. Significantly, the order excluded wage laborers and embraced a virulent nativism that was directed largely against the immigrant laborers in their communities. But Grangers saw themselves as virtuous producer-citizens in a society increasingly corrupted by monopoly and by the relentless pursuit of profit. They denounced unfair railroad practices and increasing inequalities of wealth. And they sought to curb the power of monopolies through cooperative buying and by lobbying for an income tax, anti-trust legislation, the free coinage of silver, and public regulation of the railroads.[33] Farmers on the former estates accommodated themselves to the ground rules of a capitalist order, but they continued to see themselves as a class distinct from other entrepreneurs. And they opposed the effects of that order that violated their interests as producers and their special vision of capitalism.

This, then, was a second outcome of the Anti-Rent Wars: a more complete integration of farming households into a capitalist economic, legal, and ideological order. With this development came the crystallization of a dualistic

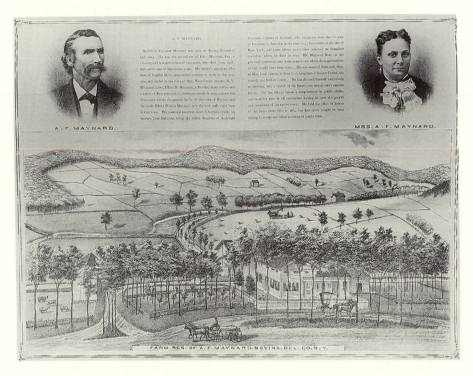

Figure 9.3. Like other members of the post–Civil War middle class, farmers in the former leasehold district idealized domestic life. Unlike their urban counterparts, they also celebrated the labor done by men (buy not by women) that took place in and around that home. Here, A. F. Maynard's Bovina home is depicted with all the trappings of bourgeois comfort, including a pleasure wagon. But by depicting haying in the background, the artist made clear that such comfort was inseparable from manual labor. From *History of Delaware County, New York.* Courtesy, American Antiquarian Society.

class identity and a Janus-faced political presence among farmers. As the nineteenth century wore on, husbandmen continued to depend disproportionately on household labor, but they made use of wage labor as well. They pursued their prosperity as both producers and property-owning entrepreneurs. In politics, they simultaneously looked after their interests as landowning entrepreneurs and fought against the expropriation of the fruits of their labor by monopolistic corporations.[34] In this, they were no different from other northern and western farmers. Western Grangers and Alliancemen shared the former leasehold farmers' dualistic identity, interest, and politics, defending the fruits of their labor from the depredations of railroads, grain elevators, and eastern financiers while making extensive use of migratory harvest laborer and crushing those workers' attempts to defend their own rights as producers.[35]

Free Soil, Free Labor, Free Men

The terms on which the leasehold system was abolished and, to a great extent, the character of the social order that would replace it depended on political power. Access to such power, in turn, depended to a great extent on the rules of the political game. The Jacksonian political order proved both liberating and constraining to tenants. Partisan leaders and the party rank and file both rejected the deferential politics that had buttressed landlords' political power and had helped assure the stability of the leasehold system before 1828. Together, leaders and rank and file created a new political order that offered tenants the leadership skills, organizational models, and indirect access to state power that they needed to mount an effective challenge to the leasehold system.

But anti-renters and political leaders differed as to how politics ought to be conducted. Militants and party men came from separate but overlapping political cultures. Party activists belonged to a partisan culture of lawyers, editors, and avocational politicians who envisioned democratic politics as a process of coalition-building and brokering between diverse constituencies. Their articles of faith included the rule of law, the sanctity of the constitution, and the beneficence of a competitive market economy based on private property, economic competition, and the commodification of land and labor.

Anti-renters participated enthusiastically in partisan culture and absorbed the teachings of party activists. But they practiced other kinds of politics as well: associationism and the localist, vigilante politics of the "Indians." In doing so, they created new institutions, activities, and social spaces that permitted them to think and act in ways that differed from the teachings of party activists. They did this primarily by reinterpreting Democratic principles, applying them to new problems, and drawing new conclusions from them. In the face of the political humiliations of 1844 and 1845, they turned those teachings into a strident critique of the political culture of their teachers. Most rejected party leaders' conception of democracy, embracing a vision of absolute popular sovereignty. Many rejected their leaders' faith in the rule of law and the sanctity of the constitution. Several explicitly rejected the parties' commitment to the rules of a capitalist political economy, challenging the sanctity of contracts or embracing the platform of the National Reformers. Many sought to use partisan methods to break with the parties and to create a new, more democratic electoral organization. Through their eclectic politics, most anti-renters hoped to transform politics, purifying it of corruption and establishing absolute popular sovereignty. Their challenge was short lived. By the end of 1845, militias and posses had crushed the Indians. Over the next three years, Whig and Hunker anti-rent leaders defeated third-party efforts and reduced the anti-capitalist politics of the National Reformers to rubble.

The Anti-Rent Wars thus reveal a process that historians of Jacksonian politics have largely ignored. Among the well-documented interparty struggles over banks, currency, incorporation, and internal improvements lay a less well understood struggle between party activists and popular movements over the boundaries of legitimate political action and the meaning of democracy. The anti-renters were not the only white, male Americans to engage in this struggle. The followers of Thomas Dorr took up arms to defend popular sovereignty in Rhode Island, sparking widespread debate over the right of "the People" to challenge constituted authority. Urban crowds vigorously defended their right to enforce their political, racial, moral, and even aesthetic norms in the streets. Radical evangelicals eschewed party politics, engaging in a politics of association, agitation, and moral suasion. They hoped to sweep aside party politics, constitutional restraints, and statute law, ushering in the Kingdom of the Redeemer. Like the anti-renters, these movements failed to change the rules of the political game.[36]

Overt challenges to the rules underlying the second party system seem to have been limited to three groups: radical evangelicals, urban workers, and white men who did not enjoy the privileges associated with citizenship in antebellum America. The Dorrites challenged the political order because their state constitution excluded them from the vote; the anti-renters were distinguished from their white, male counterparts by a lack of freehold property. Recently, however, Stuart Blumin and Gary Altschuler have suggested that discontent with party politics was far more widespread than contemporary historians have suggested. Their analysis is based on the expressions of editors, printmakers, novelists, and other cultural entrepreneurs, not on the statements of the party rank and file; while suggestive, it is less than definitive about popular attitudes toward politics. Further research is needed before we can determine whether the Dorrites, abolitionists, urban crowds, and anti-renters spoke for a broad, discontented public.[37]

Whether they addressed the grievances of a wide or narrow spectrum of the citizenry, these struggles over the boundaries of the political had critical implications for policy and for the distribution of power. The defeat of the Indians and of third-party challenges meant that popular aspirations would continue to be channeled through the parties and limited to what could be accomplished within the limits set by the constitution, the rule of law, and the requirements of capitalist development. Because of this, leasehold farmers never achieved their central aim: the right to challenge their landlords' titles in court. For all their political influence, the anti-renters would gain freehold property in a manner consistent with the constitution and the rights of property: by buying it. Similarly, the Garrisonians' pacifism and Christian anarchism went down to defeat, and their challenge to the laws protecting human property were frustrated as long as the normal rules of politics remained in force.

Neither the story of the anti-renters nor that of Jacksonian politics was one of silencing and cooptation, however. The anti-renters' relationship to their Whig and Democratic allies was one of reciprocal influence. Ira Harris, Robert Watson, and others sought to silence the unacceptable elements of leasehold militants' social vision while maintaining their electoral support. In doing so, they fused the anti-renters' ideals with the principles of liberal political economy, helping to recreate and extend a powerful ideology of free labor. Similarly, their efforts to retain the loyalties of voters who longed for universal landownership and of radical tenants who had endorsed the National Reformers' ideas about land brought forth a new commitment to a homestead act. Finally, in appealing to militants' desire for absolute popular sovereignty, some party activists embraced a new vision of the state—one in which an activist government did the precise bidding of a sovereign people.

During the Anti-Rent Wars, only a minority of political leaders embraced these innovations. The relationship between leasehold insurgents and Whig and Democratic activists nonetheless had enormous influence on the political mainstream. In the short run, it drove a wedge between reformers and conservatives in both parties, playing a prominent role in the breakup of the Whigs. In the long run, the anti-renters' influence was even more profound. H. J. Munger, a Delaware anti-rent activist, recalled that, in 1856, leasehold insurgents "united with the old Whigs and the Abolitionists and formed a new party under the name of the Republican Party." In Albany county, at least a quarter (27 out of 107) of the delegates from the anti-rent towns at Republican county conventions between 1855 and 1860 came from the ranks of former and current anti-rent activists. Nor did the influence of anti-renters end at the local level. Many of the insurgents' Whig allies—men like Ira Harris and William Seward—played a critical role in the new party's leadership, in both New York and the nation.[38]

Voters in most anti-rent towns flocked to the new party. Despite most Heldebergers' loyalty to the Democrats between 1828 and 1844, the Republicans consistently won pluralities in four of the five Helderberg towns through 1858, defeating both the Democrats and the Know-Nothings. In 1860, with the Know-Nothings out of the way, the party of Lincoln won a majority of hill towns outright. The major leasehold towns of Delaware county were slower to embrace the Republican cause. Bovina alone cast a majority for Fremont in 1856. But the new party captured two more leasehold towns in 1858 and it won four of the six towns in 1860. (See Appendix, table 21.) By 1856, three out of four former anti-rent strongholds in Columbia County voted Republican, as did all of the insurgent towns in Rensselaer County. In the core anti-rent district, only in Schoharie County did a majority of anti-rent towns remain outside the Republican camp.[39]

With a substantial cadre of anti-rent activists, politicians, and voters in Republican ranks, the ideas that had been generated in the dialogue between tenants and their Whig and Democratic allies found a hospitable reception in the new party. These ideas were not the anti-renters' alone. By 1860 they were shared by a broad spectrum of northerners and found their way into the Republican platform and ideology by numerous routes. The former anti-renters were one of many constituencies that shaped the Republican message. But they were a critically important one, having won the support of some of the most important leaders in the new party and provided them with early experience in waging political war on an "unfree" system of property and labor.

Nowhere was the influence of the ideas of the anti-renters' Whig and Democratic allies more apparent than in the Republicans' ideology of "free labor." According to William Seward, the superiority of the North's "free labor system" to southern slavery lay in its capacity to elevate labor and promote economic growth. In a formulation that harkened back to the speeches of Ira Harris and Robert Watson, he argued that the ability to compete on equal terms in a market economy guaranteed that individual ambition would result in both personal prosperity and national progress. "By opening all the fields of industrial employment, and all the departments of authority, to the unchecked and equal rivalry of all classes of men," he told an Empire State audience in 1858, the free labor system "at once secures universal contentment, and brings into the highest possible activity all the physical, moral and social energies of the whole state." Free labor was also the only sure foundation for democracy. "In states where the free labor system prevails," he said, "universal suffrage necessarily obtains, and the state necessarily becomes, sooner or later, a republic or democracy."[40]

This social and economic vision sprang from numerous sources. As numerous historians have shown, the efforts of antebellum courts and employers to justify an emerging system of wage labor were critical in forming a liberal ideology of free labor. One can also see early versions of these ideas in the thinking of Garrisonian abolitionists and Liberty Party activists. But given Seward's long alliance with the anti-renters, it is likely that his free-laborism grew to a great extent out of his and his political allies' decade-long dialogue with the anti-renters.[41]

As important as the origins of the Republicans' free-laborism were the uses to which it was put. Seward's social vision was well suited to constituencies of rural producers who, like the former anti-renters, were becoming rapidly integrated into a broader capitalist economy. Such constituencies were numerous during the late 1850s and early 1860s, and they overwhelmingly voted Republican. Estate residents' entry into the Republican party was part of a regionwide political realignment, as members of the rural middle class in commercially developed and predominantly Yankee areas throughout the North flocked to the party. To win over these voters and to cement a coalition between them and manufacturers in Republican ranks, party leaders celebrated the capacity of northern capitalism to ensure the dignity, prosperity, independence and political power of small producers.[42]

Most Republican leaders tied this producer-friendly vision of capitalism to an endorsement of universal landownership. In doing so, they drew on the legacy of the Anti-Rent Wars, the National Reform movement, and, most probably, western farmers' struggles over land. Speaking to a crowd of farmers in Madison, Wisconsin, Seward replicated the rhetoric of the antislavery–anti-rent coalition's conflation of slavery and land monopoly.

"Aristocracy," he said, was a system under which "the privileged owned the lands, and the many unprivileged work them, or in which the few privileged own the laborers and the laborers work for them." Under both slavery and land monopoly, "the laborer works on compulsion, and under constraint of force," and must yield up the bulk of the fruits of his labor to a superior class. Under both, the laborers had no political power; "the powers of the government are exercised by the owner, of labor and of land." In the Northern free-labor utopia, on the other hand, "no man can monopolize the land which another man is obliged to cultivate, much less monopolize the labor by which the lands . . . are cultivated." Because of this, northern politics and society were "entirely and absolutely established and grounded on democratic principles." Thus, Seward thundered, "the great problem of society . . . is this: Is there any danger that in the United States the citizen will not be the owner of the land he cultivates?" [43]

Seward dedicated himself to eradicating any such danger. So did other Republicans who had sought an alliance with the anti-renters—men like Ira Harris, Richard P. Herrick, and Horace Greeley, who had championed a homestead act since the mid-1840s. So too did leaders of both parties from urban, working-class districts and the West. In 1859, Seward and other pro-homestead Republicans won their national party's support for the measure, convincing Republican congressmen to push a homestead bill through the House and Senate. They rejected the National Reformers' demand that homesteads be inalienable and that the amount of land an individual could own be limited. And they ignored the former anti-renters' belief that every man had a right to the land on which he lived. Instead, they disturbed the property rights of no white man and insured that joining the ranks of the propertied would continue to require leaving home. Just as important, they also endorsed granting large sections of the public domain to railroads. Taken as a whole, their land policy ensured that farmers' land-hunger would help consolidate a capitalist order, both by winning farmers' support for the Republican party and by ensuring that those who moved west would quickly begin producing for national and international markets. At the same time, that policy helped bring into being a variant of capitalist development that promoted widespread, small-scale land ownership. [44]

A third hallmark of Republicans' politics—the use of the state to undermine "unfree" systems of property and labor—drew on the legacy of the Anti-Rent Wars, as well as on the experience and sensibilities of anti-slavery Whigs, Liberty Party supporters, National Reformers, and 10-hour advocates. [45] In advocating this use of the state, antebellum Republicans rejected the most radical anti-rent politicians' conception of the government as a powerful agent of the popular will, unconstrained by constitutional niceties. Even radicals like Seward remained loyal to the federal constitution, denying the power of the federal government to interfere with slavery in the states where it existed. But within the constraints set by the constitution, New York's Republicans labored to fulfill a goal just like that of the anti-rent Whigs and

Barnburners: to use state power to undermine a system of property and labor that they deemed anachronistic, anti-democratic, and unjust.

Nowhere was this more clear than in the senate career of Ira Harris. By far the most influential anti-rent politician, Harris joined the Republican party in the mid-1850s. In 1861, as his former constituents were facing down the state militia under the command of Walter Church, the Republican-dominated state legislature elected Harris to the U.S. Senate. There, he consistently sought to use "any and all constitutional legislation" to "roll back the tide of slavery." He avidly supported legislation to end slavery in the District of Columbia, which was constitutionally under the control of Congress. He led the floor fight for a bill that provided federal funds to compensate slave owners in an effort to convince Missouri to abolish slavery within its borders. He worked ceaselessly to emancipate the human property of those who participated in the Confederate cause. But he opposed as unconstitutional the Radical Republicans' efforts to repeal the Fugitive Slave Act and to allow military commanders to abolish slavery by fiat. "While I should be glad to see slavery abolished, while I expect to see slavery abolished," he reprimanded Charles Sumner, "I do not want to see it abolished" by an unconstitutional and anti-republican "system of legislation."[46]

As any anti-renter could have told him, Harris's constitutionalism made it impossible to destroy an existing set of class relations in the lifetime of the present generation. But under the combined pressure of military necessity and slaves' wartime efforts to free themselves, most Republicans' constitutional scruples gave way. In 1863, Republicans bypassed the Constitution and declared slaves in rebellious territories free.[47] Radicals in the party also abandoned Harris's constitutionalism in principle during the late 1860s. Then a congressional majority embraced something very much like the most radical anti-rent politicians' notion of a powerful state serving the will of a sovereign people.[48] In the meantime, Harris's desire to use the constitutional powers of government to approach social perfection, long frustrated in his efforts on the anti-renters' behalf, bore significant fruit during the crisis of the Union.

The Anti-Rent Wars in no way brought about the emergence of the Republican party, in the leasehold district or elsewhere. Nor did they alone lead the new party to endorse a homestead act or a new ideology of free labor. Rather, as one of the most politically influential social movements of the late antebellum era, the Anti-Rent Wars show that such movements provided many of the materials from which political leaders crafted partisan programs and ideologies. Like other mass-based political parties, the party of Lincoln had to forge a coalition of leaders and voters that could win elections. It is true, as William Gienapp, Michael Holt, and numerous other practitioners of the "new political history" have argued, that the Republicans found their main constituency among Yankees and other Protestants.[49] But these were not the only constituencies that the new party sought, nor were religion and culture the only commitments through which Republicans appealed to voters. Critical to the Republicans' strategy was tying their anti-slavery message

THE GREAT REPUBLICAN REFORM PARTY,
Calling on their Candidate.

Figure 9.4. Adopting the political practices of the former Liberal Whigs and Liberty Party men in their ranks, many Republicans sought the support of a variety of reform constituencies. They thus maintained a reputation for endorsing reforms that, to conservatives, threatened to undermine the foundations of social order—including radical agrarianism. In this 1856 print, a Democratic cartoonist depicts John C. Fremont, the Republican presidential candidate, receiving his constituents: a temperance man, a Woman's Rights advocate, a Fourierist, a free-love enthusiast, a Papist, and an African American. The Fourierist, dressed in rags and carrying a bottle, says, "An equal division of Property is what I go in for." *The Great Republican Reform Party, Calling on their Candidate,* 1856, by Louis Maurer. National Portrait Gallery, Smithsonian Institution.

to the experience, class interests, and reform commitments of a wide range of overlapping constituencies. Thus, in addition to appealing to the anti-slavery, nativist, and prohibitionist commitments of Yankee voters, they sought to appeal to the producerist sentiments of artisans and farmers (many of whom were Yankees) and to reconcile those sentiments to the economic liberalism championed by the manufacturers in their ranks. They also endeavored to appeal to the class interests of land-hungry farmers and sought to recruit the thousands of voters who had been influenced by the National Reformers. Finally, they sought to win the support of diverse constituencies—political abolitionists, labor reformers, textile and iron workers, National Reformers, and anti-renters—who had long been looking to the state to abolish or reform existing social relations.[50] Republicans drew on the ideas and demands of these constituencies, often only after transforming them.

Just as important, the Anti-Rent Wars provided future Republicans with important lessons in how to fight slavery. At the same moment that anti-slavery Whigs and Liberty Party activists were forging a strategy for using federal power to contain and weaken slavery, future Republican leaders among the anti-renters' allies were mobilizing tens of thousands of voters against an "unfree" system of property and labor and learning through legislative combat how to undermine (but not immediately abolish) such a system within the constraints set by the Constitution. As much as any other American statesmen, anti-rent Whigs learned early the constitutional principles and practiced the political arguments needed to mount a political attack on slavery.

This, then, was the legacy of the Anti-Rent Wars. While they did not remake their society and their political system as they wished, the anti-renters helped destroy an entire system of property and labor. They played a part in undermining the party regime in their state. They aided in creating a new party and a new, triumphant ideology of "free labor." They helped tie the political antislavery movement to land reform, and provided its leaders with lessons in using the state to undermine "unfree" systems of property and labor. Far from being crushed by the parties and the advocates of the emerging capitalist order, the anti-renters unleashed a dialectic that helped usher in a new social and political order.

STATISTICAL APPENDIX

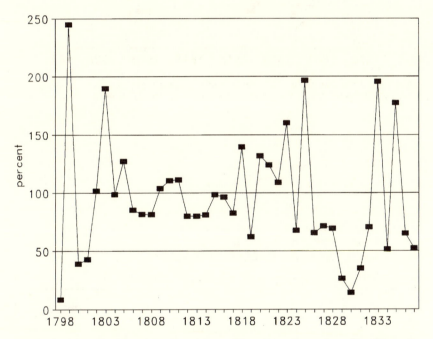

Figure A.1. Rent Payments as a Percentage of Rent Due, Rensselaerville/Westerlo, 1798–1837

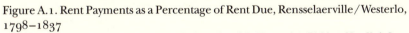

Source: Van Rensselaer Manor Rent Books, Ledgers A and B, Manuscripts Division, New York State Library.

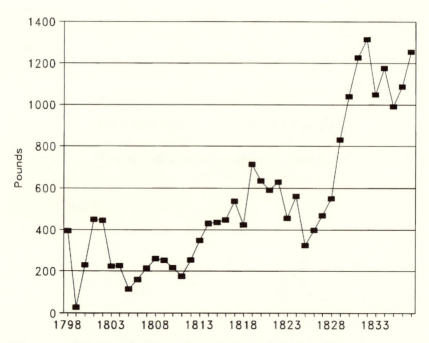

Figure A.2. Overdue Rents, Rensselaerville/Westerlo, 1799–1837
Source: Van Rensselaer Manor Rent Books, Ledgers A and B, Manuscripts Division, New York State Library.

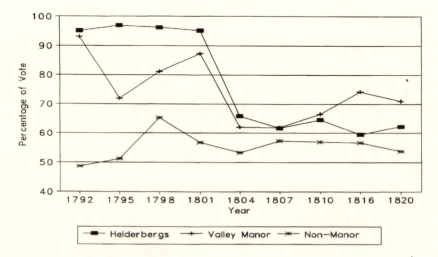

Figure A.3. Federalist Vote, Albany County, 1792–1820
Source: First American Democratization Project Files, American Antiquarian Society.

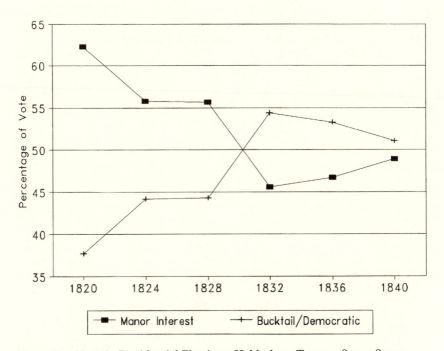

Figure A.4. Votes in Presidential Elections, Helderberg Towns, 1820–1840
Sources: First American Democratization Project Files, American Antiquarian Society, *Albany Evening Journal*, 1836–1840; *Daily Albany Argus*, 1824–1840. Stephen Van Rensselaer and his sons supported the Federalists in 1820, the Clintonian "People's party" in 1824, the National Republicans in 1828 and 1832, and the Whigs thereafter.

Table A.1. Age of Heads of Family by Real Estate Leased or Owned
Rensselaerville, 1800

Value of Real Estate	Aged 16–25		Aged 26–44		Aged 45 and up		Total	
	number	*percent*	*number*	*percent*	*number*	*percent*	*number*	*percent*
$0	13	46.4	155	32.2	53	24.7	221	30.6
$1–299	4	14.3	43	8.9	18	8.4	65	9.0
$300–499	3	10.7	81	16.8	24	11.2	108	14.9
$500–999	7	25.0	134	27.9	71	33.2	212	29.3
$1,000–1,999	1	3.6	65	13.5	42	19.6	108	14.9
$2,000 and over	0	0.0	3	0.6	6	2.8	9	1.2
Total	28	100.0	481	99.9	214	99.9	723	99.9

Source: 1800 Rensselaerville, New York Assessment Roll; 1800 Manuscript Federal Census, Population, Rensselaerville, New York.

Table A.2. Production of Selected Crops and Livestock
Helderbergs and Delaware County Leasehold Towns, 1825 and 1840

Crop	Helderbergs, 1825	Helderbergs, 1840		Delaware County, 1825	Delaware County, 1840	
		number	per person engaged in agric.		number	per person engaged in agric.
Cattle	13,530	15,990	4.1	19,690	23,758	8.5
Dairy products sold ($)	n/a	68,667	17.8	n/a	138,272	49.7
Sheep	36,479	39,436	10.2	49,941	56,546	20.3
Swine	13,911	18,387	4.8	12,786	9,847	3.5
Wheat (bu)	n/a	17,197	4.5	n/a	38,827	13.9
Rye (bu)	n/a	52,977	13.7	n/a	60,023	21.6
Buckwheat (bu)	n/a	74,326	19.2	n/a	28,192	10.1
Oats (bu)	n/a	427,659	110.7	n/a	225,510	81.0
Potatoes (bu)	n/a	313,913	81.2	n/a	315,890	113.4
Hay (tons)	n/a	27,188	7.0	n/a	33,125	11.9
Orchard products ($)	n/a	19,702	5.1	n/a	5,923	2.1
Corn (bu)	n/a	39,742	10.3	n/a	10,033	3.6
Home manufacturers ($)	131,808	30,693	2.0	141,276	24,011	1.8

Sources: *Census of the State of New York for 1825; Statistics of the United States . . . 1840.*

Table A.3. Farm Size, Westerlo and Roxbury, 1840

Farm Size (acres)	Westerlo number	percent	Roxbury number	percent
1–24	52	13.1	31	8.3
25–49	47	11.8	26	6.9
50–99	138	34.8	94	25.1
100–149	90	22.7	118	31.5
150–199	58	14.6	51	13.6
200–299	11	2.8	39	10.4
300 and over	1	0.3	16	4.3
Total	397	100.1	375	100.1

Sources: Town of Westerlo, NT, Assessment Toll, 1840; Town of Roxbury, NY, Assessment Roll, 1840.

Table A.4. Labor Force Participation in Agriculture, Commerce, Manufacturing, and the Professions, Helderbergs and Delaware County Leasehold Towns, 1820 and 1840

Economic Sector	Helderbergs 1820		Helderbergs 1840		Delaware County 1820		Delaware County 1840	
	number	percent	number	percent	number	percent	number	percent
Agriculture	2,689	84.6	3,865	83.5	2,417	89.1	2,785	80.9
Commerce	35	1.1	104	2.2	17	0.6	79	2.3
Manufactures	456	14.3	605	13.1	279	10.3	528	15.3
Professions	n/a	n/a	57	1.2	n/a	n/a	50	1.5
Total	3,180	100.0	4,631	100.0	2,713	100.0	3,442	100.0

Sources: *Fourth Census of the United States, 1820; Sixth Census of the United States, 1840.*

Table A.5: Real Estate Holdings of Heads of Families, by Age, Westerlo, 1850

Real Estate Held	Aged 16–25		Aged 26–44		Aged 45 and up		Total	
	number	percent	number	percent	number	percent	number	percent
$0	13	38.2	69	31.2	43	16.9	125	24.5
$1–499	2	5.9	13	5.9	15	5.9	30	5.9
$500–999	1	2.9	14	6.3	12	4.7	27	5.3
$1,000–1,999	9	26.5	43	19.5	45	17.7	97	19.0
$2,000–2,999	6	17.7	44	19.9	38	14.9	88	17.3
$3,000–4,999	3	8.8	28	12.7	70	27.5	101	19.8
$5,000 and over	0	0.0	10	4.5	32	12.6	42	8.2
Total	34	100.0	221	100.0	255	100.2	510	100.0

Source: 1850 Federal Manuscript Census, Population Schedules, Westerlo, NY.

Table A.6. Real Estate Holdings of Heads of Families, by Age, Roxbury, 1850

Real Estate Held	Aged 16–25		Aged 26–44		Aged 45 and up		Total	
	number	percent	number	percent	number	percent	number	percent
$0	16	59.3	90	34.1	49	24.4	155	31.5
$1–99	1	3.7	22	8.3	18	9.0	41	8.3
$100–299	2	7.4	35	13.3	21	10.5	58	11.8
$300–499	4	14.8	36	13.6	29	14.4	69	14.0
$500–999	2	7.4	34	12.9	34	16.9	70	14.2
$1,000–1,999	1	3.7	37	14.0	32	15.9	70	14.2
$2,000 and over	1	3.7	10	3.8	18	9.0	29	5.9
Total	27	100.0	264	100.0	201	100.1	492	99.9

Source: 1850 Federal Manuscript Census, Population Schedules, Westerlo, NY.

Table A.7. Whig Vote (1840) and Selected Religious and Economic Data, Rural Albany County

Town	Whig vote 1840 (%)	Evangelical and/or New England churches	Conservative churches (Dutch Reformed or Episcopalian)	Percentage of population over 20 in temperance societies, 1833	Percentage of gainfully employed in agriculture	Manufacturing capital per inhabitant ($)	Wool produced per agricultural worker (lbs.)	Dairy produce per agricultural worker ($)	Bushels wheat per agricultural worker	Home Manufacturing per inhabitant ($)
Knox	76.2	2	1	16.4	85.3	4.00	35.0	21.24	13.3	3.94
Guilderland	61.2	2	2	n/a	90.7	2.49	8.4	11.32	1.2	2.35
New Scotland	56.7	6	4	n/a	91.4	1.58	3.1	10.99	0.2	0.00
Bethlehem	54.8	2	2	34.2	91.3	8.97	7.1	9.87	0.1	2.39
Average Whig		**3.0**	**2.3**	**23.5**	**89.7**	**4.26**	**13.4**	**13.36**	**3.7**	**2.17**
Bern	48.7	7	3	25.7	81.0	4.33	25.4	19.39	5.2	2.23
Westerlo	44.3	5	2	55.8	83.9	4.35	17.7	20.11	4.3	2.35
Rensselaerville	29.6	7	1	30.1	73.0	38.95	29.2	23.33	5.2	1.8
Coeymans	27.9	3	2	n/a	73.0	9.99	16.2	21.27	2.0	1.84
Average Democratic		**5.5**	**2**	**36.7**	**77.7**	**14.41**	**22.1**	**21.02**	**4.2**	**2.05**

Sources: *Albany Evening Journal*, 19 Nov. 1840; *Census of the State of New York for 1845*; *Second Annual Report of the New-York State Society for the Promotion of Temperance* (Albany: Packard and Van Benthuysen, 1831); *Fourth Annual Report of the New-York State Society for the Promotion of Temperance* (Albany: Packard and Van Benthuysen, 1833); *Statistics of the United States . . . 1840*; *Sixth Census of the United States*.

Statistics on the proportion of the adult population enrolled in temperance societies is based on membership figures in the *Fourth Annual Report* (1833); where no information was available for a town in that report, they are from the *Second Annual Report* (1831).

Table A.8. Whig Vote (1840) and Selected Religious and Economic Data, Delaware County

Town	Whig vote 1840 (%)	Evangelical and/or New England churches	Conservative churches (Dutch Reformed or Episcopalian)	Percentage of population over 20 in temperance societies, 1833	Percentage of gainfully employed in agriculture	Manufacturing capital per inhabitant ($)	Wool produced per agricultural worker (lbs.)	Dairy produce per agricultural worker ($)	Bushels wheat per agricultural worker	Home Manufacturing per inhabitant ($)
Andes	65.0	3	0	39.4	87.7	4.32	22.7	39.36	9.1	1.10
Hamden	63.4	1	0	n/a	82.0	14.53	30.7	26.37	0.0	1.68
Bovina	58.9	4	0	10.7	83.5	3.03	33.2	86.43	13.6	2.49
Masonville	57.3	3	0	37.6	90.0	4.96	30.9	22.10	0.0	2.60
Harpersfield	55.9	2	0	n/a	81.5	3.03	36.9	48.09	0.0	2.64
Roxbury	53.1	4	2	11.3	80.8	21.11	20.7	69.58	11.4	2.10
Delhi	52.8	5	1	n/a	66.6	13.98	32.6	44.89	0.0	1.85
Meredith	50.6	3	0	13.1	87.0	3.96	46.1	52.56	0.0	1.85
Average Whig		**3.1**	**0.4**	**20.5**	**82.4**	**8.62**	**30.5**	**48.67**	**4.3**	**1.95**
Stamford	49.9	4	1	17.1	70.2	4.82	91.4	39.41	22.6	1.96
Hancock	48.8	2	0	24.0	56.2	13.11	16.0	37.38	0.0	1.22
Kortright	43.5	5	0	11.6	83.8	5.53	35.5	38.97	17.8	1.83
Middletown	43.0	0	0	21.3	79.5	14.67	24.3	32.64	11.7	1.54
Walton	39.7	3	1	29.3	82.2	3.03	30.9	16.54	0.0	1.84
Colchester	31.4	1	0	38.9	85.9	0.57	19.2	4.11	0.0	1.57
Franklin	27.5	5	0	10.5	83.0	7.32	37.0	36.12	0.0	2.81
Sidney	27.4	2	0	15.9	89.2	6.81	24.9	18.51	0.0	3.22
Tompkins	22.4	5	0	61.7	75.8	8.70	22.2	27.34	0.0	3.22
Davenport	19.8	3	0	n/a	83.5	13.65	19.6	23.68	0.0	1.15
Average Democratic		**3**	**0.2**	**23.5**	**78.9**	**7.82**	**32.1**	**27.47**	**5.2**	**1.89**

Sources: *Delaware Gazette*, 18 Nov. 1840; 18, *Census of the State of New York for 1845*; *Second Annual Report of the New-York State Society for the Promotion of Temperance* (Albany: Packard and Van Benthuysen, 1831); *Fourth Annual Report of the New-York State Society for the Promotion of Temperance* (Albany: Packard and Van Benthuysen, 1833); *Statistics of the United States . . . 1840*; *Sixth Census of the United States*.

Statistics on the proportion of the adult population enrolled in temperance societies is based on membership figures in the *Fourth Annual Report* (1833); where no information was available for a town in that report, they are form the *Second Annual Report* (1831).

Table A.9. Occupations of Anti-Rent Association Activists, 1850

Occupation	Albany County		Delaware County		Total	
	number	*percent*	*number*	*percent*	*number*	*percent*
Farmers	106	80.92	35	66.04	141	76.63
Laborers	1	0.76	0	0.00	1	0.54
Millers and Manufacturers	3	2.29	3	5.66	6	3.26
Merchants	10	7.63	9	16.98	19	10.33
Professionals	7	5.34	4	7.55	11	5.98
Craftsmen	4	3.05	2	3.77	6	3.26
Total	131	99.99	53	100.00	184	100.00

Sources: *Albany Freeholder,* 1845–46; 1850 Federal Manuscript Census, Population Schedules, Albany and Delaware Counties, New York.

Table A.10. Real Estate Holdings of Anti-Rent Association Activists Listed as Farmers, 1850

Value of Real Estate	Albany County		Delaware County		Total	
	number	*percent*	*number*	*percent*	*number*	*percent*
$0	13	12.26	0	0.00	13	9.22
$1–$999	8	7.55	3	8.57	11	7.80
$1000–$1999	11	10.38	2	5.71	13	9.22
$2000–$2999	19	17.92	12	34.29	31	21.99
$3000–$3999	17	16.04	7	20.00	24	17.02
$4000–$4999	14	13.21	7	20.00	21	14.89
$5000 and up	24	22.64	4	11.43	28	19.86
Total	106	100.00	35	100.00	141	100.00

Sources: *Albany Freeholder,* 1845–46; 1850 Federal Manuscript Census, Population Schedules, Albany and Delaware Counties, New York.

Table A.11. Age of Anti-Rent Association Activists and "Indians," Delaware County, 1845

Age in 1845	Association Activists		Indians	
	number	*percent*	*number*	*percent*
under 20	1	1.82	6	17.65
20–29	8	14.55	13	38.24
30–39	18	32.73	8	23.53
40–49	18	32.73	5	14.71
50–59	5	9.09	2	5.88
60 and older	5	9.09	0	0.00
Total	55	100.01	34	100.01

Sources: *Albany Freeholder,* 1845–46; *Delaware Gazette,* 15 Oct. 1845; 1850 Federal Manuscript Census, Population Schedules, Albany and Delaware Counties, New York.

Table A.12. Occupations of Indians and Anti-Rent Association Activists, Delaware County, 1845

Occupation	Association Activists		Indians	
	number	*percent*	*number*	*percent*
Farmers	34	65.38	18	52.94
Craftsmen	2	3.85	4	11.76
Laborers	0	0.00	10	29.41
Manufacturers	3	5.77	0	0.00
Merchants	9	17.31	1	2.94
Professionals	4	7.69	1	2.94
Total	52	100.00	34	99.99

Sources: *Albany Freeholder,* 1845–46; *Delaware Gazette,* 15 Oct. 1845; 1850 Federal Manuscript Census, Population Schedules, Albany and Delaware Counties, New York.

Table A.13. Landholdings of Anti-Rent Association Activists and Indians Listed as Farmers, Delaware County, 1850

Value of Real Estate	Association Activists		Indians	
	number	*percent*	*number*	*percent*
$0	0	0.0	1	5.6
$0–999	3	8.8	5	27.8
$1,000–1,999	2	5.9	5	27.8
$2,000–2,999	12	35.3	2	11.1
$3,000–3,999	7	20.6	1	5.6
$4,000–4,999	7	20.6	2	11.1
$5,000 and over	3	8.8	2	11.1
Total	34	100.0	18	100.1

Sources: *Albany Freeholder,* 1845–46; *Delaware Gazette,* 15 Oct. 1845; 1850 Federal Manuscript Census, Population Schedules, Albany and Delaware Counties, New York.

Table A.14. Landholdings of Anti-Rent Association Activists and Indians Listed as Farmers and Aged 35 to 54, Delaware County, 1850

Value of Landholdings	Association Activists		Indians	
	number	*percent*	*number*	*percent*
$1–999	0	0.0	3	42.9
$1,000–1,999	2	9.1	1	14.3
$2,000 and over	20	90.9	3	42.9
Total	22	100.0	7	100.1

Sources: *Albany Freeholder,* 1845–46; *Delaware Gazette,* 15 Oct. 1845; 1850 Federal Manuscript Census, Population Schedules, Albany and Delaware Counties, New York.

Table A.15. Occupations of Supporters and Nonsupporters
of National Reform, 1850

Occupation	National Reform Supporters		Not National Reform Supporters		Total	
	number	percent	number	percent	number	percent
Farmers	14	66.67	142	79.33	156	78.00
Laborers	0	0.00	1	0.56	1	0.50
Millers and Manufacturers	0	0.00	6	3.35	6	3.00
Merchants	2	9.52	18	10.06	20	10.00
Professionals	4	19.05	7	3.91	11	5.50
Craftsmen	1	4.76	5	2.79	6	3.00
Total	21	100.00	179	100.00	200	100.00

Sources: *Albany Freeholder*, 1845–46; *Anti-Renter*, 1845–46; *Young America*, 1845–46; 1850 Federal Manuscript Census, Population Schedules, Albany and Delaware Counties, New York.

Table A.16. Real Estate Holdings of Supporters and Nonsupporters of National Reform Listed as Farmers, 1850

Value of Real Estate	National Reform Supporters		Not National Reform Supporters		Total	
	number	percent	number	percent	number	percent
$0	0	0.00	14	10.69	14	9.66
$1–$999	1	7.14	10	7.63	11	7.59
$1000–$1999	1	7.14	12	9.16	13	8.97
$2000–$2999	2	14.29	29	22.14	31	21.38
$3000–$3999	3	21.43	22	16.79	25	17.24
$4000–$4999	4	28.57	18	13.74	22	15.17
$5000 and up	3	21.43	26	19.85	29	20.00
Total	14	100.00	131	100.00	145	100.01

Sources: *Albany Freeholder*, 1845–46; *Anti-Renter*, 1845–46; *Young America*, 1845–46; 1850 Federal Manuscript Census, Population Schedules, Albany and Delaware Counties, New York.

Table A.17. Party Activities of Supporters and Nonsupporters of National Reform, 1832–1846

Party Affiliation	National Reform Supporters		Not National Reform Supporters		Total	
	number	percent	number	percent	number	percent
Democrats	9	90.0	55	60.4	64	63.4
Whigs	1	10.0	36	39.6	37	36.6
Total	10	100.0	91	100.0	101	100.0

Sources: *Albany Freeholder*, 1845–46; *Anti-Renter*, 1845–46; *Young America*, 1845–46; *Albany Evening Journal*, 1834–44; *Daily Albany Argus*, 1832–44.

Table A.18. Populations of Helderberg Towns, 1840 and 1865

Town	Population 1840	Population 1865	Percent Change
Bern	3,740	2,851	−23.8
Knox	2,143	1,809	−15.6
New Scotland	2,912	3,311	+13.7
Rensselaerville	3,705	2,745	−25.9
Westerlo	3,096	2,497	−19.3
Total	15,596	13,213	−15.3

Sources: *Sixth Census of the United States, 1840; Census of the State of New York, for the Year 1865.*

Table A.19. Population of Selected Delaware County Leasehold Towns 1840 and 1865

Town	Population 1840	Population 1865	Percent change
Andes	2,176	2,815	+29.4
Bovina	1,403	1,146	−18.3
Kortright	2,441	1,897	−22.3
Middletown	2,608	3,119	+19.6
Roxbury	3,013	2,335	−22.5
Stamford	1,681	1,556	−7.4
Total	13,322	12,868	−3.4

Sources: *Sixth Census of the United States, 1840; Census of the State of New York, for the Year 1865.*

Table A.20. Production of Selected Crops and Livestock in Selected Manor Towns, Albany and Delaware County, 1840 and 1865

Crops	Albany County, 1840	Albany County, 1865	Delaware County, 1840	Delaware County, 1865
Wheat (bu.)	17,197	2,008	38,197	1,667
Rye (bu.)	52,977	43,865	60,023	15,175
Potatoes (bu.)	313,913	152,435	315,890	151,158
Peas (bu.)	n/a	4,419	n/a	342
Beans (bu.)	n/a	2,009	n/a	354
Poultry ($)	14,242	23,373	5,826	8,050
Eggs Sold ($)	n/a	18,182	n/a	3,018
Home-manufactured cloth (yards)	n/a	15,640	n/a	23,445
Hay (tons)	27,188	33,978	33,125	41,199
Hogs	18,387	6,014	9,847	4,546
Sheep	39,436	32,167	56,546	17,277
Wool (lbs.)	72,800	138,093	97,059	56,205
Cattle	15,990	8,186	23,758	25,409
Dairy products ($)	$68,667	n/a	$138,272	n/a
Butter (lbs.)	429,169 (est.)	674,273	864,200 (est.)	2,002,357

Sources: *Sixth Census of the United States, 1840; Census of the State of New York, for the Year 1865.*
To make production figures for butter comparable between years, the 1840 figures for dairy products, which were in dollars, were converted into pounds by dividing them by the average market price in Boston for the year 1840, as listed in Percy Wells Bidwell and John I Falconer, *History of Agriculture in the Northern United States, 1620–1860* (New York: Peter Smith, 1941), 502.

Table A.21. Votes
Selected Leasehold Towns, Albany and Delaware Counties, 1848, 1856–60

Town	1848 (percentages)			1856 (percentages)			1858 (percentages)			1860 (percentages)	
	Free Soil	Dem.	Whig	Rep.	Dem.	Amer.	Rep.	Dem.	Amer.	Rep.	Dem.
Berne	18.3	30.1	51.5	39.0	29.5	31.5	48.3	38.9	7.4	50.7	49.3
Knox	11.7	15.2	73.1	48.7	15.4	35.9	49.4	30.5	20.1	66.3	33.7
New Scotland	10.8	33.0	56.1	46.2	28.6	25.2	44.3	35.9	19.1	59.3	40.7
Rensselaerville	38.9	38.5	22.6	34.9	56.2	9.0	29.8	57.2	7.5	38.5	61.5
Westerlo	12.5	48.3	39.2	45.0	36.8	18.2	44.1	39.0	15.8	49.4	50.6
Helderberg Average	**19.0**	**33.9**	**47.1**	**42.2**	**34.8**	**23.0**	**42.7**	**41.1**	**13.6**	**52.0**	**48.0**
Andes	84.2	1.4	14.4	42.3	6.64	51.0	37.2	10.4	52.4	63.7	36.3
Bovina	91.5	2.7	5.8	69.0	7.54	23.4	65.9	19.0	15.1	74.9	25.1
Kortright	79.4	8.9	11.7	31.4	22.0	46.5	37.3	30.6	32.1	53.0	47.0
Middletown	80.0	7.2	12.8	19.8	45.1	35.2	44.4	48.8	6.8	48.8	51.2
Roxbury	50.2	8.2	41.6	20.5	36.2	43.3	38.7	50.2	11.1	44.8	55.2
Stamford	54.3	9.8	36.0	30.5	33.0	36.6	39.6	35.7	24.8	53.4	46.6
Delaware County Average	**70.9**	**6.6**	**22.5**	**32.5**	**26.9**	**40.7**	**42.0**	**34.4**	**23.7**	**54.9**	**45.1**

Sources: *Albany Evening Journal*; *Daily Albany Argus*; *Delaware Gazette*; Joel Silbey–Lee Benson New York Election Data, 1845–1857.

NOTES

Abbreviations

AAS   American Antiquarian Society, Worcester, Massachusetts
ACHR   Albany County Hall of Records, Albany, New York
AIHA   Albany Institute of History and Art Library, Albany, New York
CU   Department of Manuscripts and Archives, Cornell University Libraries, Ithaca, New York
DCC   Delaware County Clerk's Office, Delhi, New York
DCHA   Delaware County Historical Association, Delhi, New York
JA   New York (State) Legislature, *Journal of the Assembly of the State of New York*
JAH   *Journal of American History*
JS   New York (State) Legislature, *Journal of the Senate of the State of New York*
NYAD   *New York Assembly Documents*
NYHS   New-York Historical Society, New York City
NYPL   New York Public Library, New York City
NYSA   New York State Archive, Albany, New York
NYSD   *New York Senate Documents*
NYSHA   New York State Historical Association Library, Cooperstown, NY
NYSL   Manuscripts Division, New York State Library, Albany, NY
RPI   Rensselaer Polytechnic Archives
VRML   Van Rensselaer Manor Leases, Manuscripts Division, New York State Library, Albany, New York
VRMP   Van Rensselaer Manor Papers, Manuscripts Division, New York State Library, Albany, New York
VRMRB   Van Rensselaer Manor Rent Books, Manuscripts Division, New York State Library, Albany, New York

Introduction

1. *Albany Atlas* (weekly edition), 13 Aug. 1844; *Albany Argus,* 12 Aug. 1844; *Young America,* 17 Aug. 1844.

2. "Leasehold" estates or tenures are estates or tenures in which land is held

by lease rather than by deed. For the size and population of the estates and the extent of anti-rent support, see the sources cited in notes 6 and 7 below.

3. *Albany Atlas* (weekly edition), 13 Aug. 1844; *Albany Argus,* 12 Aug. 1844; *Young America,* 17 Aug. 1844.

4. *New York Tribune,* reprinted in *Albany Freeholder,* 17 Sept. 1845; William Elliot, *Carolina Sports by Land and Water: Including Incidents of Devil-Fishing, Wild-Cat, Deer and Bear Hunting, Etc.* (1846), quoted in Stephanie McCurry, *Masters of Small Worlds: Yeoman Households, Gender Relations, and the Political Culture of the Antebellum South Carolina Low Country* (New York: Oxford University Press, 1995); James Fenimore Cooper, *Satanstoe: A Tale of the Colony* (1845; reprint ed., New York: Funk and Wagnalls, 1969); Cooper, *The Chainbearer* (1845; reprint ed., New York: Stringer and Townsend, 1856); Cooper, *The Redskins: Or, Indian and Injun, Being the Conclusion of the Littlepage Manuscripts* (1846; reprint ed., New York: Stringer and Townsend, 1855).

5. The standard works on the movement are from the 1940s: Henry Christman, *Tin Horns and Calico: A Decisive Episode in the Emergence of Democracy* (1945; reprint, Cornwallville, NY: Hope Farm Press, 1978); David Maldwyn Ellis, *Landlords and Farmers in the Hudson-Mohawk Region, 1790–1850* (1945; reprint ed., New York: Octagon Books, 1967). See also Edward P. Cheyney, *The Anti-Rent Agitation in the State of New York,* Political Economy and Public Law Series, No. 2 (Philadelphia: Publications of the University of Pennsylvania, 1887); Isabel Thompson Kelsay, "Down With the Rent!: A Story of Social War in Rural New York" (Ph.D. dissertation, Columbia University, 1950); Albert Champlin Mayham, *The Anti-Rent War on Blenheim Hill: An Episode of the '40s* (Jefferson, NY: Frederick L. Frazee, 1906); John D. Monroe, *The Anti-Rent War in Delaware County, New York* (Jefferson, NY: privately printed, 1940); David Murray, "The Antirent Episode in the State of New York," American Historical Association, *Annual Report,* 1886; Eldridge Clarence Pendleton, "The New York Anti-Rent Controversy, 1830–1860" (Ph.D. dissertation, University of Virginia, 1974). Recently, historians have again begun to take interest in the movement. See Thomas Summerhill, "The Farmer's Republic: Agrarian Protest and the Capitalist Transformation of Upstate New York, 1840–1900" (Ph.D. dissertation, University of California, San Diego, 1993), chapters 2–4; Charles W. McCurdy, *Fettered Democracy: The Anti-Rent Era in New York Law and Politics, 1840–1865* (forthcoming, University of North Carolina Press). I am grateful to both Professor Summerhill and Professor McCurdy for allowing me to see their work before it went to press.

6. State of New York, *Messages from the Governors,* ed. Charles Z. Lincoln (Albany: J.B. Lyon, 1909), 4: 408; Bureau of the Census, U.S. Department of Commerce, *Statistical History of the United States from Colonial Times to the Present* (Stamford, CT: Fairfield Publishers, n.d.), 13. This figure almost certainly underestimates the number of leasehold tenants in the state during the early nineteenth century. It lists only those tenants who held leases in perpetuity or for a number of lives, excluding the large and growing number who held their land for a term of years. The estimate was also made in 1848, after estate populations had been declining for a decade or more.

7. NYAD 1845, 247:1, cited in McCurdy, *Fettered Democracy,* chapter 7; Albany *Freeholder,* 21 May, 27 Aug. 1845. By contrast, David Szatmary estimates that Shays' Rebellion involved some 9,000 militants; see his *Shays' Rebellion: The Making of an Agrarian Insurgency* (Amherst: University of Massachusetts Press, 1980), 58–59. Thomas Slaughter does not offer any overall estimates of support for the Whiskey Rebellion. But the largest single mobilization of the rebellion involved 7,000 mil-

itants—a number dwarfed by both anti-rent voting strength and the anti-rent "Indian" mobilizations of 1844–46. See Thomas Slaughter, *The Whiskey Rebellion: Frontier Epilogue to the American Revolution* (New York: Oxford University Press, 1986), 186–88.

8. Evidence of the leading role of New York's leaders is evident throughout the historiography of antebellum politics. See, for example, Harry Watson, *Liberty and Power: The Politics of Jacksonian America* (New York: Farrar, Straus, and Giroux, 1990); John Ashworth, *"Agrarians" and "Aristocrats": Party Political Ideology in the United States, 1837–1846* (New York: Cambridge University Press, 1987); Donald B. Cole, *Martin Van Buren and the American Political System* (Princeton: Princeton University Press, 1984); David M. Potter, *The Impending Crisis, 1848–1861* (New York: Harper and Row, 1976).

9. Like the Anti-Rent Wars, antebellum agrarian movements have been largely ignored since the 1940s but are now beginning to attract the interest of historians. See Charles Brooks, *Frontier Settlement and Market Revolution: The Holland Land Purchase* (Ithaca: Cornell University Press, 1996); Jamie Bronstein, *Land Reform and Working-Class Experience in Britain and America* (forthcoming, Stanford University Press); Paul Wallace Gates, *The Farmer's Age: Agriculture, 1815–1860* (New York: Holt, Reinhart, 1960); Gates, *Fifty Million Acres: Conflicts Over Kansas Land Policy, 1854–1890* (Ithaca, NY: Cornell University Press, 1954); Gates, *History of Public Land Law Development* (Washington, D.C.: U.S. Government Printing Office, 1968); Allan G. Bogue, *From Prairie to Corn Belt: Farming on the Illinois and Iowa Prairies in the Nineteenth Century* (Chicago: University of Chicago Press, 1963); idem, "The Iowa Claim Clubs: Symbol and Substance," *Mississippi Valley Historical Review* 45 (1959): 231–53; Paul Demund Evans, *The Holland Land Company* (Buffalo: Buffalo Historical Society, 1924); Roy Robbins, *Our Landed Heritage: The Public Domain, 1776–1936* (Princeton: Princeton University Press, 1942); Helene Sara Zahler, *Eastern Workingmen and National Land Policy, 1829–1862* (New York: Columbia University Press, 1941). Alan Taylor, in *Liberty Men and Great Proprietors: The Revolutionary Settlement on the Maine Frontier* (Chapel Hill: University of North Carolina Press, 1990), provides a model study of an earlier agrarian conflict; his book has greatly influenced this study.

10. Christopher Clark, *The Roots of Rural Capitalism: Western Massachusetts, 1780–1860* (Ithaca: Cornell University Press, 1990); Winifred Barr Rothenberg, *From Market-Places to a Market Economy: The Transformation of Rural Massachusetts, 1750–1850* (Chicago: University of Chicago Press, 1992); Allan Kulikoff, *The Agrarian Origins of American Capitalism* (Charlottesville: University Press of Virginia, 1992), 13–95; Jonathan Prude, *The Coming of Industrial Order: Town and Factory Life in Rural Massachusetts, 1810–1860* (New York: Cambridge University Press, 1985); Robert A. Gross, "Culture and Cultivation: Agriculture and Society in Thoreau's Concord," *Journal of American History* 69 (1982): 42–61.

11. The debate over farmers and the "Market Revolution" or transition to capitalism is extensive. See especially Clark, *Roots of Rural Capitalism;* Rothenberg, *From Market-Places to a Market Economy;* Kulikoff, *Agrarian Origins of American Capitalism,* 13–95; Prude, *Coming of Industrial Order;* Gross, "Culture and Cultivation."

12. Glenn C. Altschuler and Stuart M. Blumin, "Limits of Political Engagement in Antebellum America: A New Look at the Golden Age of Participatory Democracy," *Journal of American History* 84 (1997): 855–85. See also idem, "'Where is the Real America?': Politics and Popular Consciousness in the Antebellum Era," *American Quarterly* 49 (1997): 225–67. The leading Progressive

and neoprogressive historians of Jacksonian politics are, respectively, Arthur M. Schlesinger, Jr., *The Age of Jackson* (Boston: Little, Brown, 1946); Charles Sellers, *The Market Revolution: Jacksonian America, 1815–1846* (New York: Oxford University Press, 1991). The specific interpretation I cite here is Sellers's. Practitioners of the new social history who ignore formal politics include Christopher Clark, *The Roots of Rural Capitalism: Western Massachusetts, 1780–1860* (Cornell University Press, 1990); those who depict party leaders as coopting and silencing popular aspirations include Sean Wilentz, *Chants Democratic: New York City and the Rise of the American Working Class, 1788–1850* (New York: Oxford University Press, 1984) and Alan Dawley, *Class and Community: The Industrial Revolution in Lynn* (Cambridge, Mass.: Harvard University Press, 1976).

13. See, for example, Wilentz, *Chants Democratic*, 211–16; Ronald Formisano, *The Transformation of Political Culture: Massachusetts Parties, 1790s–1840s* (New York: Oxford University Press, 1984), 271–75; Amy Bridges, *A City in the Republic: Antebellum New York and the Origins of Machine Politics* (New York: Cambridge University Press, 1984), 103–24.

14. Unfortunately, the criticism they cite tells us nothing direct about ordinary voters, for it all comes from cultural entrepreneurs: novelists, commercial printmakers, P.T. Barnum, and partisan editors. For more direct evidence of popular discontent with the Jacksonian parties, see Wilentz, *Chants Democratic*, 326–35; Bridges, *A City in the Republic*, 77–82.

15. In its analysis of politics, this study draws inspiration from three bodies of scholarship. The first and most influential includes the work of Harry Watson, Amy Bridges, Joel Silbey, and Ronald Formisano, who emphasize the distance between the interests of party leaders and constituents, depicting party leaders as reshaping the demands of constituents to fit the requirements of coalition building and the needs of party organization. Except for Formisano, these historians eschew a close analysis of ideas. And they focus on the actions of party leaders, paying little attention to the ways in which constituents appropriated and reshaped partisan ideas and programs or responded to leaders' appropriation of their demands. But they provide a valuable model for investigating how the dynamics of party politics shaped political leaders' response to anti-rent ideas and initiatives. Bridges, *City in the Republic;* Silbey, *The American Political Nation, 1838–1893* (Stanford: Stanford University Press, 1991); Watson, *Jacksonian Politics and Community Conflict: The Emergence of the Second American Party System in Cumberland County, North Carolina* (Baton Rouge: Louisiana State University Press, 1981); Formisano, *Transformation of Political Culture.*

This work also draws insight from the "new institutional historians," who emphasize that politics was neither a matter of free choice nor a direct reflection of social forces, but was shaped and limited by the structure of the state and the rules of the political game. See, for example, Stephen Skowronek, *Building the New American State: The Expansion of National Administrative Capacities* (New York: Cambridge University Press, 1982); L. Ray Gunn, The Decline of Authority: Public Economic Policy and Political Development in New York State, 1800–1860 (Ithaca: Cornell University Press, 1988); Peter B. Evans, Theda Skocpol, and Dietrich Rueschemeyer, *Bringing the State Back In* (Cambridge, Eng.: Cambridge University Press, 1985); Stephen D. Krasner, "Approaches to the State: Alternative Conceptions and Historical Dynamics," *Comparative Politics* 16 (1984): 223–46.

By extending the insights of both of these groups of historians, we can move beyond narratives of triumph or cooptation and ask about the reciprocal influence of particular constituencies and the political system. And we can explore the ways in which the structure of the state and of party politics determined the limits and possibilities for popular political action.

Finally, this book is part of a broader effort to apply the methods and insights of the "new" social and cultural histories to the study of public life. See, for example, David Waldstreicher, *In the Midst of Perpetual Fetes: Parades and the Making of American Nationalism* (Chapel Hill: University of North Carolina Press, 1998); John Brooke, *The Heart of the Commonwealth: Society and Political Culture in Worcester County, 1713–1861* (New York: Cambridge University Press, 1989); Mary Ryan, *Civic Wars: Democracy and Public Life in the American City during the Nineteenth Century* (Berkeley: University of California Press, 1997); Simon Newman, *Parades and the Politics of the Streets* (Philadelphia: University of Pennsylvania Press, 1996); Alan Taylor, "'The Art of Hook and Snivey: Political Culture in Upstate New York during the 1790s," JAH 79 (1993): 1371–96; Joanne Freeman, "Dueling as Politics: Reinterpreting the Burr-Hamilton Duel," *William and Mary Quarterly*, 3d ser., 53 (1996): 289–318; Jeffrey L. Pasley, "'A Journeyman, Either in Law or Politics: John Beckley and the Social Origins of Political Campaigning," *Journal of the Early Republic* 16 (1996): 531–69.

16. Robert J. Steinfeld, *The Invention of Free Labor: The Employment Relation in English and American Law and Culture, 1370–1870* (Chapel Hill: University of North Carolina Press, 1991); Wilentz, *Chants Democratic;* Gary B. Nash, *Race and Revolution* (Madison, WI: Madison House, 1990); Gary B. Nash and Jean R. Soderlund, *Freedom by Degrees: Emancipation and its Aftermath in Pennsylvania* (New York: Oxford University Press, 1991).

17. Eric Foner, *Free Soil, Free Labor, Free Men: the Ideology of the Republican Party before the Civil War* (New York: Oxford University Press, 1970); Bruce Levine, *Half Slave and Half Free: The Roots of the Civil War* (New York: Hill and Wang, 1992); John Ashworth, "Free Labor, Slave Labor, and the Slave Power: Republicanism and the Republican Party in the 1850s," in Melvyn Stokes and Stephen Conway, eds., *The Market Revolution in America: Social, Political, and Religious Expressions, 1800–1880* (Charlottesville: University Press of Virginia, 1996), 128–46.

18. Steinfeld, *Invention of Free Labor;* Wilentz, *Chants Democratic.*

19. Foner, *Free Soil;* Ashworth, "Free Labor," 133–38.

20. Allison Bennett, *Town of Bethlehem, Albany County, New York: A Brief History* (n.p.: n.p., n.d.); George R. Howell and Jonathan Tenney, *Bi-Centennial History of the County of Albany, New York, from 1609 to 1886* (New York: W. W. Munsell, 1886); Harriet Jenkins Washbon, *Rensselaerville: Rhymes and Reminiscences* (Albany: Charles Van Benthuysen and Sons, 1888), 13; David Murray, *Delaware County, New York: History of the Century* (Delhi, NY: William Clark, 1898), 40–41, 48–49.

21. Bennet, *Town of Bethlehem,* 4, 8–10; Howell and Tenney, *Bi-Centennial History;* Ellis, *Landlords and Farmers,* 72–73, 78–80.

Chapter 1

1. Martha J. Lamb, "The Van Rensselaer Manor," *Magazine of American History* 11 (1884): 1–6; B.A. Nilsson, "The Maddening Mystery of the Dismantled Manor, Or, How Part of Albany's History Went to Pieces," *Capital Region Magazine* (July 1986): 40–41.

2. Lamb, "Van Rensselaer Manor"; Nilsson, "Maddening Mystery"; Sung Bok Kim, *Landlord and Tenant in Colonial New York: Manorial Society, 1664–1775* (Chapel Hill: University of North Carolina Press, 1978), 235–80.

3. Shays moved to Rensselaerville, on Rensselaerwyck, in 1790, only to move

on within a few years. Elmer S. Smail, "The Daniel Shays Family," *New England Historical and Genealogical Register* 140 (1986): 291–311; Amasa J. Parker, *Landmarks of Albany County* (Syracuse: D. Mason, 1897), 462. On Shays's Rebellion, see David Szatmary, *Shays's Rebellion: The Making of an Agrarian Insurgency* (Amherst: University of Massachusetts Press, 1980); Robert Gross, ed., *In Debt to Shays: The Bicentennial of an Agrarian Rebellion* (Charlottesville: University Press of Virginia, 1993). On northeastern farmers' new ideas concerning land, freedom, and political power after the Revolution, see Gross, *In Debt;* Alan Taylor, "Agrarian Independence: Northern Land Rioters after the Revolution," in Alfred F. Young, ed., *Beyond the American Revolution: Explorations in the History of American Radicalism* (DeKalb: Northern Illinois University Press, 1993), 222–25; Taylor, *Liberty Men and Great Proprietors: The Revolutionary Settlement on the Maine Frontier, 1760–1820* (Chapel Hill: University of North Carolina Press, 1990); Allan Kulikoff, "The Revolution and the Making of the American Yeoman Classes," in Kulikoff, *The Agrarian Origins of American Capitalism* (Charlottesville: University Press of Virginia, 1992), 127–51.

4. David Maldwyn Ellis, *Landlords and Farmers in the Hudson-Mohawk Region, 1790–1850* (1946; reprint, New York: Octagon, 1967), 7–10; Irving Mark, *Agrarian Conflicts in Colonial New York, 1711–1775* (New York: Columbia University Press, 1940), 19–49; J. H. French, *1860 Gazetteer of the State of New York* (1860; reprint ed., Syracuse: R. P. Smith, 1977), 49–52; Kim, *Landlord and Tenant,* vii, 235–38.

5. Edward Countryman, *A People in Revolution: The American Revolution and Political Society in New York* (Baltimore: Johns Hopkins University Press, 1981), 195–252; E. Wilder Spaulding, *New York in the Critical Period, 1783–1789* (New York: Columbia University Press, 1932), 69–70; Staughton Lynd, *Anti-Federalism in Dutchess County, New York: A Study of Democracy and Class Conflict in the Revolutionary Era* (Chicago: Loyola University Press, 1962), 55–81; Alfred F. Young, *The Democratic Republicans of New York: The Origins, 1763–1797* (Chapel Hill: University of North Carolina Press, 1987), 12, 17, 89–90; Alan Kulikoff, "Revolution and the Making."

6. Countryman, *People in Revolution,* 252–79. The political relationship between landlords and tenants will be discussed later in this chapter.

7. Robert A. Gross, *The Minutemen and Their World* (New York: Hill and Wang, 1976), 77–80; Alan Taylor, *William Cooper's Town: Power and Persuasion on the Frontier of the Early American Republic* (New York: Alfred A. Knopf, 1995), 89–91; David Murray, *Delaware County, New York: History of the Century* (Delhi, NY: William Clark, 1898), 40–41, 48–49; Harriet Jenkins Washbon, *Rensselaerville: Rhymes and Reminiscenses* (Albany: Charles Van Benthuysen and Sons, 1890), 13; Town of Berne Bicentennial Commission, *Our Heritage* (Cornwallville, NY: Hope Farm Press, 1977), 1–3; Douglas C. North, *The Economic Growth of the United States, 1790–1860* (New York: W. W. Norton, 1966), 24–45. I am indebted to Taylor's analysis on this point.

8. *Fourth Census of the United States, 1820,* 10; Kim, *Landlord and Tenant,* 238; William Bertrand Fink, "Stephen Van Rensselaer: The Last Patroon" (Ph.D. dissertation, Columbia University, 1950), 28–30; Ruth Piwonka, *A Portrait of Livingston Manor, 1686–1850* (Clermont, NY: Friends of Clermont, 1986), 62–63.

9. Land Records, DCHA; NYAD 1846, 156:5–6; Ellis, *Landlords and Farmers,* 27–29, 33, 36–37, 44–45, 59–61, 64; S. G. Nissenson, *The Patroon's Domain* (New York: Columbia University Press, 1937), 180, 247–49, 305; Kim, *Landlord and*

Tenant, 410–12; *History of Delaware County, New York* (New York: Munsell and Company, 1880), 258–59. The acreage figures given for Claverack and Rensselaerwyck are based on the original crown grant of the estates. Proprietors of both estates were compelled to give up parts of their holdings to rival claimants during the colonial and early national eras, but the secondary sources differ widely about how much land they lost.

10. NYAD 1845, 222:15; Ellis, *Landlords and Farmers,* 27–64.

11. William Strickland, *Journal of a Tour in the United States of America, 1794–1795,* Rev. J. E. Strickland, ed. (New York: New York Historical Society, 1971), 170; Last Will and Testament of Stephen Van Rensselaer, recorded 10 Apr. 1839, Book of Wills, vol. 10, 342–57, Albany County Surrogate's Court; Patricia Joan Gordon, "The Livingstons of New York, 1765–1860: Kinship and Class" (Ph.D. dissertation, Columbia University, 1959), 231–45; Young, *Democratic Republicans,* 45, 69–70, 198–99; Robert P. Swierenga, *Pioneers and Profits: Land Speculation on the Iowa Frontier* (Ames: Iowa State University Press, 1968), chapter 8; Taylor, *William Cooper's Town,* 126–30, 321–33, 372–75, 389–92; Cynthia A. Kierner, *Traders and Gentlefolk: The Livingstons of New York, 1675–1790* (Ithaca: Cornell University Press, 1992); Clare Brandt, *An American Aristocracy: The Livingstons* (Garden City, NJ: Doubleday, 1986).

12. Daniel Dewey Barnard, *A Discourse on the Life, Services, and Character of Stephen Van Rensselaer* (Albany: Hoffman and White, 1839), 33–34; Thomas J. Humphrey, "Agrarian Rioting in Albany County, New York: Tenants, Markets, and Revolution in the Hudson Valley, 1751–1801 (Ph.D. dissertation, Northern Illinois University, 1996), 61–62, 77–82; Kim, *Landlord and Tenant,* 118–23, 221.

13. Peter Schuyler Livingston to Walter Livingston, 14 Feb. 1790, quoted in Brandt, *American Aristocracy,* 150; Gordon S. Wood, "Interests and Disinterestedness in the Making of the Constitution," in Richard Beeman, Stephen Botein, and Edward C. Carter, eds., *Beyond Confederation: Origins of the Constitution and American National Identity* (Chapel Hill: University of North Carolina Press, 1987), 83–90; Taylor, *William Cooper's Town,* 154–59; Kierner, *Traders and Gentlefolk,* 128–64; Patricia U. Bonomi, *A Factious People: Politics and Society in Colonial New York* (New York: Columbia University Press, 1971); Countryman, *A People in Revolution,* 72–85, 191–279; George Dangerfield, *Robert R. Livingston of New York, 1746–1813* (New York: Harcourt, Brace, and Co., 1960).

14. "Depositions regarding Bradstreet's claim to lands between the branches of the Delaware River," NYSL; *Albany Gazette,* 9 Feb., 6, 20, 27 Mar. 1795; Bonomi, *Factious People,* 203–11; Kim, *Landlord and Tenant,* 255, 282–83, 348–67; Murray, *Delaware County,* 46; Jay Gould, *History of Delaware County and the Border Wars of New York* (Roxbury, NY: Keeny and Gould, 1856), 243–45; George R. Howell and Jonathan Tenney, *Bi-Centennial History of the County of Albany, New York from 1609 to 1886* (New York: W. W. Munsell, 1886), 292–94.

15. On the place of landownership in eighteenth-century New England family and community life, see Robert A. Gross, *The Minutemen and Their World* (New York: Hill and Wang, 1976); Philip J. Greven, *Four Generations: Population, Land, and Family in Colonial Andover, Massachusetts* (Ithaca: Cornell University Press, 1970). On the emergence of a view of land as the basis of republican freedom, see Alan Taylor, "Agrarian Independence," 222–25; Taylor, *Liberty Men ;* Kulikoff, "Revolution and the Making," 127–51.

16. Gerald F. DeJong, *The Dutch in America, 1609–1974* (Boston: Twayne, 1975), 49–50, 52, 62–64; A. G. Roeber, *Palatines, Liberty, and Property: German Lutherans in Colonial British America* (Baltimore: Johns Hopkins University Press,

1993), 158, 244, 283–84, 288, 303, 310; Roeber, "'The Origin of Whatever Is Not English among Us': The Dutch-speaking and the German-speaking Peoples of Colonial British America," in Bernard Bailyn and Philip D. Morgan, eds., *Strangers Within the Realm: Cultural Margins of the First British Empire* (Chapel Hill: University of North Carolina Press, 1991), 220–83 (quotations on 263, 276–77); Rosalind Mitchison, "Scotland 1750–1850," in F. M. L. Thompson, ed., *The Cambridge Social History of Britain* (3 vols.; New York: Cambridge University Press, 1990), 1:175–82; Ian Charles Cargill Graham, *Colonists from Scotland: Emigration to North America, 1707–1783* (Ithaca: Cornell University Press, 1956), 3–4.

17. Richard L. Bushman, *King and People in Provincial Massachusetts* (Chapel Hill: University of North Carolina Press, 1985); Robert Zemsky, *Merchants, Farmers, and River Gods: An Essay on Eighteenth-Century American Politics* (Boston: Gambit, 1971); Brooke, *Heart of the Commonwealth*, 131–229; Taylor, *Liberty-Men and Great Proprietors*, 109–112; Kierner, *Traders and Gentlefolk*, 95 n, 116–18; Countryman, *A People in Revolution*, 47–55; Roeber, *Palatines, Liberty, and Property*, 243–332.

18. *John Wigram's Proceedings on Goldsbrow Banyar's Business, 1812*, vol. 9b, Goldsbrow Banyar Papers, NYSL; *Albany Freeholder*, 31 Dec. 1845, 1 Apr. 1846; Kim, *Landlord and Tenant*, 281–333, 346–380; Ellis, *Landlords and Farmers*, 38; Amasa J. Parker, *Landmarks of Albany County, New York* (Syracuse: D. Mason, 1897), 466, 469; Porter Wright, *A Brief History of the Town of Rensselaerville* (Rensselaerville: Rensselaerville Historical Society, 1987), 3; Town of Berne Bicentennial Commission, *Our Heritage* (Cornwallville, NY: Hope Farm Press, 1977), 1–2.

19. Strickland, *Journal of a Tour*, 179; Ruth C. Bennett, *The Grafton (N.Y.) Hills of Home* (New York: Vantage Press, 1974), 3–36.

20. Charles E. Brooks, *Frontier Settlement and Market Revolution: The Holland Land Purchase* (Ithaca: Cornell University Press, 1996), 20–32, 106; Taylor, *William Cooper's Town*, 76, 320; Paul Wallace Gates, *History of Public Land Law Development* (Washington, D.C.: U.S. Government Printing Office, 1968), 125, 131.

21. Leases in VRML; Morgan Lewis Leases, Margaretville, NY, DCHA.

22. Ledger B, 5, VRMRB; Application of Justis Purdy, in Shirley A. Houck, Ann Marie Garti, and Hugh N. Riddell, *Delaware County's "War Papers"* (Walton, NY: Reporter Co., n.d.), 141–43; Petition of Woodstock inhabitants to Robert L. Livingston, quoted in Alf Evers, *Woodstock: History of an American Town* (Woodstock, NY: Overlook Press, 1987), 110; Rev. John O. Gordon, *An Historical Sermon Preached in the Presbyterian Church, Rensselaerville, New York, July 2nd, 1876* (Albany: Van Benthuysen and Sons, 1876), 12; Fink, "Stephen Van Rensselaer," 170–72; Berne Bicentennial Commission, *Our Heritage*, 70; Isabel Thompson Kelsay, "Down With the Rent!: A Story of Social War in Rural New York" (Ph.D. dissertation, Columbia University, 1950), 38; Washbon, *Rensselaerville*, 17; Gould, *Delaware County*, 192; Parker, *Landmarks of Albany County*, 511, 555, 556.

23. Van Rensselaer to Abraham Ten Broeck, 1 Feb. 1786, box 1, Ten Broeck Papers, AIHA; broadside, 14 Jan. 1795, folder 18, Van Rensselaer Family Papers, NYSL; notice, signed by Thomas Witbeck, n.d., ibid; Ellis, *Landlords and Farmers*, 37; Kim, *Landlords and Tenants*, 210.

24. Rensselaerville farm accounts, Ledger A, VRMRB. This sample includes every farm lease account for the town of Westerlo (which was taken from the town of Rensselaerville in 1815) for which I could find entries in both Ledger A (which covers the 1790s through the early 1820s) and Ledger B (which covers the 1820s and 1830s) of the VRMRB.

25. Rensselaerville farm accounts, Ledger A, VRMRB.

26. Ibid.; Clark, *Roots of Rural Capitalism*, 68, 123, 163–69. For evidence of landlords' participation in the commercial world's system of prompt, predictable payment, see Philip Van Rensselaer to Messrs. Steward and Jones, 23 July 1784, Isadore M. Fixman Collection, RPI.

27. Rensselaerville farm accounts, Ledger A., VRMRB.

28. Ibid. The estimate of Van Rensselaer's income is in Strickland, *Journal of a Tour,* 170. If we assume that average farm size on Rensselaerwyck was 100 acres, this accords with an 80 percent collection rate among all 3,000 tenants residing on Rensselaerwyck.

29. Evers, *Woodstock,* 150–53.

30. *John Wigram's Proceedings;* distress warrants against Rogers Winter, John Bartley, and Arthur Elenworth, box 2, folder 12, Hardenbergh Papers, 1776–1851, NYSL; agreement between Elizabeth Bushnell and Isaac Hardenbergh, 17 July 1815, box 1, folder 3, ibid.; agreements between Mary Demery and Isaac Hardenbergh (on back of leases from Hardenbergh to Henry Demery, dated 1 May 1796), ibid. The great landlords most likely to evict their tenants or distrain (seize and sell) their goods were the Livingstons of Livingston Manor. But available evidence suggests that all of the tenants they sued either participated in tenant revolts or refused to pay rent altogether. See Martin Bruegel, "Unrest: Manorial Society and the Market in the Hudson Valley, 1780–1850," JAH 82 (1996): 1401.

31. William Coventry Diary, NYSHA, Jan.–Feb., 14, 23 Apr., 4, 14, 15 May, 8, 9, 11, 12 June, 9, 11 July, 23 Nov. 1798, 17 Apr., 21 May, June–Aug. 1799; Isabelle Adams Swantak and Elizabeth Post, *The Valley We Love: Township* (Cornwallville, NY: Hope Farm Press, 1980), 24–30; Wright, *Brief History,* 11; Caroline Evelyn More and Irma Mae Griffin, *The History of the Town of Roxbury* (Walton, NY: The Reporter Company, 1953), 117, 119, 135; Evers, *Woodstock,* 105, 160–70.

32. Strickland, *Journal of a Tour,* 115; Lease, Samuel Verplanck to Lena Shaffer, 1 June 1806, Three Life Lease Collection, DCHA; Morgan Lewis leases; William H. Denning, power of attorney to John Kiersted, 3 May 1830, box 1, Kiersted Family Papers, 1733–1871, NYSL; Isaac Hardenbergh to Lewis Hardenbergh, 26 Mar. 1818, box 2, Hardenbergh Papers, 1776–1851; Philip Street to Abraham Ten Broeck, 30 Mar. 1809, folder 20, Ten Broeck Papers; broadside, dated 24 Jan. 1809, Ten Broeck Papers; Abel French to Abraham Ten Broeck, 4 Apr. 1808, Ten Broeck Papers; Cuyler Reynolds, ed., *Albany Chronicles: A History of the City Arranged Chronologically* (Albany, NY: J.B. Lyon, 1906), 386; Evers, *Woodstock,* 40–41, 126, 150, 164–70; Kim, *Landlord and Tenant,* 229; Wright, *Brief History,* 4.

33. Daniel Moon to Abraham Ten Broeck, 6 May 1785, Ten Broeck Family Papers, AIHA; Alexander Coventry, *Memoirs of an Emigrant: The Journal of Alexander Coventry, M.D.* (Albany: Albany Institute of History and Art, 1978), 3 Feb. 1786; Alan Taylor, "'A Kind of Warr': The Contest for Land on the Northeastern Frontier, 1750–1820," *William and Mary Quarterly,* 3d. ser., 46 (1989): 4–7; idem, *Liberty-Men and Great Proprietors,* 24–29.

34. Morgan Lewis Leases; VRML; NYAD 1846, 156: 59, 61, 64, 67; lease, Samuel Verplanck to Lena Shaffer, 1 June 1806, Three Life Leases Collection, DCHA; Kim, *Landlord and Tenant,* 179, 251.

35. "Opinion for Stephen Van Rensselaer Esq, 12 July 1792" (unsigned), Isadore M. Fixman Collection, RPI; J. Clark to Abraham Van Vechten, 20 Aug. 1835, Van Vechten Collection, NYSL; *John Wigram's Proceedings,* 3.

36. The quotation is in *Hudson Bee,* 6 Aug. 1811. My analysis here relies heavily on Alan Taylor, *Liberty Men,* 24–29; Taylor, "'A Kind of Warr?,'" 4–7.

37. Anthony to Abraham Ten Broeck, 13 Sept. 1782, box 53, folder 6, VRMP. The omissions in the letter are due to the letter being partially burned.

38. Reuben Frisbee to Lucinda _____, 27 Sept. 1788, quoted in Washbon, *Rensselaerville*, 29–30.

39. James C. Scott, *Domination and the Arts of Resistance: Hidden Transcripts* (New Haven: Yale University Press, 1990), 1–36, 45–69.

40. Frisbee to Lucinda, in Washbon, *Rensselaerville*, 29–30; *Albany Gazette*, 9 Apr. 1801. See also "Address of the Committees Appointed at Meetings of the Tenants, Freeholders of the Four Towns in the West Manor of Rensselaerwyck" (Albany, 1801; Shaw-Shoemaker No. 19).

41. Alan Taylor, "'The Art of Hook and Snivey': Political Culture in Upstate New York during the 1790s," JAH 79 (1993); Taylor, *William Cooper's Town*, 229–32; Strickland, *Journal of a Tour*, 170–71; Dangerfield, *Robert R. Livingston*, 241–55; Brandt, *American Aristocracy*, 134–35; Young, *Democratic Republicans*, 71–72, 136, 282–84, 302, 569.

42. *Albany Gazette*, 3, 10 Apr. 1800, 23 Mar., 9 Apr. 1801; Young, *Democratic Republicans*, 95–96; Taylor, "'Art of Hook and Snivey,'" 1387, 1391.

43. Albany County election data from the First American Democratization Project records, American Antiquarian Society. Many thanks to Philip Lampi for making these returns available to me.

44. "To the Electors of the County of Albany" (Albany, 1801; Shaw-Shoemaker No. 1234); Young, *Democratic Republicans*, 437–38, 561–62.

45. *Albany Gazette*, 2, 9 Feb., 6, 20, 27 Mar. 1795.

46. "Address of the Committees."

47. Albany County Election data, First American Democratization Project records; De Alva Stanwood Alexander, *A Political History of the State of New York* (2 vols.; New York: Henry Holt, 1906), 1: 115.

48. This analysis is based on biographical information on the congressmen, members of the state assembly, county sheriffs, and county judges listed in Edgar A. Werner, *Civil List and Constitutional History of the Colony and State of New York* (Albany: Weed and Parsons, 1889). To keep the research manageable, assembly members who served a single term in odd-numbered years were dropped from the group studied. Biographical information was gathered from George Rogers Howell, *Bi-Centennial History of the County of Albany, New York, From 1609 to 1886* (New York: W. W. Munsell, 1886); Parker, *Landmarks of Albany County; Biographical Directory of the American Congress* (Washington, D.C.: Government Printing Office, 1961); Charles Elliott Fitch, *Encyclopedia of Biography of New York* (4 vols; New York: American Historical Society, 1916); Reynolds, *Albany Chronicles*. In calculating the number of terms in office, I counted only those terms that were filled by men for whom biographical information could be found.

49. Young, *Democratic Republicans*, 144, 302–03, 337–38, 423, 440, 561–63; Bruegel, "Unrest," 1141; John Brooke, "The World of Martin Van Buren: Civil Society, Property, and Crisis in Columbia County, 1811–1812" (unpublished paper, 1998). My thanks to John Brooke for allowing me to read and cite his manuscript.

50. Lease between Samuel Verplanck and Lena Shaffer for land in Middletown, 1 June 1806, Three-Life Leases, DCHA; Morgan Lewis Leases; Taylor, *William Cooper's Town*, 154–98. Biographical information on Ebenezer Foote comes from Werner, *Civil List; History of Delaware County*, 165–66; Gould, *History of Delaware County*, 221–22; Murray, *Delaware County*, 162–65; "Estate of Julian Verplanck, Deceased" (1803), Peters Collection, DCHA; Powers of Attorney Collection, DCHA.

51. Delaware County election returns, the First American Democratization Project files; *Second Census of the United States, 1800,* 29–30. My analysis of office-holders is based on an analysis of all state representatives, members of the U.S. House of Representatives, county sheriffs, and county judges listed for Delaware County in Werner, *Civil List.* Biographical information on these officers was gathered from *Biographical Review . . . of the Leading Citizens of Delaware County, New York* (Boston: Biographical Review Publishing Company, 1895); *History of Delaware County, New York;* Gould, *History of Delaware County;* Murray, *Delaware County;* John D. Monroe, *Chapters in the History of Delaware County, New York* (Delhi: Delaware County Historical Association, 1949); *Biographical Directory of the American Congress.*

52. See especially Kim, *Landlord and Tenant,* 281–415; Edward Countryman, "Out of the Bounds of the Law: Northern Land Rioters in the Eighteenth Century," in Alfred F. Young, ed., *The American Revolution: Explorations in the History of American Radicalism* (DeKalb: Northern Illinois University Press, 1976), 37–69; Countryman, *People in Revolution,* 47–55; Mark, *Agrarian Conflicts,* 107–94; Ruth Piwonka, *Portrait of Livingston Manor;* Brooke, "World of Martin Van Buren"; Ellis, *Landlords and Farmers,* 34–36, 151–55.

53. "The Case of the Inhabitants of New Canaan," New York Land Papers, quoted in Kim, *Landlord and Tenant,* 358; *Hudson Bee,* 6 Aug. 1811; William Cronon, *Changes in the Land: Indians, Colonists, and the Ecology of New England* (New York: Hill and Wang, 1983), 56–57, 73, 77; Alan Taylor, "Agrarian Independence," 222–25; Taylor, *Liberty Men and Great Proprietors,* 101–14. See also the petition of Petrus Luver and others, reprinted in E. B. O'Callaghan, ed., *Documentary History of the State of New York* (Albany: Weed and Parsons, 1850) 3:501.

54. Kim, *Landlord and Tenant,* 290–333, 357, 396–414; Brandt, *American Aristocracy,* 133–35, 148, 174–75; Piwonka, *Portrait of Livingston Manor,* 62–63, 70–77; Ellis, *Landlords and Farmers,* 151–55; Countryman, "Out of the Bounds," 42–43, 45; Mark, *Agrarian Conflicts,* 119–20; Bonomi, *Factious People,* 211–24; Franklin Ellis, *History of Columbia County, New York* (Philadelphia, Everts and Ensign, 1878), 42–43, 368, 386; Elizabeth L. Gebhard, *The Parsonage Between Two Manors: Annals of Clover-Reach,* 3d. ed. (Hudson, NY: Hudson Press, 1925), 185–87.

55. Countryman, *People in Revolution,* 173–74, 187, 207–208; Lynd, *Anti–Federalism,* 55–81; Kim, *Landlord and Tenant,* 327–45, 398–412; Ellis, *History of Columbia County,* 368–86; Piwonka, *Portrait of Livingston Manor,* 62–63, 70–77; Ellis, *Landlords and Farmers,* 35–36, 154–55; Young, *Democratic Republicans,* 206, 533–35.

56. Ellis, *Landlords and Farmers,* 151–52.

57. For a fuller, superb discussion of Martin Van Buren and the Livingston tenants, see Brooke, "World of Martin Van Buren." See also Martin Van Buren, *Autobiography of Martin Van Buren,* ed. John C. Fitzpatrick, *Annual Report of the American Historical Association,* 1918 (Washington: Government Printing Office, 1920), 22–24; Donald B. Cole, *Martin Van Buren and the American Political System* (Princeton: Princeton University Press, 1984), 28–30; Ellis, *Landlords and Farmers,* 152–54.

58. *Brooke,* "World of Martin Van Buren"; *Autobiography of Martin Van Buren,* 24; Ellis, *Landlords and Farmers,* 151–55; Alexander, *Political History,* 1:206–210.

59. "Depositions regarding Bradstreet's claim"; *Albany Gazette,* 2, 9 Feb., 6, 20, 27 Mar. 1795; VRML, *passim.*

60. Ursyn Niemcewicz, *Under Their Vine and Fig Tree: Travels through America in 1797–1799, 1805* (Elizabeth, NJ: Grassman Publishing, 1965), 13; Gebhard, *Parsonage Between Two Manors,* chapters 17–18, 27–28; Evers, *Woodstock,* 148; Brandt, *American Aristocracy,* 94, 139; Fink, "Stephen Van Rensselaer," 172–213; Gordon S. Wood, *The Creation of the American Republic, 1776–1787* (Chapel Hill: University of North Carolina Press, 1969), 479–80, 496–97; Dangerfield, *Robert R.. Livingston,* 183–84; Louise Livingston Hunt, *Memoir of Mrs. Edward Livingston: With Letters Hitherto Unpublished* (New York: Harper Brothers, 1886), *passim.*

61. Werner, *Civil List;* Fink, "Stephen Van Rensselaer," 45–79, 106–43; Brandt, *American Aristocracy,* 144–45; Dangerfield, *Robert R.. Livingston,* 399–402, and *passim;* William B. Hatcher, *Edward Livingston: Jeffersonian Republican and Jacksonian Democrat* (Baton Rouge: Louisiana State University Press, 1940); Dixon Ryan Fox, *The Decline of Aristocracy in the Politics of New York* (New York: Columbia University Press, 1919), 31–46, and *passim.*

62. *Transactions of the Society for the Promotion of Agriculture, Arts, and Manufactures* (Albany: Charles R. And George Webster, 1801), *passim;* Dangerfield, *Robert R. Livingston,* 186–87, 282–97, 426–37, 403–16; Stephen Van Rensselaer to J. W. Moulton, 29 Jan. 1820, Stephen Van Rensselaer Papers, 1752–1851, RPI; Fink, "Stephen Van Rensselaer," 145, 170–213, 243–45; Elizabeth W. McClave, *Stephen Van Rensselaer III: A Pictorial Reflection and Biographical Commentary,* 17; Reynolds, *Albany Chronicles,* 373, 439, 486, 516; Berne Bicentennial Commission, *Our Heritage,* 72.

63. Robert R. Livingston to Arthur Young, 10 Jan. 1794, quoted in Brandt, *American Aristocracy,* 144; draft of an address, dated 1794, quoted in Dangerfield, *Robert R. Livingston,* 428.

64. Stephen Van Rensselaer to J. W. Moulton, 29 Jan. 1820, Stephen Van Rensselaer Papers, RPI; Robert R. Livingston, *Essay on Sheep* (New York: T. and J. Swords, 1809), 119–56; Fink, "Stephen Van Rensselaer," 203.

65. Robert R. Livingston, "Draft of Oration to the Society of the Cincinnati, given July 4, 1787," quoted in Dangerfield, *Robert R. Livingston,* 210. Livingston's vision of patrician rule did not change when he joined the Republican party. See, for example, his letter to Thomas T. Tillotson, 29 May 1803, quoted in ibid., 398. On the gentry's economic and political vision, see Taylor, *William Cooper's Town.*

66. Wills A–B, Delaware County Surrogate's Court, Delhi, NY; Book of Wills, vols. 2–4, Albany County Surrogate's Court, Albany, NY; Norma Basch, *In the Eyes of the Law: Women, Marriage, and Property in Nineteenth-Century New York* (Ithaca: Cornell University Press, 1982), 70–110.

67. Coventry Diary, 1798–1800, 1808; Beriah Holcom Account Book, 1808–1819, NYSHA; Laura Thatcher Ulrich, *A Midwife's Tale: The Life of Martha Ballard, Based on Her Diary, 1785–1812* (New York: Alfred A. Knopf, 1990), 75–90.

68. Will of Daniel Smith, 31 Oct. 1805, in Albany County Book of Wills, vol. 3. See also will of William Smith, 1803, Delaware County Wills, A–B.

69. Slaves accounted for between 7 and 13 percent of the 1790 population in valley leasehold towns like Rensselaerwyck and Clermont, but made up less than 1 percent of the inhabitants of hill towns like Rensselaerville, Stephentown, and Woodstock. U.S. Bureau of the Census, *First Census, 1790,* vol. 5: *Heads of Families, New York* (Washington, D.C.: Government Printing Office, 1908), 9–10. On taking in children from other families, see Will of Benjamin Fowler, 6 Oct. 1808, Albany County Book of Wills, vol. 4; Ulrich, *Midwife's Tale,* 80–84. On work exchange and collective labor, see Holcolm Account Book; testimony of Moses Lyon

in the People v. Peders Simmons, Summaries of Testimony Before the Circuit Court and Court of Oyer and Terminer, New York, 1824, NYSA; Evers, *Woodstock,* 232–33.

70. Holcolm Account Book; Coventry Diary, Appendix B; Ellis, *Landlords and Farmers,* 102–103.

71. More and Griffin, *History of the Town of Roxbury,* 133–55; Evers, *Woodstock,* 230–31; *Our Heritage,* 36; Murray, *Delaware County,* 39; Swantak and Post, *The Village We Love,* 30–34; Mary Fisher Torrance, *The Story of Old Rensselaerville* (New York: Privately Printed, 1939), 18; Thomas H. Blaisdell, *Town of Westerlo, Then and Now* (n.p.: n.p., n.d.), 20.

72. Holcolm Account Book; Coventry Diary; Strickland, *Journal of a Tour,* 112–13, 178–79; Lewis Hardenbergh Day Book, Roxbury, NY, 1811–1820, NYSHA; Ellis, *Landlords and Farmers,* 105–14; Evers, *Woodstock,* 126, 160–70; Murray, *Delaware County,* 39, 106; *Our Heritage,* 49; Bruegel, "Uncertainty," 257–60.

73. Bruegel, "Uncertainty," 256–57.

74. Good introductions to the implements and livestock needed for various crops can be found in Percy Bidwell and John I Falconer, *History of Agriculture in the United States, 1620–1860* (1925; reprint ed., Clifton, NJ: A.M. Kelley, 1973) and Clarence Danhoff, *Change in Agriculture: The Northern United States, 1820–1870* (Cambridge: Harvard University Press, 1969). For the implements of spinning, see Henry Conklin, *Through 'Poverty's Vale': A Hardscrabble Boyhood in Upstate New York, 1832–1862* (Syracuse: Syracuse University Press, 1974), 26.

75. Holcolm Account Book; Ellis, *Landlords and Farmers,* 101.

76. Hardenbergh Day Book; Ellis, *Landlords and Farmers,* 80–82, 87–89, 101, 108; More and Griffin, *History of the Town of Roxbury,* 133–55; Evers, *Woodstock,* 230–31; Berne Bicentennial Commission, *Our Heritage,* 36; Murray, *Delaware County,* 39; Torrance, *Old Rensselaerville,* 14, 18, 38.

77. Strickland, *Journal of a Tour,* 115, 170; Coventry diary, 3 Aug. 1799.

78. Rensselaerville Town Minute Book, 1795–1833, NYSA, 3, 31, 37, 40, 100–101, 124–25, 154–55, 196, 231, 250, 287; Town Book of the Town of Roxbury, vol. 1 (1799–1844), microfilm copy in DCC, 18, 60, 73–77, 83, 109, 113.

79. Rensselaerville, NY Assessment Roll, 1800, NYSA; Roxbury, NY Assessment Roll, 1800, NYSA. Leasehold tenants were listed as landowning taxpayers on New York assessment rolls, since leases universally required them to pay all land taxes. Thus they are included as property owners in this analysis. Since Roxbury was still being rapidly settled in 1800, much of its land was still held by nonresident landowners. I have excluded the property owned by nonresidents in the figures above. In the Connecticut Valley towns of western Massachusetts, the richest 10 percent of taxpayers claimed between 27 and 50 percent of their towns' wealth in 1798; farther east in Concord, the wealthiest fifth held 54 percent of local property in 1795 (compared to 43 percent in Rensselaerville and 44 percent in Roxbury). Clark, *Roots of Rural Capitalism,* 22–23; Robert A. Gross, *The Minutemen and Their World* (New York: Hill and Wang, 1976), 231.

80. Only 9 percent of men between 16 and 25 years old headed their own households, as compared to 90 percent of those aged 26 to 44 and all of those aged 45 and older. 1800 Manuscript Census, Population, Rensselaerville, New York.

81. A profile of the landholdings of various age groups was created by cross-tabulating the 1800 assessment roll with the population schedule for the 1800 federal census for Rensselaerville. The age categories are those of the 1800

census. Rensselaerville, NY Assessment Roll, 1800; 1800 Manuscript Census, Population, Rensselaerville, NY.

82. Rensselaerville Assessment Roll, 1800; Roxbury Assessment Roll, 1800; Town Book of Roxbury, vol. 1; Rensselaerville Town Minute Book, 1795–1833; Wilentz, *Chants Democratic*, 401; Edward Pessen, *Riches, Class, and Power Before the Civil War* (Lexington, MA: D.C. Heath, 1973), 47–48, 62–70; Washbon, *Rensselaerville*, 14. For evidence of local elites acting as intermediaries between poorer neighbors and powerful outsiders, see Jonathan Brown to Stephen Van Rensselaer, 21 May, no year, VRMP; A. Van Deusen to Abraham Ten Broeck, 27 Feb. 1809, Ten Broeck Papers.

83. Rensselaerville, NY Assessment Roll, 1800; Wright, *Brief History*, 4–5; Washbon, *Rensselaerville*, 14; Blaisdell, *Westerlo*, 15–16; Howell and Tenney, *Bi-Centennial History*, 809, 815, 817, 441. The analysis of officeholders was based on biographical information regarding officers listed in Werner, *Civil List*. Biographical information was gathered from Howell, *Bi-Centennial History* and Parker, *Landmarks of Albany County*.

84. U.S. Census, Population Schedules, 1800, Rensselaerville, New York; Rensselaerville Assessment Roll, 1800. Figures on property holding were gathered in two ways: by looking for Rensselaerville household heads listed in the 1800 U.S. census schedules in the town's 1800 assessment roll, and by comparing the aggregate number of landowning taxpayers found in the assessment roll to the total number of heads of household listed in the census schedules. The former method indicated that 31 percent of household heads owned or leased no land. This method overestimates the number of landless household heads, for it counts as landless those people who left town between the census and tax enumerations, heads of household who had passed their land on to sons who were living in their own households, and those who could not be matched because of inconsistent spelling and poor handwriting. The latter method indicates that 26 percent of household heads had no access to land. This underestimates landlessness, since it assumes that every landowner headed his or her own household when, in reality, some landowners doubtless lived under the same roof as their landed fathers, mothers, or brothers. Leasehold tenants were listed as landholders in their local tax lists because leases universally required tenants to pay all taxes on the land; thus they are counted as landholding residents in this analysis.

Of household heads between the ages of 16 and 25, 36 percent (10 out of 28) could not be found on the tax list, compared to 25 percent (119 out of 481) of those aged 26 to 44 and 19 percent (41 out of 173) of those 45 or older.

85. Houck, Garti, and Ridell, *Delaware County's "War Papers."*

Chapter 2

1. Clare Brandt, *An American Aristocracy: The Livingstons* (Garden City, NY: Doubleday, 1986), 70, 73, 86; Patricia Joan Gordon, "The Livingstons of New York, 1675–1860: Kinship and Class" (Ph.D. dissertation, Columbia University, 1959), 1–3; Kiliaen Van Rensselaer, *The Van Rensselaer Manor: Address Delivered at the Third Annual Meeting of the New York Branch of the Order of Colonial Lords of Manors in America* (Baltimore: n.p., 1929), 8, 60; Abraham Kingsley, "Chart of the Van Rensselaers, their Patroonship and Family Descent from Holland to Rensselaerwyck Manor, Claverack, and Greenbush, etc., in New York State, USA" (n.p.: n.p., n.d.).

2. Elizabeth Gebhard, *The Parsonage between Two Manors: Annals of Clover-Reach*

(Hudson, NY: Hudson Press, 1925), 145–46; Alf Evers, *Woodstock: History of an American Town* (Woodstock, NY: Overlook Press, 1987), 94–95, 178; Brandt, *American Aristocracy*, 148; Ruth Piwonka, *A Portrait of Livingston Manor, 1686–1850* (Clermont, NY: Friends of Clermont, 1986), 59–60; Cuyler Reynolds, comp., *Albany Chronicles: A History of the City Arranged Chronologically* (New York: J. B. Lyon, 1906), 396; Carolyn More and Irma Mae Griffin, *History of the Town of Roxbury* (Walton, NY: The Reporter Company, 1953), 274; C. Edward Skeen, *John Armstrong, Jr., 1758–1843* (Syracuse, NY: Syracuse University Press, 1981), 223; Gordon S. Wood, *The Radicalism of the American Revolution* (New York: Alfred A. Knopf, 1991), 180–84; Nancy F. Cott, *The Bonds of Womanhood: "Woman's Sphere" in New England, 1780–1835* (New Haven: Yale University Press, 1977), 46, 84–92; Mary P. Ryan, *The Cradle of the Middle Class: The Family in Oneida County, New York, 1790–1865* (New York: Cambridge University Press, 1981), 60–75, 98–104.

3. Brandt, *American Aristocracy*, 53–54, 63 n, 64–65, 82, 105. On the importance of economic considerations in marriage among colonial elites, see Arthur W. Calhoun, *A Social History of the American Family, From Colonial Times to the Present* (3 vols., Cleveland, Ohio: Arthur H. Clark, 1917–19), 1:59, 165, 244, 153, 269; Jan Lewis, *The Pursuit of Happiness: Family and Values in Jefferson's Virginia* (New York: Cambridge University Press, 1983), 24–26.

4. Brandt, *American Aristocracy*, 105, 132 n, 137–39 (quotation on 181); Skeen, *John Armstrong*, 222; Calhoun, *American Family*, 28–29.

5. Evers, *Woodstock*, 155–56, 687 n. 9; George Dangerfield, *Chancellor Robert R. Livingston of New York, 1746–1813* (New York: Harcourt, Brace, 1960), 426; Brandt, *American Aristocracy*, 82, 178–81.

6. Charles Havens Hunt, *Life of Edward Livingston* (New York: D. Appleton and Company, 1864), 310, 313, and *passim; History of Delaware County, New York* (New York: W. W. Munsell, 1880), 259; David Maldwyn Ellis, *Landlords and Farmers in the Hudson-Mohawk Region, 1790–1850* (1946; reprint ed., New York: Octagon Books, 1967), 233.

7. William Bertrand Fink, "Stephen Van Rensselaer: The Last Patroon" (Ph.D. dissertation, Columbia University, 1950), 212–20; Brandt, *American Aristocracy*, 172–80.

8. Ellis, *Landlords and Farmers*, 105, 136–37, 186–88.

9. *Census of the State of New York for 1825; Statistics of the United States . . . 1840*, 88–89, 112–13; *Delaware Gazette*, 9 Dec. 1840; Ellis, *Landlords and Farmers*, 142–51, 194–205.

10. Gurdon Evans, *The Dairyman's Manual: Being a Complete Guide for the American Dairyman* (Utica, NY: John W. Fuller and Co., 1851), 8, 70–86, 140–50. Farmers' diaries indicate that they used most, if not all, of the specialized buildings and implements recommended by Evans. See James H. Thompson Diary, 8 Apr., 13 June 1840, NYSHA; George Holcolm Diary, 17 Apr. 1840, NYSL. My estimate of the size of herds is based on the assumption that a typical farm would contain two or three men active in agriculture—a father and one or two sons or laborers. The corresponding figures for a typical Albany County farm are between $160 and $300 in cows and between 24 and 36 acres in meadow and pasture.

11. George Holcolm diary, 9, 12, 17 Apr. 1830, 13, 15, 16, 28 Apr., 4 , 5, 8, 13, 14 May, 5 , 6 June 1840; James H. Thompson Diary, 12 Apr., 8, 17 Aug. 1839; *A Statistical Report of the County of Albany, For the Year 1820* (Albany: Packard and Van Benthuysen, 1823); *Delaware Gazette*, 28 Jan., 5 Oct. 1824, 26 Mar., 17 Sept. 1828, 16 May 1832, 1 July 1840.

12. The population of the Helderbergs grew from 2,771 in 1790 to 12,424 in

1820. By 1845, the population was 15,632, with 57.8 inhabitants per square mile—as compared to 44.2 in Concord, Massachusetts in 1754. The population of the main leasehold towns of Delaware County grew from 4,437 in 1800 to 13,142 in 1845—29.3 inhabitants per square mile in the latter year. But much Delaware County land was unsuitable for farming; these towns had 87 inhabitants per square mile of improved farmland in 1845, as compared to 78 in the Helderbergs. *First Census of the United States, 1790*, vol. 5: *Heads of Families, New York*, 9; *Second Census of the United States, 1800*, 29–30; *Fourth Census of the United States, 1820*, 9, 10; George R. Howell and Jonathan Tenney, *Bi-Centennial History of the County of Albany, New York, from 1609 to 1886* (New York: W. W. Munsell, 1886), 72, 73, 76, 77, 80; Robert A. Gross, *The Minutemen and Their World* (New York: Hill and Wang, 1976), 209 n. 18; Philip Greven, *Four Generations: Population, Land, and Family in Colonial Andover, Massachusetts* (Ithaca: Cornell University Press, 1970), 177. The area of Delaware County towns in 1845 was provided by the Delaware County Assessor's Office, Delhi, NY. On land prices in the Helderbergs in 1820, see *A Statistical Report of the County of Albany, For the Year 1820* (Albany: Packard & Van Benthuysen, 1823).

13. Eleven of the 12 Helderberg men who wrote wills between 1801 and 1811 divided their land among several sons, but 14 of 26 will writers (54 percent) between 1840 and 1842 either passed their land on to a single child or required that the land be sold and the proceeds divided. Book of Wills, vols. 2–4, 10–11, Albany County Surrogate's Court, Albany, NY; Town of Westerlo, NY, Assessment Roll of 1840, Westerlo Town Clerk's Office, Westerlo, NY. In Roxbury, (151 of 375=) 40 percent of farms in 1840 contained fewer than 100 acres, while (57 =) 15 percent contained fewer than 50. But the mountainous terrain of that town often increased the acreage required for a viable farm. While only (2 of 11=) 18 percent of wills registered by inhabitants of the main leasehold towns of Delaware County between 1794 and 1805 passed land on to only one child or required that the land be sold and the proceeds divided among heirs, (7 of 18=) 39 percent did so between 1828 and 1842. Town of Roxbury, NY, Assessment Roll, 1840, Roxbury Town Clerk's Office, Roxbury, NY; Wills A–B, Wills D–E, Delaware County Surrogate's Office, Delhi, NY.

14. George Holcolm Diary (typescript), 1830, NYSL. In 1840, Holcolm made 45 marketing trips, selling goods worth $338.60. Ibid., 1840.

15. H.S. Tanner, *The Traveler's's Hand Book for the State of New York and the Province of Canada*, 2d ed. (New York: T.R. Tanner, 1844); *Fourth Census of the United States, 1820*, 9–10; *Sixth Census of the United States, 1840* (Washington, D.C.: Blair and Rives, 1841), 82–83, 88–89; *Delaware Gazette*, 13 Sept. 1821, 5 Nov. 1822, and 1820–40, *passim; Daily Albany Argus*, 1820–1840, *passim;* handbill, dated 1821, box 28, folder 2, Samuel A. Law Papers, NYSL–M; handbill, signed by James Robertson, dated June 1823, box 28, folder 3, Law Papers; Ellis, *Landlords and Farmers*, 159–83; More and Griffin, *History of the Town of Roxbury*, 125–29.

16. *Census of the State of New York, 1825; Census for the State of New York for 1845;* Holcolm Diary, 13, 15, 16 Apr., 3, 5, 8, 13 May, 6 June, 5, 30 Nov. 1840; Thompson Diary, 28, 29, 30 Nov., 2, 4 Dec. 1839.

17. Holcolm Diary, 1830 and 1840; Thompson Diary, 1838–41; Joan Jensen, *Loosening the Bonds: Mid-Atlantic Farm Women, 1750–1850* (New Haven: Yale University Press, 1986); Sally McMurry, *Transforming Rural Life: Dairying Families and Agricultural Change, 1820–1885* (Baltimore: Johns Hopkins University Press, 1995). For aggregate statistics on cloth and dairy production, see Appendix, table 2.

18. Holcolm Diary, 4 Sept. 1840; Thompson Diary, 1839–40; *Delaware Gazette*, 26 Dec. 1821, 23 Jan. 1828, 21 May 1834; *Albany Morning Atlas*, 25 May 1842; George Hardenbergh to Lewis Hardenbergh, 1837, box 2, folder 7, Hardenbergh Family Papers, NYSL; Theodore Devereaux and Company Account Book, 1830, NYSL; Ellis, *Landlords and Farmers*, 210; Mary Fisher Torrance, *The Story of Old Rensselaerville* (New York: Privately Printed, 1939), 35–37; Evers, *Woodstock*, 126, 160–70.

19. *Fourth Census, 1820*, 9–10; *Sixth Census, 1840*, 82–83, 88–89; Harriet Jenkins Washbon, *Rensselaerville: Rhymes and Reminiscences* (Albany: Charles Van Benthuysen, 1888), 60; Evers, *Woodstock*, 233; Torrance, *Rensselaerville*, 51; Porter Wright, *A Brief History of the Town of Rensselaerville* (Rensselaerville, NY: Rensselaerville Historical Society, 1987), 9; Ellis, *Landlords and Farmers*, 210.

20. Assessment Roll, 1800, Rensselaerville, New York, microfilm copy at NYSA; Westerlo Assessment Roll, 1840; Assessment Roll, 1800, Roxbury, NY, microfilm copy at NYSA; Roxbury Assessment Roll, 1840.

21. 1800 Federal Manuscript Census, Population Schedules, Rensselaerville, New York; 1850 Federal Manuscript Census, Population Schedules, Westerlo and Roxbury, New York. In Westerlo, 57 out of 278 men aged 26 to 44 remained dependents in 1850; in Roxbury, 91 out of 351 such men did so. The decrease in landlessness in Rensselaerville/Westerlo was probably due to Westerlo's being set off from Rensselaerville. When this happened, most of the town's manufacturing and commerce—and probably most of its landlessness—remained in Rensselaerville.

22. Henry Conklin, *Through 'Poverty's Vale': A Hardscrabble Boyhood in Upstate New York, 1832–1862* (Syracuse: Syracuse University Press, 1974), 10–11, 22–24, 26–29, 32–34, 38–39, 40–48, 62, 69.

23. Holcolm Diary, 1830 and 1840; Henry Bull Account Book, 1820–1853, NYSHA; 1850 Federal Manuscript Census, Population, Westerlo and Roxbury. See also Work Record/Diary, Delhi, NY, 1830, DCHA; will of Noah Davenport of Stamford, 1 Aug. 1840, Wills D–E, Delaware County Surrogate's Court, 92–93.

24. Evans, *Dairyman's Manual*, 8. George and Lucinda Holcolm's use of wage labor went down dramatically as their sons and daughters grew older. The Thompson family of Roxbury, with three sons over the age of 14 but only one daughter, almost never hired male laborers but had a constant stream of female servants coming through their household. Holcolm Diary, 1830, 1840; Thompson Diary, 1838–41. For a superb discussion of the labor requirements of dairying and the ways in which dairying families drew on family and hired labor to meet those requirements, see Sally McMurry, *Transforming Rural Life: Dairying Families and Agricultural Change, 1820–1885* (Baltimore: Johns Hopkins University Press, 1995), 62–71.

25. 1850 Federal Manuscript Census, Population, Westerlo and Roxbury, New York; Holcolm Diary, 2, 8, 15, 16, 20, 21, 26 Apr., 3 Nov., 5 Dec. 1830; Conklin, *Through 'Poverty's Vale,'* 39, 62. Ninety-four out of 134 Westerlo laborers and landless farmers and 247 out of 331 Roxbury laborers and landless farmers were under the age of 30.

26. 1850 Federal Manuscript Census, Population, Westerlo and Roxbury, New York; Holcolm Diary, 8, 26 Apr., 5 Dec. 1830; Conklin, *Through 'Poverty's Vale,'* 39, 62. In Westerlo, 117 out of 444 men aged 30 or older (26.4 percent) and 67 out of 310 men (21.6 percent) aged 40 or older were laborers or landless farmers. In Roxbury, 131 out of 474 men aged 30 or older (27.6 percent) and 79 out of 296 men aged 40 or older (26.7 percent) were laborers or landless farmers. A

small proportion of these were most likely older, prosperous men who had already passed their farms on to one or more sons.

27. Holcolm Diary, 1830 and 1840; Bull Account Book, entries for Moses Chamberlin, Peter Wiles, William Martin, Orsamus Ellis, John Palmer, Henry Bates, John Richmond, Orpheus Haskins, Richard Tibbets, Joseph Haskins, Elijah Young, William Bates, Nehemiah Smith, Comfort Smith, John Brooks, Daniel Right, William Marting, and Elisha B. Richtmeyer.

28. Holcolm Diary, 1830 and 1840; Rensselaer County Deeds, Book 12: 32, 33, 421; Book 18: 341; Book 24:17; Book 86:365; Book 96:286, all in Rensselaer County Hall of Records, Troy, NY; Holcolm Family Genealogy, George Holcolm Papers, NYSL.

29. Conklin, *Through 'Poverty's Vale,'* xiii, 7, 10–11, 13, 15, 23, 27, 32–34, 40–48, 54–56, 80; Wills, Rensselaer County Hall of Records; Deeds, Rensselaer County Hall of Records; Wills, Schoharie County Clerk's Office; Deeds, Books A–Z, 1–34, Schoharie County Clerk's Office; *Index to the Public Records of the County of Albany, Grantees, 1630–1894; Index to the Public Records of the County of Albany, Wills, 1630–1894.*

30. Conklin, *Through 'Poverty's Vale,'* 10–11, 13, 15, 64, 69–71, 80; *Delaware Gazette*, 26 May, 3 Nov. 1824, 9 June 1830, 13 Nov. 1839.

31. Holcolm Diary, 23, 28 Oct. 1830; *Delaware Gazette*, 29 July 1820 and 1820–40, *passim; Daily Albany Argus*, 20 May 1841, 18 Nov. 1844, Testimony of Moses Lyon and Alanson Webb in People vs. Peders Simmons, Delaware County, 1824, Summaries of Testimony Given in Circuit Courts of Oyer and Terminer, 1823–1828, NYSA.

32. *Delaware Gazette*, 17 Feb. 1820, 3 Mar. 1824 and 1820–40, *passim;* Thompson Diary, 29 June, 19 July 1839; Rensselaerville Town Board Minutes, 1795–1833, 417; Town Book of the Town of Roxbury, vol. 1 (1799–1844), 197. Westerlo voters continued to allow the running of livestock on the commons; see Westerlo Town Board Minutes, Apr. 4, 1815–Apr. 12, 1870, *passim.*

33. *Memorial of the Farmers, Manufacturers, Mechanics, and Merchants, of the County of Rensselaer in the State of New York, Praying for a Revision of the Tariff, January 26, 1824* (Washington: Gales and Seaton, 1824), in U.S. Docs. Serial Vol. 94, Doc. No. 48. See also *Petition of Sundry Inhabitants of the County of Delaware, Praying for the Passage of a Law Imposing Additional Duties on Certain Imported Materials and Fabrics,* in U.S. Docs. Serial Vol. 174, No. 229; *Delaware Gazette*, 27 Feb. 1828.

34. *Delaware Gazette*, 16, 30 July 1828, 11 Jan. 1832, 18 Sept., 2 Oct., 18 Dec. 1833, 29 Jan. 1834, 28 Oct., 23 Dec. 1835, 23 Mar., 4 May, 3 Aug. 1836, 3 May 1837, 8, 22 May, 5 June, 18 Dec. 1839, 1 Apr. 1840.

35. *Albany Cultivator,* quoted in McMurry, *Transforming Rural Life,* 52; *New York State Agricultural Society Transactions,* 1861, quoted in ibid., 52–53; *Albany Evening Journal,* 18 July 1837.

36. *Daily Albany Argus,* 2 Aug. 1832; *Delaware Gazette*, 21 May, 20 Aug. 1834; McMurry, *Transforming Rural Life,* 49, 51–53.

37. The best discussion of New York politics in the 1820s and 1830s remains Lee Benson, *The Concept of Jacksonian Democracy: New York as a Test Case* (1961; reprint ed, New York: Athaneum, 1964), 4–62. But see also DeAlva Stanwood Alexander, *A Political History of New York State* (2 vols.; New York: Henry Holt, 1906), 1:253–405; Jabez Hammond, *History of Political Parties in the State of New York* (3 vols.; Syracuse: Hall, Mills, and Co., 1852); Alvin Kass, *Politics in New York State, 1800–1830* (Syracuse: Syracuse University Press, 1965).

38. Benson, *Concept of Jacksonian Democracy,* 4–62; Alexander, *Political History,* 1:253–405; Hammond, *History of Political Parties.*

39. Only three political meetings with participation from hill-town tenants published their proceedings in the *Albany Gazette* in 1800, but 15 such gatherings were reported by the *Albany Argus* and *Albany Evening Journal* in 1840. Similarly, the number of political meetings announced or reported in the *Delaware Gazette* increased from two in 1820 to 22 in 1840. *Albany Gazette,* 1800, passim; Albany Evening Journal, 1840, passim; *Daily Albany Argus,* 1840, passim; *Delaware Gazette,* 1820, 1840, passim.

40. Of the 11 Westerlo Democrats who served as officers at town meetings, delegates to county conventions, or members of town vigilance committees during the 1840 election and who could be found on the 1840 tax list, 7 (64 percent) were among the wealthiest fifth of propertied townspeople and all but one were among the top half of property owners. Of the 12 who could be located in the 1840 census, 10 (83 percent) were farmers and 2 (17 percent) were engaged in commerce. Westerlo Whig activists were slightly less wealthy, with 4 of the 8 who could be found on the tax list in the wealthiest fifth of town residents and 6 (75 percent) in the top half. They were also less likely to be farmers. Only 4 of the 9 who could be found in the manuscript census (44 percent) were engaged in agriculture, while 1 (11 percent) was engaged in commerce, another 2 (22 percent) were in the learned professions, and 3 (33 percent) were manufacturers or craftsmen.

Delaware County's Whig newspaper has not survived, so we do not know who Whig activists were. Of the eight Roxbury Democratic activists who could be found in the census schedules, half were farmers, 2 (25 percent) were engaged in commerce, and 1 each (12.5 percent) earned their living in manufacturing and the professions. Of the 9 who could be found in the town assessment roll, 5 (56 percent) were among the top fifth of Roxbury property owners, and all were among the wealthiest half. Westerlo Assessment Roll, 1840; Roxbury Assessment Roll, 1840; Manuscript Population Census, Westerlo and Roxbury, 1840. The names of Whig and Democratic activists were drawn from partisan conventions reported in the *Daily Albany Argus,* the *Albany Evening Journal,* and the *Delaware Gazette.* I am grateful to Cathleen Dooley for tracing these activists in the census schedules.

41. *Delaware Gazette,* 1828–40, passim; *Daily Albany Argus,* 1828–40, passim; *Albany Evening Journal,* 1828–40, passim.

42. *Delaware Gazette,* 9 July 1834. See also ibid., 9 July 1828, 10 Oct. 1832, 23, 30 Sept. 1840; *Albany Evening Journal,* 9, 10, 14, 15 July, 25 Aug. 1840. On the significance of partisan ritual, see Jean Baker, *Affairs of Party: The Political Culture of the Northern Democrats in the Mid-Nineteenth Century* (Ithaca: Cornell University Press, 1983), 291–304; David Waldstreicher, *In the Midst of Perpetual Fetes: The Making of American Nationalism* (Chapel Hill: University of North Carolina Press, 1997), 177–245.

43. Voting returns before 1828 are for gubernatorial votes and are from the First American Democratization Project files, American Antiquarian Society; my thanks to Philip Lampi for allowing me access to these returns. Returns from 1828 on are for Presidential elections in presidential election years and for governor in other years, and are from the *Delaware Gazette, Daily Albany Argus, and Albany Evening Journal,* 1828–1840. The total number of eligible voters for 1801–1824 was estimated by adding half the white males between the ages of 16 and 26

to all the white men over the age of 26 counted in the *Second Census of the United States, 1800; Third Census of the United States, 1810;* and *Fourth Census of the United States, 1820.* Total voters for 1826–28 and 1836–38 were drawn from the *Census of the State of New York,* 1825 and 1835. Total voters for 1840 were estimated by adding 90 percent of the white men between the ages of 20 and 30 to all the white men listed as 30 and older in *Sixth Census of the United States, 1840.* On partisan competition for town offices, see *Delaware Gazette,* 18 Apr. 1831, 28 Mar. 1838, 13 Mar. 1839, 26 Feb. 1840. For estimates of participation in partisan rituals, see ibid., 30 Sept. 1840, *Albany Evening Journal,* 9, 15 July, 25 Aug. 1840.

44. Stephen Van Rensselaer to John Dickinson, 1 Oct. 1832, Stephen Van Rensselaer Papers, RPI; Van Rensselaer to Nicholas Low, 29 Dec. 1825, ibid.; William A. Duer to Van Rensselaer, 21 July 1827, Isadore M. Fixman Collection, RPI; Fink, "Stephen Van Rensselaer," 108–43 (quotation on p. 128); Fink, "Stephen Van Rensselaer and the House Election of 1825," *New York History* 32 (1951): 324; Edgar A. Werner, *Civil List and Constitutional History of the Colony and State of New York* (Albany: Weed, Parsons, and Co., 1889); Bruegel, "Unrest," 1410–12.

45. Van Rensselaer to Judge Woodworth, quoted in Fink, "Stephen Van Rensselaer," 128; Alexander, *Political History,* 1: 253–405, 2: 1–47, *passim;* Harry L. Watson, *Liberty and Power: The Politics of Jacksonian America* (New York: Hill and Wang, 1990), 65–72; Donald B. Cole, *Martin Van Buren and the American Political System* (Princeton: Princeton University Press, 1984), 9–98; Edward Pessen, *Jacksonian America: Society, Personality, and Politics,* rev. ed. (Homewood, IL: Dorsey Press, 1978), 174–78.

46. For a full discussion of this crackdown and of tenants' response, see chapter 3 below.

47. First American Democratization Project files; election returns, *Daily Albany Argus,* 1828–1840. Van Rensselaer's interest sought votes for the Federalists until 1820, the Clintonian "People's Party" in 1824, the National Republicans between 1828 and 1832, and the Whigs from 1834 on.

48. This analysis is based on biographical information on all the congressmen, members of the state assembly, county sheriffs, and county judges listed for Albany County in Werner, *Civil List.* Biographical information was gathered from George Rogers Howell, *Bi- Centennial History of the County of Albany, New York, From 1609 to 1886* (New York: W. W. Munsell, 1886); Amasa J. Parker, *Landmarks of Albany County, NY* (Syracuse: D. Mason, 1897); *Biographical Directory of the American Congress* (Washington, D.C.: Government Printing Office, 1961); Charles Elliott Fitch, *Encyclopedia of Biography of New York* (4 vols.; New York: American Historical Association, 1916); Cuyler Reynolds, comp., *Albany Chronicles: A History of the City Arranged Chronologically* (10 vols.; Albany: J.B. Lyon, 1906). The quotation is in Fink, "Stephen Van Rensselaer," 143.

49. Werner, *Civil List; Biographical Review . . . of the Leading Citizens of Delaware County, New York* (Boston: Biographical Review Publishing Company, 1895); *History of Delaware County;* Jay Gould, *History of Delaware County and the Border Wars of New York* (Roxbury, NY: Keeny and Gould, 1856); David Murray, *Delaware County, New York: History of the Century* (Delhi, NY: William Clark, 1898); John D. Monroe, *Chapters in the History of Delaware County, New York* (Delhi: Delaware County Historical Association, 1949); *Biographical Directory of the American Congress.*

50. *Albany Evening Journal,* 29 Aug. 1840; Eldridge Honaker Pendleton, "The New York Anti-Rent Controversy, 1830–1860" (Ph.D. dissertation, University of Virginia, 1974), 164–66. For sources on officeholders' occupations, see note 48.

51. The proportion of Albany County assembly members, sheriffs, congressmen, and county judges whose public careers lasted only one or two years grew from 35 percent in the first decade of the nineteenth century to 56 percent during the 1830s. In that same period, the proportion of officeholders whose careers spanned more than a decade dropped from 26 percent to 9 percent. In Delaware County, the proportion of officeholders whose careers lasted one or two years grew from 45 percent in the 1800s to 52 percent between 1830 and 1840. Officers serving 10 or more years dropped from 32 percent to 18 percent of the total. Werner, *Civil List.*

52. *Albany Evening Journal,* 1 Oct. 1838, 29 Sept., 21 Oct. 1840; *Daily Albany Argus,* 15, 23 Oct. 1830; *Delaware Gazette,* 6 Oct. 1824; Stephen Van Rensselaer to Martin Van Buren, 22 Aug. 1832, 12 Apr. 1834, Martin Van Buren Papers, Series 2, Library of Congress; Van Buren to Van Rensselaer, 1 Sept. 1832, ibid; Van Rensselaer to Walter ____, 1833, Isadore M. Fixman Collection, RPI; Peter R. Livingston to Frances Granger, 9 Mar. 1841, ibid; Charles Hathaway, Account Book of Lands Bought at Tax Sales, Peters Collection, DCHA; John Kiersted to Henry Overing, 30 Nov. 1830, Kiersted-Overing Letters, NYSL; C. Edward Skeen, *John Armstrong, Jr.: A Biography* (Syracuse: Syracuse University Press, 1981); *History of Delaware County,* 166.

53. See works cited in note 48.

54. *Delaware Gazette,* 12 Sept. 1832; Murray, *Delaware County,* 341–42; Gould, *Delaware County,* 218–406; Pendleton, "New York Anti-Rent Controversy," 164–66. For sources on the distribution of offices among towns, see the sources listed in note 49.

55. Mrs. Jean D. Worden, comp., *Church History of the Rensselaerville Presbyterian Church* (privately printed, 1993), 61; Worden, comp., *Albany County, New York: Rensselaerville Presbyterian (or Congregational) Church 1794–1920* (privately printed, 1993), n.p.; *Delaware Gazette,* 16 July 1828, 21 July 1830, 7 Sept. 1831.

56. *Delaware Gazette,* 12 Mar., 25 June, 16 July 1828, 18 July, 29 Aug. 1832, 17, 24, 31 July 1833, 23 July 1834, 29 July 1835, 9 Nov. 1836, 26 July 1837, 1 July 1840; Howell and Tenney, *History of the County of Albany,* 340; *First Annual Report of the New-York State Society for the Promotion of Temperance* (Albany: Packard and Van Benthuysen, 1830), 15–17, 19, 28; *Second Annual Report of the New-York State Society for the Promotion of Temperance* (Albany: Packard and Van Benthuysen, 1831), 36–37, 53, 78–80, 82; *Fourth Annual Report of the New-York State Society for the Promotion of Temperance* (Albany: Packard and Van Benthuysen, 1833), 22, 34, 39, 40, 45.

57. *First Annual Report,* 15–17, 28; *Second Annual Report,* 53, 78–80; *Delaware Gazette,* 20 June 1832.

58. *Delaware Gazette,* 16 July 1828, 11 July 1832, 22 Nov. 1837.

59. Ibid., 1 July 1829, 27 March 1833, 22 Nov. 1837.

60. *First Annual Report,* 15–17, 28; *Second Annual Report,* 36, 53.

61. Local temperance societies in the Helderberg towns of Bern, Knox, Rensselaerville, and Westerlo claimed 1,892 members in 1833—33.1 percent of the 5,709 men and women over the age of 20 in 1830. Societies in the main leasehold towns of Delaware County claimed 979 members—17.7 percent of the 5,537 men and women over 20. *Fourth Annual Report,* 22, 45; *Fifth Census of the United States, 1830; Delaware Gazette,* 16 July 1828, 26 July 1837.

62. *Delaware Gazette,* 6 Apr., 3, 10 Aug. 1836, 4 Jan., 8 Feb., 31 May, 5 July 1837, 31 Jan., 7, 14, 21 Feb. 1838, 20 Feb. 1839.

63. *Delaware Gazette*, 4 Dec. 1822, 29 Oct. 1834, 1 July 1840.

64. Ibid., 8 July 1840; *Daily Albany Argus*, 17 Oct. 1832.

65. *Delaware Gazette*, 21 May, 20 Aug. 1834, 10 Oct. 1838 (quotation in 10 Oct. 1838); *Argus*, 27 Aug. 1829, 1, 28 Aug. 1832 (quotations in 27 Aug. 1829 and 1 Aug. 1832).

66. *Gazette*, 29 Aug., 24 Oct. 1832; *Argus*, 15 Oct. 1832.

67. *Gazette*, 27 Aug. 1828, 16 June 1830, 6 July 1831, 9 July 1834, 12 Aug., 23 Sept. 1840; *Argus*, 3, 9, 15 June 1830.

68. *Gazette*, 3 Apr. 1833, 22 May, 19 June, 31 July 1839; *Argus*, 5, 11 June, 3 July 1829, 25 July 1832.

69. *Gazette*, 13 Feb., 9 July, 27 Aug., 22 Oct. 1828, 27 Oct. 1830, 2 Nov. 1831, 9 Oct. 1833, 19 Feb. 1834, 19 Aug. 1835, 11 Apr., 10 Oct. 1838, 6 Mar., 11 Sept., 23, 30 Oct. 1839; *Argus*, 6 Aug. 1832.

70. *Gazette*, 16 April 1828, 7 Oct. 1835, 22 June, 6 July 1836, 11 July 1838, 16 Jan, 10 July, 11 Dec. 1839; *Argus*, 7 July 1828, 11 July 1829, 7 July 1830.

71. *Albany Evening Journal*, 29 Aug., 4 Nov. 1840.

72. Ibid., 8 Sept. 1837. See also *Albany Evening Journal*, 21 Aug. 1838, 9 Oct. 1840.

73. Ibid.,13 July 1837, 5, 23 Sept., 29 Oct., 5 Nov. 1838, 23 July 1840. The quotation is from 23 Sept. 1840.

74. Ibid.,29 Oct. 1838.

75. Ibid.,28 Aug., 22 Sept. 1838, 31 July 1840.

76. William H. Seward, Annual Message to the Legislature, 1 Jan. 1839, in *The Works of William H. Seward*, George E. Baker, ed. (5 vols.; Boston: Houghton, Mifflin, 1884), 2: 197–98.

77. Baker, *Affairs of Party*, 27–70; Joel H. Silbey, *The American Political Nation, 1838–1893* (Stanford: Stanford University Press, 1991), 160–62; Paul F. Bourke and Donald A. DeBats, "The Structures of Political Involvement in the Nineteenth Century: A Frontier Case," *Perspectives in American History*, new series, 3 (1987): 207–38.

78. *Albany Evening Journal*, 19 Nov. 1840; *Census of the State of New York for 1845* (Albany: Carroll and Cook, 1846).

79. Whig towns, on the other hand, felt the benefits more than the costs of the new economy. Farmers in the foothill and valley towns enjoyed fertile land and easy transportation to the Albany, Troy, Erie Canal, and New York markets. The opening of the Erie Canal had made wheat production in these towns unprofitable, but local husbandmen found remunerative alternatives that required little capital investment: barley, rye, and corn for the Albany and Troy distilleries and breweries; fruits, vegetables, and swine for urban markets. Farmers in Knox, the sole Whig town in the Helderbergs, were switching rapidly from wheat to livestock in 1840, but did so with far more success than husbandmen in the Democratic towns. They produced far more wool and dairy products than other Helderbergers, without sacrificing their production of wheat and cloth for home use—a clear indication of prosperity. Farmers like these were most likely to appreciate the Whigs' message that government-sponsored capitalist development would raise the material, intellectual, and moral standards of all segments of society without sparking significant social conflict. *Albany Evening Journal*, 19 Nov. 1840; U.S. Bureau of the Census, *Statistics of the United States . . . 1840* (Washington, D.C.: Blair and Rives, 1841), 88–89; idem, *Sixth Census of the United States, 1840* (Washington, D.C. Blair and Rives, 1841), 82–83.

80. *Delaware Gazette*, 18 Nov. 1840; *Statistics of the United States . . . 1840*, 112–

13; *Sixth Census of the United States, 1840*, 88–89; *Census of the State of New York for 1845*.

81. *Argus*, 14 July 1832; *Gazette*, 1 July 1829, 25 July 1832; *Journal*, 24 Oct., 3 Nov. 1837, 9 July, 4 Nov. 1840.

82. Evers, *Woodstock*, 180–81.

83. Brandt, *American Aristocracy*, 172–80, 194.

84. James Fenimore Cooper, *The American Democrat: A Treatise on Jacksonian Democracy* (1838; reprint ed., New York: Funk and Wagnalls, 1969), 110–11, 115–16, 143; Brandt, *American Aristocracy*, 191–92; Albany *Freeholder*, 30 April, 13 Aug., 17 Sept. 1845.

85. Kosciuszko Armstrong to Henry B. Armstrong, 9 Aug. 1846, Miscellaneous Manuscripts, John Armstrong, NYHS; Skeen, *John Armstrong*, 218; Hunt, *Edward Livingston*, 219.

86. Alexander, *Political History*, 145–62, 204, 217–18, 251, 255, 287, 342, 376, 395, 400–403; Hammond, *History of Political Parties*, 2:95, 106, 265, 323–24, 262, 405, 430; Craig Hanyan and Mary L. Hanyan, *De Witt Clinton and the Rise of the People's Men* (Montreal: McGill-Queen's University Press, 1996), 11, 24, 31, 53, 69, 80, 111–12, 119, 139, 143–45, 168, 263; Fink, "Stephen Van Rensselaer," 106–143.

87. Marvin Meyers, *The Jacksonian Persuasion: Politics and Belief* (Stanford, CA: Stanford University Press, 1957), esp. chapter 4. For interpretations of partisan differences as a division between producerists and elitists, see especially John Ashworth, *"Agrarians" and "Aristocrats": Party Political Ideology in the United States, 1837–1846* (New York: Cambridge University Press, 1987); Charles Sellers, *The Market Revolution: Jacksonian America, 1815–1846* (New York: Oxford University Press, 1991).

88. Daniel D. Barnard, *Man and the State, Social and Political* (New Haven: B. L. Hamlen, 1846), 8, 12–15, 17–19, 33–34.

89. Ibid., 11, 20, 25, 26, 48.

90. Ibid., 26, 46.

91. Cooper, *American Democrat*, 39. On the Jacksonians' egalitarian liberalism, see Ashworth, *"Agrarians" and "Aristocrats"*, 21–34.

92. Ibid., 84–87, 132–33, 145–46.

93. Ibid., 84–87.

94. On the social vision of large-scale manufacturers, see Jonathan Prude, *The Coming of Industrial Order: Town and Factory Life in Rural Massachusetts* (New York: Oxford University Press, 1983), 110–116; Cynthia J. Sheldon, *The Mills of Manayunk: Industrialization and Social Conflict in the Philadelphia Region, 1787–1837* (Baltimore: Johns Hopkins University Press, 1986), 100–115; Anthony F. C. Wallace, *Rockdale: The Growth of an American Village in the Early Industrial Revolution* (New York: W. W. Norton, 1972), 296–337, 350–471; T. W. Dyott, *An Exposition of Moral and Mental Labor, Established at the Glass Factory of Dyottville, in the County of Philadelphia* (Philadelphia: n.p., 1833); Robert F. Dalzell, *Enterprising Elite: The Boston Associates and the World They Made* (Cambridge, Mass.: Harvard University Press, 1987). On the social vision of the Federalists, see Linda K. Kerber, *Federalists in Dissent: Imagery and Ideology in Jeffersonian America* (Ithaca, NY: Cornell University Press, 1970); James Roger Sharp, *American Politics in the Early Republic: The New Nation in Crisis* (New Haven: Yale University Press, 1993); Alan Taylor, *William Cooper's Town: Politics and Persuasion on the Frontier of the Early American Republic* (New York: Alfred A. Knopf, 1995). On the social vision of small manufacturers, see Sean Wilentz, *Chants Democratic: New York City and the Rise of the*

American Working Class, 1788–1850 (New York: Oxford University Press, 1984), 35–42, 145–53, 271–86.

Chapter 3

1. Robert R. Livingston Diary, quoted in Alf Evers, *Woodstock: History of an American Town* (Woodstock, NY: Overlook Press, 1987), 155–56.

2. William Bertrand Fink, "Stephen Van Rensselaer: The Last Patroon" (Ph.D. dissertation, Columbia University, 1950), 212–20. Van Rensselaer's correspondence from the early nineteenth century has been destroyed; I have imputed his actions toward his tenants from the latter's subsequent behavior. See Westerlo Accounts, Ledgers A and B, VRMRB.

3. Westerlo Farm Accounts, Ledgers A and B, VRMRB; Douglass C. North, *The Economic Growth of the United States, 1790–1860* (New York: Norton, 1966), 182–88.

4. Westerlo Farm Accounts, Ledgers A and B, VRMRB.

5. Ibid; declarations, Stephen Van Rensselaer vs. various tenants, folders 45, 46, 47, Abraham Van Vechten Papers, NYSL.

6. "Clarke and Van Alstynes Account—Timber at Bath," 1818, box 115, VRMP; Account of Robert Hall, n.d. [1830s?], folder 45, Van Vechten Papers; Pruyn to Marshall, 27 Dec. 1837, box 66, VRMP; notes on the case against Moses Winne, n.d. [1824?], Van Vechten Papers, folder 46; injunction against David W. Crandall and James N. Vars, New York Supreme Court, 18 April 1833, ibid., folder 45; narrative of the case of Stephen Van Rensselaer v. Thomas Dill, New York Supreme Court, Jan 1834, ibid.

7. Declarations against Jacob Sheldon, David Baker, and James Farquar, 10 July 1837; William Reynolds, 10 July 1837; Nicholas Brouck, 16 Oct. 1833; Isaac Crary, 18 July 1837; Richard Oliver, 10 July 1837; John Blair, Jr., 11 Feb. 1835; Benjamin Allen and Nicholas Allen, 4 Feb. 1836; J. Clark to Abraham Van Vechten, 20 Aug. 1835; Casparus V. Pruyn to Abraham Van Vechten, 23 Dec. 1833; all in Van Vechten Papers, folder 45; Writ of Possession against John Blair, Jr., 13 Jan. 1836, ibid., folder 47.

8. "Statement of Sawmills in Knox and Bern," 14 Jan. 1834, box 58, folder 6, VRMP.

9. Evers, *Woodstock*, 157, 687 n. 9.

10. Ibid., 164, 171–76.

11. Leases in box 1, folder 3 and box 2, folders 5, 9, 10, Hardenbergh Papers, NYSL; lease to Samuel Bushnell, 1 May 1800, box 1, folder 3, ibid.; lease to Henry Demery, 1 May 1796, ibid.; deed from Henry, Christina, and Regina Laraway to Lewis Hardenbergh, 1826, box 2, folder 10, ibid.; deed from Margaret Laraway to Lewis Hardenbergh, 3 Jan. 1829, ibid.; deed from Aaron Sturges to William Sturges, 26 Oct. 1812, box 1, folder 3, ibid.; Sheriff's deed to the Sturges farm, 24 May 1813, ibid; Isaac to Lewis Hardenbergh, 3, 6 Jan 1818, 30 June, 28, 31 July 1819, all in box 2, folder 3, ibid; Delaware County Land Records, DCHA; Land Record Summary Sheet, Rapelje Patent, DCHA; Albany *Freeholder,* 25 Mar. 1846, 29 Dec. 1847.

12. Lease from James Wands to William Sturges, 23 April 1828, box 2, folder 5, Hardenbergh Papers; lease from Frances Becker to John Bush, 1822, box 2, folder 10, ibid.; lease from Lewis and George Hardenbergh to Peter Moote, 25 Dec. 1833, box 2, folder 9, ibid.; lease from John Hardenbergh to Zachariah Turk, box 2, folder 5, ibid.; lease from James Wands to Hubbard Van Horn, April 1831, box 2, folder 5, ibid.

13. Lease from Isaac Hardenbergh to William Sturges, 4 Feb. 1813, box 1, folder 3, Hardenbergh Papers. See also lease from John Hardenbergh to Lawrence and Nathan Cronk, n.d., box 2, folder 5, ibid.; lease from Lewis Hardenbergh to Richard Laraway, 1 Apr. 1827, box 2, folder 10, ibid.; John Kiersted to "Dear Brother," 1 Oct. 1838, box 1, folder 1, Kiersted Family Papers, NYSL; Leases, 1807–1829 and Leases, 1830–1839, box 20, Samuel A. Law Papers, NYSL.

14. Lease from John Hardenbergh to Lawrence and Nathan Cronk, n.d., box 2, folder 5, Hardenbergh Papers; lease from Samuel A. Law to C. Simonson, 18 Jan. 1836, in Leases, 1830–39, box 20, Law Papers.

15. Law to James C. Fisher, 2 March 1830, in letters, 1830–31, box 5, Law Papers; Law to David Dart, 11 Feb. 1830, ibid.; lease from John Reed to James Gibson and John Lewis, 21 April 1823, in Leases, 1807–1829, box 20, ibid.; Isaac Hardenbergh to Lewis Hardenbergh, 1820, box 2, folder 3, Hardenbergh Papers.

16. Isaac Hardenbergh to Lewis Hardenbergh, 15 July 1820, box 2, folder 3, Hardenbergh Papers; George Hardenbergh to Lewis Hardenbergh, 4 May, 28 July 1837, box 2, folder 7, ibid.

17. Lease from Samuel A. Law to C. Simonson, 18 Jan. 1836, Leases, 1830–39, box 20, Law Papers; "Compromise and Variation," 7 Oct. 1836, ibid.

18. Evers, *Woodstock*, 157, 164–76, 687 n. 9.

19. Complaints against Peter Stanard, David Palmer, Valentine Cropsey, Minard T. Cole, David Comstock, and Nicholas Brouck; injunction against David W. Crandall and James N. Vars; judgments against Frederick Saddlemeyer, Samuel Coleman, and Ezra Olcutt and James Olcutt; warrants against George Saddlemeyer, Jacob Rishew, and Jonathan Burdick; declaration against David G. Smith; Van Vechten's notes in the case of Van Rensselaer vs. Rufus Austin and David Kendall; "Notice of Intent"; Pleas before Justices of the Supreme Court of Judicature in the case of Van Rensselaer vs. Frederick Spawn and [Jehoviakim?] Speeder; all in folder 45, Van Vechten Papers.

20. Van Vechten's notes on Moses Winne vs. Lansing, n.d., folder 46, Van Vechten Papers. It is not clear when this case was initiated, but Van Vechten's notes refer to a case in 1824, making clear that the suit took place after that date.

21. Ledgers A and B, VRMRB; Stephen Hungerford to Martin Van Buren, 10 August 1830, Series 2, *Martin Van Buren Papers*, Library of Congress, Washington, D.C., reel 9; Ellis, *Landlords and Farmers*, 234–35.

22. John Kiersted to Henry Overing, 30 Nov. 1830, Kiersted-Overing Letters, NYSL; Evers, *Woodstock*, 185; *Albany Freeholder*, 10 Feb. 1847.

23. Van Vechten Papers, Folder 45; *Argus*, 1830–40; Ellis, *Landlords and Farmers*, 235.

24. Hungerford to Van Buren, 10 Aug. 1830, Van Buren to Hungerford, 16 Aug. 1830; Van Buren to Sutherland, 17 Aug. 1830; all in Van Buren Papers, Series 2, reel 9.

25. *Daily Albany Argus*, 28 Jan. 1839; Last Will and Testament of Stephen Van Rensselaer, recorded 10 Apr. 1839, Book of Wills, vol. 10: 342–57, Albany County Surrogate's Court, Albany, NY; Inventory Log of Stephen Van Rensselaer, RPI; Henry Christman, *Tin Horns and Calico: A Decisive Episode in the Emergence of Democracy* (1945; reprint ed., Cornwallville, NY: Hope Farm Press, 1978), 15.

26. *Daily Albany Argus*, 1, 2 Feb. 1839.

27. Deposition of William Henry Anderson before the Supreme Court, 23

Jan. 1840, folder 6114 ("Helderberg War 1840"), Governor's Papers, William Henry Seward Papers, Clements Library, Ann Arbor, MI, reel 177.

Chapter 4

1. *Daily Albany Argus*, 6 Dec. 1839.
2. Ibid.; "Inventory Log of Stephen Van Rensselaer III" (1839), RPI.
3. Pruyn to Van Rensselaer, 9, 16, 24 Jan. 1840 and n.d., box 2, folder 1, William Patterson Van Rensselaer Papers, AIHA; NYAD 1841, 261: 5; Last Will and Testament of Stephen Van Rensselaer, recorded 10 Apr. 1839, Book of Wills, vol. 10: 342–57, Albany County Surrogate's Court, Albany, NY.
4. Pruyn to Van Rensselaer, 16, 21, 24 Jan. 1840, box 2, folder 1, William Patterson Van Rensselaer Papers; *Daily Albany Argus*, 25 Sept. 1839. The quotation is in Pruyn to Van Rensselaer, 24 Jan. 1840.
5. Pruyn to Van Rensselaer, 24 Jan. 1840, box 2, folder 1, William Patterson Van Rensselaer Papers. See also Pruyn to Van Rensselaer, 16, 21 Jan. 1840, ibid. On the depressions of 1837–39 and 1839–43, see Paul Wallace Gates, *The Farmer's Age: Agriculture, 1815–1860* (New York: Holt, Reinhart, and Winston, 1960), 405–406, 410; Peter Temin, *The Jacksonian Economy* (New York: W. W. Norton, 1969), 113–20, 148–57, 160–62; Douglass C. North, *The Economic Growth of the United States, 1790–1860* (New York: W. W. Norton, 1966), 201–202; Samuel Rezneck, "The Social History of an American Depression, 1837–1843," *American Historical Review* 40 (1935): 662–87; NYSD 1846, 92: 25–27.
6. Pruyn to Van Rensselaer, 16, 24 Jan. 1840, box 2, folder 1, William Patterson Van Rensselaer Papers.
7. *Daily Albany Argus*, 6 Dec. 1839.
8. Ibid.; deposition of William Henry Anderson, 29 Jan. 1840, in folder 6114 ("Helderberg War 1840"), Governor's Papers, William Henry Seward Papers, Clements Library, Ann Arbor, MI, reel 177. The towns that appointed committees were Knox, Bern, Rensselaerville, Westerlo, and New Scotland.
9. The names of the tenant representatives are in *Daily Albany Argus*, 6 Dec. 1839. Biographical information is from 1840 Manuscript Federal Census, Population, Albany County, New York; 1850 Manuscript Federal Census, Population, Albany County, New York; Westerlo, New York Assessment Roll, 1840, Westerlo Town Clerk's Office, Westerlo, NY; *Daily Albany Argus*, 20 May 1841; Amasa J. Parker, *Landmarks of Albany County* (Syracuse: D. Mason, 1897) 299, 314; George R. Howell and Jonathan Tenney, *Bi-Centennial History of the County of Albany, NY, from 1609 to 1886* (New York: W. W. Mansell, 1886), 870, 872. By July of 1839, the tenants' committee had expanded from its original 25 members to 30 members, as a sixth town—Guilderland, in the Hudson Valley at the foot of the Helderbergs—elected representatives to the committee. All percentages presented in my discussion include the five Guilderland members.
10. Patricia Hanks and Flavia Hodges, *A Dictionary of Surnames* (New York: Oxford University Press, 1988); Elsdon C. Smith, *New Dictionary of American Family Names* (New York: Harper and Row, 1956). In religion, too, available evidence suggests that committee members were drawn from all segments of the community. Local histories list two Methodists, a Lutheran, and three members of the Dutch Reformed Church as tenant leaders. Howell and Tenney, *Bi-Centennial History*, 809, 811, 812, 900; Parker, *Landmarks of Albany County*, Part 3: 257. For my method in determining the political affiliations of tenant leaders, see note 11. Two historians give an ethnic interpretation to the eighteenth-century tenant and

squatter rebellions in New York: Dixon Ryan Fox, *Yankees and Yorkers* (New York: University Press, 1940); Patricia Bonomi, *A Factious People: Politics and Society in Colonial New York* (New York: Columbia University Press, 1971), 196–228.

11. Howell and Tenney, *Bi-Centennial History*, 88–89, 809, 811–12, 817, 847–48, 871, 900, 920, 928. The names of county-level party activists and their political affiliations are drawn from the lists of delegates, nominees, and committees of correspondence listed in the Albany county Anti-Mason, Whig, and Democratic nominating conventions that preceded the November elections in each year, 1832–1838. The Anti-Mason conventions (1832–33) and Whig conventions (1834 on) are in the *Albany Evening Journal;* the proceedings for the Democratic meetings are in the *Daily Albany Argus.* If we count committee members who were active in 1839 and 1840, the number of partisan activists increases to eighteen—60 percent of the total.

12. *Daily Albany Argus,* 6 Dec. 1839; *Albany Freeholder,* 5 Nov. 1845; Thomas Ainge Devyr, *Our Natural Rights: A Pamphlet for the People, by One of Themselves* (n.p: n.p., n.d.), 53–54; Henry Christman, *Tin Horns and Calico: A Decisive Episode in the Emergence of Democracy* (1945; reprint ed., Cornwallville, NY: Hope Farm Press, 1978), 18–20.

13. *Daily Albany Argus,* 6 Dec. 1839.

14. Ibid.

15. Ibid.

16. Ibid.

17. Ibid.

18. Ibid. Emphasis added.

19. Ibid.

20. Ibid.

21. Deposition of William Henry Anderson, 28 Jan. 1840, folder 6114 ("Helderberg War 1840"), Governor's Papers, William Henry Seward Papers, Reel 177; *Daily Albany Argus,* 6 Dec. 1839.

22. *Daily Albany Argus,* 6 Dec. 1839; Michael Artcher to William H. Seward, 4 Dec. 1839, in NYSD 1840, 70: 19.

23. Deposition of Amos Adams, 28 Aug. 1839, in NYSD 1840, 70: 21–22.

24. Ibid.; James C. Scott, *Domination and the Arts of Resistance: Hidden Transcripts* (New Haven: Yale University Press, 1990); E. P. Thompson, *Whigs and Hunters: The Origin of the Black Act* (New York: Pantheon, 1975); Eugene D. Genovese, *Roll, Jordan, Roll: The World the Slaves Made* (New York: Vintage, 1972); E. J. Hobsbawn and George Rude, *Captain Swing* (New York: Pantheon, 1968); Alan Taylor, *Liberty Men and Great Proprietors: The Revolutionary Settlement on the Maine Frontier, 1760–1820* (Chapel Hill: University of North Carolina Press, 1990).

25. Deposition of D. I. Leonard, n.d., NYSD 1840, 70: 22–24.

26. Ibid.; Michael Artcher to William H. Seward, 4 Dec. 1839, ibid., 18–20.

27. Ibid.; William Seward to Michael Artcher, 5, 7 Dec. 1839, ibid., 26; Rufus King to ____, 8 Dec. 1839, ibid., 27; Michael Artcher, W. Bloodgood, and Jesse Buel to William Seward, 9 Dec. 1839, ibid., 28; "General Orders" signed by Rufus King, 9, 10 Dec. 1839, ibid., 28–30; *Daily Albany Argus,* 13 Dec. 1839; *New York Herald,* 13, 14 Dec. 1839; Frederick W. Seward, *William H. Seward: An Autobiography from 1801 to 1834, with a Memoir of his Life, and Selections from his Letters, 1831–1846* (3 vols.; New York: Derby and Miller, 1891), 2: 449–53.

28. Proclamation, dated 10 Dec. 1839, in NYSD 1840, 70: 31–32.

29. Henry Wheaton and Azor Taber to William Seward, 11 Dec. 1839, ibid.,

34–35.; S. S. Benedict to William Seward, 10 Dec. 1839, ibid., 32; William Seward to Michael Artcher, 11 Dec. 1839, ibid., 33; William Bloodgood to Rufus King, 10 Dec. 1839, ibid.; Michael Artcher to William Seward, 13 Dec. 1839, ibid., 37; "General Orders," signed by Rufus King, 14, 16 Dec. 1839, ibid., 38–39; *Daily Albany Argus,* 21 Dec. 1839.

30. Pruyn to William Van Rensselaer, 14, 17, 29, 30 Nov. 1839, box 2, folder 1, William Patterson Van Rensselaer Papers.

31. Pruyn to Van Rensselaer, 3, 15, 28 Dec. 1839, 24 Jan., 24 Feb. 1840, ibid; JA 1840–42; J.S. Hakes to William P. Van Rensselaer, n.d., box 4, folder 1, William Patterson Van Rensselaer Papers.

32. NYAD 1844, 189:14; *Albany Freeholder,* 10 Feb. 1847; *Radical* 1 (1841): 62; Deposition of John O'Brien, 29 Mar. 1842, file 6211 ("Schoharie County Riots"), Governor's Papers, William H. Seward Papers, reel 180; petition of John O'Brien, 26 Apr. 1842, ibid.

33. *Daily Albany Argus,* 29 Feb. 1840, 12 Mar., 23 June, 8, 10, 21, 22 Sept. 1841, 11 Mar. 1844; *Radical* 1 (1841): 61–62, 137; deposition of John O'Brien, 29 Mar. 1842, in file 6211 ("Schoharie County Riots"), Governor's Papers, Seward Papers, reel 180; deposition of Abraham Decker, 6 June 1842, ibid.; deposition of Jacob M. Swart, 18 Mar. 1842, ibid.

34. *Daily Albany Argus,* 21 Dec. 1839, 19 Mar. 1840; JA 1840, 91, 107, 163, 170, 178, 247, 260, 292, 308, 312, 335, 356, 362, 368, 448, 504, 515, 633, 634, 654–57, 677, 755; NYAD 1840, 271: 3–4.

35. NYAD 1840, 271: 3; *Helderberg Advocate,* quoted in Devyr, *Our Natural Rights,* 53–54.

36. For a brilliant study of how political leaders sought to deal with the lease-hold controversy in this framework, see Charles McCurdy, *Fettered Freedom: The Anti-Rent Era in New York Law and Politics, 1840–1865* (forthcoming, University of North Carolina Press).

37. De Alva Stanwood Alexander, *Political History of the State of New York* (3 vols.; New York: Henry Holt, 1906), 2: 16–18, 25–26, 51; Jabez Hammond, *History of Political Parties in the State of New York* (3 vols.; Syracuse: Hall, Mills, and Company, 1852), 2: 479, 528, 3: 248, 290–91, 481–82.

38. JA 1840, 91, 107; NYAD 1840, 271: 4.

39. Ibid., 5–6.

40. Karl Marx, *Capital: A Critique of Political Economy* (3 vols.; New York: International Publishers, 1967), 1: 713–74; Eric Hobsbawm, *The Age of Revolution: Europe, 1789–1848,* 180–201; Karl Polyani, *The Great Transformation: The Political and Economic Origins of Our Time* (Boston: Beacon Press, 1944), 68–76, 178–91.

41. *New York Assembly Documents* 1840, 271: 6–20; Gary B. Nash, *Race and Revolution* (Madison: Madison House, 1990); Nash and Jean R. Soderlund, *Freedom by Degrees: Emancipation and its Aftermath in Pennsylvania* (New York: Oxford University Press, 1990); David Brion Davis, *The Problem of Slavery in the Age of Revolution, 1770–1823* (Ithaca: Cornell University Press, 1975), 255–342; Louis S. Gerteis, *Morality and Utility in American Antislavery Reform* (Chapel Hill: University of North Carolina Press, 1987), 4–19, 86–148.

42. NYAD 1840, 271: 20–21; JA 1840, 699–700, 1390–91, 1424, 1479.

43. On most landlords' Democratic loyalties and the Democrats' constitutional thought, see chapter 2. See also Hammond, *Political History,* 3: 247; Ashworth, *"Agrarians" and "Aristocrats",* 7–20; Lee Benson, *The Concept of Jacksonian Democracy: New York as a Test Case* (1961; reprint ed., New York: Athaneum, 1964), 86–109.

44. JA 1842, 49, 889; NYAD 1842, 181; NYAD 1842, 177.

45. Autobiographical sketch by Smith A. Boughton (typescript), Henry Christman Papers, NYSHA.

46. *Daily Albany Argus*, 6 Dec. 1839, 11 Mar. 1844; deposition of John O'Brien, 29 Mar. 1842, file 6211 ("Schoharie County Riots"), Governor's Papers, William H. Seward Papers, reel 180; Devyr, *Our Natural Rights*, 530–54; NYAD 1844, 189: 6–8, 13–15.

47. McCurdy, *Fettered Democracy*, chapter 4.

48. Smith A. Boughton Autobiography; Smith Boughton to William C. Bouck, 18 Dec. 1843, box 2, Bouck Papers, CU; Burton A. Thomas to William C. Bouck, 5 Aug. 1844, box 3, ibid.; Thomas to Bouck, 23 Dec. 1844, box 2, ibid.; Burton A. Thomas to Martin Van Buren, 8 Jan. 1844, Series 2, Martin Van Buren Papers, Library of Congress, Washington, D.C.; JA 1844, 105, 127, 139, 153, 161, 168, 179, 212, 226, 232, 240, 251, 258, 266, 271, 286, 342, 371, 381, 439.

49. McCurdy, *Fettered Democracy*, chapter 4.

50. NYAD 1844, 183 and 189; JA 1844, 63, 105, 622; McCurdy, *Fettered Democracy*, chapter 3.

51. NYAD 1844, 183: 7–19.

52. Ibid., 15.

53. Ibid., 20–22, 27–45.

54. JA 1844, 945; *Young America*, 1 June 1844.

55. "A Democratic Anti-Rent Tenant of the Manor of Rensselaerwyck" to William C. Bouck, 1 Sept. 1844, box 3, Bouck Papers.

56. Burton A. Thomas to ____, *Young America*, 1 June 1844.

57. Ibid.; John J. Gallup to ____, ibid.

58. *Daily Albany Argus*, reprinted in *Young America*, 17 Aug. 1844; testimony of Jonathan C. Allaben before the Delaware County grand jury, 22 Aug. 1845 (typescript), in Anti-Rent War Documents, DCC; "Newspaper Clippings Relating to Anti-Rent Disturbances in New York State with Some Account of the Resulting Legal Trials," 13, NYSL; Charles Hathaway to Henry Overing, 12 July 1844, NYSL; *Albany Morning Atlas*, 27 July 1844; *Young America*, 21 Dec. 1844.

59. *Young America*, 8 June, 31 Aug., 21 Dec. 1844, 4 Jan., 1 Feb. 1845; *Albany Evening Atlas*, 10 July 1844; "Newspaper clippings," 38; D. Lawyer to William C. Bouck, 8 July 1844, box 3, Bouck Papers.

60. *Young America*, 5 Oct., 9 Nov. 1844; *Albany Morning Atlas*, 23, 26 Sept. 1844; *Daily Albany Argus*, 27 Sept. 1844; Jay Gould, *History of Delaware County and the Border Wars of New York* (Roxbury, N.Y.: Keeny and Gould, 1856), 263; Edgar A. Werner, *Civil List and Constitutional History of the Colony and State of New York* (Albany: Weed and Parsons, 1889), 446–47. The Rensselaer County anti-renters' nominee for the U.S. House of Representatives (who won the Whig nomination as well) was also elected.

61. *Young America*, 21 Dec. 1844, 1, 8 Feb. 1845; *Daily Albany Argus*, 10 Feb. 1845.

Chapter 5

1. *Albany Freeholder*, 21 May, 27 Aug. 1845, 13 Oct. 1847; NYAD 1845, 247:1, cited in Charles W. McCurdy, *Fettered Democracy: The Anti-Rent Era in New York Law and Politics, 1840–1865* (forthcoming, University of North Carolina Press), chapter 7.

2. *Freeholder*, April–May, 6 Aug. 1845, 21 Jan., 8 April, 10 June 1846; *Young*

America, 1 Feb. 1845; *Anti-Renter* (Albany, New York), 13 Sept. 1845; *Equal Rights Advocate* (Hudson, New York), 17 June 1846.

3. Albany *Freeholder,* 28 May, 9, 16 July, 3 Sept., 8, 29 Oct. 1845, 25 Feb., 11 Mar., 8, 15 July, 2, 30 Dec. 1846.

4. The list of anti-rent activists was compiled from lists of anti-rent association officers and the proceedings of town, county, senatorial district, and state meetings printed in the Albany *Freeholder* and the *Anti-Renter,* 1845–46. The list includes association officers; delegates to nominating conventions; speakers, secretaries, chairmen, and members of committees on resolutions at local and county meetings; and men appointed to various ad hoc committees, election-time committees of vigilance, and committees to collect funds. These activists were then traced to the 1850 federal manuscript census, population schedules for Albany and Delaware Counties, and to the 1840 assessment rolls for Westerlo, Albany County. Unfortunately, these statistics must be read with some skepticism, for they indicate the occupation, landholding, and other attributes of anti-rent leaders four to five years *after* the period under study in this chapter. I chose to trace anti-rent leaders to the 1850 census because the 1840 census enumeration was filled with errors and ambiguities, did not list property holdings, and listed only heads of household; and because the 1845 New York manuscript census did not survive for Albany and Delaware Counties.

5. Town of Westerlo, NY Assessment Roll of 1840, Westerlo Town Clerk's Office, Westerlo, NY; 1850 Manuscript Census, Population Schedules, Albany and Delaware Counties, NY. Seven out of 40 leaders from Westerlo (17.5 percent) could not be found in that town's 1840 assessment rolls; though some of these may have moved to Westerlo after 1840, been omitted by error, or been the dependent sons of landowning fathers in 1840, others probably were landless. Some of the landless farmers found in the 1850 census may have already passed their land on to heirs; four were 60 years old or older. Others may have farmed cooperatively with a neighboring sibling or parent or sold their land in anticipation of emigrating or buying a new farm. Still, at least some of these activists were doubtless subtenants who leased land from their neighbors or who scratched together a living from wage labor and a variety of other enterprises. On the problems associated with determining whether or not farmers before 1880 were indeed landless, see Alan Bogue, *From Prairie to Corn Belt: Farming on the Illinois and Iowa Prairies in the Nineteenth Centuries* (Chicago: University of Chicago Press, 1963), 63–64; John T. Houdek and Charles F. Heller, Jr., "Searching for Nineteenth-Century Farm Tenants: An Evaluation of Methods," *Historical Methods* 19 (1986): 55–61.

6. These figures were created by cross-tabulating the names of anti-rent activists with the names of delegates, nominees, and committees of correspondence listed in the reports of county Anti-Mason, Whig, and Democratic nominating conventions that preceded the November elections of each year, 1832–1844. The Anti-Masonic and Whig conventions for Albany County are reported in the *Albany Evening Journal.* The Democratic conventions for Albany County are reported in the *Daily Albany Argus;* those for Delaware County are reported in the *Delaware Gazette.* Unfortunately, the Whig newspaper for Delaware County, the *Delaware Express,* has not survived for the 1830s and 1840s.

These figures greatly underestimate the actual number of party activists among the anti-rent leadership. Delaware County anti-rent activists who had served in the Whig Party are not counted. Just as important, many more activists were likely to have served the major parties on the town rather than the county level.

7. *Freeholder,* 7, 28 May, 13 Aug. 1845, 21 Oct. 1846.

8. Ibid., 11 Mar. 1846.

9. Ibid., 28 May, 8 Oct. 1845; *Young America,* 8 Feb. 1845.

10. *Freeholder,* 28 May, 9 July, 13 Aug. 1845; Sean Wilentz, *Chants Democratic: New York City and the Rise of the American Working Class, 1788–1850* (New York: Oxford University Press, 1984), 157–58 and *passim.* See also Albany *Freeholder,* 20 Jan., 30 Apr., 21, 28 May, 13, 27 Aug., 26 Nov. 1845. New York workers' use of the labor theory of value were transmitted to the tenants by Thomas Devyr and other members of the National Reform Association, a land-reform organization based in the New York City journeyman's movement. See *Helderberg Advocate,* quoted in Thomas Ainge Devyr, *The Odd Book of the Nineteenth Century* (2 vols.; New York: privately printed, 1882), 2: 42–43. Although many Democrats endorsed the labor theory of value, Democratic newspapers in the leasehold district did not do so explicitly. See *Delaware Gazette,* 1819–1840, *passim; Daily Albany Argus,* 1837–1840, *passim.*

11. *Freeholder,* 25 Mar. 1846. See also ibid., 25 June, 13, 27 Aug., 17 Sept. 1845, 1 April 1846.

12. *Anti-Renter,* 4 Oct. 1845; *Young America,* 1 June 1844, 8 Feb. 1845; *Freeholder,* 21 May, 23 July, 3 Sept. 1845, 1 April 1846. Quotation is in *Anti-Renter,* 4 Oct. 1845.

13. *Freeholder,* 26 Nov. 1845.

14. Ibid., 23 July 1845.

15. "A Tenant" to Sheriff Michael Artcher, 9 Sept. 1839, reprinted in NYSD 1840, 70:31.

16. *Young America,* 4 Jan. 1845; *Freeholder,* 7 May, 27 Aug. 1845.

17. *Freeholder,* 25 Mar. 1846.

18. Ibid., 21 Jan. 1846.

19. *Young America,* 4 Jan 1845. See also *Freeholder,* 3 Dec. 1845.

20. Silas Wright, "Address to the New York State Agricultural Society," quoted in Ashworth, *"Agrarians" and "Aristocrats,"* 22.

21. Jay Gould, *History of Delaware County, and the Border Wars of New* York (Roxbury, NY: Keeny and Gould, 1856), 258; Albert Champlin Mayham, *The Anti-Rent War on Blenheim Hill: An Episode of the '40s* (Jefferson, NY: Frederick L. Frazee, 1906), 28–32; *Freeholder,* 27 Aug. 1845.

22. *Freeholder,* 17 Feb. 1847.

23. *Daily Albany Argus,* 12 Mar., 8, 10 Sept., 1 Oct. 1841; Deposition of Almerin Marks, File 6211 ("Schoharie County Riots"), Governor's Papers, William H. Seward Papers, Clements Library, University of Michigan, Ann Arbor, Michigan; Deposition of Jacob M. Swart, 18 Mar. 1842, ibid.; Deposition of John O'Brien, 29 Mar. 1842, ibid.; Petition of John O'Brien, 26 Apr. 1842, ibid.; Deposition of Abraham Decker, 6 June 1842, ibid.; Smith A. Boughton, auto-biographical sketch (typescript), Henry Christman Papers, 7–8, NYSHA; "Newspaper Clippings Relating to Anti-Rent Disturbances in New York State with Some Account of the Resulting Legal Trials," NYSL, 13, 80. The quotations are in the *Daily Albany Argus,* 12 Mar. 1841; Boughton autobiography, 7; "Newspaper Clippings," 13.

24. "Newspaper Clippings," 12, 108; testimony of Henry L. Russell, Delaware County Grand Jury, 22 Aug. 1845, *Anti-Rent War Documents,* vol. 3, DCC; Testimony of David P. Boughton, 22 Aug. 1845, ibid.; Boughton autobiography, 7–8; *Freeholder,* 9 Apr. 1845, 21 Oct. 1846; *Young America,* 9 Nov. 1844. The quotations are from "Newspaper Clippings," 12; testimony of David P. Boughton; and Boughton autobiography, 7–8.

25. 1850 Manuscript Federal Census, Population Schedules, Delaware County, NY. Table 11 yields a Pearson chi-square of 18.306, with a significance of .003, indicating a low 0.3 percent chance that the age distribution of association activists and Indians was random. It also yields a Cramer's V of .454, indicating a very strong level of association.

The list of Indians was drawn from a list of all who were convicted of Indian-related activities by the Delaware County Court, published in the *Delaware Gazette,* 15 Oct. 1845. These individuals were then traced to the 1850 federal manuscript census population schedules for Delaware County. Of the 73 who were convicted, only 34 could be found in the 1850 census—weak evidence that many were land-less, either because of their youth or for other reasons. On how statistics on association activists were compiled, see note 4, this chapter.

This method tends to underestimate the age difference between Indians and association activists. Delaware County juries convicted older, established farmers for the crimes the Indians committed in their defense; they also proved reluctant to send underage defendants to jail. Eldridge H. Pendleton has found that over half of the Delaware County residents who had been indicted for Indian activities (as opposed to those who were convicted) and who remained in their communities until 1850 were between 20 and 25 years of age in 1845. In addition, younger men were the members of the community who were most likely to move to other areas in search of land or jobs; the 1850 census was far more likely to record the presence of older Indians, who were more likely to have accumulated the land that made people stay put. See Eldridge H. Pendleton, "The New York Anti-Rent Controversy, 1830–1860" (Ph.D. dissertation, University of Virginia, 1974), 184.

26. 1850 Manuscript Federal Census, Population Schedules, Delaware County, NY; "Anti-Rent War Documents," vols. 5, 6, and 9. Table 12 yielded a Cramer's V of .529, demonstrating a very high degree of association, and a Pearson chi-square of 24.077, with a significance of .000, showing less than one-tenth of one percent chance of having occurred randomly. Table 13 yielded a Cramer's V of .515 and a Pearson chi-square of 13.789, with a 3.2 percent probability that the distribution occurred randomly.

27. 1850 Manuscript Federal Census, Population Schedules, Delaware County, NY. Table 14 yielded a Cramer's V of .529, indicating a very strong level of association, and a Pearson chi-square probability of 0.000, indicating an extremely low probability that the distribution was random. Because the sample on which this table is based is so small, however, the measure of significance should be regarded with some skepticism.

28. I wish to thank Sarah Deutsch for suggesting this line of analysis to me. See her *No Separate Refuge: Culture, Class, and Gender on an Anglo-Hispanic Frontier in the American Southwest, 1880–1940* (New York: Oxford University Press, 1987), 133–34.

29. *Freeholder,* 9 Apr. 1845, 30 Dec. 1846, 13 Oct. 1847; "Newspaper Clippings," 63; *Albany Evening Atlas,* 12, 13 Aug. 1844; *Albany Atlas,* 13 Aug. 1844; *Young America,* 21 Sept., 1844; Henry Christman, *Tin Horns and Calico: A Decisive Episode in the Emergence of Democracy* (1945; reprint, Cornwallville, NY: Hope Farm Press, 1976), 326–29.

30. Julia Hull Werner, "A Skimeton," *New York Folklore Quarterly* 20 (1964):134–36; letter from C. L. Fernald, *American Notes and Queries* 1 (Oct. 13, 1888): 288; letter of Alice C. Chace, ibid. 1 (Sept. 29, 1888): 263–64; ibid., 1 (May 5, 1888): 8; Bryan D. Palmer, "Discordant Music: Charivaris and White-capping in Nineteenth-Century North America," *Labour/Le Travailleur* 3 (1978):

3–62; Natalie Zemon Davis, "The Reasons of Misrule," in *Society and Culture in Early Modern France* (Stanford: Stanford University Press, 1975), 97–123.

31. Testimony of John Davis before the Delaware County grand jury, 19 Aug. 1845, Acc. No. Test. 6, p.37, reprinted in "Anti-Rent War Documents," vol. 3; testimony of Miles Bromley before the Delaware County grand jury, 22 Aug. 1845, Acc. No. Test 8, p. 9, ibid.; *Albany Atlas*, 13 Aug. 1844; *Freeholder*, 9 Apr. 1845. See also testimony of Isaac L. Burhans before the Delaware county grand jury, 8–11 Aug. 1845, Acc. No. Test. 1½ p. 8, "Anti-Rent War Documents," vol. 2; *Kingston Journal*, in "Newspaper Clippings," 38; *Albany Evening Atlas*, 10 July 1844; *Daily Albany Argus*, 28 Dec. 1844.

32. Deposition of John O'Brien, 29 Mar. 1842, file 6211 ("Schoharie County Riots"), Governor's Papers, Seward Papers; Deposition of Almerin Marks, ibid.; Jacob Livingston to Silas Wright, 28 Mar. 1844, Azariah C. Flagg Papers, NYPL; *Daily Albany Argus*, 28 Nov. 1844; *Young America*, 30 Nov. 1844; "Newspaper Clippings," 32; *Freeholder*, 9, 16 April 1845. For other political uses of the charivari, see Kevin Kenny, *Making Sense of the Molly Maguires* (New York: Oxford University Press); Edward Ayers, *Vengeance and Justice: Crime and Punishment in the Nineteenth-Century American South* (New York: Oxford University Press, 1984), 155–65.

33. *Albany Morning Atlas*, 15 Aug., 2 Sept. 1844; *Young America*, 7, 21 Sept. 1844; William Bouck to Azariah Flagg, 3 Sept. 1844, Flagg Papers.

34. *Radical*, April 1841, 61–52, Sept. 1841, 137.

35. Deposition of Abraham Decker, 6 June 1842, file 6211 ("Schoharie County Riots"), Governor's Papers, Seward Papers. See also Samuel B. Rollo to William C. Bouck, 26 Aug. 1844, box 3, Additional Papers, William C. Bouck, CU; Indictment, People v. Jonas Piester and nine others, 27 Sept. 1845, "Anti-Rent War Documents," 5: 1; *Young America*, 14 Sept. 1844; *Albany Morning Atlas*, 2 Sept. 1844; "Newspaper Clippings," 16–17, 23, 39, 94.

36. Deposition of John O'Brien, 29 Mar. 1842, file 6211 ("Schoharie County Riots"), Governor's Papers, Seward Papers; Rollo to Bouck, 26 Aug. 1844, Additional Bouck Papers; *Young America*, 17 Aug. 1844; *Daily Albany Argus*, 24 Dec. 1844.

37. For a brilliant analysis of the meanings white people have assigned to "playing Indian," see Philip J. Deloria, *Playing Indian* (New Haven, Yale University Press, 1998).

38. The braves themselves confirmed these claims. Between public appearances, they claimed to retire to the "CAMP OF THE LEATHERHEADS" (a reference to their sheepskin masks) in the "ROCKY MOUNTAINS." And they made clear that they were "the *original owners of the soil*." When driving lawmen and landlords' agents from the estates, they warned that distress warrants and eviction notices were not to be served on "Indian ground" and told the intruders never to return to "their dominions." H.J. Munger, "Reminiscences," 7–8; *Guardian of the Soil*, paraphrased in *Young America*, 21 Sept. 1844; "Tar and Feather Letter," DCHA; testimony of Barbour Stafford before the Delaware County Grand Jury, 18 Aug. 1845, Acc. No. Test, 5, p. 1, in "Anti-Rent War Documents," vol. 3; *Young America*, 16 Aug. 1845; deposition of Jacob M. Swart, 18 Mar. 1842, file 6211, Governor's Papers, Seward Papers; *Daily Albany Argus*, 31 Jan., 27 Mar. 1845.

39. Robert F. Berkhofer, Jr., *The White Man's Indian: Images of the American Indian from Columbus to the Present* (New York: Alfred A. Knopf, 1978), 29–30, 88–91.

40. "Tar and Feather Letter"; *Daily Albany Argus*, 23 June 1841; *Albany Evening Atlas*, 12 Aug. 1844; Christman, *Tin Horns and Calico*, 42–44, 326–27.

41. Testimony of Barbour Stafford before the Delaware County grand jury, 18 Aug. 1845, Acc. No. Test. 5, p.1, "Anti-Rent War Documents," vol. 3; testimony of Zadock P. Northrup, Acc. No. Test. 4, p. 6, ibid., vol. 2; testimony of Alonzo Sanford, 15 Aug. 1845, Acc. No. Test. 4, p. 25, ibid.; *Delaware Gazette*, 15 Oct. 1845; Deposition of Almerin Marks, file 6211 ("Schoharie County Riots"), Governor's Papers, Seward Papers; "Anti-Rent Clippings," 12.

42. My analysis here relies heavily on David R. Roediger, *The Wages of Whiteness: Race and the Making of the American Working Class* (New York: Verso, 1991). See my discussion of changes in the patterns of farm labor and rural culture in chapter 3, above.

43. "The Brave Indian," reprinted in Christman, *Tin Horns and Calico*, 328–29.

44. *Albany Evening Atlas*, 12, 13 Aug. 1844; Davis, "The Reasons of Misrule," in Davis, *Society and Culture*, 97–123.

45. *Daily Albany Argus*, 10 Mar. 1845; *Young America*, 28 Dec. 1844, 15 Mar. 1845.

46. *Freeholder*, 25 Feb. 1846. See also ibid., 12 Nov. 1845.

47. Ibid., 15 July 1845; Thomas Ainge Devyr, *Our Natural Rights: A Pamphlet for the People, by One of Themselves* (n.p., n.p., n.d.), 56–60. See also the *Anti-Renter*, 6 June 1846.

48. *Freeholder*, 20 May 1846.

49. *Freeholder*, 15 July 1846, 15 Sept. 1847; *Young America*, 21 Feb. 1846. See also *Freeholder*, 16 July 1845. On notions of republican womanhood, see Linda Kerber, *Women of the Republic: Intellect and Ideology in Revolutionary America* (Chapel Hill: University of North Carolina Press, 1980), 11–12, 84, 199–200, 228–30, 283–87; Mary Beth Norton, *Liberty's Daughters: The Revolutionary Experience of American Women* (Boston: Little, Brown, 1980), 242–50, 297–99; Nancy Cott, *The Bonds of Womanhood: "Woman's Sphere" in New England, 1780–1835* (New Haven: Yale University Press, 1977), 94–95. On the cult of domesticity and antebellum beliefs in women's moral superiority, see ibid., 63–100, 120, 146–48; Kathryn Kish Sklar, *Catherine Beecher: A Study in American Domesticity* (1973; reprint ed., New York: W. W. Norton, 1976); Mary P. Ryan, *Cradle of the Middle Class: The Family in Oneida County, New York, 1790–1865* (New York: Cambridge University Press, 1981), 60–144.

50. Westerlo, NY, Assessment Roll, 1840, Westerlo Town Clerk's Office, Westerlo, NY; Roxbury, NY, Assessment Roll, 1840, Roxbury Town Clerk's Office, Roxbury, NY; Norma Basch, *In the Eyes of the Law: Women, Marriage, and Property in Nineteenth-Century New York* (Ithaca: Cornell University Press, 1982), esp. 70–110; Nancy Grey Osterud, *Bonds of Community: The Lives of Farm Women in Nineteenth-Century New York* (Ithaca: Cornell University Press, 1991), 1–2, 64–66.

51. *Freeholder*, 25 Jan., 28 May, 9, 16, 30 July, 3 Sept. 1845, 1, 8, 15 July 1846; *Anti-Renter*, 14 Feb. 1846; "Newspaper Clippings," 25. The quotations are in *Freeholder*, 9 July 1845, 8 July 1846; "Newspaper Clippings," 25.

52. *Freeholder*, 31 May 1845; *Young America*, 11 Jan., 23, 30 Aug. 1845; Carolyn Evelyn More and Irma Mae Griffin, *The History of the Town of Roxbury* (Walton, NY: Reporter Company, 1953), 257; Alf Evers, *Woodstock: History of an American Town* (Woodstock, NY: Overlook Press, 1987), 197; *Albany Citizen* in "Newspaper Clippings," 105. Quotation is in *Young America*, 11 Jan. 1845.

53. *Young America*, 7 June 1845; *Freeholder*, 23 July 1845. See also ibid., 25 Feb. 1846; *Young America*, 29 Nov. 1845.

54. Temma Kaplan, "Female Consciousness and Collective Action: The Case of Barcelona, 1910–1918," *Signs* 7 (1982): 545–66.

55. Jeanne Boydston, *Home and Work: Housework, Wages, and the Ideology of Labor in the Early Republic* (New York: Oxford University Press, 1990), 42–55, 142–63. The Delaware county petitioners did acknowledge one of their productive duties when they asked, "Now, sir, what private gentleman of honor, or what court of justice, could censure females under these circumstances, for proving the prowess of their feeble arm (accustomed chiefly to the spinning wheel) in vindication of their honor ; but we are threatened with immediate death if we make the least remonstrance . . . ?" This parenthetical mention of women's production of cloth, however, was part of a broader discourse that emphasized women's helplessness and need of male protection. *Young America,* 7 June 1845.

56. *Freeholder,* 13 Aug. 1845; Roediger, *Wages of Whiteness,* 65–87.

57. For other examples of the construction of a nonwhite "other" and its relation to both class-based movements and cross-class political alliances, see Roediger, *Wages of Whiteness;* and Alexander Saxton, *The Rise and Fall of the White Republic: Class Politics and Mass Culture in Nineteenth-Century America* (London: Verso, 1990).

58. Here I am defining politics broadly as public, collective action that aims at shaping the terms of collective life. By this definition, the Indians and the anti-rent associations as well as anti-rent electoral efforts qualify as politics. And by this definition, urban artisans' and laborers' political lives encompassed not just electoral politics, but also rioting, civic ritual, ethnic and reform associations, and the labor movement, while middle-class politics included evangelical reform and associational activities as well as electoral politics. See, for example, David Waldstreicher, *In the Midst of Perpetual Fetes: The Making of American Nationalism, 1776–1820* (Chapel Hill: University of North Carolina Press, 1997); Wilentz, *Chants Democratic;* Mary P. Ryan, *Civic Wars: Democracy and Public Life in the American City during the Nineteenth Century* (Berkeley: University of California Press, 1997); Paul A. Gilje, *The Road to Mobocracy: Popular Disorder in New York City, 1763–1834* (Chapel Hill: University of North Carolina Press, 1987); Mary P. Ryan, *Cradle of the Middle Class: The Family in Oneida County, New York, 1790–1865* (New York: Cambridge University Press, 1981); James Brewer Stewart, *Holy Warriors: The Abolitionists and American Slavery* (New York: Hill and Wang, 1976).

Chapter 6

1. *Albany Freeholder,* 4 June 1845.

2. Ibid., 11 June 1845, 25 Mar. 1846. See also ibid., 16, 23 July, 8 Oct. 1845.

3. Gordon S. Wood, *The Creation of the American Republic, 1776–1787* (Chapel Hill: University of North Carolina Press, 1969), 519–606; Richard Hofstadter, *The Idea of a Party System: The Rise of Legitimate Opposition in the United States, 1780–1840* (Berkeley: University of California Press, 1969), 212–71; Marc Harris, "How Does the Sovereign Speak? Associationism and Popular Sovereignty in the Early Republic" (paper presented at the Society for Historians of the Early American Republic, Newton, MA, July 14–17, 1994).

4. *Young America,* 15 Feb. 1845 (quotation); *Albany Morning Atlas,* 23 Sept. 1844; *Daily Albany Argus,* 24, 25, 27 Sept., 1 Oct. 1844; *Albany Evening Journal,* 10, 27 Oct. 1844.

5. *Daily Albany Argus,* 14, 22 Nov. 1844.

6. DeAlva Stanwood Alexander, *A Political History of the State of New York* (3 vols.; New York: Henry Holt, 1906), 2: 45, 55, 89, 120.

7. William Seward to Christopher Morgan, quoted in Alexander, *Political*

History of the State of New York (2 vols.; New York: Henry Holt, 1906), 2: 51; ibid., 47–50, 83–85; John Ashworth, *"Agrarians" and "Aristocrats": Party Political Ideology in the United States, 1837–1846* (New York: Cambridge University Press, 1987), 111–25, 147–70.

8. Alexander, *Political History*, 2: 52–64, 76–78, 90–95, 112, 126; Herbert D. Donovan, *The Barnburners: A Study of the Internal Movements in the Political History of New York State and of the Resulting Changes in Political Affiliation* (New York: New York University Press, 1925), 19–21, 24–51, 57–59; Ashworth, *"Agrarians" and "Aristocrats"*, 87–110, 136–46.

9. Greeley to Schuyler Colfax, 23 Sept. 1845, Horace Greeley Papers, NYPL (quotation); *Albany Evening Journal*, Mar. 1845, in "Newspaper Clippings Relating to Anti-Rent Disturbances in New York State," NYSL; *Albany Evening Journal*, reprinted in *Freeholder*, 1 Oct. 1845; *New York Tribune*, reprinted in ibid., 27 Aug., 17 Sept., 17 Dec. 1845.

10. Timothy Corbin, Jr. to William C. Bouck, 13 July 1844, Burton A. Thomas to Bouck, 5 Aug. 1844, Thomas and William J. Potter to Bouck, 12 Aug. 1844, all in Box 3, William C. Bouck Papers, CU; Bouck to A. Gallup, 29 Aug. 1840, Box 1, Additional Bouck Papers, CU; Bouck to ____, 7 Aug. 1844, Timothy Corbin to Bouck, 7 Aug. 1844, Box 3, ibid.; *Albany Evening Atlas*, 12 Aug. 1844; *Albany Weekly Atlas*, 13 Aug. 1844; *Daily Albany Argus*, 13 Aug., 21, 23, 28 Dec. 1844. For evidence of the Barnburners' continuing hostility to the anti-renters, see Michael Hoffman to A.C. Flagg, 25 Mar. 1845, Azariah Flagg Papers, NYPL; Silas Wright to A.C. Flagg, n.d., 24, 25 Oct., 4 Dec. 1844, ibid.

11. John A. King to Stephen Van Rensselaer, 24 Dec. 1844, box 4, folder 1, William Patterson Van Rensselaer Papers, AIHA; Circular from the Freeholders' Committee of Safety, 20 Feb. 1845, Uncatalogued Broadsides, AAS; De Peyster Collection, Vol. 4, 49, NYHS; Charles Hathaway to James Dexter, 12 Mar. 1845, NYSL; J. Blount to William P. Van Rensselaer, 21 Dec. 1844, box 4, folder 1, Van Rensselaer Papers, AIHA; Henry B. Armstrong to George Folsom, 27 July 1846, Folsom Papers, NYHS.

12. Daniel D. Barnard, *The 'Anti-Rent' Movement and Outbreak in New York* (Albany: Weed and Parsons, 1846); James Fenimore Cooper, *Satanstoe: A Tale of the Colony* (1845; reprint ed., New York: Stringer and Townsend, 1855); Cooper, *The Chainbearer* (1845; reprint, New York: G. P. Putnam's Sons, n.d.); Cooper, *The Redskins, or, Indian and Injun* (1846; reprint, New York: Stringer and Townsend, 1855). Unless otherwise noted, quotations of Cooper are from the introductions to Cooper's books, and in his own authorial voice. There is ample evidence, however, that in these books, Cooper abandoned his usual detachment from his elite characters, employing them as mouthpieces for his own disillusionment with American politics and society. At the end of *The Redskins,* he endorses the "moral and political principles" of his main character, Hugh Littlepage, while distancing himself from the passionate language in which Littlepage voices them. Ibid., 473.

13. Barnard, *Anti-Rent Movement*, 4, 22; Cooper, *Chainbearer,* v; Cooper, *Redskins,* xiii.

14. Barnard, *Anti-Rent Movement*, 3, 8–15. Quotations are on pp. 3, 14.

15. Barnard, *Anti-Rent Movement*, 22–24; Cooper, *Redskins,* ix, 443–44.

16. Barnard, *Anti-Rent Movement*, 3, 14; Christopher L. Tomlins, *Law, Labor, and Ideology in the Early American Republic* (New York: Cambridge University Press, 1990), 223–92.

17. Cooper, *Redskins,* 117–18, 194–95, 215, 232, 273–74; Barnard, *Anti-Rent Movement,* 1–3, 5, 24.

18. Horace Greeley, *Why I Am A Whig: Reply to an Enquiring Friend* (New York: New-York Tribune, n.d.), 3. My generalizations about the anti-renters' allies are based on biographical information on six reformers and party activists who allied with the anti-renters: Ira Harris, Robert D. Watson, Thomas Ainge Devyr, William H. Gallup, Calvin Pepper, and Samuel Gordon. On Harris, Watson, and Devyr, see the text and notes below, this chapter. Gallup was a Whig editor in Schoharie County; he published the anti-renters' first newspaper, the *Helderberg Advocate*. Pepper was a Whig lawyer, an abolitionist, and a land and labor reformer. He served briefly as clerk of the Albany County board of supervisors during the 1830s but never again gained a political post—perhaps because of his commitment to controversial causes. Samuel Gordon served as a district attorney, state assemblyman, and member of the U.S. House of Representatives during the 1830s and early 1840s, but he found his political career cut short by his loss in a series of personal rivalries with other Delaware County Democrats. Entry for William H. Gallup, Manuscript Population Census, 1850, Schoharie County; *American Biographical Archive*, sheet 590, frame 215; Henry Christman, *Tin Horns and Calico: A Decisive Episode in the Emergence of Democracy* (1945; reprint ed., Cornwallville, NY: Hope Farm Press, 1978), 55; George R. Howell and Jonathan Tenney, *Bi-Centennial History of the County of Albany, New York, from 1609 to 1886* (New York: W. W. Munsell and Co., 1886), 89; Edgar A. Werner, *Civil List and Constitutional History of the Colony and State of New York* (Albany: Weed and Parsons, 1884), 248; *Daily Albany Argus*, 3 Jan. 1840, 21 Sept. 1841; *Young America*, 14 June 1845; *Freeholder*, 18 June 1845. On the rise of a new class of politicians, see Watson, *Liberty and Power*, 66–70, 174–77; Edward Pessen, *Jacksonian America: Society, Personality, and Politics* (Homewood, Ill.: Dorsey Press, 1978), 149–96.

19. Thomas Ainge Devyr, *The Odd Book of the Nineteenth Century, or "Chivalry" in Modern Days, a Personal Record of Reform, Chiefly Land Reform, for the Last Fifty Years* (2 vols.; Greenpoint, N.Y.: the author, 1882), 1: 45–46, 51–55, 77, 89, 92–93, 136, 147–49, 154–208, 2:25–43; *Biographical Dictionary of American Labor*, ed. Gary M. Fink (Westport, CT: Greenwood Press, 1984), 185–86; Thomas Ainge Devyr, *Our Natural Rights: A Pamphlet for the People, by One of Themselves* (n.p.: n.p., n.d.); Helene Sara Zahler, *Eastern Workingmen and National Land Policy, 1829–1862* (New York: Columbia University Press, 1941), 32–43.

20. Devyr, *Our Natural Rights*, 56–60; *Freeholder*, 14 May 1845. On natural law theory, Anglo-American radicalism, and the Jacksonian Democrats, see Eric Foner, *Tom Paine and Revolutionary America* (New York: Oxford University Press, 1976), 154–55; Ashworth, *"Agrarians" and "Aristocrats,"* 21–23. On the National Reformers' program, see *Young America*, 1844–46, passim; *Principles and Objects of the National Reform Association, or Agrarian League* (New York: Young America, n.d.); *The Jubilee: A Plan for Restoring the Land of New-York or (Incidentally) of Any Other State to the People* (New York: Young America, n.d.); Zahler, *Eastern Workingmen*, 33–36.

21. *Freeholder*, 11 June 1845.

22. *Freeholder*, 23, 30 Apr., 7 May, 4 June 1845; Devyr, *Our Natural Rights*, 56–60.

23. *Freeholder*, 30 Apr., 4 June 1845; Devyr, *Our Natural Rights*, 56–60.

24. Devyr, *Our Natural Rights*, 56–60; *Freeholder*, 14 May 1845. See also ibid., 7, 21 May, 18 June 1845; *Anti-Renter*, 31 Jan. 1846. Other National Reformers showed a similar ambiguity, sometimes disavowing any intention to interfere with existing ownership of land, at other times insisting that obtaining freedom of the public lands was merely an "entering wedge" toward the goal of breaking up all

large accumulations of land. *Young America,* 26 July 1845, 14 Feb., 11 July 1846; *Principles and Objects,* 3; *The Jubilee,* 6, 8–10.

25. Biographical information on Ira Harris was drawn from *Memorial of Ira Harris* (Albany: J. Munsell, 1876); *Dictionary of American Biography* (20 vols.; New York: Charles Scribner's Sons, 1928–1936), 8: 310; *National Cyclopedia of American Biography* (63 vols.; New York: James T. White, 1898–1984), 2: 96; *Biographical Directory of American Congress, 1774–1971* (Washington, DC: Government Printing Office, 1971), 1074; Howell and Tenney, *Bi-Centennial History,* 147–48; Charles Elliot Fitch, *Encyclopedia of Biography of New York: A Life Record of Men and Women of the Past* (Boston: American Historical Society, 1916), 1: 232–33; W. W. Hunt, *American Biographical Sketch Book,* reprinted in *American Biographical Archive,* sheet 703. On Ambrose Spencer's efforts to abrogate the quarter sale, see Ellis, *Landlords and Farmers,* 151–52.

26. *Daily Albany Argus,* 17 July 1841, 24 Sept. 1844; *Albany Morning Atlas,* 23 Sept. 1842; *Albany Evening Atlas,* 16 Nov. 1843; *Hoffman's Albany Directory,* 1839–46; Ira Harris, *Abolition of Distress for Rent: Remarks of Mr. Ira Harris of Albany, upon the Bill to Abolish Distress for Rent* (Albany, NY: Freeholder, 1846), 23; Autobiographical sketch by Smith A. Boughton (typescript), Henry Christman Papers, New York Historical Association, Cooperstown, NY, 6; Alexander, *Political History,* 2: 117.

27. *Hoffman's Albany Directory, and City Register,* 1839–46 (Albany: L.G. Hoffman, 1839–46); *Albany Evening Atlas,* 10, 11, 15 Nov. 1843; *Daily Albany Argus,* 14 Oct. 1844; *Freeholder,* 6 Aug. 1845, 9 Sept. 1846.

28. *Albany Freeholder,* 28 May, 4 June 1845; Harris, *Abolition of Distress,* 4–7, 20; Harris, *Speech of Mr. Harris of Albany, in Committee of the Whole Upon the Anti-Rent Question* (Albany: Albany Freeholder, n.d.), 18–19.

29. Harris, *Anti-Rent Question,* 21; Harris, *Abolition of Distress,* 22; *Freeholder,* 9 July 1845.

30. *Freeholder,* 28 May, 9 July, 20 Aug. 1845; Harris, *Abolition of Distress,* 3–7; emphasis added in first Harris quotation.

31. Robert J. Steinfeld, *The Invention of Free Labor: The Employment Relation in English and American Law and Culture, 1370–1870* (Chapel Hill: University of North Carolina Press, 1991), 73–93, 138–72.

32. Joyce Appleby, *Capitalism and a New Social Order: The Republican Vision of the 1790s* (New York: New York University Press, 1984).

33. Wilentz, *Chants Democratic,* 271–86; Bruce Laurie, *Artisans into Workers: Labor in Nineteenth-Century America* (New York: Noonday Press, 1989), 51–57; Eric Foner, *Free Soil, Free Labor, Free Men: The Ideology of the Republican Party before the Civil War* (New York: Oxford University Press, 1970), 11–39.

34. *Young America,* 1 Feb. 1845; *Freeholder,* 9, 23 April, 7, 28 May, 4, 11, 18, 25 June, 2 July 1845. The quotations are in 28 May, 23 July 1845.

35. *Delaware Gazette,* reprinted in *Freeholder,* 18 June 1845. My discussion of the "rules" of politics under the second party system has been informed by Harry Watson's, Amy Bridge's, and Joel Silbey's fascinating discussions of how party politics worked at the local level. See Watson, *Liberty and Power: The Politics of Jacksonian America* (New York: Farrar, Straus, and Giroux, 1990), 65–72, 87–95, 172–97; Bridges, *A City in the Republic: Antebellum New York and the Origins of Machine Politics* (New York: Cambridge University Press, 1984), 11–14, 61–82; Silbey, *The American Political Nation, 1838–1893* (Stanford: Stanford University Press, 1991), 46–71, 109–124.

36. *Freeholder,* 28 May, 4 June, 9 July 1845. The quotation is in ibid., 28 May 1845.

37. Ibid., 28 May, 4 June, 9 July, 24 Dec. 1845, 21, 28 Jan., 4 Feb. 1846; *Daily Albany Argus*, 1, 4 Nov. 1844; Calvin Pepper, *The Manor of Rensselaerwyck* (Albany: Albany Freeholder, 1846).

38. *Freeholder*, 13 Oct. 1847; *Daily Albany Argus*, 23 Dec. 1844; *Young America*, 28 Dec. 1844, 14 Jan. 1845; Christman, *Tin Horns and Calico*, 105–106, 109.

39. *Daily Albany Argus*, 23, 25, 28, 31 Dec. 1844, 1, 11 Jan. 1845; *Albany Evening Journal*, 22 Mar. 1845; *Young America*, 28 Dec. 1844, 11 Jan., 15, 22 Mar. 1845; *Freeholder*, 11 June, 2 July 1845; New York (State), *Messages from the Governors*, ed. Charles Z. Lincoln (11 vols; Albany: J.B. Lyon, 1909), 4: 140, 149–50.

40. *Daily Albany Argus*, 4, 6, 8, 14, 20 Jan., 10 Feb. 1845; *Young America*, 11, 18 Jan., 15 Feb. 1845; *Freeholder*, 16 July 1845. The quotations are in *Daily Albany Argus*, 6 Jan., 10 Feb. 1845.

41. Ibid., 6, 14 Jan. 1845.

42. Ibid., 1, 14, 31 Jan., 4, 10, 17 March, 30 April 1845; *Young America*, 11, 18 Jan., 1, 8 Feb., 8, 15 Mar., 3, 31 May, 16 Aug. 1845; *Freeholder*, 7, 28 May 1845; "Newspaper Clippings," 16–17.

43. *Freeholder*, 9, 16, 23, 30 July 1845. The quotation is from July 9.

44. Ibid., 28 May 1845. See also *Young America*, 20 Dec. 1845.

45. *Daily Albany Argus*, 13 Jan. 1845; *Young America*, 16 Aug. 1845. See also ibid., 20 Dec. 1845.

46. *Young America*, 15 Mar., 31 May, 7 June 1845; *Daily Albany Argus*, 14, 17, 18 Mar. 1845; *Freeholder*, 28 May 1845; indictments against Abel Gould, Asa B. Fuller, Thomas Deury, and others, Anti-Rent War Documents, vol. 8.

47. *Freeholder*, 21 May, 13 Aug., 1 Oct. 1845; "Newspaper Clippings," 109.

48. *Freeholder*, 13, 27 Aug., 3 Sept., 1, 8, 22 Oct., 5 Nov. 1845, 20 May 1846; *Young America*, 20 Sept. 1845; *Delaware Gazette*, 20, 27 Aug., 3 Sept., 15 Oct. 1845; "Newspaper Clippings," 7, 11, 27, 79; S.C. Wilcox to E.S. Edgerton, 15 Aug. 1845, Edgerton Papers, DCHA; Christman, *Tin Horns and Calico*, 182–203, 220–33.

49. *Freeholder*, 27 Aug., 10, 17, 24 Sept., 8 Oct., 5 Nov. 1845; "Newspaper Clippings," 14, 19, 23, 25, 26, 94.

50. *Freeholder*, 30 April, 9 July 1845, 25 Feb., 6 May 1846.

51. Ibid., 10 Jan. 1846, 10 Feb. 1847. See also ibid., 6 Aug., 23 Sept. 1846.

52. Ibid., 29 Oct. 1845, 5 Aug. 1846. See also ibid., 23 April, 21 May, 25 June, 22 Oct. 1845, 21 Oct. 1846. On party leaders' justification of partisanship and party discipline, see Richard Hofstadter, *The Idea of a Party System: The Rise of Legitimate Opposition in the United States, 1780–1840* (Berkeley: University of California Press, 1969), 212–71; Watson, *Liberty and Power*, 67–70.

53. *Freeholder*, 16, 23 Apr., 28 May, 25 June, 2, 9 July, 10 Sept., 19 Nov., 17 Dec. 1845; 14 Jan., 28 Oct. 1846; *Young America*, 15 Feb. 1845.

54. *Freeholder*, 9, 16, 30 Apr. 1845; *Daily Albany Argus*, 3, 10 Apr. 1845; *Young America*, 1 Mar., 12, 19 Apr. 1845; "Newspaper Clippings," 2.

55. *Freeholder*, 14 May, 1 Oct. 1845; *Daily Albany Argus*, 1, 8, 13 Oct. 1845; *Anti-Renter*, 4 Oct. 1845; *Young America*, 4 Oct. 1845.

56. Calculated from the official returns in *Freeholder*, 3 Dec. 1845.

57. *Freeholder*, 9 July, 13 Aug., 8 Oct., 12 Nov. 1845; see also ibid., 16 July, 13, 24 Sept. 1845.

58. *Freeholder*, 3 Sept. 1845, 18 Feb. 1846.

59. *Delaware Gazette*, 15 Oct. 1845.

60. *Freeholder*, 22 Oct. 1845.

61. *New-York Tribune*, reprinted in *Freeholder*, 19 Nov. 1845; *Freeholder*, 25 Feb. 1846.

62. Charles W. McCurdy, *Fettered Democracy: The Anti-Rent Era in New York Law and Politics, 1840–1865* (forthcoming, University of North Carolina Press), chapter 10.

63. NYAD 1846, 156: 7–8.

64. Ibid., 10–21.

65. Ibid., 8, 29.

66. The votes in the Assembly were as follows. On the bill outlawing distress: Whigs 38–4, Democrats 53–3; on the tax bill: Whigs 32–6, Democrats 49–3; on the revision of the laws of inheritance (also known as Wright's devise-and-descent bill): Whigs 22–11, Democrats 38–7. Votes in the Senate were as follows. To amend the distress bill to apply only to future leases: Whigs 3–3, Democrats 8–13; on final passage of the tax bill: Whigs 3–2, Democrats 12–8. JA 1846, 1105–12; JS 1846, 594–95, 611, 662–63, 672, 691–95, 698, 700, 725–27, 732, 734–38, 745, 763, 773–74.

67. *Freeholder,* 25 Mar. 1846.

68. Ibid. See also the *Anti-Renter,* quoted in *Freeholder,* 24 June 1846.

69. Kosciuszko Armstrong to Henry B. Armstrong, 9 Aug. 1846, Miscellaneous Manuscripts, John Armstrong, NYHS; NYAD 1846, No. 156:37; JS 1846, 695, 745. On leases' guarantee of the power to eject, see leases from Stephen Van Rensselaer to Peders Planck, 1793; John and Hendrick Van Dyck, 1797; and Josiah Beach, 1795, in VRML; leases from Isaac Hardenbergh to George Bloombergh, 1 May 1811; Elisha Stephens, 1 May 1813; Samuel Bushnell, 1 May 1804; and Henry Demery, 1 May 1796, in box 1, folder 3, Hardenberg Family Papers, NYSL; leases from Morgan Lewis to Stephen Palmer, 1800; Joseph Larabee, 1799; Aaron Hull, 1796; Michael Weaver, 1804, in Morgan Lewis Leases, Margaretville, DCHA; lease from Samuel Verplanck to Lena Shaffer, 1 June 1806, Three-Life Leases, DCHA; and lease from Edward P. Livingston to Nathan Arbuckle, 21 Nov. 1833, ibid.

70. *Freeholder,* 3 June 1846.

71. *Freeholder,* 10, 24 June 1846; *Anti-Renter,* 6 June 1846. On Devyr's conflict with Whig and Democratic anti-renters, see chapter 7.

72. McCurdy, *Fettered Democracy,* chapters 5, 8; Alexander, *Political History,* 97–102.

73. *Freeholder,* 28 May, 25 June 1845; McCurdy, *Fettered Democracy,* chapters 5, 8; *Young America,* 28 June 1845, quoted in ibid., chapter 9. A formal alliance between the two movements had been an objective of the National Reformers since the Association was formed in 1844, and many anti-rent leaders had been sympathetic to the idea from the start. See, for example, *Young America,* 1 June 1844.

74. For the story of the conflict between the National Reformers and the Whig and Democratic allies of the anti-renters, see chapter 7.

75. *Freeholder,* 4, 18 Mar., 1, 22 Apr., 26 Aug., 23 Sept. 1846; *Equal Rights Advocate* (Hudson, NY), 15 July 1846; *Young America,* 11 July 1846; Roy Robbins, *Our Landed Heritage: The Public Domain, 1776–1936* (Princeton: Princeton University Press, 1942), 100–103.

76. S. Croswell and R. Sutton, *Debates and Proceedings in the New–York State Convention for the Revision of the Constitution* (Albany: Albany Argus, 1846), 72, 143, 681, 802–805, 815–18.

77. *Freeholder,* 23 Sept. 1846; Croswell and Sutton, *Debates and Proceedings,* 802–805.

78. *Young America,* 11 July 1846; *Equal Rights Advocate,* 5 Aug. 1846; *Freeholder,* 24 June 1846.

79. L Ray Gunn, *The Decline of Authority: Public Economic Policy and Political Development in New York State, 1800–1860* (Ithaca: Cornell University Press, 1988), 184–94, 232–45.

Chapter 7

1. *Albany Freeholder,* 9 July, 6 Aug. 1845; *Young America,* 9 Aug. 1845.
2. *Young America,* 2, 9, 16, 23, 30 Aug., 6, 13 Sept., 8 Nov. 1845; *Anti-Renter,* 31 Jan., 6 June 1846.
3. *Young America,* 10 May, 21 June, 9, 23, 30 Aug., 6 Sept. 1845, 21, 28 Feb. 1846 and passim, 1845–46; *Freeholder,* 21 Jan., 25 Feb., 26 Aug. 1846; *Equal Rights Advocate* (Hudson, NY), 15 July, 19 Aug. 1846; *Anti-Renter,* 14, 21 Feb., 6 June 1846 and passim.
4. *Freeholder,* 15 May, 27 Aug. 1845. See also ibid., 17 Sept., 5 Nov. 1845.
5. Ibid., 28 May, 23 July, 27 Aug. 1845.
6. Ibid., 27 Aug., 17 Sept. 1845.
7. Ibid., 16 July 1845.
8. In Schoharie County, where anti-rentism thrived but where movement leaders shunned the National Reformers, Devyr's efforts to unite the two movements found little support. The radicals also found scant support in places like the valley towns of Albany or Rensselaer counties or anywhere in Greene, Montgomery, Ulster, or Oneida counties, where the movement remained weak. *Young America,* 13 Sept. 1845 and passim, 1845–46; *Freeholder,* passim, 1845–46; *Anti-Renter,* passim.
9. A table correlating anti-rent activists' factional affiliation with their occupation resulted in a Pearson chi-square of 9.286 with a probability of 0.098, indicating a likelihood of 10 percent that the relationship was random. The table correlating the factional affiliations to landholdings of farmers yielded a Pearson chi-square of 3.929, with a whopping probability of .686, indicating a likelihood of 69 percent that the relationship was random. When factional affiliation was converted to a dummy variable, simple linear regressions linking leaders' landholdings and age in 1845 yielded paltry R^2's of .001 and .006 respectively. In other words, activist's landed wealth accounts for only 0.1 percent of the variation in their factional affiliation, while their age accounts for 0.6 percent of that variation.

I located anti-renters who supported the National Reformers through the lists of officers and speakers at meetings that explicitly endorsed the National Reform Association or helped collect funds for the *Anti-Renter,* through a list of men who served as agents for Devyr's newspaper, and through scattered instances of anti-rent leaders attending National Reform conventions or publicly declaring themselves supporters of National Reform. These were all in the *Anti-Renter,* 17 Jan., 14, 21 Feb., 6 June 1846; *Young America,* 17 May, 12 July, 30 Aug., 28 Nov. 1845; *Freeholder,* 26 Aug., 9 Sept. 1846. I have excluded from this group those who participated in meetings that endorsed part of the National Reform program without declaring their allegiance to the organization, since many town associations did so without supporting Devyr against his Whig and Democratic rivals. My aim is to count as National Reform supporters only those who explicitly sided with Devyr and his allies when the movement split into factions.

For my methods in locating association activists and in tracing them and the National Reform supporters through the 1850 census, the Westerlo tax list, and Whig and Democratic conventions, see chapter 5, note 4.

10. The names of anti-rent activists from both factions were compared to a list

of delegates, nominees, and electoral committees listed in the Albany County Whig and Democratic nominating conventions that preceded the November elections of each year, published in the *Albany Evening Journal*, 1834–44; and *Daily Albany Argus*, 1832–44. On the National Reformers' Jacksonian proclivities, see John Ashworth, *"Agrarians" and "Aristocrats": Party Political Ideology in the United States, 1837–1846* (New York: Cambridge University Press, 1987), 97–99; Jonathan Earle, "The Undaunted Democracy: Jacksonian Antislavery and Free Soil, 1828–1848" (Ph.D. dissertation, Princeton University, 1996), chapter 2. On Democratic anti-renters' fears of a Whig campaign to control their movement, see N. K. Wheeler to Azariah Flagg, 11 Oct., 26 Dec. 1846, both in box 2, Flagg Papers, NYPL.

A table correlating factional affiliation with county-level Whig activism yielded a Pearson chi-square of 2.940 with a probability of .086; one tabulating faction and Democratic activism yielded a Pearson chi-square of 0.830 and a probability of .362; and a table correlating factional loyalty to activism in either party resulted in a Pearson chi-square of 0.165 and a probability of .685. In each case, this means that there was no statistically significant correlation. These statistics should therefore be taken as suggestive, not conclusive. I am indebted for this interpretation to Jonathan Earle, who saw the significance of my statistics before I did.

11. *Young America*, 7 Mar. 1846; *Anti-Renter*, 13 Sept. 1845, 28 Feb. 1846; *Freeholder*, 3, 10, 17 Sept. 1845, 25 Feb., 8 Apr., 14 Oct. 1846.

12. *Freeholder*, 9, 16 April 1845; quotation in *Anti-Renter*, 17 Jan. 1846.

13. *Freeholder*, 21 May, 8 July, 23 Sept. 1846; *Equal Rights Advocate*, 22 July 1846.

14. Horace Greeley to Schuyler Colfax, 28 Feb., 22 April 1846, Horace Greeley Papers, NYPL; New York *Courier and Enquirer*, reprinted in *Equal Rights Advocate*, 5 Aug. 1846; *Freeholder*, 29 July, 12 Aug. 1846.

15. *Equal Rights Advocate*, 19 Aug. 1846; *Freeholder*, 2 Sept. 1846.

16. *Freeholder*, 26 Aug., 2, 9 Sept., 21 Oct. 1846; *Equal Rights Advocate*, 2 Sept. 1846.

17. *Freeholder*, 30 Sept. 1846.

18. JA 1845, 728–29; ibid. 1846, 1109–11; De Alva Stanwood Alexander, *A Political History of the State of New York* (3 vols.; New York: Henry Holt, 1906), 2: 116–18.

19. *Freeholder*, 14 Oct. 1846; *Anti-Renter*, 17 Oct. 1846.

20. Helene Sara Zahler, *Eastern Workingmen and National Land Policy, 1829–1862* (New York: Columbia University Press, 1941), 44–46, 95; *Daily Albany Argus*, 21 Sept. 1841; *Young America*, 14 June 1845.

21. Henry Christman, *Tin Horns and Calico: A Decisive Episode in the Emergence of Democracy* (1945; reprint ed., Cornwallville, NY: Hope Farm Press, 1976), 272–73.

22. Horace Greeley to Thurlow Weed, 8 Oct. 1846, Miscellaneous Manuscripts, Horace Greeley, NYPL; New York *Courier and Enquirer*, reprinted in *Equal Rights Advocate*, 21 Oct., 25 Nov. 1846 and in *Freeholder*, 14 Oct. 1846; *New York Express*, reprinted in *Equal Rights Advocate*, 21 Oct. 1846; *New York Tribune*, reprinted in *Freeholder*, 11 Nov. 1846.

23. *Anti-Renter*, 17 Oct. 1846; *Freeholder*, 2 Sept., 28 Oct., 9 Dec. 1846.

24. N. K. Wheeler to Azariah C. Flagg, 26 Dec. 1846, box 2, Flagg Papers; *Equal Rights Advocate*, 21, 28 Oct. 1846; Albany *Atlas*, 3 Nov. 1846; *Freeholder*, 21 Oct. 1846.

25. *Freeholder*, 25 Nov. 1846; *Equal Rights Advocate*, 11 Nov. 1846.

26. *Freeholder*, 11 Nov. 1846.

27. *Freeholder,* 25 Nov., 16 Dec. 1846; Thomas Ainge Devyr, *The Odd Book of the Nineteenth Century, or, "Chivalry" in Modern Days, a Personal Record of Reform — Chiefly Land Reform, for the Last Fifty Years* (2 vols.; New York: privately printed, 1882), 2: 50–51.

28. *Freeholder,* 17 Dec. 1845. Emphasis mine.

29. *Equal Rights Advocate,* 2, 9, 23 Dec. 1845; *Freeholder,* 24 June 1846; *Anti-Renter,* 14 Feb. 1846; *Young America,* 4 Oct. 1845.

30. *Freeholder,* 17, 30 Dec. 1846.

31. Ibid., 8 Apr., 13 May 1846.

32. NYSD 1846, 107: 20–21.

Chapter 8

1. David Potter, *The Impending Crisis, 1848–1861* (New York: Harper and Row, 1973), 90–144.

2. L. Ray Gunn, *The Decline of Authority: Public Economic Policy and Political Development in New York State, 1800–1860* (Ithaca: Cornell University Press, 1988), 198–257; Potter, *Impending Crisis,* 1–89; DeAlva Stanwood Alexander, *A Political History of the State of New York* (3 vols.; New York: Henry Holt, 1906), 2: 101–102, 126–58.

3. New York (State), *Messages from the Governors,* ed. Charles Z. Lincoln (11 vols.; Albany: J. B. Lyon Co., 1909), 4: 363–80; *Equal Rights Advocate,* 13, 20 Jan., 3 Feb. 1847; Albany *Freeholder,* 6, 27 Jan. 1847.

4. JA 1847, 135, 420, 457, 1117, 1463; NYAD 1847, 162: 1–2. On the efforts of radical Whigs, "workie Democrats," and frontier politicians to integrate the National Reformers' programs and insights into their own political messages during the 1840s and 1850s, see Roy Robbins, *Our Landed Heritage: The Public Domain, 1776–1936* (Princeton, NJ: Princeton University Press, 1942), 92–116; Helene Zahler, *Eastern Workingmen and National Land Policy, 1829–1862* (New York: Columbia University Press, 1941), 147–76; Alexander Saxton, *The Rise and Fall of the White Republic: Class Politics and Mass Culture in Nineteenth-Century America* (New York: Verso, 1990), 209–212; Sean Wilentz, *Chants Democratic: New York City and the Rise of the American Working Class, 1788–1850* (New York: Oxford University Press, 1984), 330, 337–38, 341–43, 383–86; Jonathan Earle, "Free Soil, Free Men, Free Farms: The Jacksonian Origins of the Homestead Act, 1828–1862" (paper presented at the annual meeting of the Society for Historians of the Early American Republic, Harper's Ferry, WV, July 16–19, 1998).

5. NYAD 1847, 162: 6.

6. Ibid., 6–8.

7. On the Republicans' use of free labor ideology, see Eric Foner, *Free Soil, Free Labor, Free Men: The Ideology of the Republican Party before the Civil War* (New York: Oxford University Press, 1970), 11–39. On the Radical Republicans' conception of the state, see David Montgomery, *Beyond Equality: Labor and the Radical Republicans, 1862–1872* (1967; reprint, Urbana: University of Illinois Press, 1981), 72–89.

8. Democrats voted 21–17 against the bill, while Whigs voted against it 28–20. JA 1847, 1885–86.

9. N. K. Wheeler to Azariah C. Flagg, 11 Oct, 26 Dec. 1846, box 2, Azariah C. Flagg Papers, NYPL.

10. *Equal Rights Advocate,* 26 May, 2 June 1847; *Freeholder,* 17 Mar., 15 Sept., 27 Oct. 1847, 12 Jan., 8 Mar. 1848; *Voice of the People,* reprinted in ibid., 15 Dec. 1847.

11. *Equal Rights Advocate*, 3 Feb. 1847; N. K. Wheeler to Azariah Flagg, 26 Dec. 1846, Flagg Papers; Horace Greeley to Thurlow Weed, 13 Jan. 1847, Miscellaneous Manuscripts, Horace Greeley, NYHS; *Freeholder*, 27 Sept. 1848; *Albany Atlas*, reprinted in ibid., 20 Sept. 1848; Alexander, *Political History*, 2: 139.

12. *Messages from the Governors*, 4: 410–12.

13. NYAD 1848, No. 126:3; *New York Revised Statutes*, 3d. ed., 2: 391, paragraph 1.

14. NYAD 1848, 126: 4–5; JA 1848, 1011–15; JS, 1848, 535, 575.

15. *New-York Daily Tribune*, 16 Sept. 1848.

16. *Freeholder*, 19 Jan., 23 Feb. 1848.

17. *Freeholder*, 28 June, 5 July, 9, 16, 30 Aug., 6, 13, 20, 27 Sept., 15 Nov. 1848, 3 Jan., 28 Mar., 4, 11 Apr., 16 May, 20 June, 5 July, 1, 22 Aug., 5 Sept., 3, 31 Oct., 14, 28 Nov., 5 Dec. 1849, 13 Mar., 23 Oct. 1850. Quotation is in ibid., 1 Aug. 1849.

18. *Freeholder*, 22 Sept., 27 Oct. 1847, 8, 15 March, 30 Aug., 1848, 7 March 1849, 26 Feb. 1851; *Young America*, 23 Sept. 1848. See also *Equal Rights Advocate*, 2 June 1847; *Freeholder*, 26 May 1847, 20 Mar. 1850, 12 Feb. 1851.

19. Alexander, *Political History*, 2: 101–146; Glyndon G. Van Deusen, *William Henry Seward* (New York: Oxford University Press, 1967), 105–107, 110–11; Potter, *Impending Crisis*, 89.

20. *Freeholder*, 24 Mar., 27 May, 15, 29 July 1847, 8 Mar., 5 May, 21 June 1848, 3, 17 Jan., 23 May, 29 Aug. 1849; *Equal Rights Advocate*, 3 Feb., 10 Mar., 19 May 1847 and 1847, passim; Horace Greeley to Thurlow Weed, 13 Jan. 1847, Miscellaneous Manuscripts, Horace Greeley.

21. *Equal Rights Advocate*, 19, 26 May, 2, 16 June 1847; *Albany Atlas*, 17 June 1848; *Freeholder*, 22 Nov. 1848; *Freeman's Advocate* (Hudson, NY), reprinted in ibid., 15 Aug. 1849.

22. *Freeholder*, 27 Sept., 4 Oct. 1848; *Albany Atlas*, 29 Sept. 1848. The anti-rent alliances of the Albany County Free-Soilers were determined by comparing a list of anti-rent association officers, candidates, committee members, officers and speakers at anti-rent meetings, and delegates to anti-rent conventions drawn from the *Anti-Renter*, 1845–46 and the *Albany Freeholder* 1845–48 to the delegates to the Albany County Free-Soil convention, reported in the *Albany Atlas*, 17 Oct. 1848.

23. Jonathan Earle, "The Undaunted Democracy: Jacksonian Antislavery and Free Soil, 1828–1848" (Ph.D. dissertation, Princeton University, 1996); Alexander, *Political History*, 2: 135–44, 149–51; Potter, *Impending Crisis*, 81–82, 142; Robbins, *Our Landed Heritage*, 105–116; Zahler, *Eastern Workingmen* 127–76; Saxton, *Rise and Fall of the White Republic*, 209–212, 247–51.

24. On the Radical Whigs' endorsement of a homestead act, see Horace Greeley to Joshua R. Giddings, 3 Apr. 1848, Miscellaneous Manuscripts, Horace Greeley; *Freeholder*, 19 Jan. 1848; William Henry Seward, speech in the U.S. Senate, 27 Feb. 1851, in George E. Baker, ed., *The Works of William H. Seward* (5 vols.; Boston: Houghton, Mifflin, 1884), 1: 162–71; Robbins, *Our Landed Heritage*, 105–116. On Garrisonian abolitionism and the emergence of antislavery politics, see James Brewer Stewart, *Holy Warriors: The Abolitionists and American Slavery* (New York: Hill and Wang, 1976), 74–123; Aileen Kraditor, *Means and Ends in American Abolitionism: Garrison and His Critics on Strategy and Tactics, 1834–1850* (New York: Pantheon, 1969), 179–224; Richard H. Sewell, *Ballots for Freedom: Antislavery Politics in the United States, 1837–1860* (1976; reprint ed., New York: Norton, 1980), 152–230, 254–320; Eric Foner, "Racial Attitudes of the New York Free Soilers," in *Politics and Ideology in the Age of the Civil War* (New York: Oxford University Press, 1980), 77–93.

25. *Albany Atlas,* 28 Oct. 1847, 21 Feb., 19 June, 22 Sept. 1848; *Freeholder,* 12 July 1848; Edward O'Connor to Martin Van Buren, 29 Aug. 1848, series 2, reel 31, Martin Van Buren Papers, Library of Congress, Washington DC; Eric Foner, "Racial Attitudes of the New York Free Soilers"; Saxton, *Rise and Fall of the White Republic,* 153–54, 205–212.

26. *Freeholder,* 17 May, 30 Aug., 27 Sept. 1848; *Equal Rights Advocate,* 24 Mar., 21 Apr. 1847.

27. Other than his work on the court challenge to the landlords' titles, there is no evidence that Seward publicly addressed the leasehold issue during the late 1840s or 1850s.

28. Benson-Silbey Election Returns, New York, 1845–1857. My thanks to Joel Silbey and to John Kirn for making these returns available to me.

29 James W. Beekman to Campbell P. White, 13 March 1850, box 1, Miscellaneous Manuscripts, J.W. Beekman, New-York Historical Society, New York City.

30. John Kiersted to Henry Overing, 30 Nov. 1850, Kiersted-Overing Letters, Manuscripts Division, NYSL.

31. Duncan C. Pell to Campbell P. White, 11, 13, 26 Mar., 7 Apr. 1850, and n.d., Campbell P. White Papers, NYHS.

32. Pell to White, n.d. and 13, 21 Mar., 8 May 1850, White Papers; Albany *Daily State Register,* 1850, passim; *Freeholder,* 6 Nov. 1850.

33. Thomas Machin to George Clarke, 2 Mar. 1850, box 45, folder 8, George Hyde Clarke Family Papers, CU.

34. JA 1850, 101–102, 335, 871, 1193–94, 1350–52; JA 1851–52, passim; JS 1851–52, passim; *Freeholder,* 16 Jan, 6 Feb., 20, 27 Mar., 3, 10, 16 Apr. 1850; Pell to White, n.d, n.d., 13, 20, 27 Mar., 3 Apr. 1850, White Papers.

35. Vigorous prosecutions for rent or evictions took place in Albany, Rensselaer, Columbia, Delaware, Schoharie, Otsego, and Sullivan Counties between 1848 and 1851. *Freeholder,* 3 June 1846, 13 Jan., 3 June 1847, 26 Apr., 3 May, 14 June, 5 July, 27 Dec. 1848, 3, 10, 17 Jan., 7, 14, 21, 28 Mar., 18 Apr., 2, 16 May, 6 June, 3 Oct., 21 Nov. 1849, 23 Jan., 13 Feb., 7, 21 Aug. 1850, 5, 12 Feb., 5 Mar. 1851; Thomas Machin to George Clarke, 2 Mar. 1850, box 45, folder 8, Clarke Papers; A. G. Johnson, *A Chapter of History, or, The Progress of Judicial Usurpation* (Troy, NY: A. W. Scribner, 1863), 19.

36. Duncan C. Pell to Campbell P. White, 13, 21 Mar. 1850, White Papers.

37. Albany *Daily State Register,* 2 Oct. 1850; Alexander, *Political History,* 45–51, 145–49, 153–55; Van Deusen, *William Henry Seward,* 105–106, 110–111, 124–28, 132–35.

38. *Daily State Register,* 2 Oct. 1850; Duncan C. Pell to Campbell P. White, 21 Mar. [1850?], White Papers.

39. *Daily State Register,* 27 Mar. 1850; New York *Commercial Advertiser,* reprinted in ibid., 1 Apr. 1850. See also ibid., 23, 24, 25 Mar., 2, 3, 4, 5, 6, 16, 20 Apr. 1850.

40. Pell to White, 21 Mar. [1850?], White Papers; *New York Daily Tribune,* 27, 18, 30 Sept. 1850; *Daily State Register,* 1, 2, 7, 9, 18, 19, 21 Oct., 1 Nov. 1850; *Freeholder,* 6 Nov. 1850; Alexander, *Political History,* 153–58, 165–68, 175–79, 189, 198–204, 211–14.

41. *Freeholder,* 20 Aug. 1845, 24 Mar. 1847, 20 Dec. 1848; Douglass C. North, *The Economic Growth of the United States, 1790–1860* (New York: W. W. Norton, 1966), 204, 206, 209, 212; Mary Fisher Torrance, *The Story of Old Rensselaerville* (New York: privately printed, 1939), 51; Arthur Harrison Cole, *Wholesale Commodity Prices in the United States, 1700–1861* (Cambridge: Harvard University

Press, 1938), 135–36; David Maldwyn Ellis, *Landlords and Farmers in the Hudson-Mohawk Region, 1790–1850* (1946; reprint ed., New York: Octagon Books, 1967), 185–86, 196–97, 202, 204, 210–11, 221; Percy Wells Bidwell and John I. Falconer, *History of Agriculture in the Northern United States, 1620–1860* (1832; reprint ed., New York: Peter Smith, 1941), 493–504.

42. *Freeholder,* 25 Mar., 2 Apr., 10 June, 1, 15 July 1846, 3 Mar. 1847.

43. *Freeholder,* 25 Mar., 15 July 1846.

44. *Freeholder,* 20 Jan. 1847, 2, 23 Apr. 1851; Ellis, *Landlords and Farmers,* 182, 216–18; Oliver Wendell Holmes, "The Turnpike Era," in Alexander C. Frick, ed., *History of the State of New York* (5 vols.; New York: Columbia University Press, 1934), 5: 272–73.

45. *Freeholder,* 28 Mar., 18 July 1849, 7 Aug. 1850.

46. *Freeholder,* 30 May 1849, 22 May, 7 Aug. 1850.

47. Ibid., 31 Jan, 14, 21, 28 Feb., 28 Mar., 18 Apr., 23 May, 15, 29 Aug., 5 Sept., 7 Nov., 5, 19, 26 Dec. 1849, 16 Jan., 6, 27 Mar., 22 May, 4 Sept. 1850.

48. John Kiersted to Henry Overing, 1 Feb., 25 Nov. 1847, 9 Oct. 1848, 6 Aug. 1851, Kiersted-Overing Letters, Manuscripts Division, New York State Library, Albany, New York; *Freeholder,* 8 Sept. 1847, 20 Nov. 1850; Roxbury, NY Assessment Roll, 1864, Roxbury Town Clerk's Office, Roxbury, NY; Alf Evers, *Woodstock: History of an American Town* (Woodstock, NY: Overlook Press, 1987), 200–202; David Murray, *Delaware County, New York: History of the Century* (Delhi, NY: William Clark, 1898), 95–96; Caroline Evelyn More and Irma Mae Griffin, *History of the Town of Roxbury* (Walton, NY: Reporter Company, 1953); Albert Champlin Mayham, *The Anti-Rent War on Blenheim Hill: An Episode of the '40s* (Jefferson, NY: Frederick L. Frazee, 1906); J. H. French, *1860 Gazetteer of the State of New York* (Syracuse: R. P. Smith, 1860), 157 n; Thomas Summerhill, "The Farmers' Republic: Agrarian Protest and the Capitalist Transformation of Upstate New York, 1840–1900" (Ph.D. dissertation, University of California, San Diego, 1993), 521–44.

49. Church and Tyler Rent Ledger, Rensselaerville and Westerlo, 1838–1890, Walter S. Church Business Records, Manuscripts Division, New York State Library, Albany, NY; Ellis, *Landlords and Farmers,* 196–97, 221–23.

50. *Freeholder,* 6, 20 May, 3, 10 June 1846, 3, 17 Feb. 1847; Torrance, *Old Rensselaerville,* 35–37, Ellis, *Landlords and Farmers,* 221, 310–11.

51. U.S. Bureau of the Census, *Sixth Census of the United States, 1840* (Washington, DC: Blair and Rives, 1841), 82–83, 88–89; *Census of the State of New York, for the Year 1865* (Albany: Charles Van Benthuysen and Sons, 1867), 3–4; Ellis, *Landlords and Farmers,* 310.

52. *Albany Atlas,* 25 July 1848; *Freeholder,* 4 Apr., 12 Sept., 17, 31 Oct., 7 Nov., 19 Dec. 1849, 15 May, 21 Aug., 25 Sept., 2, 30 Oct. 1850.

53. *Opinion of Hon. Judge Cady, in Supreme Court. The People of the State of New York,* v. *George Clarke* (Albany: Joel Munsell, 1851), 19–21.

54. *Livingston Manor Case. Opinion of Mr. Justice Wright, in the Case of the People* agt. *Hermon Livingston. Supreme Court—Columbia County.* (Hudson: Hudson Gazette, 1851), 17.

55. G. Clarke to Campbell P. White, 26 Sept. 1851, White Papers; Ellis, *Landlords and Farmers,* 286–87.

Chapter 9

1. B.A. Nilsson, "The Maddening Mystery of the Dismantled Manor, Or, How Part of Albany's History Went to Pieces," *Capital Region* (July 1986):40–41;

Kiliaen Van Rensselaer, *The Van Rensselaer Manor: An Address Delivered at the Third Annual Meeting of the New York Branch of the Order of Colonial Lords of Manors in America* (Baltimore: n.p., 1929), 36.

2. Martha J. Lamb, "The Van Rensselaer Manor," *Magazine of American History* 11 (1884): 3; A.G. Johnson, *A Chapter of History, Or, the Progress of Judicial Usurpation* (Troy, NY: A. W. Scribner, 1863), 19; Albany *Freeholder,* 11 Oct., 20 Dec. 1848.

3. Johnson, *Chapter in History,* 14, 21; 6 NY 467.

4. Ibid., 14–20; NYAD 1862, 237: 6–8.

5. "Public Meeting," dated 10 Feb. 1855; "Notice to the Tenants of Stephentown," dated 5 Mar. 1855; "To the Tenants of Knox, Bern, Westerlo, and Rensselaerville," dated 14 Sept. 1855, all in Broadside Collection, AIHA.

6. Church and Tyler Rent Ledger, Rensselaerville and Westerlo, 1838–1890, Walter S. Church Business Records, NYSL; "Mass Convention," 16 Aug. 1856, Broadside Collection, AIHA.

7. Johnson, *Progress of Judicial Usurpation,* 21–41; Andrew J. Colvin, "Anti-Rentism in Albany County," in George Rogers Howell and Jonathan Tenney, eds., *Bi-Centennial History of the County of Albany, New York, from 1609 to 1886* (New York: W. W. Munsell, 1886), 277–85; "Fiat Justicia," *Anti-Rent Controversy* (Albany: n.p., 1865), 1, 10–11; *Landlord and Tenant: Speech of Hon. John I. Slingerland, in Assembly, March 13, 1860* (n.p.: n.p., 1860); Henrietta Riter, ed., *People Made it Happen Here: History of the Town of Rensselaerville, 1788–1950* (Rensselaerville, NY: Rensselaerville Historical Society, 1977), 21.

8. Church and Tyler Rent Ledger, Rensselaerville and Westerlo, 1838–1890; The exact percentage of Westerlo farms listed in this account book that had been purchased varies according to the method of counting used. If we assume that rent accounts that were transferred to another account book, now lost, were sold, we find that 73 percent of the acreage listed in the account book was sold by 1870 and 99 percent was sold by 1900. If, on the other hand, we assume these farms were not sold, we find that 52 percent of the acreage listed had been purchased by 1870, and 67 percent had been released by Church by 1900.

9. Johnson, *Chapter in History,* 19–23.

10. Rev. Rufus W. Clark, "A Discourse, in Memory of Stephen Van Rensselaer, Preached in the First Reformed Church, Albany, Sunday Morning, May 31, 1868," *In Memoriam. Stephen Van Rensselaer* (Albany: Joel Munsell, 1868), 4, 12–14; Albany *Argus,* 26 May 1868, reprinted in ibid., 25; *New York World,* reprinted in ibid., 27–32; Johnson, *Progress of Judicial Usurpation,* 23; Lamb, "Van Rensselaer Manor," 3.

11. Clare Brandt, *An American Aristocracy: The Livingstons* (Garden City, NY: Doubleday, 1986), 180, 181, 187. Other members of the Livingston clan and Henry Overing, a Delaware County landlord, faced heavy debts and possible bankruptcy. See *Freeholder,* 22 Dec. 1847, 25 July 1849; John Kiersted to Henry Overing, n.d., 1 Feb. 1847.

12. Thomas Summerhill, "The Farmer's Republic: Agrarian Protest and the Capitalist Transformation of Upstate New York, 1840–1900" (Ph.D. dissertation, University of California, San Diego, 1993), 533–44, 546–50.

13. On the courts' adoption of the law of master and servant, see Christopher L. Tomlins, *Law, Labor, and Ideology in the Early American Republic* (New York: Cambridge University Press, 1993), 223–92. On the destruction of what came to be seen as "unfree" labor relations in the North, see Gary B. Nash, *Forging Freedom: The Formation of Philadelphia's Black Community, 1720–1840* (Cambridge, MA: Harvard University Press, 1988); idem, *Race and Revolution* (Madison, WI:

Madison House, 1990); Gary B. Nash and Jean R. Soderlund, *Freedom By Degrees: Emancipation in Pennsylvania and its Aftermath* (New York: Oxford University Press, 1991); Robert J. Steinfeld, *The Invention of Free Labor: The Employment Relation in English and American Law and Culture, 1370–1870* (Chapel Hill: University of North Carolina Press, 1991); Christopher Tomlins, *Law, Labor, and Ideology;* David Montgomery, *Citizen Worker: The Experience of Workers in the United States with Democracy and the Free Market during the Nineteenth Century* (New York: Cambridge University Press, 1993).

14. Caroline Evelyn More and Irma Mae Griffin, *The History of the Town of Roxbury* (Walton, NY: Reporter Company, 1953), 134–55; Nancy Grey Osterud, *Bonds of Community: The Lives of Farm Women in Nineteenth-Century New York* (Ithaca, NY: Cornell University Press, 1991), 139–226.

15. *Census of the State of New York, for the Year 1865* (Albany: Charles Van Benthuysen and Sons, 1867), 274–81, 298–305; U.S. Bureau of the Census, *Sixth Census of the United States, 1840* (Washington, DC: Blair and Rives, 1841), 88–89, 112–13; More and Griffin, *History of the Town of Roxbury*, 134–55. In order to make production figures for dairy products comparable, I converted the 1840 figures, which were in dollars, to pounds of butter by dividing them by the average market price per pound for the year 1840 in Boston—the only city for which I was able to find price figures. For the purposes of conversion, I assumed that farmers had produced only butter—by far the most prominent dairy product in Delaware County. Prices were taken from Percy Wells Bidwell and John I. Falconer, *History of Agriculture in the Northern United States, 1620–1860* (New York: Peter Smith, 1941), 502.

16. *Census for the State of New York, for 1865*, 274–81, 298–305.

17. For a discussion of the capital costs of livestock raising, see chapter 2 above.

18. Albany *Freeholder*, 30 Jan. 1850; Torrance, *Old Rensselaerville*, 35–37; Knox, New York Publications Committee, *Knox, New York Sesquicentennial: 1822–1972* (n.p.: n.p., n.d.), 78; Ellis, *Landlords and Farmers*, 210–11.

19. Church and Tyler Rent Ledger, Rensselaerville and Westerlo, 1838–1890, Walter S. Church Business Records, 1.

20. Ibid., 44.

21. Ibid., 78.

22. The statistics are even more dramatic when one measures how many purchasers had been on their farms during the 1840s. Only 19 of 66—29 percent—of all buyers had cultivated the farms they bought at any time during that decade. Ibid.; Ellis, *Landlords and Farmers*, 219.

23. U.S. Manuscript Population Census, 1850, Roxbury and Westerlo, NY; U.S. Manuscript Population Census, 1860, Roxbury and Westerlo, NY. In 1860, 120 out of 480 Westerlo male heads of household were laborers or landless farmers, while 100 out of 382 men aged 35 and older pursued those occupations. In Roxbury, 74 out of 417 male heads of household and 60 out of 324 men aged 35 or older worked as laborers or landless farmers. Many thanks to Cathleen Dooley for coding and entering this data for me.

24. For a discussion of the extent of emigration, see chapter 8.

25. "Life of Harvey M. Seaman," handwritten manuscript, Harvey M. Seaman Papers, DCHA. For an excellent discussion of emigration from settled eastern farming communities, see Hal Barron, *Those Who Stayed Behind: Rural Society in Nineteenth-Century New England* (New York: Cambridge University Press, 1984), 78–111.

26. My discussion here is heavily influenced by Barron, *Those Who Stayed Behind*, 51–111.

27. *Freeholder*, 25 Mar. 1846.

28. Sean Wilentz, *Chants Democratic: New York City and the Rise of the American Working Class, 1788–1850* (New York: Oxford University Press, 1984); Helene Zahler, *Eastern Workingmen and National Land Policy, 1829–1862* (New York: Columbia University Press, 1941); Carl Guarneri, *The Utopian Alternative: Fourierism in Nineteenth-Century America* (Ithaca: Cornell University Press, 1991); Teresa Ann Murphy, *Ten Hours' Labor: Religion, Reform, and Gender in Early New England* (Ithaca: Cornell University Press, 1992); Aileen Kraditor, *Means and Ends in American Abolitionism: Garrison and His Critics on Strategy and Tactics, 1834–1850* (New York: Pantheon, 1969); Douglas M. Strong, "A Political Millennium: Evangelical Perfectionism and the Liberty Party" (paper presented at the sixteenth annual meeting of the Society for Historians of the Early American Republic, Boston College, July 14–July 17, 1994).

29. Wilentz, *Chants Democratic*; Steven Hahn, *The Roots of Southern Populism: Yeoman Farmers and the Transformation of the Georgia Upcountry, 1850–1890* (New York: Oxford University Press, 1983); Henrietta Larson, *The Wheat Market and the Farmer in Minnesota, 1858–1900*, Studies in History, Economics, and Public Law, Vol 122, no. 2 (New York: Columbia University Press, 1926).

30. Harriet Friedmann, "Household Production and the National Economy: Concepts for the Analysis of Agrarian Formations," *Journal of Peasant Studies* 7 (1980):158–84; Friedmann, "Simple Commodity Production and Wage Labour in the American Plains," *Journal of Peasant Studies* 6 (1978): 71–100; Friedmann, "World Market, State, and the Family Farm: Social Bases of Household Production in the Era of Wage Labor," *Comparative Studies in Society and History* 20 (1978):37–43.

31. Smith Boughton, autobiographical sketch (typescript), in Henry Christman Papers, NYSHA.

32. Harriet Jenkins Washbon, *Rensselaerville: Rhymes and Reminiscences* (Albany: Charles Van Benthuysen, 1888), 60–61.

33. Summerhill, "Farmer's Republic," 585–88, 597–99, 605, 617–45.

34. For a superb analysis of the agricultural economy, farmers' social and economic practices, and rural inhabitants' political and social thought in the late nineteenth century, see Summerhill, "The Farmer's Republic," chapters 7–9.

35. Solon J. Buck, *The Granger Movement: A Study of Agricultural Organization and its Political, Economic and Social Manifestation, 1870–1880* (Cambridge, MA: Harvard University Press, 1933); D. Sven Nordin, *Rich Harvest: A History of the Grange, 1867–1900* (Jackson: University Press of Mississippi, 1974); Fred A. Shannon, *American Farmers' Movements* (Princeton, NJ: Van Nostrand, 1957), 136–41; Lawrence Goodwyn, *Democratic Promise: The Populist Moment in America* (New York: Oxford University Press, 1976); Paul S. Taylor, "Origins of Migratory Labor in the Wheat Belts in the Middle West and California: Second Half of the Nineteenth Century," in U.S. Congress, Senate, Subcommittee on Migratory Labor, *Migrant and Seasonal Farmworker Powerlessness*, 91 Cong., 1970, 6265–66; Peter H. Argersinger and Jo Ann E. Argersinger, "The Machine Breakers: Farmworkers and Social Change in the Rural Midwest of the 1870s," *Agricultural History* 58 (1984): 393–410.

Many thanks to William J. Cronon, who first gave me the idea to explore the "Janus-faced" self-presentation of nineteenth-century farmers (the phrase is his).

36. Paul A. Gilje, *The Road to Mobocracy: Popular Disorder in New York City, 1763–*

1834 (Chapel Hill: University of North Carolina Press, 1987); George M. Dennison, *The Dorr War: Republicanism on Trial, 1831–1861* (Lexington, KY: University Press of Kentucky, 1976); Marvin E. Gettleman, *The Dorr Rebellion: A Study in American Radicalism, 1833–1849* (New York: Random House, 1973); Kraiditor, *Means and Ends.*

37. Glenn C. Altschuler and Stuart M. Blumin, "Limits of Political Engagement in Antebellum America: A New Look at the Golden Age of Participatory Democracy," JAH 84 (1997): 855–85; Altschuler and Blumin, "'Where is the Real America?': Politics and Popular Consciousness in the Antebellum Era," *American Quarterly* 49 (1997): 225–67. Many thanks to Harry Watson for urging me to rethink this point; he bears no responsibility for my revised interpretation.

38. H. J. Munger, "Reminiscences of the Anti-Rent Rebellion" (typescript), NYSHA. Lists of delegates and officers at Republican conventions were drawn from the *Albany Evening Journal,* 1855–1860. The lists of convention delegates and officers were compared to lists of anti-rent activists in Albany County drawn from the Albany *Freeholder,* 1845–52, the *Anti-Renter,* and anti-rent broadsides, 1850–1860, in Broadside Collection, AIHA.

39. *Albany Evening Journal,* 27 Nov. 1855, 25 Nov. 1856, 16 Nov. 1858, 8 Nov. 1860; *Delaware Gazette,* 19 Nov. 1856; 17 Nov. 1858; 21 Nov. 1860; Silbey-Benson New York Election Data, 1845–1857. Many thanks to Joel Silbey and John Kern for allowing me to use this data.

40. George E. Baker, ed., *The Works of William H. Seward* (5 vols.; Boston: Houghton, Mifflin, 1884), 4: 291, 379–80.

41. Wilentz, *Chants Democratic;* Steinfeld, *Invention of Free Labor;* Richard H. Sewell, *Ballots for Freedom: Antislavery Politics in the United States, 1837–1860* (1976; reprint, New York: W. W. Norton, 1980); James Brewer Steward, *Holy Warriors: The Abolitionists and American Slavery* (New York: Hill and Wang, 1976).

42. On the Republicans' constituencies, see Eric Foner, *Free Soil, Free Labor, Free Men: The Ideology of the Republican Party Before the Civil War* (New York: Oxford University Press, 1970); William Gienapp, *The Origins of the Republican Party, 1852–1856* (New York: Oxford University Press, 1987); David Montgomery, *Beyond Equality: Labor and the Radical Republicans, 1862–1872* (1967, reprint, Urbana: University of Illinois Press, 1981); Michael Holt, *Forging a Majority: The Formation of the Republican Party in Pittsburgh, 1848–1860* (New Haven: Yale University Press, 1969). On northern rural producers' integration into a broader capitalist economy during the late 1840s and 1850s, both through developing markets for farm produce and through an increasing use of wage labor and tenancy, see Christopher Clark, *The Roots of Rural Capitalism: Western Massachusetts, 1780–1860* (Ithaca: Cornell University Press, 1990); John Mack Faragher, *Sugar Creek: Life on the Illinois Prairie* (New Haven: Yale University Press, 1986); Allan G. Bogue, *From Prairie to Corn Belt: Farming on the Illinois and Iowa Prairies in the Nineteenth Century* (Chicago: University of Chicago Press, 1963); Eric E. Lampard, *The Rise of the Dairy Industry in Wisconsin: A Study in Agricultural Change, 1820–1920* (Madison: State Historical Society of Wisconsin, 1963). On the social import of the Republicans' ideology, the classic account is Foner, *Free Soil, Free Labor, Free Men,* 11–39.

43. Baker, *Works of William H. Seward,* 4: 321–22. On western agrarian conflicts see Paul Wallace Gates, *The Farmer's Age: Agriculture, 1815–1860* (New York: Holt, Reinhart, 1960); Gates, *Fifty Million Acres: Conflicts Over Kansas Land Policy, 1854–1890* (Ithaca, NY: Cornell University Press, 1954); Gates, *History of Public*

Land Law Development (Washington, DC: U.S. Government Printing Office, 1968); Allan G. Bogue, *From Prairie to Corn Belt* (Chicago: University of Chicago Press, 1963); idem, "The Iowa Claim Clubs: Symbol and Substance," *Mississippi Valley Historical Review* 45 (1959): 231–53; Roy Robbins, *Our Landed Heritage: The Public Domain, 1776–1936* (Princeton: Princeton University Press, 1942).

44. Baker, *Works of William H. Seward*, 1: 156–71, 4:29, 31, 58–59; Ira Harris, *Abolition of Distress for Rent: Remarks of Mr. Ira Harris of Albany, Upon the Bill to Abolish Distress for Rent* (Albany: Freeholder, 1846), 11; Robbins, *Our Landed Heritage*, 105–107, 178–82.

45. Foner, *Free Soil, Free Labor, Free Men*, 11–72; Sewell, *Ballots for Freedom*, 277–320, 343–65; Montgomery, *Beyond Equality*, 45–134; idem, *Citizen Worker*, 132–34; Zahler, *Eastern Workingmen*, 147–76; Robbins, *Our Landed Heritage*, 150–216; Alexander Saxton, *The Rise and Fall of the White Republic: Class Politics and Mass Culture in Nineteenth-Century America* (New York: Verso, 1990), 227–62.

46. *Congressional Globe*, 37 Cong., 2 sess., 1191, 1526, 3139; ibid., 37 Cong., 3 sess., 625, 805, 897, 903; Ira Harris, *Confiscation of Rebel Property. Speech of Hon. Ira Harris, of New York, in the Senate of the United States, Monday, April 14, 1862* (Washington, D.C.: Scammell and Co., 1862), 7–8 and passim.; Allan G. Bogue, *The Earnest Men: Republicans of the Civil War Senate* (Ithaca, NY: Cornell University Press, 1981), 165–66, 183, 194, 223. Bogue convincingly characterizes Harris as a "moderate"; probably, like Seward and Greeley, he began as a radical in the mid-1850s and became a "moderate" when he failed to shift to the left as quickly as other Republicans during the late 1850s and the Civil War. Nonetheless, his commitment to the use of all constitutional powers of the government to abolish slavery is unmistakable; on this, his only quarrel with Senate radicals was his willingness to endorse gradual emancipation in West Virginia and in his unwillingness to use what he saw as unconstitutional means to end human bondage. See ibid., 98, 105–106.

47. Ira Berlin et al., *Freedom: A Documentary History of Emancipation*, ser. 1, vol. 1: *The Destruction of Slavery* (New York: Cambridge University Press, 1985).

48. Montgomery, *Beyond Equality;* Eric Foner, *Reconstruction: America's Unfinished Revolution, 1863–1877* (New York: Harper and Row, 1988).

49. Gienapp, *Origins of the Republican Party;* Michael F. Holt, *The Political Crisis of the 1850s* (New York: Norton, 1983); Paul Kleppner, *The Third Electoral Party System, 1853–1892: Parties, Voters, and Political Cultures* (Chapel Hill: University of North Carolina Press, 1979).

50. Foner, *Free Soil, Free Labor, Free Men*, 11–72; Sewell, *Ballots for Freedom*, 277–320, 343–65; Montgomery, *Beyond Equality*, 45–134; idem, *Citizen Worker*, 132–34; Zahler, *Eastern Workingmen*, 147–76; Robbins, *Our Landed Heritage*, 150–216; Saxton, *Rise and Fall of the White Republic*, 227–62.

INDEX

Conklin, Samuel and Mary, 51–52, 54
constitutional convention of 1846, 158–61
constitutionalism, 65–66, 100–02, 132, 146, 148, 161, 188–89, 215–17
contract law, 100–02, 136, 205
Cooper, James Fenimore, 4, 70–71, 73–74, 135–37, 188
Copake Flats, 120
Council of Appointment, 31–32, 34
Coventry, William, 27, 39–40, 41
Crawford, William Henry, 57, 71

dairy industry, 47–50, 52, 56, 68–69, 201, 222, 224–25, 229, 245n10, 278n15
Davenport, 225
deference, 17–19, 21, 28–29, 89
    and politics 30–32
    decline of, 72–75
Delaware County, 8, 14, 50, 241n51, 246nn12–13;
    agriculture in, 39–43, 47–56, 69, 201, 222, 225, 229
    anti-rent movement in, 104, 117, 149–50, 153–54, 178–79, 226–27, 262n25
    dairy farming in, 48
    elections in, 32, 58, 60, 133, 154, 171–72, 225, 230
    politics in, 32, 58, 60–61, 65, 69, 153–54
    population of, 229
    poverty in, 44
    religion in, 62–64, 225
    temperance movement in, 62–64, 225
    title disputes in, 83
Delhi, 61, 153–54, 225
Democratic Party
    and anti-rent movement, 100–02, 132–35, 145–46, 152–56, 158–61, 168–72, 178–81
    Barnburners, 134–35, 153–55, 183
    characteristics of supporters, 224–25
    and constitutionalism, 65–66, 100–02
    and contracts, 100

Delhi Regency, 61, 153–54
    election returns for, 133, 154, 230
    factions within, 134–35
    Hunkers, 134–35, 152, 172
    landlords and, 71–72, 73–74
    and producers' rights, 65
    and property rights, 100
    reactionary wing of, 71–72, 73–74
    in second party system, 57
    social vision of, 64–66
Devyr, Thomas Ainge, 138–40, 145, 152, 157–60, 163–66, 168, 170–72
distress, right of, 26, 155–57
Dix, John, 183
Dorr, R. G., 170
Dorr, Thomas, 211
Duchess County, 13, 14, 33

Earle, Jonathan, 167
Earle, Moses, 149
economy
    changes after 1820, 47–56
    changes after 1845, 160–61, 189–94
    and expanding markets, 6, 50
    and manufacturing, 51
    of tenant farms, 39–43, 47–56
    and wage labor, 52–53
    See also agriculture; capitalism; dairy industry; grain production; home manufacturing; livestock; wool
Edgerton, Erastus, 149
elections, 30, 60–61, 133, 168–72, 220, 221, 224, 225, 230
    See also anti-rent movement and electoral politics
Emmet, Thomas, 34
Erie Canal, 36, 38, 47
Esopus Creek Navigation Company, 79
estates
    destruction of, 195–98
    expansion of, 13–14
    family life on, 38–41
    financial troubles of, 45–47
    improvements to, 27–28
    and primogeniture, 45–46
    population growth on, 14, 49
    and the Revolution, 11–13, 45–46

estates (*continued*)
    settlement of, 13, 22–24
    See also titles
evangelicals, 61–64, 224–25
Evans, George Henry, 158–59, 168
Evans, John, 164, 168

family life on leasehold farms, 38–41
farming, changes in, 47–56, 189–92,
    201
    See also agriculture; dairy industry;
        grain production; home manu-
        facturing; livestock; wool
Federalist Party, 13–14, 30, 31, 34,
    220
Fish, Hamilton, 171
Foote, Ebenezer, 32
Ford, Elijah, 188
Formisano, Ronald, 234n15
Franklin, 58, 225
freedom
    and agrarian traditions, 12, 21–22,
        33, 111–16
    as freedom of contract, 136
    and free labor, 200, 204
    as free markets, 113, 144
    as free transfer of land, 99, 142–43,
        155
    and hierarchy, 129
    and homestead act, 172–73, 184–
        85
    as universal land ownership, 111,
        113–14, 139, 164, 204–05
Freeholders' Committee of Safety,
    135, 186–87
free-labor ideology, 7–8, 145, 200,
    202, 206, 212, 213, 217
Freeman's Advocate, 183
Free-Soil Party, 170–72, 183–86, 230
Frisbee, Reuben, 29
Fugitive Slave Act, 215

Gallup, Albert, 60
Gallup, John, 103, 170
Gallup, William H., 267n18
Gansevoort, Leonard, 31–32
Gardiner, Addison, 171
gentry, 17–19, 21, 35–38, 46, 70–75
    See also deference; landlords
Gienapp, William, 215

Gordon, Samuel, 145, 267n18
Grafton, 147
grain production, 47, 222, 224, 225,
    229
Grant, Hiram, 185
Greeley, Horace, 4, 134, 137, 159,
    168, 171, 182–83, 188
Guilderland, 224

Hamden, 225
Hancock, 225
Hardenbergh, Isaac, 17, 20, 26, 79–
    80
Hardenbergh, Lewis, 41, 81
Hardenbergh patent, 16, 19, 79, 104,
    182
    anti-rent movement on, 104
Harpersfield, 225
Harris, Ira, 133, 153, 158, 164, 167,
    185, 205, 281n46
    and abolition, 182, 215
    and constitutionalism, 215
    and free market in land, 141–44,
        165
    on leasehold system, 159–60
    nomination for governor, 168,
        169–70
    on Tilden Committee, 155
Hayner, Henry Z., 83, 153
Helderbergs, 59, 89–94, 120, 153,
    198, 245–46n12
    agriculture in, 201, 222
    election returns in, 59, 61, 220–21,
        230
    Helderberg War, 87–94, 96, 99
    population in, 229
hierarchies, 17–18, 73–75, 125, 129,
    136–37, 200
Hoag, Joseph, 112, 125
Holcolm, Beriah, 40, 41, 52
Holcolm, George, 49, 52, 53–54
Holcolm, Lucinda, 49, 50, 53
Holt, Michael, 215
home manufacturing, 41, 50, 51, 53
homestead act, 172–73, 183–85, 214,
    274n24
households, farm, 21, 38, 51, 200,
    204
Hun, Thomas, 25–26, 29, 32
Hungerford, Stephen, 83–84

McCurdy, Charles, 101, 155
Mann, Charles, 188
manors. *See* estates
manufacturing, 51, 55, 224–25
markets, 41–43, 49–50, 142–44,
    201, 205
Masonville, 225
Masquerier, Lewis, 170
Mayham, John, 103–04
Maynard, A. F., 209
Melville, Herman, 175
Meredith, 225
Meyers, Marvin, 72
Middletown, 32, 225, 229, 230
migration, 13, 22
militia, 33–35, 94
Miller, Henry, 118, 120
monopolies, rejection of, 31, 111–16,
    139, 158–61, 164
Montgomery, Janet, 24

National Reform and Anti-Rent
    Vanguard Association, 164
National Reform Association
    convention of 1846, 168–69
    and Democrats, 166–67
    landholdings of supporters, 228
    and land reform, 137, 138, 140, 158
    political affiliation of supporters, 228
    occupations of supporters, 228
    support among anti-renters for,
        158, 164–67, 182
    See also Devyr, Thomas; Evans,
        George Henry
New Scotland, 224, 229, 230

O'Connor, Edward, 150

patriarchy, 38, 40, 73, 204. *See also*
    deference; households; women
Patrons of Husbandry, 208
patroonery. *See* landlords; leasehold
    system
Pell, Duncan, 186–89
Pepper, Calvin, 164, 169, 170, 185,
    267n18
Perkins, Bishop, 155
politics
    and anti-renters, 6–7, 98–102, 129,
        132–35, 145–46, 152–56, 158–
        61, 168–72, 178–81

and election of 1846, 168–72
factionalism in, 56–61, 134–35,
    186–89, 212–17
grass-roots mobilization, 58–59, 61,
    132–33
of landlords, 30–36, 59–61, 70–
    75, 135–37
and legitimate action, 210–11
and second party system after 1820,
    56–61, 181, 187–88, 211
See also anti-rent movement;
    Democrats; Republicans; tenants;
    Whigs
popular sovereignty, 64–66, 131–32,
    147–48, 151, 161, 177–78
population, 14, 49–50, 229
prices. *See* agriculture; dairy industry;
    wool
primogeniture, 45–46, 199
property
    accumulation of, 27–28
    as commodity, 164–65
    distribution, 5–6, 33, 166, 173
    and eminent domain, 102
    and family prestige, 17–19, 29, 35–
        38
    ideas about, 5–6, 28, 33, 55–56,
        99–102, 107, 111–16, 122, 141–
        44, 159–61, 122, 204–05
    and land reform, 5–6, 158–61
    monopolies of, 111–16, 139, 158–
        61, 164, 172
    natural right to, 113–14, 129, 136,
        138–40, 146, 164–65, 172–73
    private ownership of, 141–44,
        159–61
    public, 172–73, 184–85
    See also improvements; leasehold
        system; titles
Pruyn, Casparus V., 87–88, 95–97

Reidsville, 93–94
Rensselaer County, 14, 152–53
    Anti-Rent Association of, 103
Rensselaer School, 36, 47
Rensselaerville, 25, 179, 219–20,
    243–44nn79–84, 247n21
    common land in, 42, 55
    distribution of wealth in, 42
    election returns for, 30–31, 224,
        230

tenants
ambition for property ownership, 38–44
and capitalism, 47–56, 191–92, 205–09
committees of, 88–91
distribution of wealth among, 42–44, 47–56
emigration of, 191
and farm economy, 39–43, 47–56, 160–61, 189–94
gender roles among, 38–41, 125–29
and goods produced, 41, 47–56
indebtedness of, 24–26, 78
and individual morality, 190–92
and leases, 23–24, 27–28, 79–82, 155–60, 195–96
and land improvements, 27, 79
and religion, 61–64
occupations of, 203, 223–226, 278n23
petitions to legislature, 98–102, 154–61
politics of, 30–35, 57–61, 68–70, 75, 129, 131–46, 151–61
and purchases of farms, 191–92, 196–99, 202–04
rebellions of (1750–1813), 13, 33–35
and resistance to landlords: individual, 27–28, 80–82; collective, 82–84, 88–90, 92–94
wage labor and subtenancy among, 40–41, 52–53
See also anti-renters; anti-rent movement; "Indians"
textiles. See wool
Thomas, Burton, 103, 170
Tilden Committee, 155–57
Tilden, Samuel, 155–56
titles, estate
attorney general's suit against landlords, 181–82, 192–93
Clintonian attacks on, 31–32
and dubious claims, 19–20
and final court decision (1851), 193–94
to George Clarke's lands, 34, 182, 193
Governor Young's challenge to, 180

to Hardenbergh patent, 19–20, 83, 104, 182
Harris and Watson on, 146
Indians and, 121–22
legislative attacks upon, 34–35
to Livingston estates, 19, 34, 83, 101, 182
and Martin Van Buren, 34
pre-1815 challenges to, 33–34, 35
to Rensselaerwyck, 31, 35, 83–84, 92, 101, 182
to Scott patent, 83, 101
Tilden Committee on, 155–57
title-test bill, 101–02, 115, 143, 155, 156–57, 176–77
timber, 27–28, 50–51, 55, 79, 82, 124, 201–02
Tompkins, 225

Van Buren, John, 155
Van Buren, Martin, 59, 60, 84, 134, 155
and Bucktails, 57
and 1830 challenge to Van Rensselaer title, 83–84
criticism against, 66, 69
and Free-Soilers, 184
representation of Livingston tenants, 34–35
Van Rensselaer, Jeremiah, 17
Van Rensselaer, Johannes, 45
Van Rensselaer, John, 14, 34
Van Rensselaer, Stephen, III, 11, 21, 23, 26, 27, 101
death of, 85
deference shown to, 29
financial plight of, 46, 77–78, 85
leniency towards tenants, 17–18, 24, 25, 28–29
political career of, 30–31, 36, 59–61, 74, 221
public activities of, 36, 38, 46–47
lawsuits against tenants, 24–25, 78, 82–83
Van Rensselaer, Stephen, IV, 71, 85, 182, 188
financial plight of, 87–89, 195
and Helderberg tenants, 87–92
sale of estate, 196–98
lawsuits against tenants, 88, 92, 103